Critical Pedagogy for Healing

Also available from Bloomsbury

Assessment for Social Justice: Perspectives and Practices within Higher Education, Jan McArthur
Ecopedagogy: Critical Environmental Teaching for Planetary Justice and Global Sustainable Development, Greg William Misiaszek
Education, Equality and Justice in the New Normal: Global Responses to the Pandemic, edited by Donaldo Macedo and Inny Accioly
International Perspectives on Critical Education, Peter Mayo and Paolo Vittoria
On Critical Pedagogy, Henry A. Giroux
Pedagogy, Politics and Philosophy of Peace: Interrogating Peace and Peacemaking, edited by Carmel Borg and Michael Grech
Race, Politics, and Pandemic Pedagogy: Education in a Time of Crisis, Henry A. Giroux
Reinventing Pedagogy of the Oppressed: Contemporary Critical Perspectives, edited by James D. Kirylo
The Student Guide to Freire's "Pedagogy of the Oppressed", Antonia Darder
Transnational Feminist Politics, Education, and Social Justice: Post Democracy and Post Truth, edited by Silvia Edling and Sheila Macrine

Critical Pedagogy for Healing

Paths beyond "Wellness," toward a Soul Revival of Teaching and Learning

Edited by
Tricia M. Kress, Christopher Emdin,
and Robert Lake

BLOOMSBURY ACADEMIC
LONDON • NEW YORK • OXFORD • NEW DELHI • SYDNEY

BLOOMSBURY ACADEMIC
Bloomsbury Publishing Plc
50 Bedford Square, London, WC1B 3DP, UK
1385 Broadway, New York, NY 10018, USA
29 Earlsfort Terrace, Dublin 2, Ireland

BLOOMSBURY, BLOOMSBURY ACADEMIC and the Diana logo are trademarks of Bloomsbury Publishing Plc

First published in Great Britain 2022

A catalogue record for this book is available from the British Library.

Library of Congress Cataloging-in-Publication Data
Names: Kress, Tricia M., editor. | Emdin, Christopher, editor. | Lake, Robert, editor.
Title: Critical pedagogy for healing : paths beyond "wellness", toward a soul revival of teaching and learning / Edited by Tricia M. Kress, Christopher Emdin, and Robert Lake.
Description: London ; New York : Bloomsbury Academic, 2021. | Includes bibliographical references and index.
Identifiers: LCCN 2021026764 (print) | LCCN 2021026765 (ebook) | ISBN 9781350192676 (hardback) | ISBN 9781350192683 (paperback) | ISBN 9781350192690 (pdf) | ISBN 9781350192706 (epub)
Subjects: LCSH: Critical pedagogy. | Mental healing. | Mental health. | Social justice and education. | School environment.
Classification: LCC LC196 .C75654 2021 (print) | LCC LC196 (ebook) | DDC370.11/5–dc23
LC record available at https://lccn.loc.gov/2021026764
LC ebook record available at https://lccn.loc.gov/2021026765

ISBN: HB: 978-1-3501-9267-6
PB: 978-1-3501-9268-3
ePDF: 978-1-3501-9269-0
eBook: 978-1-3501-9270-6

Typeset by Newgen KnowledgeWorks Pvt. Ltd., Chennai, India

To find out more about our authors and books visit www.bloomsbury.com and sign up for our newsletters.

Contents

Figures

Contributors

Inny Accioly is Professor of Education at the Fluminense Federal University, Brazil. Her research interests focus on critical pedagogy in a multidisciplinary perspective that relates environmental education, grassroots movements, policy analysis, and international and comparative education. She is coeditor of *Commodifying Education: Theoretical and Methodological Aspects of Financialization of Education Policies in Brazil* (2016). Her most recent book, coedited with Donaldo Macedo, is *Education, Equality and Justice in the New Normal: Global Responses to the Pandemic* (2021).

Jennifer D. Adams is a Tier 2 Canada Research Chair of Creativity and STEM and Associate Professor at the University of Calgary, Canada, where she holds a dual appointment in the Department of Chemistry, Faculty of Science and Werklund School of Education. Her research focuses on the intersection between creativity and STEM teaching and learning in postsecondary contexts. She has scholarly expertise in STEM teaching and learning in informal science contexts including museums, science centers, National Parks, and community-based learning. She was awarded a National Science Foundation Early CAREER award to study informal learning contexts and formal/informal collaborations for STEM teacher education. Her research portfolio also includes youth learning and identity in informal science contexts, with a focus on underrepresented youth and place/identity in transnational communities and environmental education. Her work emphasizes critical and sociocultural frameworks and participatory, qualitative, post-structural approaches to data collection and analysis.

Benedito Alcântara is a history teacher in the public-school system of the State of Amapá, in the Amazon in Brazil. He received a master's degree in environmental law and public policy and has been working for several years with traditional communities. He is a representative of the Pan-Amazonian Ecclesial Network (REPAM), working with the Justice and Peace Commission (CJP), the Social Pastorals of the Macapá Diocese, and coordinating the project "Young Environmental Guardians from Riverside Communities."

Curtis Acosta is Assistant Professor in Teaching, Learning, and Sociocultural Studies and Director of the MEd in Secondary Education, alternative path program at the University of Arizona, USA. He is also the founder of the Acosta Educational Partnership, a consultation firm that helps educators create culturally sustaining and humanizing educational practices in their classrooms, schools, and communities.

Prior to that, he was a high school teacher for nearly twenty years, where he developed and taught Chicanx and Latinx literature classes for the renowned Mexican American Studies program in Tucson, USA.

e alexander is a recent graduate in educational studies from the Ohio State University, USA. They are interested in higher education as a global neocolonial project, Black womxn as neocolonial subjects therein, and exercises of neocolonial resistance through anti-hegemonic pedagogy, scholarship, and community engagement. alexander is also concerned with Black womxn's wellness as they engage in resistance efforts on and through all locations of knowledge construction. They have a decade of experience in higher education, having worked in a variety of roles, institution types, and world regions.

Carolyne Ali-Khan is Associate Professor in the Department of Teaching, Learning and Curriculum at the University of North Florida (UNF), USA. Her research interests include critical pedagogy and autoethnography. Prior to joining UNF, she spent twenty years as a high-school teacher in New York City, USA.

Laura Apol is Associate Professor at Michigan State University, USA and Lansing-area poet laureate. Her poetry has been published in four full-length collections including, most recently, *Nothing but the Blood* (2018), which was winner of the Oklahoma Book Award for poetry and the Independent Publishers Award silver medal for poetry. She is the author of *Poetry, Poetic Inquiry and Rwanda: Engaging with the Lives of Others* (2021), which centers around therapeutic writing and ethical arts-based inquiry, and her newest collection of poetry is *A Fine Yellow Dust* (2021).

Robin Brandehoff is Assistant Clinical Professor in culturally and linguistically diverse education and oversees the Latinx Schools and Communities EdD program at University of Colorado, Denver, USA. In connection to her work as a scholar and researcher, she is also a theater arts practitioner driven to work alongside students and teachers in communities facing conflict and marginalization using critical race theory and performance to investigate, educate, and liberate. Her research examines the oppressions and traumas of marginalized Communities of Colour through mentorship, performance, and counter-stories to support and educate Latinx gang-affiliated youth and the educational leaders and mentors that work with them.

Alex Chisholm is a doctoral candidate in the Educational Theory and Practice Department at the University of Georgia, USA, where he also teaches undergraduate courses in Middle Grades Education. His studies center on the pedagogical practices of Black teacher-coaches and athlete activism as civic engagement. He is the coauthor of *A Radical Doctrine: Abolitionist Education in Hard Times* (2021).

Donna DeGennaro is Associate Professor of Educational Leadership at the University of North Carolina, Wilmington, USA, and the founder of Unlocking Silent Histories.

She is the author of *Designing Critical and Creative Learning Designs with Indigenous Youth: A Personal Journey* (2016).

Damaris C. Dunn is a doctoral student in the Mary Frances Early College of Education at the University of Georgia, USA. She is a former social studies teacher and youth developer. Her research centers on the embodied and lived experiences of Black girls and their joy inside and outside of K–12 spaces.

Christopher Emdin is Associate Professor and Associate Director of the Institute for Urban and Minority Education at Teachers College, Columbia University, USA. He is the author of the *New York Times* best-selling *For White Folks Who Teach in the Hood … and the Rest of Y'all Too* (2017).

Gene Fellner is Assistant Professor of Education at City University of New York, USA, where he teaches master's pre-service special education teachers at the College of Staten Island and occasional arts-based research courses at the Graduate Centre. He has written, often with his students, on special education, teacher dispositions, and arts-based research. His most recent articles include "The Demon of Hope: Race, Disability and the White Researcher's Complicity with Injustice" (2019); "You Get Tenure, What Do I Get? Using Art to Interrogate a Researcher's Dilemma" (2018); and, with Helen Kwah, "Transforming the Embodied Dispositions of Pre-service Special Education Teachers" (2017).

Isabelle Gatt is a Senior Lecturer in the Arts, Open Communities and Adult Education Department at the University of Malta, Malta. She runs the Drama Education Masters in Teaching and Learning as well as the Arts and Creativity Modules for Primary and Early Years teacher training programs. Her research interests are in applied theater, drama education, and creative processes. She is also a theater practitioner and consultant working with schools (the Teatru Qroqq Projects, the Trikki Trakki Youth Theatre Festival) and marginalized communities (Rehab Centres, Active Aging Centres). She is presently a collaborator/researcher in the Horizon 2020 EU project AMASS (Acting on the Margins: Arts as Social Sculpture) working with marginalized communities through the arts.

David S. Greene has been a popular educator for more than fifty years. He cofounded several alternative educational institutions, including the Southern Appalachian Labor School (1979) in West Virginia, The Paulo Freire Institute for Popular Education and Social Change (1997) in New York City, and the Freedom School in Licking County, Ohio (2012). His book, *Unfit to be a Slave: A Guide to Adult Education for Liberation* (2015), describes this work and lessons learned from experience and coworkers in industry and community. More recently, he has focused on the development of critical class consciousness and emerging leadership.

Janet Wells Greene is a labor historian and adult educator. She was assistant professor of labor studies at the Harry Van Arsdale Center for Labor Studies at Empire State

College, State University of New York, USA and historian and director of the Library of the General Society of Mechanics and Tradesmen of the City of New York, USA. She was a cofounder of The Freedom School in Licking County, Ohio and a faculty member of the Southern Appalachian Labor School, West Virginia. Her publications include *From Forge to Fast Food: Child Labor in New York State from the Colonial Period to the Civil War* (1994).

Perpetual Anastasia Hayfron is a multiple humxn with a ferocious passion for critical inquiry, mental health, and the spiritual liberation of Black people. Her Ghanaian and Liberian ethnicity has informed her doctoral research at the University of Massachusetts at Boston, regarding the impact global anti-Blackness has on the mental health of Black millennial womxn pursuing postsecondary education. In the spirit of healing, advocacy, and radical self-love, Perpetual utilizes her skills as a social worker to aid marginalized individuals and families across the birth continuum in her vocation as full spectrum doula.

James D. Kirylo is Professor of Education at the University of South Carolina, USA. Kirylo has published works in a variety of educational journals, and among other books, he is the author of *The Thoughtful Teacher: Making Connections with a Diverse Student Population* (2021), *Paulo Freire: The Man from Recife* (2011) and, with Drick Boyd, coauthor of *Paulo Freire: His Faith, Spirituality, and Theology* (2017).

Tricia M. Kress is Associate Professor in the Educational Leadership for Diverse Learning Communities EdD program at Molloy College in Rockville Centre, New York, USA. She is co-editor of *Paulo Freire's Intellectual Roots: Toward Historicity in Praxis* (2013), which received the Society of Professors of Education 2014 Book Award. She is a coeditor of *Imagination and Praxis: Criticality and Creativity in Education and Educational Research* book series with Brill/ Sense Publishers and *Transformative Imaginings: Critical Visions for the Past-Present-Future of Education* book series with DIO Press.

Patricia Krueger-Henney is Associate Professor at the University of Massachusetts Boston, USA in the Urban Education, Leadership, and Policy Studies doctoral program. Before entering academia, Krueger-Henney taught social sciences in high schools and organized with multiple youth communities around issues of (in)justice. Her research responds to the power and wisdom of young people.

Helen Kwah is an independent scholar, artist, and educator. Her most recent publications explore the use of contemplative/artistic practices and social theory to address issues of race, embodiment, gender, identity, communal healing, and well-being.

Robert Lake is Professor of Social Foundations and Curriculum Studies at Georgia Southern University in Statesboro, Georgia, USA. Lake is the author of *Vygotsky on Education* (2012) and *A Curriculum of Imagination in an Era of Standardization: An*

Imaginative Dialogue with Maxine Greene and Paulo Freire (2013). He is a coeditor of the Imagination and Praxis: Criticality and Creativity in Education and Educational Research book series and the Transformative Imaginings: Critical Visions for the Past-Present-Future of Education book series.

Irwin Leopando is Associate Professor of English at LaGuardia Community College, City University of New York, USA. He is the author of *Pedagogy of Faith: The Theological Vision of Paulo Freire* (2017).

Ian P. Levy is Assistant Professor and Director of the School Counseling Program at Manhattan College, USA. He is the 2016 New York State School Counselor of the year. His work exploring the use of hip-hop and spoken word therapy in urban schools has been featured on various news outlets, including the *New York Times* and CNN, and has been published in a variety of reputable academic journals. He is the author of *Hip-Hop and Spoken Word Therapy in School Counseling: Developing Culturally Responsive Approaches*. Levy is also an emcee and released his album *And Then It Glistens* in 2020.

Jamila Lyiscott is a community-engaged scholar, national speaker, and the author of *Black Appetite. White Food: Issues of Race, Voice, and Justice within and beyond the Classroom*. She currently serves as an assistant professor of social justice education at the University of Massachusetts Amherst, where she is the founding codirector of the Center of Racial Justice and Youth Engaged Research, and coeditor of the *Equity & Excellence in Education* journal. Lyiscott is most well known for being featured on TED.com where her video, "3 Ways to Speak English," has five million views.

Aldineia Fernandes Monteiro is a Portuguese language teacher in the state of Pará in Brazil, specializing in Portuguese language methodology and literature and higher education management and Teaching. She is the pedagogical coordinator of the Amapá-Pará Educational Institute (IEAP) and the project "Young Environmental Guardians from Riverside Communities," in the Amazon region of Brazil.

Aldenice Monteiro is an activist, philosophy teacher in the state of Pará, Brazil, specializing in higher education management and teaching and also in Portuguese language methodology. She coordinates the Amapá-Pará Educational Institute (IEAP) and the project "Young Environmental Guardians from Riverside Communities," in the Amazon region of Brazil.

Victoria Restler is Assistant Professor of Educational Studies and Director of the Youth Development Master's Program at Rhode Island College, USA. Her award-winning dissertation research engages arts-based methods to interrogate teacher evaluation and value. Her recent articles include "Rubbing the Room: Tactile Epistemologies of Teacher Work" (2020) and "Countervisualities of Care: Re-visualizing Teacher Labor" (2019). Her current collaborative study explores institutional whiteness through image archives, narrative research, and teacher workshops.

Jennifer Somma-Coughlin is a doctoral candidate in the Educational Leadership for Diverse Learning Communities EdD program at Molloy College in Rockville Centre, New York, USA. Her research examines narratives of everyday mindfulness practices and special education teacher burnout.

Shirley R. Steinberg is Research Professor of Critical Youth Studies at the University of Calgary, Canada. She is the author and editor of many books in critical pedagogy, urban and youth culture, and cultural studies. Originally a social/improvisational theater creator, she has facilitated happenings and flash mobs globally. A regular contributor to CBC Radio One, CTV, the *Toronto Globe* and *Mail*, the *Montreal Gazette*, and *Canadian Press*, she is an internationally known speaker and teacher. She is also the founding editor of *Taboo: The Journal of Culture and Education*, *The International Journal of Youth Studies*, and the managing editor of *The International Journal of Critical Pedagogy*. She is the cofounder of the Paulo and Nita Freire International Project for Critical Pedagogy and the co-organizer of International Institute of Critical Pedagogy and Transformative Leadership. She is committed to a global community of transformative educators and community workers engaged in radical love, social justice, and the situating of power within social and cultural contexts, specifically involving youth.

Kathryn (Katie) Strom is Associate Professor with the Educational Leadership for Social Justice EdD program at California State University, East Bay, USA. Her research interests include critical preparation of teachers and leaders, critical/feminist posthuman theories, and intimate forms of scholarship. Katie's recent work includes "Toward a Complex Framework of Teacher Learning-Practice" (2020), "Learning from a Lost Year: An Auto-theoretical Journey through Anxiety and Panic" (2020), and a double special issue, "Non-Linear Perspectives on Teacher Development: Complexity in Professional Learning and Practice" in *Professional Development in Education*.

Gregory Tewksbury is Adjunct Associate Professor in the School of Education at Brooklyn College, USA. Education for social justice and empowerment is at the center of his thinking and practice. He had the opportunity to work with and write about the inspirational Brazilian educator Paulo Freire. Tewksbury's essay "From Oppression to Freedom: Paulo Freire's Legacy and Challenge" appeared in a collection in Brazil. In his work on educational leadership in New York City public schools, Tewksbury brings a focus on realizing racially equitable practices. He holds a PhD in urban education from the Graduate Center at the City University of New York and an MA in social psychology from Stony Brook University.

dorothy vaandering is Associate Professor at the Faculty of Education, Memorial University, Newfoundland, Canada, and was a primary-elementary educator for twenty years. She draws on her life, teaching, and research experiences to explore the implementation and sustainability of restorative justice in education. Most recently, she is grappling to understand the realities of colonization past and present and working to understand reconciliation as a settler-Canadian. She is the author and coauthor of a variety of academic and professional publications including *The Little Book of Restorative Justice in Education*. She is the director of Relationships First: Restorative Justice Education Research & Resource Consortium in Newfoundland and Labrador.

John Wesley White is Associate Professor in the Department of Teaching, Learning and Curriculum at the University of North Florida, USA. His research interests include critical pedagogy, critical literacy, and redefining the literary canon for sixth- to twelfth-grade English Language Arts curricula.

Introduction: Pathways toward a Soul Revival

Tricia M. Kress, Christopher Emdin, and Robert Lake

Healing for Soul Revival in Teaching and Learning

Never in our lifetimes has "healing" been as prominent in public discourse as it is in the contemporary moment. By the time our readers have this volume in their hands, the world will have already been feeling the effects of the Covid-19 pandemic for more than a year. The physical and emotional toll of this year escapes easy description, as the world has been struggling with the mortal risk of a deadly virus but also with deadly racism, which continues to put the lives of people of color at risk. Life itself, as well as the foundations of modern social institutions, feel incredibly fragile. Countless people are simultaneously experiencing deep epistemic, psychological, and physical pain, albeit in different ways and to different degrees. Gasps for "healing" have begun to emerge from the lips of politicians and community members alike. Humanity, with all its racist, classist, colonialist, exploitative, and destructive baggage on full display, is waking up to what Fromm (1955) more than half a century ago called a "social sickness." While many people may dream of a "return to normal," we don't. "Normal" is what brought us here to this moment where humanity is bruised and broken, a husk without a soul. "Normal" was cruel and violent for much of humanity and the natural world. And so, we offer this volume to you in solidarity; we too are feeling and witnessing pain, our own and that of those around us. At the same time, we also see a world of resilience and hope. We ache from the pain that was and is, but we also ache with desire for what could be. We don't know what a world beyond this moment might look like, but we know that healing is life-changing, perhaps world-changing, and we want to be part of that change.

While it is fitting that we are publishing this volume in such a time, this work has been many years in the making, at least as far back as 2009 when Tricia began thinking about critical pedagogy and healing at an international critical pedagogy conference. Later in 2013, Tricia and Robert began incorporating Erich Fromm's theories about social sickness, having versus being, and biophilia and necrophilia into their conceptualizations of transformative curriculum (Fromm, 1955). Since then, they have been writing about the role of embodiment, place, and human and nonhuman relations in critical pedagogy (see Kress & Lake, 2017, 2018, 2019). Similarly, Chris has been writing for over a decade about the need for healing in urban schools where teachers and students alike have been systematically oppressed and exploited by dehumanizing US society and its institutions of schooling (see Emdin, 2016). Chris's work about integrating hip-hop and science education has emerged as a practice of healing for many young people and their teachers (Adjapong & Emdin, 2015). The moral imperative for moving ahead with this collaboration came when Chris gave a talk at Molloy College (Tricia's institution) in 2019. He provoked the audience to contemplate how society can expect teachers with broken spirits to be in a healthy position to educate young people with broken spirits. That moment brought the three of us together on this journey to considering not just wellness in education, but how to revive the very spirit, the very soul, of what it means to teach and learn through and beyond the trauma of the colonial-capitalist-racist-classist-patriarchal legacy of European imperialism. So, while our coming together with like-minded colleagues from around the world has occurred over the span of just two years, this work is far from new. Indeed, it would be irresponsible for us to not point out that critical pedagogy elders have been calling for healing for more than half a century. What we are experiencing now with such deep and widespread intensity is simply where we have always been but rubbed raw from a constant assault on our bodies and minds over the past year. However we might describe "normal" pre-pandemic life, it was incredibly unhealthy for people's bodies and minds as well as for the planet and all organisms with whom we share this earth that we call home. Humanity needs healing in order to become more humane.

Over the past decade, the neoliberal marketplace has tuned in to this need for healing, churning out an entire wellness industry that responds to much of the dis-ease that people are feeling in day-to-day life. For all its horrors, the neoliberal marketplace is terribly astute at identifying people's deepest needs and desires and finding innovative ways to satiate them through consumerism. The tendrils of the neoliberal wellness discourse have slowly begun infiltrating social institutions. "Self-care" and "mindfulness," in particular, have become buzzwords in popular discourse about schools. On the one hand, teachers are encouraged to engage in mindfulness and self-care to reduce stress and burnout. On the other hand, students are encouraged to engage in social and emotional learning and mindfulness to cope with personal life and school life stressors. While we are supportive of self-care and mindfulness as general concepts, how they are often integrated into society and schools is where we take issue. First, we cannot help but notice how the push for "wellness," "self-care," and "mindfulness" has hastened alongside increasing social inequalities. And, we cannot accept that it is simply coincidental that wellness, self-care, and mindfulness industries have taken off at the same time that tax cuts on the wealthy have exacerbated global income inequality. As noted by Hope and Limberg (2020), the past fifty years of "trickle-down economics" has been disastrous for most people, except, of course, the wealthy. Likewise, the shift toward high-stakes accountability in schools, and the general defunding of education at the federal level, has created incredible stress for teachers and students, especially those working in or attending schools with many students living in poverty. The ostensible reason for the push toward high-stakes testing and accountability was to provide a better education for students so they could access college and careers. And while we would never argue that quality education is unimportant, the entire premise misses the mark, especially when placed within the context above—what careers are we preparing young people for? How do we expect students to afford college tuition? Again, we do not accept as coincidence the emergence of high-stakes testing and accountability, which in the United States was jump-started by the Reagan administration in 1983 and then furthered by George W. Bush in 2002, in parallel with trickle-down economics and a changing labor market where job creation was shifting toward low-wage, hourly paid employment in retail and service sectors.

While the above economic trends were making the futures of the world's young people more precarious, the tearing down of social safety nets in the United States and elsewhere has intensified the urgency for something to be done. Unfortunately, education is an easy patsy. In the United States, at least, because there is such an intense hegemony of individualism and meritocracy, the source of this social predicament cannot be understood as collective; therefore, it must be understood as individual, which shifts the blame for inequality from society and economy to workers. This was baldly stated in *A Nation at Risk*, the 1983 US policy brief that claimed America was under assault by a "rising tide of mediocrity" because the education of young people, the future workforce, was so dismal. Schools had been saddled with the responsibility to ensure students would pursue college and ostensibly lucrative careers. This myth hides the reality that there simply are not enough jobs that pay a living wage, and as young people compete with each other, many are set up for a life of struggle. Teachers, too, experience the effects of living in an inequitable and inhumane society, with many teachers receiving wages that are disproportionately low in comparison to other industries. For instance, in New York City, where Chris and Tricia live, the starting public school teacher's salary *with a master's degree* (that means at least six years of higher education) is $65,000. However, the cost of living in New York is 129 percent higher than the national average, which makes it difficult to support a family on such an income. Meanwhile, the conversations around wellness, self-care, and mindfulness are out of step with what young people and their teachers are up against on a daily basis. The wellness and self-care industries tend to be rooted in individualism and linked to middle-class consumerist practices. There are clothing lines, food products, magazines, machines, spas and retreats, and even whole communities designed to, supposedly, encourage a healthy and happy lifestyle. For the more than 11.9 million children living in poverty in the United States (Children's Defense Fund, 2020), wellness of this sort is simply not reality. For their teachers whose wages do not situate them squarely in the middle class, this sort of wellness is also unrealistic. For us, injecting wellness discourse of this sort into schools in most need of social healing is beyond tone-deaf; it borders on abusive. Yet again, the source of social sickness and the remedy for solving it have been placed squarely on the bodies and minds of young people and their teachers, who are told they need to "fix" themselves in order to make their lives and society better.

Numerous scholars have pointed to the need for education that recognizes teachers and learners and their lives for their fullness (van Manen, 1991/2016), embodiedness (Pinar & Grumet, 2014; Darder, 2014), and humanity (Thomas & Kincheloe, 2006). Others have pointed out the need to relearn how to be in relation to each other and the living and nonliving world (e.g., Braidotti, 2019; Gruenwald, 2003). Indeed, any avid reader of Paulo Freire would be quick to point out that critical pedagogy is as much about love and honoring the materiality of people's bodies in the world as it is about print and political literacy (see Freire, 1978, 1987). And, as Bettina Love (2018) so poignantly asserts, education should be about young people (and their teachers) "mattering," and schools should be homeplaces where students (and their teachers) experience respect, nurturing, and love. Yet, Miller (2000) calls attention to the pervasive emptiness of modern institutions and how in consumerist societies people are increasingly unhappy with life. They are exhausted, hollowed out, and compelled to "fill the void" by purchasing new products, consuming more media, immersing themselves in school/work, indulgences, or self-destructive addictions. To us, this speaks to a sickness of the soul, and perhaps more troubling, it speaks to neoliberal capitalism's need for soul sickness. It is a vicious cycle—life feels empty, fill the void with consumption; life feels more empty because the void is still there, fill the void with more consumption—and the self-care discourse becomes yet another void-filler in a soul-sucking capitalist world. According to Miller (2000), "*Soul is a deep and vital energy that gives meaning and direction to our lives*" (p. 9, emphasis original). For us, soul is this, but it is also so much more. As Lyiscott (this volume, Chapter 1) says, it is "the spirit of the thing" that you feel deep in your bones, that allows history to come alive in the aches in one's body or the effervescence of shared moments of joy. Despite what neoliberalism wants us to believe about people needing to "fill the void," humanity is all about soul, and soul is within and around us, even when the turbines of neoliberalism begin to suck our lives into a consumerist vortex. Throughout time people have tapped into soul and soul-healing in many ways that have been shared around dinner tables, in front of fireplaces, in music halls or places of worship, in love letters, carefully crafted art, improvised comedy and music jams, and yes, even in classrooms when the flow is just right and teachers and students experience the embodied, synchronous jouissance of learning that feels oh so good and you carry that moment's memory in your back pocket for a lifetime. This is soul. We all have it. And we, as editors, want to revive it, share it, multiply it, and let it thrive so we can thrive too.

Overview of the Book

The chapters in each section share some common themes; hence, readers will notice that the divisions between the sections are imperfect. Each chapter could easily fit into a different category other than the one to which it was assigned. For the ease of our readers, we have arranged the chapters thematically into five sections.

In Part I: Spirituality, Faith, and Hope, the authors discuss how spiritual practices can inform, contradict, and live alongside critical pedagogy. In Chapter 1, Jamila Lyiscott discusses Black liberation theology in relation to critical pedagogy by examining her own "life notes"; her reflexivity opens up opportunities for healing via "racio-spiritual remembering." Chapter 2, by Irwin Leopando, taps into the spiritual dimensions of critical pedagogy to illuminate how teaching and learning can foster wholeness, meaningfulness, and agency that usher forth healing through individual flourishing and social transformation. In Chapter 3 James D. Kirylo asserts that teachers can bring meaning to their practice through a "spirituality of inclusion" founded on "dispositions of significance" including love, faith, hope, humility, compassion, and persistence. Christopher Emdin, in Chapter 4, illuminates how critical pedagogy in urban science education can provide "soul healing" for urban young people and their teachers. Finally, Helen Kwah, in Chapter 5, explores her own history with Buddhist practices in relation to racism. She encourages a spiritualism that embraces embodied awareness to afford healing and social justice.

Part II: Mental and Physical Well-Being draws attention to the physical and mental dimensions of critical pedagogy for healing. In Chapter 6, Tricia Kress and Jennifer Somma-Coughlin use co-autoethnography to explore the psychological and physiological effects of burnout in their lives pre- and mid-Covid-19 pandemic in order to theorize and disrupt the effects of "neoliberal urgency" and technorationality on their minds and bodies. Kathryn Strom calls for a "pedagogy of vulnerability" in Chapter 7, as she sheds light on her own struggles with anxiety and panic disorder and how being vulnerable in her pedagogy enabled her to begin to heal while also providing healing opportunities for students. In Chapter 8, Victoria Restler provides insights about teachers' embodied pedagogies of self-care as they participated in social justice activism in their schools. Ian Levy in Chapter 9 offers a discussion of hip-hop and spoken word therapy (HHSWT), a healing intervention for school counselors to engage in when working with youth of color. Lastly, in Chapter 10, Carolyn Ali-Khan and John Wesley White call for educators to not ignore that young people are more than just "brains on stems," and their physical health, including their sexual health, is crucial for combatting disembodied and dehumanizing public schooling.

Part III: Creativity and the Arts recognizes the immense power of creativity and forms of self-expression to bring about soul healing. In Chapter 11, Robert Lake taps into nature and music to immerse readers in the healing potential of sound. Isabelle Gatt, in Chapter 12, shares how her collaborations in rehab centers reveal the healing potential of dramatic performance and theater. In Chapter 13, Laura Apol shares her own experiences with poetry writing and healing and how her poetry classroom also serves as a site of healing for future teachers. Chapter 14 presents the work of Gene Fellner who introduces preservice special education teachers to the healing possibilities of arts-based pedagogies. In Chapter 15, the final piece in this section, Damaris C. Dunn explores hip-hop as a means of honoring the historical contributions of Black women activists and facilitating Black girl joy in the social studies classroom.

Part IV: Community and Connection recognizes the role of human collectives in providing support and creating necessary conditions for healing. In Chapter 16, Robin Brandehoff recounts her time working with youth who had experienced trauma and how providing mentoring, community, and leadership opportunities allowed for individual and collective healing. In Chapter 17, e alexander connects with the wisdom of Black womxn elders as they explore the relationship between their praxes and the writings of bell hooks. In Chapter 18, dorothy vaandering revisits her work on restorative justice to bring to the surface how restorative practices can facilitate rehumanization for individual and collective healing. Gregory Tewksbury, in Chapter 19, explores the potential of critical pedagogy for transforming social relations and creating a "relational home" where people can address their social injuries and work together to begin to heal. Lastly in Chapter 20, Alex Chisholm explores the importance of Black teacher-coaches in facilitating healing by supporting the academic and social well-being of Black and Brown student-athletes.

In the final section of the book, Part V: Space, Place, and Land, authors draw attention to the connections between people and places and the human and nonhuman world. In Chapter 21, Curtis Acosta opens this section with his recollection of the fight for the Mexican American and Raza Studies program (MARS) which had been banned from his school in Tucson, Arizona. The chapter chronicles the ensuing court battle and victory, as well as the ongoing healing of teachers, students and the community. David S. Greene and Janet Greene follow with Chapter 22, "Schools for Liberation." In this chapter, the authors recount their time working with a rustbelt town to create a community-based adult learning school. In Chapter 23, Inny Accioly, Benedito Alcântara, Aldineia Fernandes Monteiro, and Aldenice Monteiro share the praxes of the "Young Environmental Guardians from Riverside Communities" project in the Brazilian Amazon. This project integrated environmental education with a critical interrogation of the colonial legacy of Brazil and its current manifestations of destruction and oppression for Amazon peoples and lands. In Chapter 24, Patricia Krueger-Henney and Perpetual Hayfron weave an interrelational space from which to conceptualize individual and collective healing praxes fueled by radical love to resist and transform systemic violence. In Chapter 25, Donna DeGennaro reflects on resiliency and healing in Unlocking Silent Histories, a youth leadership and digital film making nonprofit organization she founded with Maya youth in Guatemala. Finally, Jennifer D. Adams, in Chapter 26, draws her readers into the embodied knowledge of growing up in relation to urban nature and offers urban Shinrin-Yoku as a way of healing in relationship with urban land.

Conclusion

In publishing this volume, we are inspired by critical pedagogy elders and social activists like Paulo Freire, Antonia Darder, Maxine Greene, bell hooks, Joe Kincheloe, and Audre Lorde. We choose to not ignore the realities of living in a world of ongoing physical and epistemological violence. At the same time, we also recognize the incredible wealth of embodied knowledge and the many diverse healing pedagogies that have been cultivated to revive people's souls. We want to illuminate these knowledges and pedagogies, vistas of healing, that bring soul to teaching and learning. We invite you to join us on these pathways toward healing through critical pedagogy.

Part I

Spirituality, Faith, and Hope

1

And Let the Church Say "Amen": Racio-spiritual Re-membering as a Pedagogy of Healing

Jamila J. Lyiscott

The Spirit of the Thing

A Black. Woman. Christian. Scholar. Activist. All of these I carried with me as we emerged from the dungeons of the Cape Coast slave castle in Ghana during the month of January 2020. And perched atop the male dungeon of the slave castle, our tour guide gestured, was a small church for the slave traders to worship between the catching, shipping, starving, beating, stacking. A church. And a small opening in the ground at the door of the church to overhear any unwanted contestation below them. My body stiffened. The faces around me distorted in disgust. The "hmph" of a Black mother holding her baby girl close was enough for us to all know. My own motherland ravaged by the "white man's religion," as they say. They named the slave ships after Jesus, Mary, and every clichéd Christian phrase the mind could think of, the tour guide told us. My throat dried. Black. Woman. Christian. Scholar. Activist. A cluster of social identities that coexist courageously and with contradiction. I stood in the auction hall of the castle. In the very steps where my ancestors were betrayed by the terror of white "Christian" men. I knew in that moment, more deeply than ever before, that the work of contending with my interrelated spiritual and racial identities has long played a salient, but silenced role in my pedagogy of liberation for Black lives. While religion and spirituality are indeed different, it is through the religious construct of Christianity that my personal navigation of the metaphysical and spiritual takes place. And it is here, at this here crossroad, that I am perpetually faced with what it means "to be both unapologetically black and Christian at the same time" (National Public Radio, 2008) in my commitment to Black liberation within and beyond education.

This chapter explores how, in my work that prepares both classroom and community educators to forward the disruption of anti-Blackness in their praxes, my pedagogical choices emerge out of what I call a racio-spiritual re-membering that creates room for navigating the contradictions of being Black within predominantly white contexts, broadly. Racio-spiritual re-membering acknowledges that racial oppression does not just operate at the material level of systemic disenfranchisement and individual harm, but it seeks to break the very spirits of the racially oppressed. It also acknowledges that our holistic healing is found in the (re)turn to who we have always powerfully been. The unlearning of white supremacist and colonial conditioning. Finally, racio-spiritual re-membering is grounded in the fact that Black history and identity are marked by an unapologetic assertion of transcendent spiritual fortitude that has operated in the service of our individual and collective healing. This assertion operates in the vein of the of Dillard's work, which explores the intersections of spirituality and education. She writes,

> Given the reward structure and cultural milieu of the academy, spiritually minded academicians have often received the implicit message to hang their spirituality outside the doors of the university and to pick it up again … on the way out … While this might work for those who view spirituality as optional, it is an act of violence against us and those like us whose cultural norms dictate the centrality of spirituality in our lives.
>
> (Dillard, 2000, p. 449)

My refusal to abandon my Blackness or my Christianity within the Eurocentric ethos of the institutions that I navigate as a scholar-activist has come to function as an orientation of resistance. Beholden to this, when I work with educators to cultivate critical pedagogies—pedagogies which question systems of power and act to disrupt the status quo—I do not fall prey to the desire for a one-sheet. A set of bullet points. A slide show of tactics and thinly veiled tricks for sounding woke in the classroom. Rather, through the evocation of my own racio-spiritual re-membering, with my Black Christian woman self, I invite the spirit of the thing. My classroom is an experiential embarkment on the very essence of the thing. Yes, the spirit of the thing.

The spirit of the thing cannot be taught in the rigid and finite ways that we are used to in traditional educational contexts. It sways you at the level of the soul and invites a holistic approach to the work of teaching and learning. It is always amusing how unnerved and excited students are when we create space for this work. It is the dissonance of engaging in new ways of knowing and being within a space where we have only been taught to operate, think, and feel in ways that are still beholden to white colonial logics. The dissonance is felt across the room. When I do hip-hop cyphers with teachers, I watch as they work to calculate how to participate in the cultural tradition correctly. I invite emotion, they work toward efficiency. I invite rhythm, they get stuck in rigidity. I invite spirit, they feel haunted by the standard. But the spirit of the thing is what moves through the hip-hop cypher as freestyle and the rocking of bodies and ancestral rhythm flows through the people. It is the extemporaneity of worship in the Black church. The freeness of scat and jazz. The mass influence that Black culture has on the popular realm of our world.

When we extend our material understanding of structural inequity to understand how social diseases operate in the spheres of spiritual and psychic violences, we find that evoking and attending to the "spirit of the thing" has been an enduring strategy for Black people to engage in individual, collective, and systemic healing. Through a critical analysis of my own life notes (Bell-Scott, 1994), I examine the spiritual ethos, racial hauntings, and liberatory consciousness that frame my identities as a Black Christian scholar-activist committed to healing the social disease of racism and the myriad contradictions navigating psychic, bodily, and spiritual racial violence imposes. To do this, I utilize racio-spiritual re-membering as an analytic, theoretical, and pedagogical tool for unearthing how my commitments to being unapologetically Christian and unapologetically Black have informed my duty to healing, disruption, and re-membering in both the classroom and the community. My own racio-spiritual re-membering illuminates how navigating the tensions between my Blackness and my Christianity equips me to challenge the systems of power that I navigate daily while sustaining my own commitments to wholeness and wellness. I take up the life notes to establish how re-membering through a racio-spiritual lens informs how I navigate, transcend, and dream beyond the racial trauma imbued in our society against Black lives.

Communion

> *I sit in communion and fellowship with the work of several scholar activists to conceptualize racio-spiritual re-membering. I break from the bread of this comm(unity) as a source of nourishment and connection. I share also in the life blood of our collective commitment toward racial healing.*

It is no surprise that DuBois's most seminal work takes up issues of racial hatred, alienation, and structural oppression in ode to the very souls of Black folks (Dubois, 1968). Speaking of the impact of racial oppression in America, DuBois laments, "One ever feels his twoness,—an American, a Negro; two souls, two thoughts, two unreconciled strivings; two warring ideals in one dark body, whose strength alone keeps it from being torn asunder" (Du Bois, 1903). This metaphysical wounding speaks to an undertheorized realm of resistance that Black people have engaged in for centuries. It is what Patricia Williams calls "spirit-murder," effected by the ongoing systemic racial violences that play out on the very spirits of the racially oppressed in myriad ways. It is "a slow death, a death of the spirit, a death that is built on racism and intended to reduce, humiliate, and destroy people of color" (Love, 2019).

Spirit-murder operates in the realm of what the world witnessed in the final eight minutes and forty-six seconds of George Floyd's life on May 25, 2020, when the murderous officer, Derek Chauvin, stole the very breath from Floyd's body for us all to see. For Black people to see. For everyone to see. And to know what we have already known. We have known this, because its psychic violence has deep historical resonance so much so that Williams in her 1987 theorization of spirit-murdering evokes a similar violence. She writes,

> Taking the example of the man who was stabbed thirty-nine times out of the context of our compartmentalized legal system, and considering it in the hypothetical framework of a legal system that encompasses and recognizes morality, religion, and psychology, I am moved to see this act as not merely body murder but spirit-murder as well. I see it as spirit-murder, only one of whose manifestations is racism-cultural obliteration … I see spirit-murder as no less than the equivalent of body murder (p. 151).

For the field of education, attention to spirit-murder and the two-ness imposed on souls of Black folks is an acknowledgment of the education system's complicity in perpetuating harm against Black lives. The kinds of harms that necessitate critical pedagogies so that we are held accountable for how education and schooling enact Black suffering. Love (2019) tells us,

> Physical and psychological attacks on Black and Brown children's bodies and culture are more than just racist acts by misguided school educators; they are the spirit murdering of Black and Brown children. This type of violence toward children of color is less visceral and seemingly less tragic than physical acts of murder at the hands of White mobs and White self-appointed vigilantes, the shooting of unarmed people of color by police officers in their own homes and communities, or the senseless violence in some Black communities, which are all conditions of racism.

How then do we attend to the "spirit of the thing" in education? That tabooed realm that sustains such woundings, and at the same time is a realm of resistance and possibility for Black people across the world?

In a "spiritual offering" that refuses the hegemony of Eurocentricity in the academy and its tyranny over what ways of knowing and being should be centered, Dillard asserts, "many scholars and activists involved in the reformation of the academy have worldviews deeply embedded in the spiritual" (Dillard, 2000, p. 448). Her work then puts forth "alternative offerings of 'truth,'" which calls for attention to the spiritual in African-centeredness and to the myriad ways that spirituality and education already function in the lives of Black educators. As one of her research participants shares, "Spirituality in education is education with purpose, education that is liberatory work, education that is emancipation" (p. 447).

While I join this line of scholarship that calls for attention and attending to the spirit of the thing in addressing racial healing, I am faced with the reality that my own spiritual orientations shape me as unapologetically Christian in a society where Christianity has been weaponized against Black, Indigenous, and People of Color through a heinous history of slavery, colonialism, and imperialism. I am faced with the fact that right here in my communion, my brother DuBois makes plain, "I flatly refused again to join any church or sign any church creed. From my 30th year on I have increasingly regarded the church as an institution which defended such evils as slavery, color caste, exploitation of labor and war" (Du Bois, 1968). My racio-spiritual re-membering, then, begins in the crosshairs of this contention, which then frames my pedagogical and methodological approaches to enacting individual and systemic resistance as a scholar-activist.

For making sense of this invitation to attend the spiritual alongside my personal Christian orientations as a Black woman scholar-activist, I turn to the work of the late James Cone. In his seminal work, *The Cross and the Lynching Tree* (2011), the theologian contends with the symbolic and material violences of both the lynching tree and the burning cross to expose the Christianization of racial oppression against Black lives. As the father of Black liberation theology (BLT), Cone's taking up of these charged symbols has opened up powerful possibilities for the tensions of being both Black and Christian by disrupting the violent white hegemonic history of Christianity and prioritizing the liberation and healing of the oppressed, as Christ did throughout scripture. These possibilities hold deep implications for Black realities broadly, since the tensions and inherent contradictions of being both Black and *insert white-dominated institutional affiliation here* saturate Black experiences daily. At its core, BLT rejects the white-dominated construction of Christianity and works to heal the violences of this history by repositioning Christianity through the lens of the oppressed in both the theorization and implementation of Black Christian practices. Thus, it positions the work of healing (racial) violence as a necessary praxis of the liberation that it offers.

Re-membering through a Racio-Spiritual Lens

Taking the above conceptual commitments into account, racio-spiritual re-membering recognizes that systems of power acting against Black lives have inflicted spiritual wounds, and that Black people have long engaged in both individual and systemic healing through the audacity of spirit, survival, and song. The concept of re-membering that I take up for my methodological framing was first introduced to me in Toni Morrison's (2004) *Beloved*, where the central figures of the story, set in the early postbellum South, were newly freed from American chattel slavery. For Morrison, any hope of wellness or healing against the backdrop of racial hatred in the nineteenth-century South, occurred through remembering—the evocation of memories from the trauma of slavery and the triumphs of survival—and re-membering—the bringing together of self and community and past and present and future. This play on words and call for individual and collective healing is perhaps most well epitomized in the sermon of the matriarchal figure of the text, Baby Suggs, who exhorts her Black community to re-member. She proclaims,

> Here … in this here place, we flesh; flesh that weeps, laughs; flesh that dances on bare feet in grass. Love it. Love it hard. Yonder they do not love your flesh. They despise it. They don't love your eyes; they'd just as soon pick em out. No more do they love the skin on your back. Yonder they flay it. And O my people they do not love your hands. Those they only use, tie, bind, chop off and leave empty. Love your

> hands! Love them. Raise they up and kiss them. Touch others with them, pat them together, stroke them on your face 'cause they don't love that either … You got to love it. This is flesh I'm talking about here. Flesh that needs to be loved. Feet that need to rest and to dance; backs that need support; shoulders that need arms, strong arms I'm telling you. And O my people, out yonder, hear me, they do not love your neck unnoosed and straight. So love your neck; put a hand on it, grace it, stroke it and hold it up. And all your inside parts that they'd just as soon slop for hogs, you got to love them … and the beat and beating heart, love that too. (pp. 103–4).

Re-membering is to refuse the devaluation of Blackness. To recall, to hold, to care, to love, to see, and to own the self in ways that have been disparaged by whiteness for generations. Remembering who we are is re-membering who we are. For Black educators and scholar activists committed to critical pedagogies of healing, committed to acknowledging how the whiteness of educational contexts continues to murder the spirit of the thing, there is an essential re-membering that must occur to break free from the curricular impositions, norms, and values of schooling that are still violently rooted in white colonial logic. That is, a returning to what we have always known to be valuable and valid, even in the face of white supremacy. I have done this work as forged by my own complex navigation of re-membering and (re)turning to the reality of Christianity—which has its beginnings in North Africa and the Middle East—against the backdrop of the Christianity of the Western world with its violent history of anti-Blackness. The urgency of my racio-spiritual re-membering began in the contradictions of the Black church. To exist in the Black church is to at once know the power of Black cultural practices in shaping our connection to the spirit through the rhythm of our praise and at the very same time be faced with images of a white Jesus, the respectability politics of the suit and tie, and standards of decorum rooted in white supremacy that persists in the Black church. It is to know that there is a "Black church" because the white "Christians" who shared the gospel with our ancestors wouldn't dare also worship alongside Black people. These painful contradictions have deeply informed how I bring healing, wholeness, and resistance to all of the predominantly white institutions that I navigate as a scholar-activist.

I draw on re-membering as a methodological tool to excavate from my past and present interrelated inner worlds of spirituality and racial identity as they shape my personal and professional experiences as a scholar-activist. To do this, I draw from the methods laid out in the work of Cynthia Dillard, which utilize life notes (Bell-Scott, 1994) to examine "constructed personal narratives such as letters, stories, journal entries, reflections, poetry, music, and other artful forms" that inhere the complex lived realities of the subject as situated within sociocultural realities that shape meaning. Data sources for my life notes included poetic writings, journal entries, and personal reflections. For each life-note, I chose moments where my Christian values and orientations were saliently operating in my decisions as a scholar-activist. I used open coding to explore major themes in answer to two salient questions: What does being a Black Christian mean for the ways that I engage in scholar-activism? How does a liberatory Black Christian-centered paradigm influence my pedagogical choices through racio-spiritual re-membering?

Racio-spiritual Re-membering

The following life notes represent the ways that my spiritual ethos interacts with my journey toward a liberatory consciousness (Love, 2010) as a Black woman scholar-activist that is contending with the racial hauntings (Johnson, 2017) of being Black in America. The first two life notes are Facebook posts created during the 2020 Black Lives Matter uprisings following the murders of Ahmaud Arbery, Breonna Taylor, and George Floyd. The final life note is an excerpt from a spoken-word poem that I share with students as a teacher-educator to invoke the spirit of rhythm and orality that are tied to both my cultural traditions and my spiritual traditions in the Black church.

Life note #1

Many people who claim to follow Christ don't seem to realize that the reason Jesus was murdered and the reason He gave His life are two different things. Jesus was not murdered for our sins. His murderers were not like "let's kill this guy and save the world." He was murdered because He was a political threat who stood in solidarity with the oppressed in a radical and outspoken commitment to peace, equity, love, and justice that is of divine order. Jesus gave His life/died for us because God knows how to work human evil into His divine plan. But He was murdered because in the minds of the social elite, He dared to take a stand against their corruption. So the next time you're feeling like Christianity means some kind of ethereal apolitical existence, please note that anything that threatens equity, peace, love and justice is anti-Christian in the worst possible way. #Blacklivesmatter

Life note #2

The Black Lives Matter movement is not fighting for symbols of white repentance. We are not fighting for you to take a knee. We are fighting for you to take a stand against the ways that anti-Blackness is systemically embedded into your institutions. We are not fighting for street names. If I can be murdered by an officer on Black Lives Matter Plaza with no accountability, then this is nothing more than an empty promise. We are not fighting for white tears, we are fighting for you to tear down the statues to white supremacy that live in your hiring practices, in who is labeled as "difficult," in who is silenced and who is heard, in your loan decisions, in your dress codes, in your white Jesus, in who gets suspended and erased in schools, in your prison industrial complex, and so much more. We are not fighting to be featured on your brochure or website if we are not also represented in your leadership. The good Lord knows we are NOT fighting to see white people put on kente cloth. We are fighting for white people to take off white privilege. We are not fighting for police to cupid shuffle their way into our hearts, we are fighting for you to defund police and redirect those funds to community policing models, education, healthcare, and all of the social services that are constantly defunded in our communities. We are not fighting for you to make thinly veiled public statements that protect your brand and economic interests. We are fighting for you to burn down the way things were and radically reimagine your role in dismantling systemic oppression. "Mattering is the minimum."
#Blacklivesmatter

13 Comments 480 Shares

Life note #3

For those who don't know, over 83% of our urban educators are not people of color and live outside of the racially diverse communities where their students reside
So I bring in the cypher, a practice within hip hop culture with West African roots
Essentially, it's a circle of people who come together to share in extemporaneous freestyle or newly written ideas over a beat
The goal is to exhibit mastery
Lyrical and rhetorical dexterity
Sometimes using the African Diasporic tradition of signifying

So every semester for some years now I have taught these teachers some fundamental skills and features of hip hop writing so that they dare participate in the art of the cypher
And every semester I witness the same exact patterns during the lesson …
In a nutshell, terror and fear
The beat is in the background and as I watch the anxiety and hesitation in the room reach a boiling point I lower the music to invite some truth
Honest reflection about what is being felt
Vulnerability, fear of failure, fear and discomfort about being inauthentic, my lines suck!
These are some of the feelings that are agreed upon in the room
It is at this point
When I can see the anxious excitement of some
And fear and shame in the eyes of others that I ask
How many of your students do you label illiterate by societal standards
While they can demonstrate mastery over this complex form that intimidates YOU in this cypher?
How inauthentic it must feel for them to speak in a language that regards their own as inferior?
I tell this 83% that for marginalized peoples, a truly diverse society is not about simply being included in dominant culture

Theorizing through the Lens of Racio-spiritual Re-membering

Black educators are perpetually faced with what it means to navigate the dissonance of educational structures that are rooted in whiteness and anti-Blackness while holding onto the spirit of education that we believe in dearly. An analysis of my own racio-spiritual re-membering demonstrates how I have made sense of this dissonance to elucidate what being a Black Christian means for the ways that I engage in scholar-activism, and how my liberatory Black Christian-centered paradigm influences my pedagogical choices through racio-spiritual re-membering. Each of the life notes above were either created or employed in my work as a scholar-activist during the 2020 Black Lives Matter uprisings. My analyses offered three themes: *re-membering history, re-membering resistance, and re-membering the spirit of the thing.*

The 2020 outcry of the Black Lives Matter movement across the globe represents a railing against the pervasiveness of whiteness and anti-Blackness across all facets of our social reality. In the wake (Sharpe, 2016) of such blatant sins against humanity, I found that the theme of *re-membering history* was a prominent pattern in my work as a Black educator. My analyses of notes one and two were directly informed by the lens of BLT, which invites us to re-member history by directly challenging the white-washed history of the Bible distorted through its translation into European languages and its use as an oppressive rather than liberating tool. These distortions, a key player in "the white man's burden" to colonize, civilize, and Christianize indigenous groups, were used to placate the oppressed and even teach us that to follow Christ is to passively and meekly accept their oppression as divinely ordered. Today, America's radical right still clings to Christianity as the guise and guard of their white supremacist capitalist ideologies. In direct contrast to this, BLT shows us that when stripped away from its whiteness, the Bible in its original context is not at all a "white man's religion" but finds its roots in North Africa and the Middle East. And I am left to sit with the complicity of schooling in forwarding a "white man's history," which explicitly does not teach or acknowledged the historical contributions of racially diverse groups. BLT teaches us how violent the lie of a blue-eyed blonde-haired Jesus is. And I am left to sit with the parallels of how the history books in our schools disproportionately feature white heroes in an act of psychic violence and spirit-murder against millions of Black, Indigenous, and students of color who do not see themselves represented in the text. BLT re-members biblical history as the story of a God who stands with the oppressed and exacts justice for the marginalized throughout. As a Black Christian scholar-activist, my own racio-spiritual re-membering of biblical history directly shifts my responsibility to draw on my spiritual values as a Christian and align with the oppressed in resistance to the oppressor. Note one represents my proclamation that Jesus was indeed a political agitator and not just a passive recipient of violence.

Re-membering resistance was the second theme that cut across all of my life notes. Note three represents one way that I actualized resistance particularly in teacher education contexts where I share spoken word poetry as a natural part of the lesson plan. Evoking the rhythm, orality, and spirit found in the traditions of the Black church, the poem acts as a tool of resistance against the traditional ethos of schooling. Life notes #1 and #2, though on Facebook, almost function as sermons. The combined 904 likes and 833 shares represents a socio-digital "amen" having ripple effects across timelines as people join me in re-membering resistance through the historical re-membering of who Christ truly was.

The final theme that emerged in my analysis was *re-membering the spirit of the thing*. The spirit of the thing can be found in the rhythm and bold truth of note number three, the sermonesque stylings of life notes #1 and #2, and the linguistic dexterity across all three notes. Rhythm, truth-telling, and engaging linguistic style are lauded features of Black cultural and spiritual traditions. This represents a re-membering of who I am both spiritually and racially, which permeates my work as a Black scholar-activist fighting for racial justice in education.

2

Toward a Critical Pedagogy of Spirituality and Healing

Irwin Leopando

We are living through a time of converging crises: skyrocketing income and wealth inequality, eroded democratic institutions, resurgent authoritarianism and white supremacy, ecological collapse. In the face of so many challenges, we critical educators have the responsibility to persist in the struggle to build a more compassionate, equitable, and sustainable world. To do so, we must marshal the inner resources to orient our work and keep us from succumbing to apathy, fatalism, pessimism, and despair. Accordingly, the questions of vision, meaning, purpose, and hope should precede all concerns, including those which routinely take up the bulk of our time and energy (e.g., classroom techniques, assessments, instructional technologies). Without the consistent and conscious effort to foreground our most fundamental commitments and aspirations in our day-to-day work, we can easily become divorced from our sense of idealism, energy, and vocation. In time, this alienation will likely lead to stagnation and bitterness.

In this chapter, I attempt to explore the pedagogical substance and significance of these foundational questions, including: What is the larger purpose of our teaching? What kinds of persons are we helping our students to grow into? What educational structures and conditions can cultivate or hinder this development? What kind of society are we helping to create? How can we contribute toward healing a broken world? I am convinced that engaging seriously with such concerns leads us into the realm of spirituality, which is the natural domain for investigating the deepest questions of human existence. By centering and embracing the intrinsic spirituality of our profession, we can reenergize and strengthen this crucial work. Along similar lines, I envision the classroom as a potential site of healing, which I define as fostering the wholeness, growth, and agency of teachers and students alike. Such critical pedagogies of healing affirm the uniqueness and full personhood of all participants, thereby opposing the market-driven logic of instrumentalization, standardization, and surveillance, which pervades contemporary schooling. To this end, I will draw attention to key themes in the educational praxis of Paulo Freire (1921–1997), the influential Brazilian activist, philosopher, and seminal figure in the development of critical pedagogy. Freire's work, in my view, offers a powerful vision of a vibrant and enlivening pedagogy, which is grounded upon human flourishing.

A Tentative Definition of Spirituality

Before proceeding, I want to briefly explain what I mean by "spirituality." For the purposes of this discussion, I posit that spirituality does not require adherence to any specific creed or doctrine. Rather, it is akin to Paul Tillich's (2001) definition of authentic faith as "the state of being ultimately concerned" (p. 1). It is that which "matters infinitely" for one's life (2001, pp. 4–5). In other words, spirituality is the realm of the highest values and meanings for any given person. In addition, spirituality involves actions, not just beliefs. As an integral phenomenon, it encompasses one's thoughts and everyday choices. Spirituality can also be understood as the depth dimension of human existence. It is the ontological field on which each person wrestles with the eternal problems of mortality, purpose, and meaning. Moreover, I understand spirituality as a profoundly social phenomenon. As Michael Dallaire (2001) explains:

> [Spirituality] must include the wider world around us, the demands of solidarity, and the story of the universe. It must take up the feminist challenge to be inclusive and concerned with grounding in relationship and interrelationship, between self and other, between selves and the world. It must take into account the global village we live in, a village marked by pluralism and diversity. It must include the public dimension and the areas of politics and economics. Finally, spirituality must be life affirming in promoting the deepest needs and aspirations for life that reside in the human person and which are connected to the global and ecological community. (p. 35)

As such, authentic spirituality moves both inward *and* outward. It cannot be purely individualistic; without an abiding concern for the welfare of others, it is hollow. Finally, I propose that spirituality is nondualistic. It integrates mind and body, intellect and emotions, self and other, inner growth and the common good.

A Selfish Society

The societal context for a pedagogy of spirituality is the hyper-individualistic, winner-take-all ethos that has long pervaded US culture. George Monbiot (2016) identifies the most corrosive aspects of this ultra-capitalistic philosophy: "[It] sees competition as the defining characteristic of human relations. It redefines citizens as consumers, whose democratic choices are best exercised by buying and selling, a process that rewards merit and punishes inefficiency." Indeed, the past four decades have seen the relentless penetration of virtually every facet of human life by the values and logic of capitalism. As Peter Roberts (1999) has pointed out, educational system has assimilated this worldview, with market-based concepts and frameworks such as "efficiency," "quality assessment," and "performance indicators" dominating the professional discourse (pp. 99–101). Explicitly or otherwise, educational institutions at all levels have defined their primary mission as imbuing students with the "knowledge" and skills to compete in an unforgiving globalized marketplace. Disciplines of study that are considered less "useful" or "marketable" have been devalued and defunded (pp. 99–101). In effect, the fundamental purpose of education has been recast as worker training. As a result, teachers are forced to spend inordinate amounts of time and energy on one the most insidious (and archetypically capitalist) forms of coercion and control within the educational system—the use of grades.

To be sure, I acknowledge that we have a professional responsibility to help our students to develop "practical" skills. Likewise, completely ignoring the need to prepare our students for their desired careers would be pedagogical malpractice. Nevertheless, the near-absolute capture of the US educational system by market imperatives has shaped an educational status quo that is largely stultified, depersonalized, and anti-intellectual. Excessively focused on "pragmatic" means and ends, it has alienated countless students from their full personhood. David E. Purpel (2010) describes tragic results:

> The society and the schools urge us to work hard, strive for personal success, and compete with ourselves, our colleagues, and our enemies. Some (too many) people respond with drugs, crime, suicide, and depression. The society and schools extol individual achievement and indeed equate it with virtue. Some (surely too many) people respond with divorce, loneliness, and anomie. The society and the schools exhort us to be "number one" and that we are risking our loss of economic and political supremacy. Some (far too many) people respond with racism, sexism, jingoism, and homophobia. The society demands more control, discipline, hard work, and competition and the profession responds with more sophisticated tests and more clever modes of monitoring students and teachers. The people cry out for meaning, wisdom, and deliverance—and the society and school respond fearfully with more control, more jargon, more retrenchment, and less meaning and wisdom than ever. (p. 8)

Purpel correctly points out how the instrumentalism and anti-personalism of the educational system both reflects and feeds into the malaise, fragmentation, and destructiveness of the wider culture. Excessively oriented toward competition and management, schools have come to resemble factories in which students are the products which need regular evaluation for quality control (Kirylo and Nauman, 2006, p. 198). Given such woeful conditions, the pedagogical orientation toward supporting the growth and flourishing of each student as a unique and irreplaceable human being is too frequently and readily surrendered, even by educators with the best of intentions.

Indeed, the marketization and depersonalization of education is not just harmful for students; it is spiritually corrosive for teachers as well. As James D. Kirylo (2006) notes, educators are frequently reduced into "mechanical functionaries" who are handcuffed by an avalanche of externally mandated curricula and bureaucratic requirements "from fostering critical thought, innovation, and [cultivating] … the love of learning" (p. 198). For his part, Clifford Mayes (2003) recounts how innumerable teachers have experienced "relentless institutional pressure" to become "pedagogical agents of the corporate state" when they are forced to serve as transmitters and enforcers of top-down "competencies" in the service of market-based goals which are frequently not their own (p. 5). Moreover, the linkage of testing outcomes to institutional funding has resulted in "teachers and administrators working in fear, creating an unhealthy school environment that is immersed in a discourse focused on numbers, ratings, and scores" (Kirylo and Nauman, 2006, p. 202). Far too many educators are compelled to lead profoundly divided lives, with their day-to-day work reduced to performances of "professionalism" that bears little connection to their inner selves. The result: schools blighted by teacher burnout and turnover, where 20 percent of new educators leaving the profession within their first three years (Kirylo and Nauman, 2006, p. 203). This is an untenable situation, one which calls out for a fundamental reimagining and transformation of schooling.

Freire's Pedagogy of Spirituality and Healing

Given this bleak educational landscape, the praxis of Paulo Freire (1921–1997) can serve as a point of departure for envisioning a more humane, healing, and spiritually nourishing pedagogy. Freire's theory and practice, which grew out of his various Latin American literacy campaigns, aimed to challenge the material, structural, and ideological sources of injustice. Through years of working with adult peasants and urban workers, Freire grew convinced that education can foster either adaptation to the status quo (i.e., "domestication") or critical analysis, political agency, and solidarity (i.e., "liberation"). Pedagogies which purport to be "neutral" or "apolitical" are tacitly legitimating the status quo and must be rejected. Even during his lifetime, Freire achieved near-mythical status among radical and progressive educators, activists, and intellectuals. His writings, especially *Pedagogy of the Oppressed* (1970), continue to spark study and debate more than two decades after his death. His work inspires teachers and activists in adult literacy programs, church groups, labor unions, community organizations, and formal educational institutions throughout the world (Weiler, 1996, p. 353).

As I (2017) have written elsewhere, the spiritual dimension of Freire's thought has received relatively little recognition among much of his Western audience. Many of these readers tend to view him primarily as a revolutionary Marxist thinker. Viewing Freire's lifelong educational project exclusively through a secular lens overlooks an even more foundational influence—his lifelong Catholicism. As he asserted in his final years:

> All arguments in favor of the legitimacy of a more *people-oriented* society have their deepest roots in my faith. It sustains me, motivates me, challenges me, and it has never allowed me to say, "Stop, settle down; things are as they are because they cannot be any other way."

(1997, p. 104)Without question, Freire's moral core, social concern, and educational philosophy flowed from the wellspring of his faith. Regrettably, this aspect of his praxis has often been downplayed by much of the Western intellectual Left (Perkins, 2001, p. 590). This is a tragic erasure, given the potential of Freire's spiritual vision to enrich the desperately needed project of rethinking and revitalizing our educational praxis.

To begin, we can consider one of Freire's most lasting contributions to educational thought: his critique of the "banking method." According to Freire (2000), traditional pedagogies turn students into uncritical "containers" or passive "receptacles" for prefabricated, officially sanctioned knowledge (p. 72). In addition, it is detached from political or ethical considerations—a practice that he derides as "training rather than educating" (2004, p. 19). Students are conditioned into accommodating themselves to the world as it is because they are kept from "awakening" to their intrinsic capacity to resist and reshape oppressive societal conditions (1998c, pp. 499–500). In his view (1998a), the greatest injury of such pedagogy is that it "impoverishes what is fundamentally human in [the learning] experience: namely, its capacity to form the human person" (p. 39). Which is to say, it is essentially immoral because it negates the learner's "vocation of becoming more human" (2000, p. 72). Along these lines, he (2005) references Jacques Maritain, the prominent twentieth-century French Catholic theologian who greatly influenced his educational philosophy:

> As Jacques Maritain has pointed out, "If we remember that the animal is a specialist and a perfect one, all of its knowing power being fixed upon a single task to be done, we ought to conclude that an educational program which would only aim at forming specialists ever more perfect in ever more specialized fields, and unable to pass judgement on any matter that goes beyond their specialized competence, would lead indeed to a progressive animalization of the human mind and life." (p. 36)

Freire (by way of Maritain) is contending that educational practices which aim solely at preparing students for specialized careers, and which leave them incapable of critical thought in any other area of life, are profoundly dehumanizing. Speaking in line with Catholic tradition, both thinkers affirm a radical ontological discontinuity between persons and nonhuman creatures. The latter are limited to instinctual, reactive, and habitual behaviors. While they are capable of motion, perception, and reaction, they lack the human capacity for self-consciousness, moral intelligence, and the godlike capacity to infuse genuine newness into the universe. Moreover, Freire (2005) asserts that only human beings have the potential to enter "the domain which is theirs exclusively—that of History and of Culture" (p. 4). They are the only living creatures who *exist* rather than merely *survive*. They have the potential to transcend "mere being in the world" through conscious acts of transformation, production, decision, creation, and communication (1998b, pp. 499–500). In contrast, animals must "adapt" to the world as it is because they are incapable of transcending their biological conditioning (1997, p. 32). For Freire, the purely instinctual ways of inhabiting the material world, which are characteristic of the animal sphere, are symptoms of degradation when practiced by humans (2005, p. 4).

Bracketing any objections to Freire's assumption of human exceptionalism, my basic point is that his view of "humanization" constitutes the foundation of his educational project. It undergirds his core views about the nature and purpose of human existence. The centrality of this concept to his work is writ large in the opening lines of *Pedagogy of the Oppressed*, where he declares that the struggle for "humanization" is the axis of historical struggle (2000, p. 43). Importantly, Freire (1998a) insists that all persons possess the capacity—and responsibility—to become "more fully human" by cooperating with others to build a more just, compassionate, and beautiful world. This journey involves forming relationships of mutuality and participating in collective struggle for societal transformation helps us to grow less passive and selfish (p. 55). In other words, we grow into our full humanity as part of a community of self-sacrificial struggle (1998a, p. 79). Humanization is thus a deeply relational and collective phenomenon. Indeed, Freire scorns purely individualistic forms of growth, freedom, or well-being. Against privatized notions of "success," he reaffirms that human beings can only flourish through interdependence and solidarity: "No one saves another, no one saves himself [sic] all alone, because only in communion can we save ourselves. We work out our [liberation] in communion" (1972, p. 10). As Peter Roberts (1996) notes, Freire understood personhood as a thoroughly relational phenomenon (p. 192). It is only in reference to others that we grow into our full stature as human beings. This is one of the greatest paradoxes of genuine healing; we become more ourselves, more authentic, and more whole by *turning toward* one another.

These spiritually grounded ideas about the human personhood informed Freire's entire educational praxis. For instance, Freire affirms that "liberating" pedagogies are grounded in the very nature of persons are "unfinished" beings (i.e., capable of further growth): "In this incompletion and this awareness [of this incompleteness] lie the very roots of education as an exclusively human manifestation" (2000, p. 84). Along similar lines, he (1998a) asserts that "the open-minded teacher cannot afford to ignore anything that concerns the human person" (p. 127). Education is always a "strictly human experience," which can never be reduced to "something cold, mental, merely technical, and without soul, where feelings, sensibility, desires, and dreams had no place" (1998a, p. 129). He (1997) repudiates the rationalist epistemologies which dominate traditional Western intellectual and educational discourse: "I know with my entire body, with feelings, with passion, and [not only] with reason" (p. 30). Rejecting dualistic categories (i.e., mind and body, intellect and emotion, ethical and technical), he affirms an integrative and healing vision of what it means to be a full human person. In addition, Freire (1998a) calls upon educators to cultivate a wide range of virtues, including "a generous loving heart, respect for others, tolerance, humility, a joyful disposition, love of life, … a disposition to welcome change, perseverance in the struggle, a refusal of determinism, a spirit of hope, and openness to justice" (p. 108). As all teachers know, this is a daunting challenge. It demands great courage, steadfastness, and devotion, especially in the face of institutional structures, working conditions, and societal expectations that hinder the practice of these pedagogical commitments at every step. Importantly, Freire (1998a) contends that the source of these virtues is not the "merely scientific, technical mind," which is incapable of giving rise to them (108). Rather, they flow from the same "mysterious" ground which gave rise to the educator's sense of vocation. Drawing on this spiritual bedrock, teachers can "persist with so much devotion despite the immoral salaries they receive. And do it with love" (1998a: 126). Above all, Freire affirms that teachers and students become "more fully human" through relationships that are grounded in mutuality, vulnerability, and humility. Ultimately, he envisions a pedagogy of healing and care, grounded on a fundamental commitment to nurturing each learner's sacred personhood.

Implications and Final Reflections

In this anguished historical moment, those of us who have chosen teaching as our life's work have the chance to contribute toward healing a broken world. As I have maintained throughout this chapter, this project will only emerge in its fullness if we deepen our work beyond technocratic improvements to our teaching methods. While pursuing such reforms are necessary and admirable efforts, confining our inquiry to this pedagogical level only perpetuates the constricted, instrumentalist, anti-person ideologies that have created to the status quo. (As Albert Einstein famously said, "No problem can be solved from the same level of consciousness that created it.") Rather, we must conduct our praxis on a more fundamental dimension, which is that of spirituality and healing. As I mentioned at the beginning of this piece, we must foreground the first principles of our vocation: What is the ultimate purpose of our teaching? What kinds of persons are we helping our students to grow into? What educational conditions can foster or hinder this growth? What kind of society are we helping to build? As a faculty member in a chronically underfunded urban community college, I recognize how difficult it can be to keep these concerns at the forefront of our consciousness as we navigate the demands and stresses of our professional lives. Yet we must make the constant effort to wrestle with them. For unless we commit ourselves to an enduring, energizing, and meaning-filled vision of our "ultimate concern" as educators, I fear that we will be cast adrift. Without a clear and enduring sense of purpose and possibility, we can easily—perhaps inevitably—fall prey to cynicism, sterility, and hopelessness.

In this vein, I have presented Paulo Freire's praxis as a potential point of departure for developing a spiritually grounded pedagogy. His "ultimate concern" was to foster the full flourishing of human beings *and* the wider society. This total commitment was the guiding light and final arbiter for his lifelong project. It led him to advocate, sometimes at great personal risk, for "humanizing" educational structures, material conditions, and public policies. To be sure, we need not—indeed should not—replicate every aspect of Freire's philosophy or practice. Instead, we should adapt them to our own cultural, institutional, and disciplinary contexts, considering our students' needs and aspirations, and in accordance with our own unique identities and deepest values. In the end, regardless of our various pedagogical methods, I am convinced that bringing to light, affirming, and cultivating the spiritual dimension of our work can be profoundly sustaining and clarifying. It can orient and move toward a more humane, socially conscious, and genuinely transformative educational system. In an era awash in selfishness, exploitation, and alienation, such a pedagogy can hardly more essential to healing our social bonds, our nation, and our planet.

3

A Spirituality of Inclusion and Six Dispositions of Significance: Bringing Eternal Meanings to Our Pedagogical Practice

James D. Kirylo

To be a teacher is to respond to a call from the heart. Teaching thus becomes an autobiographical venture, moving from the inside out, suggesting an inherent spiritual dimension to its process. The assumption is that spirituality is something we innately possess as a natural impulse, as a way of seeing life as a whole, to live more deeply (Helminiak, 1987; Leean, 1988; Warren, 1988; Kolander & Chandler, 1990; Nouwen, 2016).[1]

When Parker Palmer (1993) argues that education is a journey into the spiritual, indicating that "teaching and learning can be renewed upon spiritual wisdom" (p. x), he is not engaging us in a sectarian argument of any sort; but, rather, he is exhorting a way of thinking that is dedicated to truth, justice, and goodness in the effort to cultivate relationship, to build community. Moreover, echoing Palmer's thought, Dwayne Huebner (1995) further stresses the intentional living out the spiritual life in schools, emphasizing that education ultimately embarks on a "journey of the soul" (p. 20).

The idea of entering this journey is naturally linked to personalist thought, that which is particularly espoused by Emmanuel Mounier (1905–1950).[2] For Mounier, the person as a spiritual being, acting as a subject (i.e., participant in the making of history) implies that one is not an object but rather exists through action moving the subjective self from the center in order to realize that purposeful existence occurs through relationship with the other (Kirylo & Boyd, 2017; Williams & Bengtsson, 2016; Sawchenko, 2013; Inglis, 1959), working toward "humanizing" humanity (Mounier, 1952).[3]

Collectively drawing from the above and through an ecumenical prism in light of being an educator, a certain spirituality of inclusion is a way of being that regardless of one's faith position, belief system, or religious affiliation recognizes the uniqueness of every individual—not in competition with one another—but rather in collaboration with each other to justly, rightly, and lovingly build the community. Yet, the idea of fostering the latter is perilously being challenged.

That is, consider the racial animus that continues to pervade within an era of hyper-political partisanship, tribalism, and mean-spirited divisiveness both in and out of education circles. In that light, therefore, the notion of a critical pedagogy for healing is not only timely but also suggests an intentionality toward renewal, toward wholeness, in a concerted effort that collaboratively works to lovingly and justly build the community. To work toward that end requires us to examine our collective hearts, while at that same realizing the decisive relevance of our individual dispositions.

The Decisive Relevance of Dispositions

John Dewey (1933) suggests that dispositions ought to be cultivated through an attitude of open-mindedness (i.e., to consider multiple points of view and possibilities), wholeheartedness (i.e., an undivided heart in order to absorb what we learn; a genuine enthusiasm), and responsibility (i.e., taking into thoughtful consideration one's beliefs and their consequences to responsibly engage students in meaningful subject matter).

The cultivation of these three attitudes are integral to what Dewey (1933) describes as a "habit of thinking" influencing the formation of character. Therefore, the routine of habit in the context of thinking implies that habits are not some mindless rulings that direct us; rather, thought informs our habits as a way of being, thinking, and doing (Dewey, 1983). In that light, the habit of mind needed to appropriate behaviors and actions that are intentionally thoughtful and intelligent—is a disciplined mind (Costa & Kallick, 2000).

Realizing the necessity of a disciplined mind in order to appropriate dispositional patterns, the cultivation of mindfulness (i.e., a state of being where one feels a sense of control of one's life, guided by creativity, flexibility, information, memory, and retention [Ritchart & Perkins, 2000]) is an integral aspect to that process, which is also inclusive of a psychological element comprised of three constituents: sensitivity (i.e., "an awareness of and alertness to occasions for engaging in certain behavior."), inclination (i.e., "the motivation or habit toward carrying out a particular behavior."), and ability (i.e., "the capability of carrying out that behavior") (Ritchart & Perkins, 2000, p. 30).

The inference of the three components suggests that the mindfulness infused in one's disposition is the engine that propels behavior, parallel to the thinking that explains the idea of activating intentional habits of the mind. For the teacher, Lovewell (2012) would characterize this way of thinking and doing as mindful teaching, which emanates from a heart-centered approach, always linked to the spiritual, to who we are.

As teachers, responding to who we are, in light of our intimate awareness of the decisive relevance of our individual dispositions, we come to realize that the desirable dispositions of a teacher can vary from context, setting, circumstance, student population, and the political, social, and religious landscape,[4] making teaching what Eisner (2006) calls a custom job. And while there are natural dispositional differences that teachers must consider relative to setting, circumstance, and time, there are, however, foundational humanizing dispositions all teachers ought to possess. Infused by a certain spirituality of inclusion and characterized as *dispositions of significance*, these foundational dispositions bring a sense of healing, wholeness, and indeed, eternal meanings to our pedagogical practice.

Dispositions of Significance

Love

When educators assert they teach because "I love children," the suggestion is that they desire to engage in relationship with young people, including the establishing of relationships with the parents of students, colleagues, and with the community at large. This implies that a loving relationship entails a flow of integrity, dialogue, devotion, and mutual respect, and that the idea of love is moved by a deliberate decision, which promises to nourish meaning and good for the other (Fromm, 2006). Mother Teresa (1983) shares that, "Love cannot remain by itself—it has no meaning" (p. 75). Thus, in order for love to have meaning, it must not only be an emanation from the heart, but it also must be demonstrated in meaningful purpose.

From the act of preparing to deliver a lesson, to how collegial, parent, and student relationships are natured, to how we view ourselves and others, to the body language (or nonverbal cues) that we convey, to the words we use or not use in our verbal communication to the tone of our voice, to how we make pedagogical and curricula decisions, to the other five dispositions discussed here—radiating a sense of love as an educator is in reality the well from which all else flows. Love is the foundation; love is the measure.[5] Not as some kind of sentimentality intention without substance, but, rather, as an authentic illumination of love in concrete practice.

And, finally, within this concrete practice, this kind of love is one that does not seek for any return, suggesting an *agape* type of love that understands the place of humility, appreciates a sense of keeping the ego in check, monitors motives, and stays focused on what Martin Buber (1958) calls an *I and thou* relationship as opposed to an *I–it* relationship pattern. The former is driven by a sense of love and respect, illuminated through authentic dialogue in a coexisting relationship between persons; the latter is propelled by the idea that the "I" is the creator of things and manipulator of the other. The notion of an "it" with respect to relationships views the other as an object, not only subverting the fostering of dialogue, but also representing a deformation of education (Freire, 1994). In the context of education, therefore, the idea of the unfolding of an I–thou relationship functions through a teacher's ability to lovingly, respectively, and intentionally be available and present with her/his students. That is, the I and the thou suggest we are not alone; we coexist; there is a between with one to another, all of which is an encounter of inclusion.

Faith

Because of their eternal significance and even characterized as theological virtues, a discussion about love is necessarily linked to the concepts of faith and hope. The idea of faith is naturally associated with one's belief system often expressed in one's religion or spirituality. It is reasonable to assume the authenticity of one's faith is determined through the manifestation of how one communicates, what is communicated, as well as in behaviors and actions. And while faith is naturally linked to things of the spirit and religious belief systems, there is also the idea of faith expressed in the context of possessing a fundamental faith in the human family, which is revealed in how we relate to one another.

Drawing from William Fowler's *Stages of Faith* and H. Richard Niebuhr's *Radical Monotheism and Western Culture*, Purpel (1989) emphasizes the value of faith in the context of how we care, trust, and interact among ourselves. In his text *Does Civilization Need Religion?*, Reinhold Niebuhr (1927) succinctly states, "Men [and women] cannot create a society if they do not believe in each other" (p. 62). Said otherwise, because education is an endeavor that works to influence lives, it is a journey to become more fully human, which is only possible in relationships, markedly exemplified by adopting "an article of faith" that believes in the betterment of the other (Ayers, 2005). Indeed, for the teacher, the "other" in particular, is the student who stands right before him or her.

Hope

While hope is a concept that is viewed as a theological virtue, it is also a necessary psychological element that provides for human beings a sense of purpose in order to live meaningfully. As Komonchak, Collins, and Lane (1987) put it, "Hope is the presupposition behind the human 'will to live'" (p. 493). The antithesis of hope is hopelessness, which debilitates because it immobilizes, distorts, and sees reality as deterministic with no possibility of change (Freire, 1998). Therefore, for teachers, hope is not some abstract concept; it is concretized when they realize its powerful mobilizing agency not only in their own life but also in the lives of their students. To the latter, hope manifests itself in respectful communication and meaningful interaction; the giving of time; steadfast encouragement; creating a climate of healing and wholeness; the power of stirring imaginations; the sincere belief that change is possible; and, in the belief of possibilities for the other.

Humility

In the higher and admirable sense of the word, humility describes one as modest, unassuming, and unpretentious. From a spiritual perspective, humility genuinely places ego to the side, allowing one to authentically yield and be open to God (or the transcendent), others, and to grow in wisdom. In other words, as Nouwen (1983) asserts, humility, "means staying close to the ground (*humus*), to people, to everyday life, to what is happening with all its down-to-earthness. It is the virtue that opens our eyes for the presence of God on the earth" (p. 162).[6] Thus, humility necessitates a letting go of preconceived notions of what is, who we are, and perhaps even who God is.

Mother Teresa (1996) suggests that the reality of truth cannot be spoken without simultaneously considering the value and necessity of humility. In that light, Freire

(2005) makes the point, "Humility helps us to understand this obvious truth: No one knows it all; no one is ignorant of everything. We all know something; we are all ignorant of something … Humility helps me avoid being entrenched in the circuit of my own truth" (p. 72). Hence, in the act of teaching, one is also in the primal position to learn from students, implying a profound respect for students and taking the time to listen to them. A dispositional stance of humility opens wide the avenue for teachers to intimately connect with their students, allowing them "to pay attention to 'the other' " (Palmer, 1993, p. 108). Humility, as described above, is demonstrated through modest behavior, keeping one close to the ground, guiding the certainty–uncertainty tension of our truth, and is critical in fostering connection with students. It does not imply, however, a resignation, weakness, or disregard for oneself; in fact, humility is an act of courage and indicative of self-confidence (Freire, 2005).

Compassion

Compassion, which is intricately linked to the qualities of empathy and care, comes from the Latin *compati*, meaning to be conscious and aware of another's difficulty and distress while simultaneously extending a healing hand, seeking out possible solutions and alternatives to alleviate anxiety and troubles. As it relates to the concept of care, Mayeroff (1971) points out the idea of caring is not an abstract concept, or momentary event, but a way of relating with another. In other words, the process of caring is tangible, a healing balm, facilitating growth, and relationship, especially illuminating itself in realizing another's potential, particularly when facing obstacles and times of difficulty.

The motivation that drives caring actions assumes a stepping out of self and one's frame of reference in order to consider the point of view, objective needs, and welfare of the other (Noddings, 2013). For teachers, this can manifest in how they model caring in their relationships with students (even with the parents of students and colleagues), engage students in dialogue, and create opportunities that are purposeful, which fosters caring and confirms the better self in students (Noddings, 1992; Pugach, 2006). In the end, the idea of compassion and its natural association to caring is an action that is not formulistic or rule-bound, but rather a way of being, a pattern of living that responds to the moment, the event, to life itself (Noddings, 2013, 1992; Pugach, 2006; Mayeroff, 1971).

Persistence

A synonym for the word persistence is perseverance, which implies maintaining a steadfast stance amid facing obstacles, challenges, competing thoughts, emotions, and feelings. Being persistent suggests, despite the odds, circumstances, situations, and multiple other factors, because *every* child is unique and specially created, the teacher remains resolute in believing in the possibilities of each child. The other side of the coin of persistence in upholding its resolve is consistency. When teachers exude a persistent–consistent resolve pattern, students are provided with a grounded understanding of who their teachers are and where they are coming from, which nurtures a predictable regularity in a classroom setting, providing the integral sustenance of a teacher's words and actions (LaCaze & Kirylo, 2012).

Most certainly, however, a teacher's patience level will barometrically be tested in her/his practice in the effort to maintain that persistent–consistent resolve pattern. In other words, a classroom teacher generally works with children from diverse backgrounds and various personalities, and at times interacts with students and families who, for a number of reasons, are challenging or difficult. It is during these times, in particular, that the teacher not only remains grounded in the aforementioned dispositions but also recognizes a threefold fundamental task of her/his work to (a) engage in an instructional practice that is developmentally appropriate and culturally relevant in order to make connections with a child so that meaningful learning can take place; (b) deeply understand that working with challenging children obviously does not mean acceptance of disruption, inappropriate behavior, or noncompliance. It means, however, to authentically exhaust every effort to find solutions and seek appropriate ways to constructively deal with them; and (c) thoughtfully reflect on one's practice. The depth of reflection on one's practice (i.e., item c) determines the degree of insightfulness and innovation of the former.

In the end, when working with a challenging student, the notion of "can't" should not enter into the lexicon. What enters the mind and action of the teacher is concepts such as "persistence," "belief," "will," and "connection." The idea of being persistent is thusly a way of being acting in order to move, prod, and suggest, paving the way toward tapping into the unique gifts, strengths, and talents of each student.

Conclusion

We live in interesting times. Working toward healing the persistent plague of racial animosity demands allyship, justice, and commitment. Working toward community wholeness in confronting the destructiveness of extreme partisanship and tribalism requires authentic dialogue, civility, and commitment. Indeed, a critical pedagogy of healing is a concept whose time has come. It necessitates a certain intentionality in order to work toward renewal in the collective effort to lovingly and justly build the community in which schools play an obvious integral part.

Because educators work with all segments of society—intersecting race, class, political persuasion, religious affiliation, gender, and sexual orientation—they are in a prime position to enlivening a critical pedagogy of healing in the effort toward racial harmony and fostering civility, dialogue, and respect despite multiple differences. One way to move toward that end is to authentically consider the relevance of these discussed six dispositions of significance. To be sure, these dispositions are, on one hand, straightforward to conceptually grasp, but, on the other, there is a clear profundity of their depth and breadth. The idea of realizing them as an emanation of a certain spirituality of inclusion moves these dispositions as mindful habits of thought and action—bringing healing and wholeness, and ultimately eternal meanings, to one's pedagogical practice.

4

Pentecostal Pedagogy and the Rights of the Body as Restoration in Education

Christopher Emdin

The legacy of slavery in the United States permeates every aspect of our lives. Scholars like Kevin Bales and Ron Soodalter (2010) have written about the links between contemporary human trafficking and slavery. Others write about the slavery-like experiences of Black folks in corporate America (Livers and Caber, 2003). William C. Rhoden's (2010) book *Forty Million Dollar Slaves* compares professional athletes to slaves on plantations who were introduced to sports as a way to entertain their masters and distract from the toils of everyday life. Each of these comparisons provides profound insight into how the legacy of slavery persists in education and is operationalized within an education-industrial complex which coerces folks with strong and free cultural expression into a system that profits from their underperformance. This system relishes in removing Black folks from positions of power and purpose and celebrates their vilification in society. Contemporary schooling (particularly in urban schools) is often about robbing the historically marginalized of power and purpose through the provision of a formal education.

I suggest, the enslaved enacted teaching and learning with its own unique methods and educational instruments in response to plantation pedagogies. It was raw and expressive and stands in contrast to plantation pedagogy, akin to human trafficking of Africans from the continent to slave ships, which coerces genius from Black communities into institutions that ultimately function to demonize where they came from and use them as labor. The coercion of Black genius into an education-industrial complex is similar to how Black athletes are coerced into professional sports. Both the education-industrial complex and the system of professional sports render Black bodies disposable unless they entertain and/or provide income (or outputs) for a wealthy class. These systems, contemporary iterations of a model for "dealing with" Black bodies while ostensibly benefiting them, are rooted in slavery. Plantation pedagogy stands in sharp contrast to Pentecostal pedagogy which restores to the soul that has been stolen by the coercive system. The enslaved responded to their masters' plantation pedagogy with a Pentecostal pedagogy which spiritually and psychologically broke free from their conditions even as they were physically incapacitated. This chapter traces the historical roots of plantation pedagogy, drawing parallels to other similar social systems (e.g., professional sports) and explores how core identity contributes to youth's rejection of plantation pedagogy. It offers Pentecostal pedagogy as an escape rooted in Afrocentric traditions of faith and education.

Confronting the Legacy of Slavery in the White Education-Industrial Complex

The "white teaching" of Black children in contemporary America stands in stark contrast from informal (yet academically rigorous) Black teaching that has existed since and in response Black folks' education during slavery. The distinction between white teaching and the ways the enslaved taught themselves in response to it is highlighted by Webber (1978) who states,

> That the content of white teaching directly contradicted understandings, attitudes, values, and feelings which slaves had learned from birth in an educational process created and controlled by slaves themselves, was a notion too incredible and too dangerous to entertain. To suggest that slaves were capable of molding their own culture, of fashioning and maintaining their own educational instruments, would be to undermine the most fundamental arguments with which whites rationalized their enslavement of other human beings. (pp. 249–250)

This phenomenon of white folks (a) fearing models for education created by Black folks, and (b) not believing those who have been positioned as "less than" could develop a viable system for teaching and learning, is at the core of how current flawed models of education persist. I want to be clear that "white teaching" is not just about white people. It is about plantation pedagogies enacted by white slaveholders, pedagogies still being carried out today by the majority-white teaching force. Plantation pedagogy is about disregarding and demonizing what Weber (1978) describes as the "understandings, attitudes, values, and feelings which slaves had learned from birth" [TK3] (p. 250) and the implanting of different ones that do not necessarily align to the souls of Black folks.

Today, many college and professional sports leagues maintain a power structure in which athletes are pawns controlled by the white wealthy class who owns/operates universities and/or professional teams. Despite whatever compensation athletes receive, owners determine their worth or lack thereof based on their performance. The wholeness of athletes is of no significance to owners, as long as the institution profits from their performance on the field or the court. Similarly, the education-industrial complex creates an economy of jobs, real estate, and funding streams that line pockets. Such individuals and organizations are primarily concerned with Black youth performance on tests that do not capture their wholeness, genius, or potential. As with professional sports, the education-industrial complex mimics slavery. It reduces complex people to labors who entertain the masses and/or reap profits for the few.

From Role Identity to Core Identity: Youth Embodiment of Pentecostal Pedagogy

Many K–12 urban schools are eerily similar to plantation pedagogies in form and enforcement. Black bodies perform obedience and showcase worth through test performance. Loud voices bark orders and threaten punishment like suspension for expressing oneself and being free in thought, word, and action. Sociologist Jonathan Turner argues, human beings have core, social, group, and role identities2012). These multiple identities are listed in the order of emotional significance to an individual, with role identity being furthest away from the authentic self and core identity being the anchor of who a person is. Understanding role and core identities is essential for making sense of how partial, "academic" identities are enacted and strengthened at the expense of more significant parts of the core identity. In many ways, a plantation pedagogy attacks the core identity of the enslaved in order to develop a role identity that serves the institution.

Role identities are performed in different settings. People take them on because they are essential for survival. For many, being a teacher or student means taking on a role that one perceives is emblematic of "teacher" or "student." For example, a teacher who sees the beauty in their students' cultures learns to erase their love and admiration for their students' music, style, or traditions by remembering past teachers, watching other teachers, and receiving scripts from professional development. This person learns to walk, talk, and act in a socially accepted way that is defined by the understandings, attitudes, values, and feelings of the institution. They to be a plantation pedagogue – a contemporary slave master who robs young people of joy and freedom in the pursuit of "learning."

The core identity is the most important piece of who we are. Turner (2012) describes it as "accumulated cognitions and emotions that we have about ourselves as persons … [We] work very hard to make sure that people honor and verify this identity because it embodies … who we are as persons, carrying a sense of how we are treated and how we should be treated" (p. 20) The core identity is the truest self; it is the part of us we protect the most. When it is threatened, we respond viscerally and lose capacity to give measured responses or feel controlled emotions. Biologists describe this as deimatic behavior, which in animals is a threat response designed to intimidate and dissuade predators from attacking. It can involve displaying the colors of feathers or accentuating other features so an attacker pauses and gives the threatened animal an opportunity to escape. For Black youth under constant attack or threat of assault within a system of plantation pedagogy, deimatic behaviors (i.e., role identities) respond to threats to their authentic selves. They often do not have the opportunity to return to the self they were trying to protect because of the persistence of the attack on their core. As a student's sense of self is assaulted, they become less of the self they are protecting and more of the expressive (misread as aggressive) self that is the protector. They may take on the protector self for so long, they cannot find what they were protecting to begin with.[TK4]

When a person's core self is intelligent/artistic/creative/brilliant but in school there is no space to express this core self or the core self is threatened, that person experiences an authentic emotional and visceral response (Emdin, 2020). That response is ratchetness—the chief mechanism for expression in moments of threat for the marginalized. It is the attitudes, values, beliefs, and emotions that come with being who these students are in the world, simultaneously on display in their rawest form. It is the unfiltered expression of individual or collective self that runs counter to modes of expression normalized by an institution. Ratchetness is different each time it is expressed, but it is raw and unapologetic whenever it emerges. A Pentecostal pedagogy honors the expression of ratchetness, using it as the anchor of teaching and learning. It recognizes plantation pedagogies stifle the core while free expression is necessary for the core self to emerge. Pentecostal pedagogy restores and revives the spirit. To meet the needs of students, teachers must denounce their allegiance to a plantation structure that causes them to harm youth and their own core selves. This requires a recognition that teaching and learning that stifles students' free expression by making the experience about the production of work extracts joy and is a plantation pedagogy. Teachers must be deliberate about creating spaces where youth can freely and unabashedly release frustration and articulate pain in the pursuit of being intellectual or academic.

Pentecostalism: Countering Plantation Pedagogy

In the book *Deep Like the Rivers*, Webber (1978) explores education in the slave quarter from 1831 to 1865. He describes a number of examples of white slaveholder teaching and the Black response, including the quest for free, loud, joyful, and even guttural expressions among slaves in the midst of oppressive teaching. The enslaved believed in their "stylistic superiority" to whites—their better storytelling, creative singing, and energetic dancing. Webber described the sharp wit of the enslaved and the ways whites "blocked their learning" out of fear that the enslaved were too smart. The enslaved found the church services or Sabbath schools of their white masters boring and lacking in energy. They rejected the pedagogy in those places because Sabbath school instruction "required [teachers] to maintain the strictest order and [students] were prohibited from shouting, moaning or dancing" (p. 250). This distinction echoes the core difference between the plantation pedagogy of the master and Pentecostal pedagogy of the enslaved. In today's schools, where parents, school leaders, teachers, and students have been convinced that the strictest order/control over youth (particularly urban youth of color) is good teaching, there is a need to push back by embracing a Pentecostal pedagogy restores to youth what has been robbed from them in institutions that operate like slave plantations.

Pentecostalism is a distinctly American approach to Christianity born from preachers without formal training who had not been ordained by any particular church or institution. Pentecostalism embraces a freedom to worship rooted in connecting to the divine in ways that have no particular established form. Charles Parham and William J Seymour, forefathers of the movement, existed in the margins of Christianity and centered their approach to faith despite not being recognized by any particular denomination. Parham was described as "an amateur who followed his own meandering line of reason as he tried to make sense of Christian faith and practice"

(Jacobsen, 2003 p. 19). Seymour, who was a Black man, took Parham's approach and pushed it beyond Parham's imagination by advocating for freedom and liberty in a uniquely Black way which involved speech and "speaking in tongues" – which involved crying and yelling if need be for the sake of releasing inhibition in the process of getting closer to the divine.

In the United States, education has always taken cues from the church and Christianity even as Christianity, the church, and the bible have been used as a means to dominate Black folks. In her powerful article "We Slipped and Learned to Read" Janet Cornelius (1983) shares, it was the practice of plantation owners to teach the slaves to read just well enough so they could regurgitate certain biblical scriptures that supported and sustained the power of slave owners. Some slaves were "educated" by slaveholders who ensured that slaves were unable to read any text (including sections of the Bible that may be interpreted as a rebuke of slavery) or study anything about themselves that would indicate they were anything other than subjects destined to serve their masters. The slaves who were literate read and memorized scriptures and were then positioned as more intelligent than their counterparts. Many enslaved who were elevated above their peers developed greater allegiances to their masters than their peers and ended up as teachers who pushed plantation pedagogy. Yet the enslaved looked for a different way, rooted deeply in Afrocentric ways of knowing and being and centered around communal learning, the restoration of the core identity, a desire to learn, and a passion for knowledge. This "other way" involved transcendence or "catching the holy ghost", a fundamental tenet of Pentecostal Christianity reached in communal events through dancing, singing, and feeling free enough to speak in foreign tongues indiscernible to those around you (Hinson, 2010). Transcendence is at the root of a Pentecostal pedagogy that allows young people an escape from plantation pedagogy that robs them of agency and keeps them from feeling, healing and learning. What I am calling for here, through Pentecostal pedagogy, is by no means religion based or hyper-structured. It is a deliberate enactment of a new kind of teaching that is designed to restore what society has stolen from the youth and set the context for the abandonment of deimatic role identities and the replenishing of the core identity through the rights of the body.

Pentecostal Pedagogy and the Rights of the Body

By "the rights of the body," I refer to seven rights articulated within Buddhist tradition: to be here, to feel, to act, to love, to speak, to see, and to know. Educators who anchor their teaching to the restoration of these rights to young people use their pedagogy as protest against the ways that emotional and psychological violence against young people has been normalized in schools. These rights are restored through Pentecostal pedagogy. In this section, I address each right in turn.

The Right to Be Here

This is the most fundamental right of the body. In education, it must be modified to the right to be here *as you are*. Young people must feel as though their presence in the classroom, in whatever way they choose to express it, is always welcome. Pentecostal pedagogy recognizes that students—especially Black students who typically feel unwelcome in schools—have the right to be there. Their comfort and agency are compromised by the norms of the institution. Consequently, they feel as though school is not for them, which compromises their ability to learn. With Pentecostal pedagogy, this right can be restored by explicitly stating when students walk into the school and/or classroom for the first time that the entire enterprise of schooling is about them. Students must be told they have a right to be there, and they must be reminded that school is not about anything other than ensuring that they are whole and learning. Statements like, "This is your school," "This is your classroom," and "you are welcome here" become essential and are repeated in almost chant-like fashion until students understand that because of divine rights they have been born with, wherever they are they can claim as their own even if others make them feel like visitors in a strange land.

The Right to Feel

The second right ensures that students have space to express their emotions and the vocabulary to name what they are feeling. Human beings are born with the right to feel. It is an essential right to return to young people because in schools, students are only afforded a very limited range of emotions. In the eyes of teachers, Black youth (in particular) can be only angry or agreeable. A number of actions that are indictors of a bevy of emotions are attributed to anger and addressed as though they are rooted in negative intentions. If Black or Brown students are curious or unclear with instructions, they are perceived as angry and questioning authority. If they are frustrated, sad, or pensive, they are perceived as angry. In fact, for too many students anything other than blind complicity is read as anger and confronted with the wrath of the institution and its operatives. The work of the educator then becomes working with young people to name their emotions—sharing the language that helps them to identify what and how they are feeling—while creating the space for these emotions to be felt and expressed without being demonized. This right also involves creating classroom spaces where young people can share their emotions about what is going on in the world without judgment and have a teacher who can model how to work through these emotions. The right to feel gives youth the right to yell, scream, articulate frustration, "catch the holy ghost" and not be demonized for it because, it will ultimately lead to a resettling of the emotion and resetting of the body and then, the space to learn.

The Right to Act

Once students are afforded the right to feel, they must also have the right to act on how they feel in order for them to feel free. As long as the act does not violate the rights of someone else, acting on an emotion is a way to feel affirmed and confirm the right to be present and take up space. In classrooms, creating space and time for the physical expression of emotions is essential. A moment in the class to stand, stretch and even walk around demonstrates a value for the student's full self.

The Right to Love and Be Loved

This right is about agape love—the love of others for the good of humanity and betterment of society—and also about opening space for students to express a love for the people and things in their world that have significance to them even if they lack value in schools. The love of music, sports, and cultural artifacts and figures must be allowed in the classroom. The love of people and the space to express that love is also important. The Pentecostal pedagogue teaches about and with the artifacts and people that students love so that communality is built and community is centered. The right to love recognizes that there is no more compelling emotion than love, and there is no place where love is more needed than in learning[TK5]. Teachers can activate the love young people have for presumably nonacademic phenomena in classrooms when teachers love their students enough to be creative and uncomfortable in uncovering the connections between those phenomena and academic content. Love transforms the nature of teaching and learning and restores a lost right to students.

The Right to Speak

This right involves creating space where the voice of the student is not compromised or distorted in the pursuit of learning or being "better educated." The right to speak is about being welcome to speak in one's own tongue, dialect, or accent and honoring that right even if and when the discourse of power is different. The right to speak is also about speaking truth to power. The Pentecostal pedagogue creates pathways and platforms for young people to speak about issues in the school, the community, and society to those who hold positions of power and authority. This is not about providing a voice to students. It is about amplifying their voices and providing them with access to those who hold power so that their voices can be heard.

The Right to See

The sixth right recognizes that students have the right to see things from a different perspective than the teacher or the school. Students can have and express inner visions in the tradition of Stevie Wonder—a deep and reflective excavation of self as it relates to society and an expression of one's vision of the world based on one's reality. When young people are allowed to see things differently, their visions to come to life in the classroom which restores faith in their own visions of the world and transforms education to meet the needs of young people. The right to see is about educators challenging students, activating their imaginations, and creating a classroom where young people are most free to learn.

The Right to Know

This right is connected to the fact that schools deny Black children the right to know about themselves, their history, their legacy, and the causes for the inequities they endure. The right to know is compromised by teachers' low expectations of students and the belief that students are not prepared to know about the inequities of the world or understand ostensibly rigorous academic content. The right to know is also the right to be challenged academically and to have all the information needed to understand the world shared with you. Once all the other rights of the body have been provided, youth thrive when they have the right to know. Their full selves are affirmed as they are free to accept and pursue knowledge.

Pentecostal Pedagogy for Transcendence

The goal of this work is to drive teachers to be who we need to be for students and inspire them to become their best selves. I am setting those who read this on the course to "good trouble" in the tradition of the late John Lewis. Pentecostal pedagogy equates to being loud, disruptive, and unapologetic. It elicits anger and can be misread as antagonistic to school norms. I have been denied professional opportunities for being too honest and vocal contemporary education and too unorthodox in my approach to life and work. I have received "critique" that was hatred and racism. Centering the freedom of the most marginalized in the classroom requires courage to see that traditions we have upheld are rooted in the plantation. If we want our children to fly, we have to let go of the shit that weighs us down. Some might misconstrue the provision of the rights of the body and Pentecostal pedagogy as intentionally undermining established norms simply for the sake of being disagreeable. Some will misconstrue my words as a lack of value for formal education or structure or control. Neither is the case. This is not about unbridled anger or undervaluing education. It is about love—love of self, love of students, love for the community one comes from, love for ones' ancestors and most importantly, a love for education.

In 1988, hip-hop group Arrested Development was formed in Atlanta, Georgia. Its members ranged in age from early 20's to late 50's and their sound resonated across generations. They introduced Afrocentric spirituality to a critical mass of people, and although they employed a framework not rooted in the Christian tradition, they employed a Pentecostal approach to delivering their music and engaging with their audience. During live performances, they sang their hit song "Tennessee" as thousands of people chanted in unison, "Take me to another place. Take me to another land. Let me forget all that hurts me. Help me understand your plan" (Thomas, 1992, n.p.). In those moments, fans arrived at a place of transcendence, so deeply connected to each other that they wouldn't want to leave the venue. Arrested Development entranced their audience but also made them aware of their pain, in touch with who they are, and proud to be Black. This feeling can and should happen in all classrooms.

5

Embodiment and Buddhist Practices for Racial Healing and Social Justice

Helen Kwah

At the time of this writing, the Covid-19 pandemic has exposed the disproportionate inequities and traumas that Black, Indigenous, and People of Color (BIPOC) suffer in a society structured to maintain white supremacy and power. There are urgent needs to heal at the individual level and to transform systemic racial oppression at the collective level. Fortunately, as the Black Buddhist teacher, Reverend angel kyodo williams points out, these two needs are interrelated: "love and justice are not two. without inner change, there can be no outer change; without collective change, no change matters" (2020a). In the contemporary Buddhist communities to which I belong, BIPOC Buddhist teachers are sharing Buddhist teachings and practices as epistemological and practical tools for coming to terms with and transforming individual and collective suffering from racial and social injustice. In this chapter, I present the relevance and work of BIPOC Buddhist teachers along three lines of how they ground an understanding of traditional Buddhist teachings in embodiment, how they bring the focus on embodiment to Buddhist awareness practices, and how they create separate but supportive practice communities for BIPOC. I position my understandings through the frame of my own experience and through the teachings and examples of two prominent Black Buddhists, Reverend angel kyodo williams and Lama Rod Owens, who are my teachers.

Some Background

I came to Buddhism from an attraction to the possibilities I found within for a philosophy and method of practice for becoming free from the suffering that I experienced in the world. As a first-generation immigrant/ Asian-American/ middle-class/ cisgendered woman/ single mother, I have lived in and moved through various social groups and institutional settings where I sometimes experienced privileged access by virtue of my socialization and economic resources, but where I was otherwise more likely than not marginalized, objectified, and alternately bullied or ignored for being Other than the norm. In my early adulthood, I turned to psychotherapy but was not able to break out of my internalized responses to oppression, which manifested in my case as severe depression and self-sabotaging behaviors. I found Buddhism after college through books and initially sought it out as an alternative form of therapy. Eventually, in my mid-twenties, I joined a Korean Zen practice center in New York City.

In the beginning, I was fascinated by what I thought were the classic Buddhist teachings on how to "escape" from suffering by understanding the "ultimate truth" that all phenomena are impermanent, interdependently arisen, and therefore "empty" in nature. Intellectually, the notion of the ultimate and empty nature of all phenomena made sense, but what appealed was the emotional register of longing to obliterate the suffering I experienced by naming it as "emptiness." What I did not realize was that in the white (and often male)-dominated spaces of American convert Buddhism at the time, the emphasis on the "ultimate truth" teachings was a way to devalue difference and the particular, socially marked, and embodied ways that phenomena appear. In fact, when my anxieties and depression would emerge and make my meditation practice difficult, I was told instead to focus on the "ultimate nature" and not get attached to the feelings or narratives that triggered my disordered emotional states and behavior. I was also always the only or one of the few people of color in any of the American Buddhist groups that I joined, I often attracted unwanted attention as white people projected their fascination with the Asian cultural origins of Buddhist traditions on me and white men sometimes framed their fascination as fetishized desire. American Buddhism writ large refers to the Buddhist communities that have formed in the United States under the leadership of white and often upper middle-class converts to Buddhism (Sherrell & Brown, 2017). I eventually left these American Buddhist communities after many years of not finding the "escape" from suffering that I was longing for.

It was not until a few years ago that I realized there was a growing number of Black, Indigenous, and People of Color (BIPOC) Buddhist teachers who were coming to prominence and critiquing the white supremacy and privilege embedded in American Buddhist communities. Among this new generation of BIPOC Buddhist teachers, many are explicit about being social change activists with the goal of bringing about racial justice and liberation for all (williams, Owens, & Syedullah, 2016).

Embodied Understanding of the "Two Truths"

As mentioned, in my early years of Buddhist practice when I asked my then white male teacher how to cope with the depression and self-hatred that were troubling my meditations, he told me to see their "ultimate nature" as impermanent expressions of the mind. I was conscious from his answer that he could not understand the racialized experiences that produced such thoughts and feelings. In an essay on healing from racial trauma, the queer Black Buddhist teacher, Lama Rod Owens (williams, Owens & Syedullah, 2016), shares a similar story of his first experience in a Buddhist "*sangha*" (community of practitioners); note it is told in the third person:

> During the question-and-answer period after a dharma talk, he (Lama Rod Owens) explained to the white male teacher that he felt lonely and marginalized in the

> *sangha* as the only person of color. The teacher suggested that this was something the young man struggled with outside of the *sangha*. The young man agreed. The teacher advised him to just sit with what he was feeling. The young man wanted more and did sit with the feelings and knew that the *sangha* and that teacher were not safe for him. (p. 59)

The advice to sit with what one is feeling is given in meditation practice based upon the Buddhist teaching that whatever thoughts and feelings arise will eventually fall away; they are impermanent phenomena, and by observing their arising and falling, they lose their grip and one begins to "see" their ultimate true nature. This is one side of the Buddhist doctrine called the "Two Truths," that there is an "ultimate truth," which describes the way phenomena are impermanent, dependently arisen, and therefore empty but also fundamentally interconnected and inseparable. On the other side, there is the truth of relative reality, which we know as the embodied, socially conditioned, and seemingly separate ways that phenomena appear. But the Two Truths are epistemological (Garfield, 1995) in that they describe the two ways that reality can be known. Also, the Two Truths are based upon the recognition that the relative phenomenal world is the *medium* through which one comes to know the ultimate nature. Nonetheless, in contemporary American Buddhist communities, the original understanding of the Two Truths has often been glossed over while the goal of knowing the "ultimate truth" of all phenomena has instead been privileged, in line with Western Cartesian notion of the supremacy of the mind over the body (Selassie, 2020). Unfortunately, the privileging of "ultimate truth" has the effect of dismissing the different, embodied, and messy ways that all beings but especially those that are marginalized and oppressed by the dominant culture experience reality.

In contrast, BIPOC Buddhist teachers have found it necessary to bring a radical focus back to their embodied experience of relative reality because without bringing the suffering of BIPOC bodies to awareness, there is no chance for liberation and seeing the ultimate nature. This is what Lama Rod Owens found as a gay Black man raised in the Bible belt South entering into white Buddhist communities. Lama Rod went on to further training and official recognition as a teacher, or "Lama," in the Tibetan Buddhist tradition, and he, like other BIPOC Buddhist teachers, takes the Two Truths in their entirety by focusing first on the relative truth of his embodiment in order to see the larger truth of who he is:

> In the end, I am no longer the little boy having to hold the potential violence of those in stress around him, or the little boy who is afraid to claim his love for other men, or the preteen who is challenged to make meaning out of race and class, or the young teen terrified of riding the bus, or the young man othered because of his body type, or the man who is told that his feelings of marginalization are his issue not the issue of a sangha steeped in white-supremacist cultural norms. I am no longer these people, but I remember their stories. They made me who I am.
>
> (williams, Owens, & Syedullah, 2016, p. 73)

Reverend angel kyodo williams is a Black, queer Buddhist teacher who is also a writer, activist, and an ordained teacher in a Japanese Zen tradition. Reverend angel strongly advocates for the need to acknowledge and work through our embodied experiences of racialized trauma and injustice because until those experiences are truly felt and brought to awareness, there is no freedom and ultimate truth. She clarifies why generating an embodied awareness of our experience is liberating:

> You have to claim your experience for what it is, and instead of reacting, we are slowing things down in a contemplative approach, pausing, and saying "*Let me feel what that is.*" Every time someone talks about the idea that there is oneness, actually we're having really different relative experiences … If you don't allow yourself to interrogate multiplicity, diversity, (then you don't understand) the reality of the social order that makes "oneness" an easy escape hatch for those of us who have access … You can notice how that (interrogating difference) *makes you feel* and be curious … *what is that reaction in me*? (2020b)

Reverend angel has been among the first in American Buddhist communities to articulate the need to ground meditation practices in embodiment, especially as racism and social oppression have embedded themselves in our bodies. At this moment, many are acknowledging how racism is internalized and reproduced as unconscious bodily habit, including how unconscious gestures or responses belie what is now known as implicit bias (Hall et al., 2015). As racism is painfully experienced and perpetuated at the level of the body, BIPOC Buddhist teachers have been prescient in calling for more awareness, care, and healing of the suffering of BIPOC bodies.

Practices of Embodied Awareness

As the Black Buddhist teacher, Sebene Selassie (2020) notes:

> There is a call to embodiment in Buddhist teachings … but we Western meditators have not necessarily heard that invitation to embodiment … "Mindfulness" purports to encompass all of experience and lead to liberation, but in reality, it privileges the mind … In many Asian languages, mind and heart go together … But not for us: mind is mind, heart is heart, and body is devalued. Which is why we need embodied awareness. (pp. 77–8)

For this reason, Selassie (2020) uses the term "embodied awareness practice" rather than mindfulness because of how that reorients the practice to a "felt sense," which is a bodily rather than a conceptual understanding of what is happening (p. 79). Similarly, Reverend angel (williams, Owens, & Syedullah, 2016) explains:

> I introduced embodiment practice to invite people back home to their felt experience. To disrupt the disconnect among head and heart … I believe anyone

engaged in the practice of liberation must actively discover it in their own being. (pp. 99–100)

Without reconnecting head to heart and knowing what one feels, there can be no healing and liberation of others. Even within activist movements, there is a growing recognition of the need for the "inner work" of self-care and healing in order for the outer work of community organizing and social change to happen (Ginwright, 2016).

But to be clear, there is no separate category called "embodiment practices" in any of the Buddhist practice traditions. When BIPOC Buddhist teachers such as Reverend angel speak of embodiment practice, they are calling for Buddhist practices, including the practice of mindfulness (Salzberg, 2011), to be grounded in the body *as a site for healing and liberation*. The basic instructions for an embodiment practice might be to first follow the breath as it enters the body and to locate one's body in space starting with where the body meets the ground; after settling the body, the instructions might continue to bring to mind a difficult experience, including of racialized trauma, and then to watch the feelings, thoughts, and sensations as they arise in the body in response to the memory. By becoming aware of how difficult experiences are held and arise in the body, one is then more able to pause and disrupt their habitual force, release, and bring about a new response. For an example of a guided meditation on becoming aware, see Reverend angel kyodo williams' practice for sitting with discomfort.

Another Buddhist practice that can be taken as an embodiment practice is Loving Kindness meditation (Salzberg, 2011), which involves first grounding oneself in the breath and body and then generating feelings of warmth and kindness as well as repeating phrases that offer kind thoughts (such as "May you be happy, may you be at ease") to oneself and then to others. In fact, in some Buddhist traditions, the Loving Kindness practice is intended as a complement to the wisdom practices on the "nature of the mind" because of the recognition that wisdom (or the ultimate truth) cannot arise without working through one's relationship to the world (relative truth) (Kwah, 2019). Other examples of embodied practices can include any movement practices such as yoga and tai chi, taken in the context of attending to, questioning, and caring for how thoughts and feelings arise in the body (williams, 2020b).

The recognition of embodiment carries within it an understanding of the need to disrupt the habitual and unconscious ways that racism is learned and reproduced. As the sociologist, Pierre Bourdieu (2000) recognized, the social order is produced through socialization, through repeated actions and interactions with others in the social environment, resulting in the unconscious acquisition of the group's "habitus," which are the thoughts, perceptions, actions, and norms that constitute the social group. However, as Bourdieu also pointed out, habitus is difficult to change because it is habituated, unconscious, and embodied; explicit teaching can help but what is needed is a "bodily counter-training" (2000). Racism is acquired as the habitus of white supremacy, and as BIPOC Buddhist teachers have recognized, practices of embodied awareness are necessary to disrupt, pause, and create space for awareness of the habitual thoughts and emotions that arise in response to racism. Only by becoming aware of how the habits of racism and oppression arise in the body can we hope to transform how they are produced in the dominant culture.

Community and Identity Groups

A key notion in Buddhism is of taking "refuge" in not only the teachings but also in the community of practitioners (*sangha* in Sanskrit), which is a recognition of our interdependence and the need for mutual support and inspiration in order to grow. However, the American Buddhist communities that have formed around Asian-originated Buddhist teachings and practices are predominantly white spaces (Sherrell & Brown, 2017). Out of necessity, BIPOC Buddhist teachers have been creating dedicated spaces for BIPOC from Buddhist or other faith traditions to meet and practice. As Ruth King (2018) explains in her book, *Mindful of Race*, white people do not have to identify with a group identity in the way BIPOC have. When POC relate to white people in white-dominated spaces where there is no acknowledgment of racial group identity, there is an assumption that we are all "good individuals," which shifts responsibility for the dominant group away from whites. In addition, when white people are confronted about race, BIPOC often find themselves in a position of having to manage the "fragility" (DiAngelo, 2018) of white people in addition to their own pain. There is at times a need for BIPOC to heal and practice in separate spaces, including separate groups for specific BIPOC identities such as Black or Indigenous or Asian American.

I have been drawn to Reverend angel and Lama Rod Owens particularly because of the online practice communities they have created that offer spaces exclusively for BIPOC and for particular or intersecting racial and/or other group identities. According to its website description, Reverend angel's Liberated Life Network (www.liblifenet.com) is a "place to connect and caucus with new friends and old, based on identity, location, affiliation or shared interests." The accessibility of an online community of practice makes it possible to be involved with a community despite physical location or time zone, and when I first joined one of the Asian-only identifying caucuses, I experienced a palpable feeling of safety in the presence of other Asian American Buddhists. In fact, one of the issues that we shared and reflected upon as a community that we couldn't do easily in the larger BIPOC community was our difficulties in claiming our own experiences of racial injustice relative to Black people's suffering. Lama Rod Owens has also founded an online practice community called Bhumisparsha (https://www.bhumisparsha.org) that creates alternative spaces for BIPOC Buddhist practitioners to meet together in community to explore and practice traditional Tibetan Buddhist practices reframed in terms of embodied awareness and social justice. For example, Lama Rod offers the traditional Tibetan Buddhist practice of the "Medicine Buddha" with its ritual language modified to reflect not only its original intent to promote healing of self and other but also the goal of healing "the social inequities that perpetuate harm" (https://www.bhumisparsha.org/practice-texts).

A Path of Individual and Collective Transformation

The vision that teachers like Reverend angel kyodo williams and Lama Rod Owens have is of a path to individual and collective transformation that begins with full awareness and acknowledgment of the particular, the embodied, and the conditioned. The necessity to grapple with embodiment perhaps comes easily for BIPOC whose bodies have long been subject to the systemic racism and violence of white supremacist culture. BIPOC are well positioned to understand the original intent of traditional Buddhist teachings, such as the teachings on the Two Truths, which connects the embodied conditions of the world where racism and social oppression are manifest, to their transformation and revelation of the inherent interconnection of all beings. Further, the emphasis on the embodiment in Buddhist practices acknowledges the necessity to bring awareness to the body where racism and its effects are internalized, thereby enabling a conscious disruption in the habitual reproduction of racism and oppression. Finally, given the power differentials and differences in how white and BIPOC relate to dominant and subordinate group identities, BIPOC Buddhist teachers have led the way in creating separate spaces, especially online, for BIPOC to support each other through shared and intersecting group identities and affiliations. While there are other BIPOC Buddhist teachers who are doing similar work, I have primarily presented the work of Reverend angel kyodo williams and Lama Rod Owens due to my connection with them as a student. It is my hope that their examples provide inspiration and practical tools for all people, but especially BIPOC, who recognize the urgent need to heal and transform the racialized suffering that marks our current time.

Part II

Physical and Mental Well-Being

6

Mindfully Running the Course(s): Self-Care as Critical Praxis

Tricia M. Kress and Jennifer Somma-Coughlin

(September 2019)

Tricia

When I think about mindfulness and wellness, I'm not sure this is a time of arrival. I've been here before, but I always move on and circle back. I remember this topic being raised at a critical pedagogy conference (eight or more?!) years ago. How can people who feel unwell help others who also feel unwell? Yet, to remain still long enough to seriously consider wellness as central to my life and work … Well, I'm not very good at remaining still. I'm always busy even if not with work. Sometimes, my whole life seems to consist of running: to an appointment, to a meeting, errands, a household, numbers, and (literally) miles as exercise. Sometimes when the pace is particularly intense, I run in my sleep. Since starting my doctorate decades ago, I have a recurring nightmare: I am working hard to run somewhere, but I'm actually not getting anywhere. My body is stuck and I start to panic. The destination is never consistent nor is it always even clear. But that hardly matters; I will never get anywhere when my body is stuck, no matter how fast I try to run. So, how did I get here to mindfulness and wellness? I guess, I ran here. Again and again and again.

Jennifer

I never saw myself being a teacher. It was happenstance, a part time job; yet, I fell in love with it and went back to school to be a special education teacher. My role was a shiny new penny, but the shine couldn't last. Early in my teaching career, I had a student who was going to be suspended and was labeled a behavior problem; however, she begged not to be given out of school suspension because she had no heat in her home. Graduate school didn't prepare me for these daily challenges. While I felt (and still feel) enthusiasm is my best quality, there had to be a way to sustain it. This led me to mindfulness, which was in some ways was a convenience. My colleagues and I received a thirty-minute professional development about mindfulness techniques in the classroom. Research showed it could benefit students even those with behavioral and emotional needs. As with teaching, I fell in love with mindfulness. I started doing mindfulness practices with my class, and I realized I was also doing it for myself. Deep breathing, certain poses, guided meditation. It has helped me/us. I know it is important to be student-centered, but in order to help students we also need to help teachers. Mindfulness is a way to take a pause. My brain doesn't easily shut off, so mindfulness helps me pause, listen, and look from a different point of view.

Introduction

This chapter is written by a doctoral student (Jennifer) and her professor (Tricia). We are both white women educators, but we are different in our autobiographical histories, current professional roles, and responsibilities. Jennifer works on Long Island, New York, with secondary students diagnosed with social and emotional special needs. Tricia works with doctoral students who are educators in various settings on Long Island and in New York City. Given the explicit social justice mission of what we do and the psychological and physical challenges of our jobs, remaining strong and centered is essential so that we don't inadvertently reproduce oppressive social structures in our own practice. Yet, we are profoundly skeptical of the self-help and wellness deluge we see in popular media and in conversations with coworkers, friends, and loved ones. We are troubled on a personal level by the ways educators are increasingly treated like machines that are beginning to break down and are now expected to repair themselves. We cannot help but be reminded of critical pedagogy's critique of "technorationality" (Giroux, 1988; Kincheloe, 1999) and what Marx called "thingification" (Tairako, 2018).

We entered this collaboration because we were concerned about the physical and mental toll of neoliberal schooling on teachers and how burnout can lead to depression and ill health. We are also concerned that "McMindfulness" "solutions" being implemented by schools and societies are just shoddy repairs for broken-down bodies that will break again amid the abuses of an inhumane society. As Purser (2019) notes, "Anything that offers success in our unjust society without trying to change it is not revolutionary—it just helps people cope" (p. 1). The 2020 global pandemic and resulting shifts to remote learning and pandemic schooling have only deepened our concerns. In this chapter, we explore embodied knowledge generated during our pre-pandemic and mid-pandemic experiences with education, burnout, and self-care to illuminate how neoliberalism dehumanizes people into being complicit in their own dehumanization. We raise questions about how "self-care" becomes a tool for maintaining oppression and exploitation and what we can do/have done to change that. Our goal has been to reset our praxis, better care for ourselves and others, and collectively advocate for and struggle toward systemic changes in workplaces and communities.

Running toward Dehumanization: Neoliberal Urgency, Alienation, and Disposability

(July 2020)

Jennifer

Just when I thought I had embraced a steady way to navigate my world, the pandemic hit, and I was suddenly an online educator, home with twin second graders, wondering when I would be able to hug my parents again. I pride myself on connecting with my students, and I was panicked at how they would fare without their school community, which, for some, is where they receive consistent meals, snacks, attention, and love. Suddenly, we were trying to figure out how to find computers or tablets for students in need. I was quickly made aware of my privilege: I have a laptop and my daughters have two tablets each. I contacted parents and guardians, told them, "We would get through this together." These weren't empty platitudes; this was a solemn oath. Did they need anything? Food, resources, gently used devices? It was the first time I shared my personal phone number with parents and encouraged them or their children to text me. I made impersonal drop offs to their homes in the mailboxes—walking the fine line between district protocols and what I felt was right. I also realized my teaching and personality are best served face-to-face. I was compelled to adapt and succeed. But at what cost? My workdays were built around an eighteen-hour norm: feed my girls, set them up for digital learning, run to the other side of our house, try to teach. I divided myself in half to give all of myself to work or family but more often to work. It was easy to let my daughters do their assigned work at their convenience then binge-watch shows or play video games. Certainly, I thought, work needed me more. As the vice president of my local union, I faced questions from colleagues. I lay awake nightly, wracked with guilt, thinking I should have spent more time with my girls, checked on a sickly staff member, or returned a relative's call. I reminded others to take care of themselves, "put on your own oxygen mask first," but neglected my own needs. I drove myself to exhaustion; days blended together. When I reconnected with Dr. Kress and focused on this narrative, I was shaken awake. I knew how important self-care was, I knew the impact mindfulness had on me. How could I let this part of me go? It was easy to blame the pandemic, but I cannot allow myself to continue in this way and melt into the crisis.

Tricia

When the pandemic hit in New York City, life became a frenzy of adjusting to quarantine. Practically overnight, I shifted classes online, refurbished a laptop, set up my son with remote learning, and bought groceries that could last for several weeks. I was exhausted with work and family care spanning fifteen hours daily. My time was spent maintaining normalcy at home and supporting students, all of whom were overwhelmed, and some who were sick or grieving lost loved ones. I stopped going for my runs for three months. In the evening, I collapsed on the couch, watched an hour of television, and fell into dream-filled sleep. My bustling neighborhood was silent except for ambulances rushing to the nearby hospital. The sirens stopped after the peak, and death it seemed was everywhere. But work continued. I showed up to online meetings. Everyone discussed best practices for supporting students. No one discussed our struggles as faculty. Working with Jen on this chapter prepared me for what I needed to do for myself when the pandemic hit. I was too exhausted to exercise, and I confess once the peak of the crisis was over, I only worked a few hours each day so I could remain present for my family and students. I set anything extra aside because additional work hours would lead to burnout, which I was certain would lead to depression given the circumstances. I felt guilty for being selfish and not working as hard as my colleagues seemed to be. I told my students to be kind to themselves and create space to live through the crisis. It was okay to put school assignments on hold. Those words were for them but also for me. I wanted us all to have permission to do for ourselves and loved ones what we needed to while enduring trauma that would impact us for the rest of our lives.

This chapter is the culmination of a year of dialogue, shared journaling, co-researching, and cowriting. When we embarked on this journey, we sought to collaboratively explore our individual self-care practices, our challenges and successes in maintaining them, and the implications this might have for self-care as praxis. Jennifer's self-care consisted of incorporating mindfulness techniques in her classroom. Tricia's self-care was primarily outdoor, long-distance running. As we engaged in our self-care practices, often imperfectly and inconsistently, we kept track of what took place in our lives day by day, the number and duration of activities we engaged in, and what we were thinking and feeling at those times. Journal excerpts included here, and those not included, reveal discourses at play in our lives. One recurring theme was how work was always pressing, students and family needed us, "time" was always in short supply, and self-care came last if we could fit it in to our already long days. Another involved thinking about ourselves as running like "well-oiled" machines, "running in a hamster wheel," "running on a treadmill," and working as part of "the machinery" of our institutions. Such language indicates a clear self-image of dehumanization. Upon first thought, we didn't regard ourselves as bodies with needs. We were machines or cogs in a machine, which lends itself to other problematic aspects of this discourse and its associated practices. First, machines are not thinking and feeling beings. While they have "needs" like upkeep and maintenance, if a machine breaks down, a human may be able to fix it, though the machine cannot fix itself. We see some troubling connotations here; namely, our destiny is not our own. Within the person-equals-machine discourse, we have no agency, and we have no power to take care of ourselves. Someone else (i.e., the human) has the power to do that for us. The external locus of control and lack of agency in all of these images is striking. There is also a pattern of repetition or monotony. Even when we envision ourselves as humans (i.e., running on a treadmill), our bodies are kept in motion by a machine. As hamsters, we are trapped in a wheel, running in place with no way out. The well-oiled machine is particularly worrisome because if we think of ourselves as machines, and we also allow others to think of us as machines, we also need to consider that we live in a consumerist society increasingly driven by novelty and planned obsolescence. If a machine breaks down and cannot be fixed, it can be disposed of and replaced by a newer model. As machines, we are disposable and replaceable.

We began to notice that when we regarded ourselves as machines we were complicit in our own dehumanization, which in itself is problematic, but we were also more likely to be complicit in others' dehumanization by regarding people in general as mechanical. Such dehumanization led us to a sense of alienation and disaffection. We were disconnected from ourselves and our bodies, our professional work, our colleagues and students, and our families and loved ones. We went through the motions like clockwork automatons, with food and sleep simply winding our gears well enough to keep us grinding away on a daily basis. During one of our dialogues in the early fall of 2019, we realized we shared a warped sense of time when it came to work–life balance. We then calculated how much time we spent devoting to professional work, domestic work, and caring for ourselves. What we found appalled us: Neither of us spent more than three hours a week doing anything simply for ourselves, excluding "maintenance" like showering and eating. That amounted to about 3 percent of our total waking hours for an entire week. In other words, 97 percent of our waking hours (nearly one hundred hours per week) was spent doing professional work, domestic work, and caring for others. The sense of urgency we felt to incessantly "work" was deeply entrenched in our bodies. Both of us experience anxiety when the pressures in our lives culminate. But as we slowly understood, we were living in a perpetual state of "crisis" that was not, in fact, a crisis. We started asking ourselves questions like, "Will things really fall apart if we don't respond to that email until tomorrow or Monday?" "Will it make a difference if the house is messy this week?" "Will it really have a negative effect if I went for a run or to a Zoomba class for an hour instead of working?" As we thought about time and alienation, without even speaking to each other about it, we started to do better for ourselves by drawing boundaries and quieting the sirens in our minds that compelled our bodies to run themselves into the ground. Without speaking about it, we both actually stopped working on this chapter and began working on ourselves. By sharing our self-care journeys with each other, we set out on a course to be mindful about reconnecting with ourselves and those around us. We had arrived at a place in the journey where we could see most things were not truly urgent. Emerging from dehumanization slowed the urgency we felt—most things did not need immediate attention; they could wait.

And then, the pandemic hit and urgency took on a new meaning.

Resetting our Praxes: Mindfulness, Self-Care, and Self | Other Forgiveness as Resistance

(November 2020)

Jennifer & Tricia

We fell off the self-care course again. Pandemic life took its toll, and in this now legitimate crisis we fell into old mechanical patterns. We stopped exercising, taking mindful moments, dialoguing; we stopped developing self-care praxes. We lost touch;

the chapter stalled; we sunk back into dehumanization. When the worst of the crisis passed, we rested, we breathed, we grieved, we felt gratitude. We reconnected and realized while we didn't maintain our self-care praxes the way we wished we had, our bodies hadn't forgotten what we learned. We rescheduled a meeting when Jen's school went remote again. Finding time was challenging with increased work and family demands. Our email exchange before a holiday helped us resurface our mutual self-care commitment. After Jen contacted Tricia to reschedule, Tricia replied, "No worries. I'm sorry to hear about … your school. I could meet on Friday … I could [also] meet on Wednesday, but I am trying to not schedule stuff because my son is off from school. But if Friday doesn't work, we can do Wednesday." Jen replied, "Friday would be best. I too am trying to keep Wednesday open to be really off with my girls." On Wednesday Jen and her daughters went for a hike in a nature preserve. Tricia went for a run in the park and made banana pancakes with her son. We gave each other permission to be fully human.

Various cultures throughout human history have utilized mindfulness for introspection and clarity. "Mindfulness can be thought of as moment-to-moment, nonjudgmental awareness, cultivated by paying attention in a specific way, that is, in the present moment, and as nonreactively, as nonjudgmentally, and as openheartedly as possible" (Kabat-Zinn, 2015, p. 1481). This concept has spread throughout the world, transcended time and place, and been adapted as a tool in various cultures. In the United States, mindfulness has also entered popular discourse, with mindfulness practices taken up in schools and in the corporate sector. Mindfulness, at times, is marketed toward specific demographics or perceived as something that can only take place in a yoga studio; however, mindful practices can be done by anyone almost anywhere, through breathing exercises, deliberate movement of the body, with guided meditations and yoga-like poses (Tobin, Powietrzynska, & Alexakos, 2015), or in our case, by collaborating on this chapter together. As we struggle to lead balanced lives, stressors affect our home life, our work, and ultimately our health. Feelings of dissatisfaction and anxiety can lead to exhaustion and burnout. Research highlights the importance of mind–body connection and the ties that connect our emotional health to our physical health. And just as we can exercise and improve our physical health, we can similarly look to mindful practices as emotional exercises to strengthen our psychological well-being (Davidson & Begley, 2012).

As is evident in both our narratives, the pandemic changed life drastically for us and for everyone around us, near and far. But the issues of work, time, and urgency were present in our lives long before the pandemic hit and were what led us to examine mindfulness and self-care in the first place. By being intentional in writing this chapter together, we were able to reset our praxes by supporting each other and being forgiving of ourselves and those around us when we could not hold everything together. At times we needed to let go, but we needed someone to give us permission and empathy. At first, we gave each other permission to take our time, set boundaries, and not do more than what was humanly possible. Eventually, we internalized our practices of other-care as self-care, and we began assuming forgiving and empathic stances for our selves. Our mindfulness became reciprocal; we better cared for ourselves, we also better cared for others. Without saying so, we developed an individual/collective act of resistance that asserted, "I will not sacrifice my/your well-being." The praxis that emerged from our collaborative "reset" is cumulative—forgiveness begets forgiveness; mindfulness begets mindfulness; healing begets healing. We took time out, we revisited and circled back, we ran the courses prior to, into, and during the pandemic, but mindfully. And we ran in multiple ways, the courses of work, wellness, quarantine, self, family, and life.

Paulo Freire (1970) gives us tools for understanding the process we have organically gone through. He said oppressed people must locate the origin of their circumstances, turn upon it, and change it. While we are not economically and materially oppressed as were the people Freire was writing about, we have experienced dehumanization as machine metaphors were overlaid onto our bodies (Darder, 2016) and our minds. For Freire (2007), this is a key feature of neoliberalism: people are dehumanized, objectified, exploited, and made disposable by global capital. Educators are in an unfortunate predicament because they are responsible for "growing" unique young humans into healthy and happy adults, and they are cast as "self-less" and "not in it for the money." This makes them easy prey for exploitation. As we write this during the United States' third wave of the coronavirus pandemic, New York State, an early epicenter of the outbreak in the United States, is facing another round of school closures. The dehumanization of teachers is striking as there is widespread public outcry over school closures, while there is little empathy for the dangers that teachers (and their loved ones) may face simply by reentering their classrooms. As a nation, we are in a no-win situation—schools may contribute to further virus spread, but they also contribute to a healthy economy, healthy children, and keeping millions of people out of poverty and hunger because they provide childcare and food for many families. Health and wellness in schools and in the teaching force has never in our lifetimes been more important than it is at this moment in history. Yet, the physical, mental, and emotional health of teachers appears as a sidebar behind the need to get children back in schools so parents can go back to work in order to keep the economy afloat. This is no small matter as more than 250,000 Americans have already died and nearly 1,500 more are dying daily. The magnitude of suffering and death that is taking place for the sake of keeping the economy going is nothing short of appalling, but from within the current socio-political-economic ethos, there appear to be no easy escape routes.

Caring for ourselves is an expression of our recognition of and value for humanity; it is a resistance to the plunder of neoliberalism. By resetting our praxes, instead of acting more like machines, we can become more fully human. But we could not do this alone. Even though we kept stalling with our progress, sometimes not looking at this chapter for months, we kept coming back to the embrace we had created for each other. Each time we connected, we healed a little more. We opened our hearts to Freire's (1998) assertion, as humans we are "unfinished," and we continued to refine our praxis, seeking to become more fully human. Mindfully running the courses this past year has taught us: healing is collective and productive; it is not fracturing and destructive. We started in different places and with different practices and goals, but we have settled into running the courses together, providing space, motivation, and care for each other and ourselves in the process. As we close this collaborative chapter, we reaffirm our commitment to protect our bodies and minds, create space for ourselves and others to be whole, and to facilitate healing. We invite you to join us in a self-care praxis as resistance to reset a course toward healing and becoming.

7

Immanence and a Pedagogy of Vulnerability: Teaching with Anxiety and Panic Disorder

Kathryn Strom

Part 1: I Am Not, In Fact, Okay

I am a full-time faculty member in an educational doctoral program. And I am not okay.

Most of us academics are probably not okay. The pervasive mental health crisis in academia is an "open secret" (Brunila & Valero, 2018). Academia is a toxic soup of nonstop rejection, cutthroat competition, constant budget shrinkage, workaholism—plus all the institutional *isms*. As Mountz and colleagues (2015) note, "the effects of the neoliberal university are written on the body" (p. 1245).

However, dominant discourses of the academy, which privilege rationality, productivity, individualism, and independence, perpetuate academics' tendency to hide their mental health issues (Price, 2011). For one, academics rely on their minds for their work. To me, these dominant discourses and the realities of working with graduate students mean I'm supposed to keep my personal life separate from my professional life and generally be seen as "having it together" to have the credibility for guiding doctoral students.

In the first several years of my career, I generally did "have it together"—or at least was able to perform as if I did. In the summer of 2018, that illusion exploded in my face.

> *July 2018*
>
> *Self-Study of Teacher Education Practices*
> *Castle Conference*
>
> *I'm sitting in a stuffy conference room with thirty other faculty members who have flown in to Herstmonceux Castle, where the self-study conference is held every two years. Worn out and lightheaded, I decide to head back to my room to take a nap.*
>
> *I make my way back to where me and three of my closest friends are staying on the top floor of a centuries-old B&B.*
>
> *I'm (always) thinking about work.*

I'm exhausted (it's been an exhausting year).

I get into bed, plug my earphones in, start my sleep app, put my sleeping mask on. Ocean waves fill my ears, my mind goes blank.

Out of nowhere, thoughts race across my mind.

*YOU-ARE-NOTHING-BUT-YOUR-WORK-YOUR-WORK-IS-NOTHING-**YOU**-ARE-NOTHING*

Icy fingers sweep up my body.
Stomach bottoms out.
Heart pounds.
Can't breathe.
Skin crawls.
Mouth full of sand.

I'm more terrified than I've ever been in my life.
It's happened.
I've lost it.
I've gone crazy.

I was trapped in terror and bodily distress for days. Later, I learned I'd experienced waves of panic attacks that felt like one long episode. It was so traumatic that by the time I arrived back home, my brain had been rewired, my fear response constantly active, making me feel perpetually trapped on the knife-edge of a panic attack.

I was diagnosed with anxiety and panic disorders and began a year-long process of trial and error with various medications and therapies. The panic, anxiety, and medication side effects impacted every facet of my work. When school started, I did the bare minimum.

Before the attacks, I existed only for intellectual activity. My days were spent reading, writing, and talking about posthuman research, or planning and teaching. Now, my mind had seemingly shut off. Twenty-four hours a day, feelings coursed through my body on multiple simultaneous levels in an awful way that defies words. I was frozen with terror that had no discernible source. My body was on high alert, my nerve endings frayed, as if someone was raking their nails down a chalkboard on a never-ending loop. I was always exhausted from the adrenaline continuously being released to prepare my body to flee danger. I so distracted by my body's distress that I couldn't focus for more than a moment, which produced intrusive thoughts that spiraled out of control:

from
I can't think straight
I can't do any reading or writing

to
I'm never going to get better
I'm going to lose my job
to
We are going to lose our house
It's going to be all my fault
to
I don't want to live like this.

My days were a blur of misery: wake up, move from bed to couch, hide under my weighted blanket, watch television to distract myself until it was time to take a pill and sleep. As I drifted off, I always thought to myself, *maybe I'll wake up tomorrow and be okay.* But I never was.

Part 2: Disrupting Segmentarity

The logic of Western civilization is based on *rational humanism,* or "commonsense" thinking, which operates via segmentarity, or separations. Deleuze and Guattari (1987) argue, "We are segmented from all around and in every direction" (p. 208). The spaces around us are divided up—different parts of town, buildings with certain purposes, homes with areas for specific functions. We are segmented from micro- to macro-system levels, from the individual moving out in ever-widening spheres, to community, region, country, so on. Society is divided into categories that establish hierarchies and dualisms (man/woman, rich/poor, white/nonwhite, human/nonhuman, self/other). We are segmented in terms of our own body/mind, personal life, and work multiplicities. My stress, anxiety, and panic belong in the "personal life" category, so it needs to be kept out of my work.

The reasons I am supposed to keep my mental illness out of my work are all about opposing dualisms:

1. Personal/professional life: I have a particular job—teach students about education and qualitative research, apprentice them to apply critical perspectives in research. My mental health issues would be an off-topic in the classroom.
2. Mind/body: I am supposed focus on intellectual activity and not have a body. Addressing issues concerning my body might make students uncomfortable, which threatens *their* mind/body dualities.
3. Rational/irrational, expert/novice: As a woman and young-presenting academic, revealing my struggles might complicate my tenuous position of authority by communicating to my doctoral-level students (all successful educational leaders) that I am not rational, a weakness that could compromise my position as knowledgeable instructor.

The Enlightenment's rational humanism is exemplified by "I think, therefore I am," a mind/body binary. The body's existence is predicated on the mind's thinking. Hence, dualistic, hierarchical thought is the marker of humanity (Braidotti, 2013): "I think (*rationally, like a White man*), therefore I am (*human, and have access to the rights and privileges of humanity*)." Those rights and privileges are based on the idea that (human) individuals have full agency, free will, and the ability to self-determine (St. Pierre, 2000).

The mind/body binary is also a marker that defines difference in negative terms—*this* is not *that* (Braidotti, 2013)—which casts groups with onto-epistemologies different from rational humanism as inferior and not fully human. Accordingly, this Eurocentric rational, individualistic ahistorical, decontextualized way of thinking-being justifies the subordination and/or erasure of "other" groups, forces people into toxic hierarchies, and perpetuates white supremacy.

The antidote, according to Delueze and Guattari, is an *immanent* onto-epistemology. Immanence is a binary-blurring, relational perspective: everything that exists is connected, part of one giant diverse matter, which is dynamic, alive, and made up of multiplicities—temporal constellations of humans, spaces, things, ideas, forces—constantly morphing in relation to each other. This moves away from "human" (i.e., white cis-het men) as the center of reality, toward *human–nonhuman multiplicities* as the main unit of existence, which has massive implications for how we think, work, and live. For instance, boundaries do not exist but are drawn, imposed, as "agential cuts" (Barad, 2007). These cuts create our realities, and we *can* do otherwise, draw new boundaries, create new worlds.

October 2018

I take two propranolol. They calm my heart rate, telling my brain, *there's no danger here.* They mute the physical symptoms of anxiety, but not necessarily the psychological ones.

I'm dreading class. *Normal Katie* loved teaching—it was an important part of her positionality. *Anxiety-Panic Katie* is terrified of teaching.

It's yet another performance in the stage production of my professional life. I'm pretending to teach, but I'm just mouthing words from classes previously planned by *Normal Katie.* I copy and paste the class slides with slight modifications, like the date on the first slide.

I *hate it.* My students are shortchanged. I feel like I've lost another vital part of my identity—my teacher-self.

Students come in.

I'm trembling. I hope they can't see me shaking. I'm lightheaded. I've had very little to eat because my medication makes me feel nauseous. My heart would be beating furiously, but the beta-blocker is doing its job.

I feel my students' eyes on me. I am abnormally pale, dark purple smudges under my eyes.

> As I stumble through the technology set-up, a student asks how I'm doing. I consider lying but instead I say, "Not great." These students have been with me for a while; they know about my disorder, but I still try to perform normality. It's not usual for me to let on that I'm struggling.
>
> I signal that we are going to begin and lead them into the first activity. Voices scream in my head: *They'll find out I'm a fraud! I shouldn't be teaching in a doctoral program!* Along with other thoughts I can't bring myself to put into words. I don't know why I'm thinking these things—it's like an evil being filling my head with upsetting things to torture me.
>
> The voices are so consuming that when I open my mouth, I am afraid some of these terrible things will come out. My therapist says they are not voices, just intrusive thoughts; they can't hurt me. Of everything that is happening to me, these intrusive thoughts are the worst. They make me feel mentally ill.
>
> Over the voices' screech, I click to the PowerPoint slide and force myself to read the words out loud.

***

In the past, I simply pretended that I was OK, pushed these feelings aside, and focused on the teaching or interacting with other faculty. When I returned to school in the fall of 2018, however, it was impossible to keep my struggle out of the classroom and my workplace. I was *visibly* not okay. The disturbing feelings continued, keeping me in a continuous state of distress and discomfort. I was a shell of my previous self.

I needed to explain to my coworkers and my students why.

I disclosed to faculty colleagues at our first meeting of the year. Usually, colleagues shared about their summer activities, or life milestones—*we bought a house! My daughter got married!*—or work-related celebrations: *I got the grant! My article was accepted!* When it was my turn, I choked out a brief summary, sharing that I had been diagnosed with anxiety and panic disorder and was actively seeking treatment. I finished with, "I wanted to let you know that in case I don't seem like myself right now. Because I'm not." Two of my colleagues disclosed that they, too, had anxiety issues, while others expressed sympathy and support. This opening allowed me to be honest rather than adopting a painful veneer of cheerfulness.

I provided less detail to my students as I explained my recently developed anxiety and panic disorder. I asked for their patience with me as I learned how to deal with it. After class, two students wrote me privately and disclosed their own struggles with anxiety, forging a connection between us beyond the classroom. Students were more open with me about their own struggles from that point forward.

I found the more I talked about my anxiety and panic, the easier it became. In more lucid moments, I thought about how rational humanism not only constructs ways of particular thinking but also a particular "normal" individual. I decided share some of my thinking in the ability/dis-ability module of my social and cultural foundations course.

Part of the class drew on disabilities studies and critical posthuman lenses to problematize the autonomous, independent thinking-moving individual "norm." I posited, in actuality, none of us fits that "norm": we all need mediation-modification to function, to live our best and most joyful lives. I offered myself as an example. I may seem a successful early career academic with plenty of awards and publications. However, I am chemically mediated at all times. I couldn't be standing before them at that moment if I wasn't taking at least two forms of medication. Needing chemical help doesn't make me weak or less able; it makes me different, with different needs for assistive tools and practices (e.g., medication, therapy, and so on) to live my fullest life. I argued that part of disrupting the harmful norm of the pull-yourself-up-by-your-bootstraps, ahistorical-and-acontextual, independently-thinking-and-moving hu-Man is making these mediations/modifications public, normalizing them, and confronting the stigma head-on.

The concept of immanence also helped me change my perspective on my anxiety and panic disorder itself, which put me on a path to managing it. Multiple therapists told me I needed to stop fighting my anxiety—fighting it made me worse. Anxiety isn't rational; we don't have agency over it. So, the inability to control it through rational thought or intentional action amplified my anxiety, sending my body/mind into a downward spiral. Instead, my therapist told me, "You need to develop a relationship with your anxiety; think of your anxiety as a friend."

I had no idea how to do that—I *hated* my anxiety and panic. It was the stranger that took over my body, a parasite that sucked away my vitality and passion for my work and life. However, as the months passed, I finally was able to find a combination of medication, therapy, mindfulness, and body-soothing strategies that brought my anxiety level down, and with a clearer mind, I began to see what she meant. I was setting myself up *in opposition to* my anxiety, as something I needed to overcome and get rid of. I needed to accept that my anxiety was *part of me*, not some evil presence separate from me that I could battle and subdue.

From there, I began to see real progress. My therapist and I practiced a combination of exposure therapy (exercises that induced anxiety and panic-like feelings) and self-talk ("this is okay—it's okay to feel anxiety"). Over several months, I did develop a different relationship with my anxiety and panic: when I felt anxiety/panic, I repeated that it was OK to feel it, and I did not spiral any further. This exercise—in combination with my assemblage of management strategies—helped me arrive to where, although not anxiety- and panic-free, I can work with the sensations and enjoy my life.

Part 3: Developing a Pedagogy of Vulnerability

When I started feeling better in early July of 2019, I engaged in weeks of autoethnographic writing trying to analyze and understand my experiences. The more I thought and wrote about the assemblage that produced my anxiety and panic—including the toxic systems of which my students are also part—the more determined I became to share my experiences in my scholarship as well as my teaching. I decided to build on my disclosure from the previous year and more purposefully fold my experiences into our curriculum, using them to demonstrate and put to work concepts such as intersectionality, feminism, and dis/ability, as well as help introduce shifts in thinking from critical posthumanism.

I began referring to this pedagogical work as a *pedagogy of vulnerability.* I drew on bell hooks' notion of (1994) engaged pedagogy, where she discusses vulnerability as a way for teachers to mediate coercive power relations while deepening student understanding. hooks explains:

> When professors bring narratives of their experiences into classroom discussions it eliminates the possibility that we can function as all-knowing, silent interrogators. It is often productive if professors take the first risk, linking confessional narratives to academic discussions so as to show how experience can illuminate and enhance our understanding of academic material. But most professors must practice being vulnerable in the classroom, being wholly present in mind, body, and spirit. (p. 21)

Although I used my experiences in multiple lessons, I focus here on an in-depth example from my disability and education module of my social and cultural foundations of education course.

At the start of class, students were assigned either the medical or social model of disability. The medical model is a deficit-based perspective that views disability as an abnormality or problem within the disabled person, making them "less-than," and it pursues medical care to "fix" the issue. The social model views disability as caused by the normative beliefs and structures of society and promotes a difference-appreciative perspective while advocating for revisioning environments so people with a range of abilities can live full lives. Using one of our readings for that session, students worked with a partner to identify the major ideas of their perspective and brainstorm the implications of that model for K–12 and university. They then found a partner with the opposite model and discussed across them, followed by a whole-class share-out and discussion. In these conversations, my students already were poking at the dichotomy that the literature sets up between the two models.

After our discussion, I introduced the ideas of intersectionality and posthumanism to push beyond the either/or medical/social dichotomy. In small groups, students discussed a second article that delved into the intersections of disability, race, class, language, and culture. I then moved us into an overview of the conceptual shifts from rational humanism to critical posthumanism (as discussed in the previous section of this chapter), which I had foreshadowed earlier in the semester. I identified the medical perspective as one grounded in individualism/individual agency and rationality, demonstrating how this perspective would produce me/my illness, and contrasted it with a posthuman perspective (Figure 7.1).

The medical model views my illness as a problem located in my head; I am prompted to blame myself for my own choices. I should be able to overcome it, and if not, it means I'm weak, although it could be managed through pharmaceuticals. I also presented an alternative view, the posthuman, that viewed the development of an anxiety disorder as a product of a human–nonhuman, material–discursive assemblage.

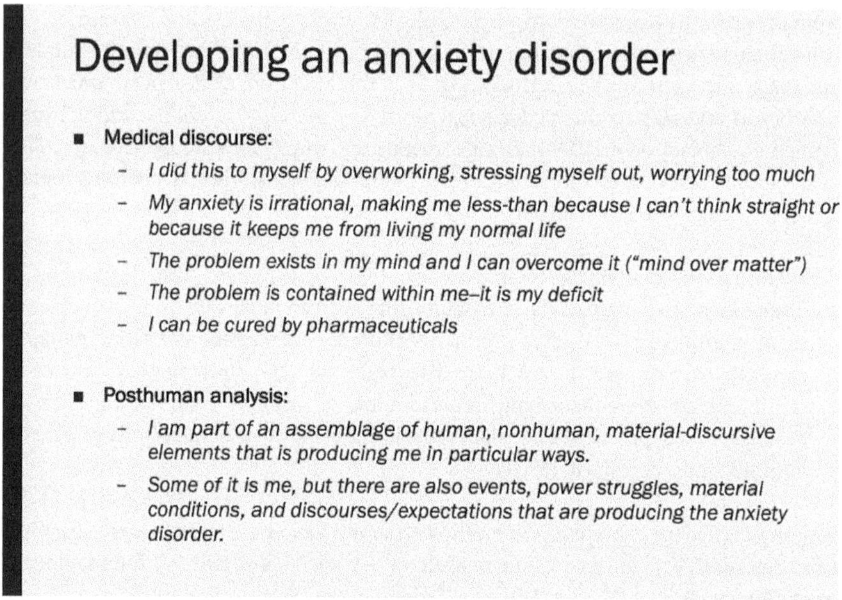

Developing an anxiety disorder

- **Medical discourse:**
  - *I did this to myself by overworking, stressing myself out, worrying too much*
  - *My anxiety is irrational, making me less-than because I can't think straight or because it keeps me from living my normal life*
  - *The problem exists in my mind and I can overcome it ("mind over matter")*
  - *The problem is contained within me–it is my deficit*
  - *I can be cured by pharmaceuticals*

- **Posthuman analysis:**
  - *I am part of an assemblage of human, nonhuman, material-discursive elements that is producing me in particular ways.*
  - *Some of it is me, but there are also events, power struggles, material conditions, and discourses/expectations that are producing the anxiety disorder.*

Figure 7.1 Slide of the medical model and posthuman perspectives on anxiety.

I then projected an alternative analysis using intersectional and posthuman concepts, shown in Figure 7.2.

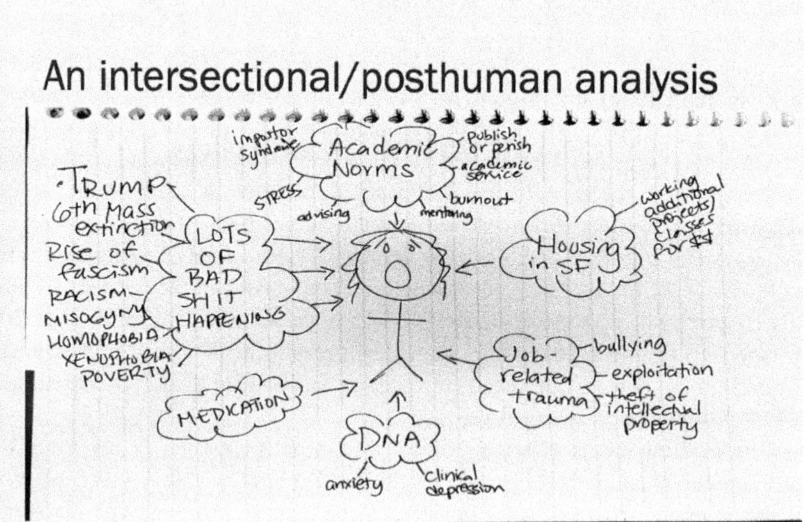

Figure 7.2 An extremely sophisticated rendering of a posthuman analysis of the production of an anxiety disorder.

I pointed out that there was no single factor caused the disorder—it developed as a result of multiple interacting human and nonhuman elements, systems, and forces. These included the academic norms and expectations I had internalized; publish or perish mentality; service requirements for tenure; teaching and advising; mentoring; imposter syndrome; and stress/burnout. Another dimension encompassed material conditions, like housing in one of the most expensive cities in the United States. We needed a down payment of 10 percent to purchase our home, so I taught extra classes, picked up additional dissertations, and took on consulting work, which contributed to my burnout and stress. I also discussed job-related traumas, including academic bullying, exploitation, and intellectual property theft.

In response, several students exclaimed angrily on my behalf. I mimicked the chirpy tone of an advertisement, telling them, "But wait—there's more!" Several students joined in on a chorus of "there's more!" We were all laughing by then. I discussed human factors (such as my DNA) and more material/chemical elements (e.g., multiple forms of medication I had been taking) and then addressed the macro-political material-discursive conditions that weighed on me and so many others. Students again laughed as I introduced this—"And then there's just LOTS OF BAD SHIT HAPPENING!"—and named all of these political-economic-social-environmental conditions that wrote themselves on my body (and the bodies of so many).

I introduced my treatment as a corpomaterial-affective assemblage and addressed two concepts we had been studying for the past several weeks—power/privilege and intersectionality—in the context of my treatment, as a way to provide a concrete example of these concepts. I laid out several intersections of power/privilege noted in the slide below, and talked through all of these with the students (Figure 7.3).

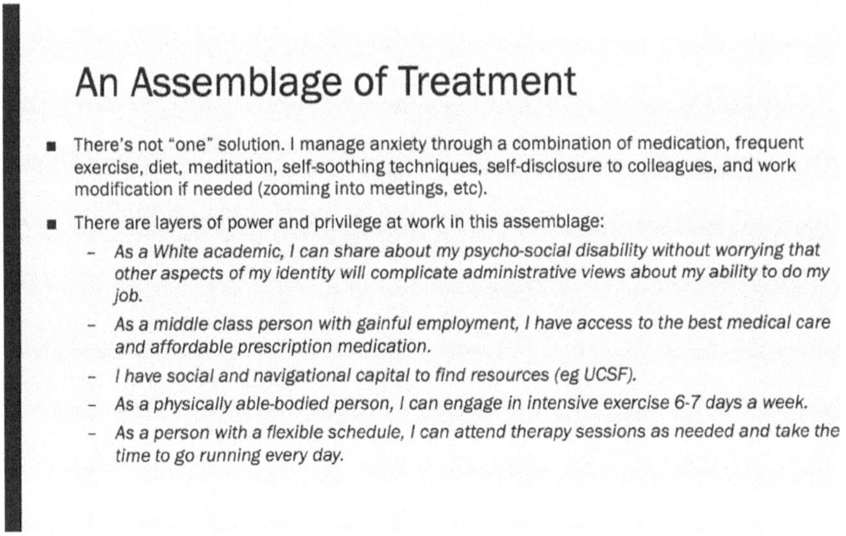

An Assemblage of Treatment

- There's not "one" solution. I manage anxiety through a combination of medication, frequent exercise, diet, meditation, self-soothing techniques, self-disclosure to colleagues, and work modification if needed (zooming into meetings, etc).
- There are layers of power and privilege at work in this assemblage:
  - *As a White academic, I can share about my psycho-social disability without worrying that other aspects of my identity will complicate administrative views about my ability to do my job.*
  - *As a middle class person with gainful employment, I have access to the best medical care and affordable prescription medication.*
  - *I have social and navigational capital to find resources (eg UCSF).*
  - *As a physically able-bodied person, I can engage in intensive exercise 6-7 days a week.*
  - *As a person with a flexible schedule, I can attend therapy sessions as needed and take the time to go running every day.*

Figure 7.3 Assemblages and layers of power and privilege in treatment of anxiety.

Afterward, we continued to discuss these ideas. Many shared that they recognized in their own lives the same, or similar, toxic conditions compromising their mental and/or physical wellness. As with the previous year, several students disclosed to me their own mental health struggles privately, and it became an important point of connection for us over the next two semesters.

Conclusion

I'm still figuring out what a pedagogy of vulnerability looks like and what its impact is, but I know the more I share my experiences, the easier it becomes to be vulnerable, and the more I center it in my teaching. This year, I foregrounded my pedagogy of vulnerability by sharing the above "I am from" poem with my doctoral students, opening myself while introducing my core values and key ideas we would discuss over the semester.

I am from

… the kind of entrenched racism no one likes to admit is reality.
… de facto segregated schools and neighborhoods.
… billboards that warn: if you aren't a good Christian,
you will burn in hell.
… parents who know to navigate systems.

I am from

… a society that tells me that "those who can't do, teach."
… portable classrooms with chipped desks and peeling walls.
… a field infected with White Savior Complex
… and Nice White Lady Teacher Syndrome.

I am from

… a feminized profession that is undervalued and underpaid.
… critical dialogue and self-interrogation about whiteness.
… "and and and," an antidote to "either/or."
… Freire, hooks, Deleuze & Guattari, Braidotti.

I am from

… assets-based and linguistically responsive pedagogies.
… classes that examine systems perpetuation
and disruption of oppressions.
… graphic organizers that scaffold doctoral level literacy.
… The maroon swivel chairs in Arts & Education 123.

I am from

... a field that has taught me that my work
takes precedence over my health.
... pounding heart rates.
... stomach knots.
... body-shaking terror.

I am from

... cognitive based therapy.
... learning to tell my body, "It is OK to feel anxiety."
... disclosure of mental health issues.
... doing differently in academia.

This process has been healing and generative—and an act of immanence. Using my life as a site for demonstrating analysis with critical theoretical concepts and complex ways of thinking with students transgresses typically imposed binaries of academia: personal/professional, lived/theoretical knowledge, and rationality/irrationality. It disrupts the shame and taboo that silences dialogue about mental health. It troubles dominant narratives around independence, individualism, and human exceptionalism. It breaks down the illusion that I am the all-knowing, perfect scholar who "has it together." It allows me to stand in solidarity with my students and acknowledge we work in toxic systems. It also offers potential for developing practices of care and compassion for ourselves and our communities. These acts of disruption and creation help heal us and sustain us to carry on our justice work another day.

8

In the "Being" and the "Doing": Teachers' Critical Embodied Pedagogies of Care

Victoria Restler

Introduction: Space + Air + Bodies in Schools

Schooling is built around a set of largely unarticulated norms and expectations about who students, teachers, and administrators are, their values, ways of knowing and being, cultures, languages, and lives outside of the classroom. Steeped in whiteness, heteronormativity, and middle-class values, these norms are enacted on and experienced in bodies—bodies forced into shapes that don't fit, bodies pushed into and out of school buildings, and bodies surveilled by racial capitalist accountability structures. In school spaces, where (some) bodies are consistently denied and devalued, it is implemented through a "pedagogy of disembodiment," that as Ohito (2019, p.3) writes, "divorces the mind from the 'weeping, living, hurting body' (Bakare-Yusuf 1999, 312)." Through the (in)visible near-totalizing norms of whiteness, schools deny the presence, needs, desires, hurts, and lived experiences of Black, Indigenous, and People of Color (BIPOC), queer, and disabled positionalities. Cleaving mind from body (Pindyck 2018), they deny bodies as vibrant vectors for teaching and learning—marginalizing forms of knowing and being that are associated with queer, Black, indigenous, femme, and non-Western forms and traditions.

Teaching and learning with young people up against these violent histories and presents—teaching toward love, justice, and freedom—demands what I call critical embodied pedagogies of care. This pedagogical orientation stretches beyond social justice curricular resources, democratic teaching strategies, and dominant white, feminized notions of care as kindness (Nieto 2008). It asks us to imagine a wider more generous (Smith 2005; Restler 2017) frame for the work of teaching that encompasses formal and informal academic work, affect, and relational engagement. And it centers the body, recognizing the social locations and specificity of bodies (both teachers' and students'), and of the emotional, physicality of the work. It is a pedagogy grounded in Rosalie Rolon-Dow's race-conscious critical care praxis (2005); Shawn Ginwright's (2015) concept of healing justice that braids care with activism; and Stephanie Cariaga's healing pedagogy of the body that positions the body as "(a) site of trauma and healing,

(b) source of wisdom, (c) channel for narrative, and (d) tool for healing pedagogy" (2018, p.26).

This chapter explores the drawings and narratives of two teacher/activists working in New York City public high schools and the ways they inhabit and mobilize their teaching bodies toward critical embodied pedagogies of care. Although both educators center critical social justice curriculum and pedagogy in their practice, this analysis focuses on moments, modes, and orientations outside of the formal—trained, tracked, evaluated, and valued—work of teaching. Through body map drawings and interview dialogue, these teacher-activists draw our attention toward often invisible aspects of their work—the bodily *being* and *doing* of radical teacher practice.

Context

The images and narratives of this chapter are drawn from a broader study on the invisible work of radical teaching in urban schools. In 2014, I joined with a group of teacher-activists through the New York Collective of Radical Educators and their "Inquiry to Action Groups" (ItAG). Rooted in Freirean praxis, this program invites groups of teachers to explore a critical topic of interest and create a collective action in the form of art, pedagogy, or protest. Our group was titled "Beyond Scores, Ranks, and Rubrics: Re-imagining Teacher Evaluation." And over five months, we met for weekly workshops where we analyzed dominant images and discourses of teacher labor and assessment and made new images to reimagine teacher practice and especially the invisible labor that urban teachers do in the face of racist and discriminatory school and social policies.

One of our projects was a form of mapping called Body Practice Maps (Restler 2017; Restler 2019). I developed the activity with Lee[1]—my ItAG co-facilitator—as a way for the teacher-activists to catalog and describe their daily labor. As I explain elsewhere (Restler 2019), I had initially imagined an abstract form of mapping, but Lee reworked the activity to focus on bodily labor. With this project, we instructed participants to "consider the different kinds of work that comprise their practice and how they map onto different parts of the body." We invited them to think about the full-bodiedness of teaching work and to include emotional, mental, and other invisible forms of labor that take shape both in and outside the classroom.

The teacher-activist's body maps are diverse in scale, aesthetic, and content. Most (eight of ten) depict a partial- or full-body self-portrait, ringed with text, annotating body parts with different forms of teacher work. In the interchange between descriptive narrative and drawn depictions, they capture something ineffable about the scope and pace of teaching work—about the deep emotional labor, the day-in-and-day-out-ness, and especially the visceral and bodily demands. These drawings help make visible much of the work of teaching that is invisible to white, patriarchal, middle-class educational policies and imaginations. With words and images, the maps draw our eyes to body work and highlight the many forms of caring labor that comprise radical teaching praxis.

In the following sections, I discuss the body maps and narratives of two teacher-activists—Sarah and V. Their multimodal analyses of identity, self-presentation, and activism blur boundaries between formal and informal practice, between work in and outside of the classroom, between interior thought and exterior action, between feeling-body and thinking-mind. The embodied pedagogies of care that Sarah and V take up dwell in the "excess," outside of dominant discourses of teaching and learning. Orner, Miller, and Ellsworth (1996) write, "what becomes contained by an educational discourse and what becomes excess or excessive to it is no accident. Excess is a symptom of histories of repression and of the interests associated with those histories." The "excessive [pedagogical] moments" that Sarah and V relay challenge repressive histories that mark bodies, queerness, activism, and Blackness beyond the frames of educational discourse.

"A Bat Signal for LGBT Students"

Sarah's portrait is a cartoonish purple line drawing sketched onto a 3 × 3 foot square of brown craft paper, circled with arrows, speech bubbles, and short marks pointing to blocks of orange, green, and purple text. Sarah renders her full-body figure in a caricature style, confident marker strokes tracing the outline of a side-swept pompadour, large smiling face, one hand reaching up in a friendly wave, the other wrapped around her tapered waistline. She wears a long-sleeved collared shirt, pants and a set of shoes

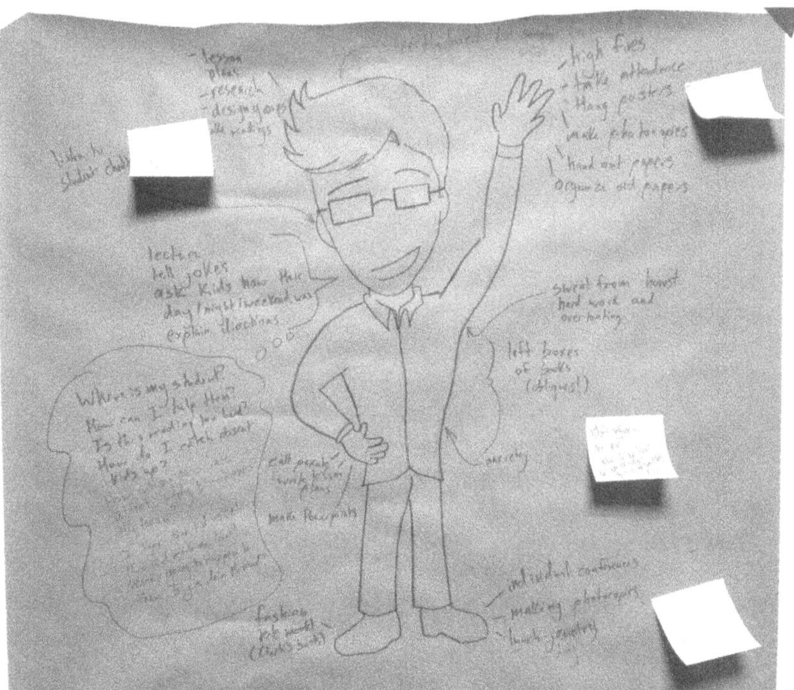

Figure 8.1 Sarah's Body Practice Map (2014).

captioned in bright orange text to read, "fashion role model (Clark's boots)." Looking at the image, I noticed Sarah's facile hand and the mix of confidence and self-deprecating humor. For example, an arrow pointing to her armpit reads, "sweat from honest hard work and overheating." Even with spare exaggerated marks, the image captures some of Sarah's essence. White and Jewish, with a mop of red hair, freckles and tortoiseshell glasses, Sarah favored a casual dapper/dandy style of dress. She was in her second-year teaching and her first at Bronx Humanities, a transfer school that serves students who the system identifies as "over-age and under-credited" (a deficit label which is highly raced, cultured, and classed). At Bronx Humanities, 98 percent of the student body are youth of color, 85 percent receive free/reduced lunch, and only 20 percent of the students graduate in four years compared with a 69 percent city-wide average. Students' experiences in school are shaped by social factors beyond school walls including racial capitalist disinvestment in social welfare and racist policing practices.

During an image-elicitation interview, Sarah spoke about her "superfly haircut," which she described as a "bat signal for LGBT students," and queer presentation, drawing out the links between her appearance and teaching work. She further explained:

> I think as an educator who has really chosen to be out to the kids, a lot of my physical appearance tends to be a subject of conversation with the kids. Like they talk about my clothes or they talk about my haircut, or they talk about my gender presentation, like, 'how come you never wear a dress?' So that does become a part of my teaching and the way I educate.

For Sarah, the pedagogy of her self-presentation is many-layered. It is expressed in the lunchtime support group she runs for queer and questioning students and what she describes as "a small fan club of queer girls" who often stay after class. Her own nonconforming gender presentation comes through in her curriculum as well. She spoke, for example, about a unit on the age of exploration where they studied: "How European viewpoints changed over time about people who look different—topics about sexuality, gender and how women are treated." Her queerness is also a form of pedagogy beyond particular lesson plans, a more deeply rooted "part of [her] teaching and the way [she] educates." She talked about coming out to students at her last job as a sixth-grade teacher and said, "With my sixth graders, they were, 'Here's a successful-ish person who's living the good life …' For them, it was enough to know you could be a human and also have this thing about you be open in public."

Sarah describes a kind of modeling work, crossed with basic facets of her own identity—her haircut, clothing choices, and the fact that as students remark, she "dresses like a man." This work is like what Maeve O'Brien (2009) says of her study of mothers' labor, a kind of care work that is "about being rather than doing, especially being available to support and encourage children and listen to their concerns" (p.165). For Sarah, the "being" is about her own identity and self-expression, being herself, as well as being there for students who need her guidance, friendship, or support. Being an out lesbian teacher with short hair who never wears dresses is a way of showing lesbian, gay, bisexual, transgender, queer (LGBTQ) and straight cisgender students alike that success and queerness (and perhaps other kinds of difference too) can go together.

When Amir, another teacher participant spoke about the drawing during our interview, he echoed this sentiment, but from the angle of "colleague" as opposed to "student." Amir is older than Sarah, then forty-four as compared with her twenty-five, and also identifies as queer. Contemplating Sarah's drawing, he called the figure "a very queer being," a representation that he saw as "so endearing and so beautiful and wonderful." When I asked him what he found special about the image, he replied, "It's that someone like that can have that kind of a self-image and be able to express it in this way. And be a teacher. And be comfortable being a teacher as a queer, in a queer body." Amir was visibly moved (eyes watery) that Sarah could so thoroughly inhabit both a teacher identity and queer identity and see them as complementary.[2]

Amir reflected on the links between Sarah's queer presentation and caring pedagogy. Commenting on her haircut and boots, he observed,

> She's using signs, she's using codes. The haircut, the fashion role model, even her being, it's interesting, even her boots and her fashion are about communicating some sense of self or community. Her hair is a code for the gay kids. Being fashionable is for the kids' sakes. Again, her need of being fashionable in society still has kids in mind.

Sarah's way of being "teacher" is intercorporeal and relational, rooted in what LaJevic and Springgay (2008) call "being-with." They explain,

> Bodies/selves cannot exist without other bodies/selves, nor are the two reducible to one another … [Being-with suggests] a with that opens self to the vulnerability of the other, a with that is always affected and touched by the other. (2008, p. 70)

The way that Sarah keeps "kids in mind," with her fashion reflects a relational orientation, a way of holding her sense of self alongside her connections to students and community. And the inherent vulnerability of coming out and being out with students opens space for their vulnerability, for being and doing against the hegemonic norms of school and society (Reimers 2020).

Sarah's portrait complicates dominant aesthetic and conceptual representations of teaching and care. Her image and analysis disrupt "controlling images" (Collins 1986) of the white, cis, hetero, femme caring teacher as angelic, as old maid, as nice, as marmy-mother. Amir takes up this juxtaposition in reflecting on Sarah's approach to care. He comments,

> It's interesting, because it's not a maternal care. The traditional image anyway, the whole notion of teaching being basically mothers in a classroom. This is not that kind of a care. This is a care based on a love of humanity, rather than maternal instincts.

Distinguishing Sarah's image from traditional depictions of "maternal care," Amir holds Sarah's portrait—sweaty, boastful, and clad in work boots—up against typical feminine representations of mothers and teachers with long hair and dresses, sweet and demure. But he also connects her presentation and approach to an investment in others—her community of students, queer culture, and queer youth— as opposed to individual white, Western conceptions of mother love. Sarah's intentional linking of "self and community" reflects a care philosophy rooted in social conceptions of identity and justice.

I Trust Them and You Should Trust Me

With brown skin, hair in a short natural style, and a smile that seems to fill her whole face, V another teacher participant, was currently in her first year teaching media arts at Newcomer High School (a fact I didn't compute for months, because she had none of the first-year teacher affects of panic or self-deprecation). V's grounding in this new role came partly from her substantial prior experience working as a music teacher and teaching artist. And it came from her well-developed art practices (rock band drummer, storyteller, and video artist) and commitment to regular meditation. As a Nigerian-born arts educator, she was passionate about the philosophy of Newcomer, a public high school for recently arrived immigrants, 90 percent of whom are students of color and 86 percent of whom are emergent bilinguals.

V's Body Practice Map depicts a cross-legged, four-armed, Ganesha-inspired pencil drawing on craft paper that visually echoes her spiritual and holistic orientation toward teaching. In describing the map, she explained,

> In the life of a teacher—if we're talking about all of our hidden work—it does feel like spiritually and emotionally we do have to grow extra limbs. We have to reach into so many different pots and we have to reach into so many different existences, so that's where that inspiration initially came from. I think my map, in particular, sort of speaks to the idea that teaching, takes a lot! It takes a lot more than you can ever know unless you've been in it, and even as you're in it, you learn every day more and more of where you need to go to continue to grow, where you need to go as a person to continue to grow, and that learning is … in conversation. It's passing between us constantly—educator/learner, learner/educator.

V's explanation speaks to the volume of teaching work, and the way that radical teaching invites or perhaps requires personal, spiritual, and emotional growth. She situates teaching in the body—growing "extra limbs," knowing by being "in it"—and slides between the almost-synonyms of growing, learning, and teaching to describe the work. Finally, she positions the practice of teaching as "passing between us constantly," the "being-with" (LaJevic & Springgay 2008) of back-and-forth conversations between educator and learner (Figure 8.2).

V often speaks through story, using interpersonal narratives to explain her thinking and approach. In talking about "the conversation" of teaching, she interrupted her discussion of the map to raise a story from earlier that week. During class, she had taken her video students outdoors to a neighboring park to film, and as she describes,

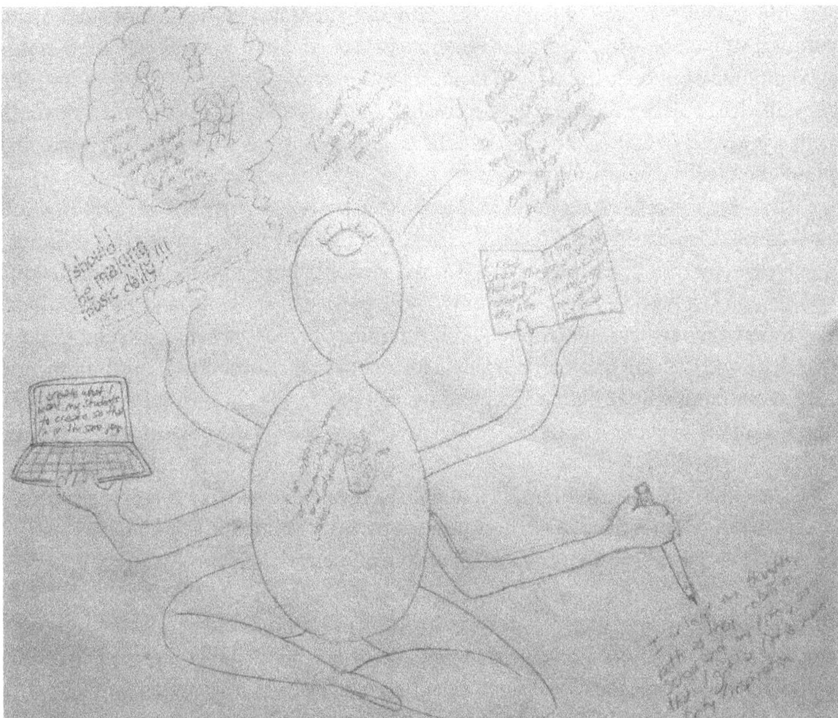

Figure 8.2 V's Body Practice Map (2014).

> When I came in security tried to make my students go through the scanner again. So I said, "But, they were just in the building. No. They're not going through it. They were with me the entire time, in my sight."

The students had already passed through the metal detectors when arriving for the start of the school day, but after this short outdoor excursion, security guards ordered them to pass through the scanners again. V explains,

> The kids started to line up because they're seeing a uniform, and they're used to that intimidation. I said to them [the students], "No, get out of line and get to the elevator," and my kids are looking like, "Should we?" So I told them to go and they did and they were kind of looking wide-eyed at security. And I said to the guard, "You can call whoever and tell them V from Newcomer High School did this. I'm not putting my kids through this."

This anecdote in the life of a New York City teacher evokes the landscape of stigma and surveillance that Black and Brown youth are daily called to confront. It also suggests the fraught context that shapes teachers' care, including the impact of school culture and community on their work. The presence of metal detectors and uniformed security guards are only one piece of a broader apparatus of neoliberal school and community policies (including zero tolerance, broken windows policing, high-stakes accountability policies, and post-9/11 immigration enforcement, criminalization, and surveillance) that brand students of color, low-income, LGBTQ, and immigrant youth with dangerous deficit frames. These policies and conditions shape the way particular populations of young people are seen by others, and the ways they see themselves.

These dynamics were at play in V's story when school security officers required this class of majority low-income, recently arrived immigrant youth of color to pass through metal detectors for a second time, when the students lined up out of "intimidation," and when V, a Black teacher, said "no." Her experience spoke to and through ideas about excessive policing practices in communities of color, social views, and policies that deny and devalue Black and Brown lives, xenophobic surveillance, and competing narratives about who these students and teacher are. In the context of these unspoken oppositions, V's act of resistance is also an act of care as explained by Ginwright (2010),

> Care within the black community is as much a political act as it is a personal gesture because it requires that the relationship prepare black youth to confront racism and view their personal trauma as a result of systemic social problems. (p. 84)

In this way, V's opposition locates the problem—the humiliation, dehumanization, and boredom of school surveillance—outside of her students' bodies and identities and onto the school's racialized security apparatus.

V's protest was an act of solidarity with her students. This caring gesture is louder, more indignant, and confrontational than the white middle-class teacher model—nor is it a likely scenario in a predominantly white middle-class school due to the racialized distribution of school metal detectors and presumptions of criminality (Kupchik & Ward 2011; Aaron & Ye 2015). It is life-lesson-level work of affirming her students' value, of advocating on their behalves, modeling nonviolent resistance tactics, and it links with V's academic pedagogy as a media educator. As she told me,

> You've got to stand up, and that's what I'm teaching my kids all day. Our documentaries [their class projects] are all about how we challenge power structures that we see as unfair. That's how they came up with the ideas [for their films on topics] like discrimination, scanners, etcetera, so you gotta, walk the walk.

This incident actualizes the creative and academic work she does with students to identify and critique unjust power structures through documentary film. V enacts this pedagogy with/in her body. And by putting her body, voice, emotion, and indignation in the way of racialized harm, she loops tight threads around these multifaceted forms of care and teaching, linking pedagogy with personal political action.

V went on to describe how the security guards called in their supervisors and forced the students to double back through the scanners again. With a heaviness in her voice, she reflected, "I think part of my frustration is … they [the security guards] were completely disregarding that I have a relationship with these students where I can say, I trust them, you know, and you [the security guards] should trust me." This interaction not only hurt her students, but it also renders invisible her relational work and discredits her central framing of teaching labor as relational, "in conversation," "passing [constantly] between" herself as educator and her class as learners.

Situated Somewhere

Esther Ohito reminds us that critical embodied pedagogy grows from the particular identities, social locations, and systems that operate on the assemblage of bodies in the room. Citing Moraga, she writes,

> Enacting a pedagogy of embodiment begins with conceptualizing the body as enfleshed—that is, by factoring the flesh as the location upon which a person's positionality meets her body's materiality, and a site whereby "the physical realities of our lives—our skin color, the land or concrete we grew up on, our sexual longings—all fuse" (Moraga in Moraga and Anzaldúa 1981, 19) into a racial body politic. (Ohito 2019, p. 14)

In the face of these violent systems, "the barbarism of whiteness [that] persists in ravaging the bodies of Black and othered persons" (Ohito 2019, p. 14), teachers must embrace the body as both a "source of wisdom" (Cariaga 2018) and a site for activism and healing. The play of body and (racial) body politic that Ohito references, draws out the inherent links between bodies that are "othered" and the social action of teacher/ activists. The embodied pedagogies of care that V and Sarah recount grow from this situated somewhere (Harraway 1988)—in the passing between their own bodies, students' bodies, and the invisible/ hyper-visible systems of oppression that structure urban schooling. Their drawings and narratives help us to image and imagine radical teaching practice as excessive, expansive, relational, and bodily.

9

Healing in Collaboration with School Counselors: Hip-Hop and Spoken Word Therapy

Ian P. Levy

Acclaimed rapper Dave East's (2019) song "*On My Way 2 School*" details a variety of emotional experiences Black and Latinx youth carry with them into the school building. Specifically, for the chorus of the song, East (2019) recites, "On my way to school / I seen everything on my way to school/ I seen people die on my way to school/ Just tryna stay alive on my way to school." As a result of structural inequities, rooted in institutionalized racism, Black and Latinx youth are subjected to higher stress than their white counterparts surrounding poverty (Knopp, 2012), racism and discrimination (Perreira, & Pedroza, 2019), as well as unaffordable housing and healthcare (Gallagher et al., 2018; Patel et al., 2019). Exposure to violence and loss, particularly through the unwarranted and unjust encounters with police officers (Smith-Lee & Robinson, 2019), further reflect systemic ills that negatively impact the daily lives of Black and Latinx youth. In 2020, research indicates Covid-19 may worsen mental health problems among youth as a result of social isolation, public health issues, and economic concerns (Golberstein et al., 2020). An understanding of these inequities and stressors should, at a minimum, lead to the establishment of robust mental health services to support the processing of emotional stress (Sanchez et al., 2013). In fact, leading organizations in the school counseling field have publicly called for an increase in culturally responsive counseling services (ASCA, 2019); however, Black and Latinx youth receive significantly less access to mental health services than white youth (Creedon & Lê Cook, 2016).

The stressors experienced by youth outside of school buildings are often compounded within schools themselves. Emdin (2016) tasks educators with pinpointing how oppressive structures in schools inflict harm on youth and strip them of opportunities to showcase their authentic voices. Emdin's position is validated by research suggesting Black and Latinx youth face more punitive discipline and zero-tolerance policies than their white counterparts (Gopalan & Nelson, 2019). Teacher referral biases contribute to disproportionate referrals for Black and Latinx youth (Villodas et al., 2019), which correlate prison sentences overtime (Bacher-Hicks et al., 2019). These exclusionary practices lead to disengagement, feeling unsupported, leading to the alienation of youth from the educational community (Parks et al., 2016).

However, in response to the lack of services to support or systems that actively curtail well-being, Black and Latinx youth have historically turned to hip-hop as an outlet for emotional expression, healing, and resilience (Chang, 2005). For example, the legendary hip-hop duo *Dead Prez* (2000) wrote a song called "They Schools," which critiques the very oppressive practices just alluded to. Lyric writing is one of many community-defined practices, available to individuals who identify with hip-hop culture, that functions as a mechanism for healing within a world that has failed to establish such outlets. For example, creating mixtapes (a collection of multiple songs) has functioned as a mechanism for marginalized youth to showcase who they are, where they are from, and push back against larger systems of colonialism that inflict harm and stunt growth and development (Ball, 2011). Understanding hip-hop's ingenuity, Washington (2018) urged counselors to use hip-hop music and lyrics in work with youth specifically to process the personal impact of oppressive systems. Hip-hop pedagogical practices discussed in the literature as social-justice work can be used to address power dynamics in classrooms, aid student engagement, and other educational outcomes (Adjapong, 2017; Kelly, 2013). An even smaller amount of literature has explored the role of hip-hop school counseling services (Gonzalez & Hayes, 2009). Very few studies have focused on the collaborative use of hip-hop practices by school counselors and teachers to aid students in processing emotional stress (Levy, Cook & Emdin, 2019; Levy & Adjapong, 2020). Therefore, in this chapter I offer theoretical and empirical support for school counseling interventions that can foster relationships, community and promote healing.

Healing within Schools

When considering emotional development, the therapeutic relationship is evidenced as the variable most predictive of student growth (Gelso, 2018). At the core of the counseling profession is the humanistic perspective, which promotes core conditions (empathic connection, unconditional positive regard, and congruence) that, if maintained, promote a strong relationship (Rogers, 1957). An explicit focus in relationship research has been placed on empathic understanding and connection to support the client's emotional disclosure (Gelso, 2018), indicating that counselors need hear and feel the emotions students are expressing. Unconditional regard is maintained when students are able to express their thoughts and feelings without receiving judgment. Lastly, students need to be able to bring their authentic selves to counseling sessions which cannot happen unless the helping professional is able to show up authentically (Rogers, 1957).

In an effort to support educators in maintaining humanistic conditions and understanding youth's authentic experiences inside and outside of school, I turn to Hannon and Vereen's (2016) research on *irreducibility* in culturally competent humanistic counseling. Irreducibility is explained as the ability of a helping professional to see Black men "in the context of their ecological world and experiences" (p. 242) and actively avoid adopting stereotypical perceptions that minimize the cultural, social, and political complexities of their lived experience. The humanistic concept of irreducibility emphasizes "holism and authentic relational encounters as the route to human connection and healing" (Hansen et al., 2014, p. 174). School counselors and teachers must engage in self-work that promotes acknowledging and shedding personal biases (Hook et al., 2016), to fully see youth in their complex contexts. Hannon and Vereen (2016) further explain how previously held negative stereotypes may "be representative of agency and meaning making, [and] seen as areas of strength to be nurtured within the counseling realm" (p. 242). Hip-hop sensibilities are a prime example of this phenomenon: the pain and resilience expressed through hip-hop are often muted by the reductionist view of hip-hop as only violent and misogynistic, preventing counselors from using hip-hop practices with youth toward healing (Levy, 2020). In this sense, educators must engage in the cultural humility work (ongoing self-critique, self-reflection, collaboration, and nonjudgmental listening; Hook et al., 2016) to be able to nonjudgmentally develop a full understanding of the intricacies of a student's emotional experience.

There is evidence that tensions rooted in implicit bias exist in relationships between Black and Latinx youth and educators. For example, Black and Latinx youth doubt the authenticity and relatability of counseling professionals, reporting feelings of skepticism, distrust, and being misunderstood (Lindsey et al., 2013). Recent national data suggest that teachers' perceptions of student future achievements vary by race and reek of bias, showing they believed 58 percent of white high school students would obtain a four-year college degree, compared to 37 percent of Black students. Additionally, white students were perceived to be twice as likely to graduate high school compared to Black youth (Gershenson & Papageorge, 2018). Further, discipline research found that Black teachers indicated more favorable expectations for Black students than white teachers, and the subjectivity of these evaluations could impact discipline practices (Gershenson, Holt, & Papageorge, 2016). This finding is backed by research from Lindsay and Hart (2017), which shows Black students received less exclusionary discipline from teachers of the same race. This data suggests that with knowledge and understanding of students' lived experiences comes empathy and irreducibility. When educators in schools and classrooms are unable to see youth in the context of their lived experiences, authentic relationships cannot be developed, youth cannot engage in the emotional disclosure necessary for healing, and youth will be subjected to educational practices that harm them. It is necessary, therefore, to instill educators with the counseling and pedagogical tools that support students' emotional processing.

Hip-Hop-Based Interventions for Healing

In the following section, I distill a series of practical hip-hop-based interventions that can be used by both counselors and teachers, to aid youth in processing difficult emotions. Hip-hop practices in schools have emerged as culturally responsive approaches, labeling youth culture as hip-hop culture (Emdin, 2016; Levy, 2019). Hip-hop was birthed by and for the Black and Latinx community (Chang, 2005) as a social justice movement responding to environmental stressors in the 1970s South Bronx (Rose, 1994). Community-defined spaces like block parties or street-corner hip-hop cyphers functioned as places where individuals congregated to express emotional experiences through rhyme (Levy et al., 2018) and promote the complexities of their identities and knowledges (Ball, 2011). Given the importance of school counselors honoring their students' cultural knowledge (Hannon & Vereen, 2016), Hip-hop and spoken word therapy (HHSWT) was developed as an approach to counseling and pedagogy that engages students in writing, recording, and performing emotionally themed hip-hop music (Levy, 2019).

As a youth-driven modality in individual counseling, group counseling, and classroom contexts, students discuss and digest difficult emotional experiences in dialogue for the sole purpose of then converting thoughts and feelings to song and/or music videos. HHSWT is inherently humanistic in that it promotes the belief that youth have, embedded within them, the answers to their own emotional struggles. It is therefore the practitioner's job to function as a mirror, allowing youth to unearth those answers through authentic self-reflection. This means that HHSWT practitioners actively listen for and ask follow-up questions about emotions that lie beneath the surface of students' lyrics. Through dialogue practitioners help students identify salient emotional themes they want to explore, to use hip-hop as a platform to explore areas tailored to their individual development. A seminal pilot study (Levy, 2019) deployed a HHSWT small-group counseling process where students produced hip-hop mixtapes about emotional challenges in their lives, finding improvements in students' stress coping skills. The use of HHSWT is positioned as an approach that enables students to present authentic accounts of their life experiences, receive validation from educators, and ultimately aids the development of the therapeutic relationship (Levy, 2020). The remaining sections of this paper illuminates how components of HHSWT (*Lyric Writing, Mixtapes,* and *Studio Construction)* offer school counselors and teachers interventions toward healing.

Lyric Writing

Lyric writing in HHSWT pulls from cognitive behavioral therapy (Beck, 1963) as well as Rogers's (1957) humanistic approach. In group or individual sessions, students engage in dialogue around an emotional theme and then convert their thoughts and feelings to rhyme. Students are also encouraged to select beats (Youtube is commonly used) that they feel sonically capture the emotions they are writing about. Outside of sessions, counselors offer youth a chance to continue processing a concern through cognitive journaling, where on a daily basis students make lyrical entries about a salient emotion they are working on. Students return to the subsequent session journal and explain the meaning of lyrics to their counselor who, through active listening, highlights discrepancies between entries, asks follow-up questions, and challenges students to create new verses that concretize what they throughout the week. Here, lyric writing functions as cognitive restructuring (Beck, 1963) where students learn to reframe thoughts to produce different feelings. Another cognitive tactic used is role-play as collaboration, where students work in small groups, pairs, or with counselors to co-construct songs that develop solutions to difficult situations. Lyric writing has been evidenced as a stress-coping skill that can deepen a student's emotional self-awareness and increase self-esteem (Levy, 2019).

In a classroom setting, Emdin et al. (2016) measured science content acquisition through rhymes about science topics. While the initial intention was to bolster content knowledge, findings suggested that students used the opportunity to construct emotionally laden lyrics in which they used science content knowledge to process stressful life events. For example, one student used the functionality of the digestive system as a metaphor for digesting the end of a romantic relationship. The Emdin et al. (2016) findings evince the healing power of lyric writing, even in the event that students are asked to write about academic content. Given the gaps in preparing teachers to sit in and navigate emotional dialogue, school counselors can push into classes to support lyric writing and group sharing. In classrooms, teachers can collaborate with school counselors to use lyric writing and explore emotional themes that naturally overlap with academic content.

Mixtapes

The Critical Cycle of Mixtape Creation (CCMC) is another distinct process using youth participatory action research (YPAR) to help teachers and counselors work with youth to select a research area of interest to them that will be explored through the researching, discussing, writing, and recording of a mixtape (Levy et al., 2018). Students select a general theme of particular importance to them, and a number of subtopics that fit within this theme. Over the course of a unit, or multiple group counseling sessions, students plan, market, and disseminate their research findings through an emotionally themed hip-hop mixtape that addresses a concern of importance to them. For example, students might construct a mixtape about stress that contains a number of relevant subtopics (e.g., feeling overworked, socially isolated, family tensions, etc.). Students would traverse the CCMC steps of identifying and researching mixtape content, discussing and digesting findings to develop a tracklist, planning the recording and release of the mixtape and then evaluating the impact of the release.

Levy and Travis (2020) found that use of the CCMC with adolescents led to significant decreases in stress, anxiety, and depression symptoms. Notable in the Levy and Travis (2020) study, the sample was split into three intervention groups, which each used the CCMC to create a distinct mixtape around different themes (immigration policy, life goals, and relationships). Regardless of the group, all youth experienced reductions in stress, anxiety, and depression, highlighting that the CCMC can address a variety of outcomes while benefiting well-being. Cook et al. (2020) found that mixtape-making as YPAR enabled students to explore solutions to school-based systems that create stress. Educators are encouraged to use the CCMC to engage youth in discussing, researching, and creating mixtapes about issues of importance to them and/or aligned with their course content.

Studios

Additional HHSWT research pertains to the physical creation of school studios as environments that support emotional disclosure. Studio construction emerged from a need to address the nonexistent guidance in constructing culturally appropriate school counseling environments (Benton & Overtreee, 2012). In schools, open, flexible, and calm environments promote engagement and the sharing of thoughts and feelings (Cook & Malloy, 2014). Levy and Adjapong (2020) assessed a process where students, a school counselor, and teacher collaborated on co-constructing a school studio as an environment for social and emotional development. During a high school elective course, students spent three months co-designing and constructing a studio where they would eventually engage in mixtape creation.

Levy and Adjapong (2020) suggested that students were given the autonomy to decide what equipment they would like to have within the studio, as well as the roles they would like to play in its physical creation. The teacher and counselor then crowdsourced funding to support the project. During class, students met to discuss the roles they wished to play (painting, furniture design, lighting, studio booth construction), and the educators collaborated on specific activities, like writing a poem about "what comfort feels like" to brainstorm design choices. Results from student focus groups indicated that students experienced "the studio as a shared space for inclusivity, comfort, and belonging; a place to make their own design choices; and a practice space to garner peer support, engage in personal self-development, and support others" (Levy & Adjapong, 2020, p. 266). Given that no prior studies existed exploring hip-hop studios as therapeutic environments, students maintained complete control over their role in the studio creation and alone created a space for their own healing. Overall, these results suggest that educators should partner with students on codesigning classroom and/or school counseling environments, trusting that students hold the knowledge to construct spaces where they feel comfortable exploring themselves.

Conclusion

The hip-hop interventions explored in this chapter can be used by both school counselors and teachers to support students in exploring emotions. The youth-driven and process-oriented nature of HHSWT can aid educators in deepening their understanding of youth's experiences, strengths, and knowledge, that otherwise might be minimized through the use of traditional approaches healing in schools. As it stands, healing, under the moniker of social and emotional learning (SEL), has emerged as a pedagogical approach for teachers to support students' emotional self-awareness (CASEL, 2016). While SEL can support student's emotional processing, teachers themselves are not trained with the skills needed to address students' mental health challenges in classrooms (Schonert-Reichl et al., 2017). Conversely, school counselors are trained in using active listening skills to facilitate emotional dialogues with students, but seldom learn pedagogical skills (Weger et al., 2010). School counselors are responsible for supporting students' academic, personal/social and career development through group, individual counseling, classroom lessons, and school-wide interventions (ASCA, 2019), making them ideal professional to deploy interventions that help students navigate stressors and promote well-being (Bowers et al., 2018). Collaborative efforts between school counselors and teacher hold the potential too, produce positive SEL outcomes for students (Cholewa et al., 2016). Therefore, this chapter's offering of hip-hop based interventions towards healing is significant, as HHSWT services encourage teacher and school counselor collaboration to maximize a school's ability to offer youth a culturally salient medium for emotional development and healing.

10

Sexual Healing: Confronting Disembodiment in Public Schooling

Carolyne Ali-Khan and John Wesley White

Let's Get Physical

When we think about teaching, why is it that such thoughts almost always ignore the body? What are the implications of the Cartesian mind–body split and what important ideas get ignored when we buy into that arbitrary dichotomy? Iconic educator and author bell hooks (1994) has cautioned educators to look for their bodies in classrooms, lest they disappear. She states, "No one talked about the body in relation to teaching. What did one do with the body in the classroom? Trying to remember the bodies of my professors, I find myself unable to recall them" (p. 91). This inability to recall is, she argues, not a memory lapse but a sign of structural erasure. She continues, "The public world of institutional learning was a site where the body had to be erased, go unnoticed" (p. 94). In 2021, the global Covid-19 pandemic chased our bodies into our homes, where they have been largely "erased" from public view. As we begin to contemplate emerging from our home-bunkers we find ourselves reflecting on the role of the body in education.

For many of us, 2020 was a year filled with pain and deep disappointment. American society was exposed as unwell in more ways that one and we collectively suffered in ways and to degrees that were unprecedented. The magnitude of both a global epidemic and the unashamed emergence of white supremacy juxtaposed against surreal (if not downright incompetent) governmental responses to suffering led many people into feelings of despair. It became easy to lose hope and to see healing as an impossibility. Critical educator Paulo Freire (1998) reminded us, however, that it is necessary to respond to pain with hope. According to him, we must first find and then deconstruct the sources of pain, particularly the pain that is hidden from view and normalized in everyday life: "the struggle for hope means the denunciation, in no uncertain terms, of all the abuses, schemes and omissions" (p. 106). Freire asks us to challenge these with a different reality, one that is rooted in hope. We heed Freire's advice to deconstruct the sources of our pain ("to read the world"), in this case looking specifically at the pain that hides in our bodies and the healing that can be possible when that pain is no longer ignored. We question how much pain is caused by an adherence to policies, practices, and mores that steer educators into treating themselves and their students via the Cartesian mind–body divide—to see themselves and their students as brains on stems. Ultimately, we posit that the denial of teachers' bodies is significant to education and comes at a great cost.

In what follows, we trace the ways that schools endorse and perpetuate practices of disembodiment while simultaneously policing teachers' and students' bodies. In order to examine the normalization of body-phobic messages that run rampant in teaching and teacher education, we also share our own experiences of denying the importance of our bodies as teachers. We note how school-based messages about physicality reflect the hegemonic (white, male, and upper-class) mores and ways of being. Additionally, we raise questions about the healing that might surface if educators were to demand that their bodies be taken seriously and as meaningful to the acts of teaching and learning. Inspired by current movements and bringing together insights from Black Lives Matter, #Metoo, and the body positive and sex positive movements, we ask: What are the possibilities that might emerge if schools were sites for reconnecting the body to the intellect and how might resistance to disembodiment help move us toward healing and wellness?

As teacher educators and former teachers, we are all too aware how often and without question teachers adhere to the notion that obedience and control are synonymous with professionalism. Recent events have further prompted us to question the myriad ways that this idea is enacted through our bodies. We have been struck, for instance, by how often teachers are mandated to use their positions to control the bodies of students and, in turn, how often their own bodies are controlled within schools. Drawing from our combined experiences, we recognize, critique, and provide alternative possibilities to these hegemonic practices. Our thinking is largely shaped by the work of Michel Foucault (2010) who exposed the ways that the human body can be disciplined, regulated, subjugated, and encouraged to strictly control self and others. It is also shaped by the work of educators who refuse to deny physicality (and sexuality) in educational space (e.g. Johnson, 2004; Kipnis, 2015) and who demand that we pay attention to bodies in schools (e.g. hooks, 1994; Darder, 2010). In what follows, we use our experiences as straight, abled bodies cis-gender educators to think about the discursive paths of bodily harm and healing in schools, highlighting how mixed messages about the body serve to alienate teachers and students from themselves and from each other.

The Professional Body?

Schools provide mixed messages about bodies; they focus on regulating the body while also promoting a narrative that our bodies do not matter (i.e., it is "who we are and not the bodies that we come in" that matters). For teachers, bodily erasure and regimented control are closely tied to ideas about professionalism, appropriateness, and morality. These ideas have been repeated so often and from so many places that they have been normalized, and for the most part, widely accepted. Teachers are encouraged if not required to fit into the machinery of schools.

Many educational historians have used the analogy of factories to describe schools (Bowles & Gintis, 1977; Liston, 1990). Frederick Taylor's approach to industry has taken root in our schools; vestiges of machine-like control, regulation, regimentation, and standardization are visible in practices such as bells and age grouping (assembly line), age and ability grouping (standardized inputs), national standards and scripted curricula (interchangeable parts), and a myopic focus on assessment (quality control). An associated focus on efficiency in schools has translated into disciplining the bodies of students and teachers. Schools control and value students in part by how well the latter demonstrate bodily regulation (that they speak, laugh, eat, defecate, and move at specific and teacher-sanctioned times). Bodily obedience is valued as "good behavior." Because teachers are, like so many of us, deeply ensconced in a hegemonic paradigm—one that is itself based in Freire's notion of the oppressors also being oppressed (Freire, 1970)—teachers enforce oppressive rules on students while they themselves adhere, often unquestioningly, to similarly oppressive expectations.

For teachers, *professionalism* equates to compliance with myriad layers of rules that control our bodies and deny our needs; these rules govern dress, use of language, body language, eating/drinking, proximity to others, and the ability to address basic human needs (i.e., using the bathroom). Modern schooling values a machine-like conformity into which the messy and organic body cannot easily fit. This situation is bound to become exponentially worse as pandemic-related educational practices further disembody teachers and students and reify an already problematic paradigm.

We believe that teachers' bodies are split into two categories: the sacred body that is pure and innocent and the profane body that is impure and unworthy of consideration. Within this are straight versus queer bodies (evidenced in common and tacit rules around which wedding or family photographs are on desks and whose marriage is "rubbing sexuality in our faces") and able machine-like bodies versus bodies that exhibit any physical needs. Narratives and practices of corporeal erasure and control operate for teachers (and in turn their students) in a paradigm of bodily shame.

Shame on You

Almost all schools have tacit, if not overt, rules for how teachers are expected to appear; the way that this is understood and enforced is instructive. Using the language of "professionalism," most schools expect teachers to look as if they belong in a *casual Friday* business environment. Accepted are khakis and button-downs, mainstream corporate logos and designer shoes (Freeburg, Workman, & Arnett, 2011) while the long list of unacceptable attire remains amorphous, its suitability for classrooms is judged against the norm of "I know it when I see it." Teacher dress codes for women also and often incessantly prohibit any non-matronly display of femininity. In this we see the old binary of Madonna/Whore in full bloom; teachers are expected to look pure and motherly and any suggestion of their own sexuality is both overtly and tacitly shamed.

The kinds of body regulation that are mandated in teacher dress codes are also rife with cultural and class biases. Piercings, for example, are expected to be limited to certain numbers and to the ears; visible tattoos are to remain covered; dreadlocks are frowned upon; bra straps are to be covered; t-shirts are forbidden; open toe shoes are not allowed; skirt and dress lengths are regulated; shorts are forbidden, and so on. This kind of control of appearance/dress also echoes the kinds of somatic control evident in militarism as the teacher "uniform" signifies broader institutional and corporeal compliance (which we touch upon later). We find it additionally troubling that the teaching body is fashioned as if the signifier of middle class (corporate) dress is intrinsic to being knowledgeable/credible. (We cannot help but note here how the idea that wealth = knowledge has been highly problematic in recent US politics.) The irony is also that this requirement of sameness sits in direct opposition to the American meritocratic myths that the way we look does not matter and the oft-touted notion that we are a country that values a culturally diverse "individuality." We believe it is important to point out the disconnect between telling students to "be themselves" and not fall prey to peer pressure while expecting both students and teachers to visibly conform to a hegemonic norm.

The regulations on teachers' bodies also include regulations of the sounds bodies make via language, discourse, and acceptable noises. Teachers' voices—in the sound that bodies make while speaking—are conscripted to a set of tacit rules that govern the volume, pitch, magnitude, as well as language and words. For example, "Standard" English—what Lisa Delpit (1995) refers to as the "codes of power" (p. 24)—is the de jure language for classrooms. Delpit notes that both actual words and syntax (e.g., African American Vernacular English [AAVE]–Black vernacular) are strictly policed. Despite decades' worth of research on code-switching and code-meshing in classrooms and a wealth of evidence that these approaches are "culturally sustaining" pedagogies (Paris, 2012), many if not most educators continue to demand of teachers and their students strict fidelity to standard English. The use of words considered obscene or profane, regardless of curricular and classroom contexts, are often for teachers heavily policed and punished. Meanwhile the tacit rules regulating the sounds that bodies make through control of speaking volume, the duration of laughter, patterns of interruption, eating/chewing noises, et cetera, are framed as issues of "respect." But here again these mechanisms of shaming and corporeal control have an obvious cultural and class bias generally, and furthermore model a form of cultural assimilation that seldom gets noticed or challenged.

This normalization of control is particularly evident when it comes to the topics to which teachers may or may not give voice. Official school curriculum is tightly controlled and regulated (Apple & Christian-Smith, 1991; White, 2012). Such regulation is arguably most salient in issues of sex and sexuality in schools. Teachers do students a disservice when they allow policymakers' and their own discomfort about sex to silence classroom conversations (White & Ali-Khan, 2020). Schools reinforce, via omission and censorious messages, the notion that we all live in cis-gender, straight bodies and that any topics pertaining to the body are not legitimate forms of knowledge. They reify specific cultural norms about what is and is not appropriate for our classrooms by celebrating some ideas and relegating others to the taboo. In keeping with this hidden curriculum of shame, teachers (and by default students) are taught to deny any voicing of the somatic experiences regardless of how much these impact their lives (Ali-Khan, forthcoming).

Practices of disembodiment for teachers extend into the ways that bodies are dismissed as having little influence on work opportunities, social mobility, and overall life trajectories. The deeply rooted, uniquely American, and ultimately hegemonic myth of meritocracy stresses that our minds are separate from and more important than our bodies. Schools focus almost solely on students' cognitive development (and give only tertiary attention to physical well-being through electives like health class and physical education). We posit that such practices serve to reduce a focus on the body and thereby to hide the fact that sexism, racism, ableism, homophobia, and transphobia are endemic in our society. Despite a ubiquitous focus on the body in media and pop culture, teachers are expected to behave as if we are a society that is blind to the bodies we are in. Any discussion otherwise was considered too political and both overtly and tacitly forbidden in schools. (It is our hope that the Black Lives Matter and Trans Lives Matter movements will encourage educators and educational policymakers toward a deeper understanding of the importance of the bodies to questions of equity.)

On top of this, many schools also enforce bodily parameters with strict rules around physical proximity and touch. Although there is a wealth of evidence that highlights the connectedness and comfort that comes with physical proximity and the power of the human touch (e.g., Sin & Koole, 2013), many schools have—due to salacious news stories, narratives of teachers as predators, and fears of litigation—implemented fear-based expectations regarding touch. It is common for schools to impose strict rules around physical contact with students (excepting handshakes, high-fives, or fist bumps). Secondary teachers are not to be trusted alone in classrooms or other school sites with students. Even elementary teachers who desire to respond to the clearly expressed needs of young children are increasingly reticent to physically touch their students for the purposes of comfort or celebration (Owen & Gillentine, 2011). The fear of teachers' bodies as enacted in touch-phobic policies and practices is counterproductive in that it silences any actual discussion of what real consent looks like (Ali-Khan, forthcoming).

One of the most common, and we believe most dehumanizing, of school rules is the regulation of basic human functions, for example the ability to use a bathroom. Ignoring individuals' specific needs and contexts, many if not most schools have specific and severely limiting rules for when students may and may not use the bathroom. Though these rules do not officially pertain to teachers, we posit that teachers' bodies are even more regulated than are those of their students. In contrast to virtually every other profession, finding ways to go to the bathroom can be excessively onerous for teachers. Teachers must try to carve out brief moments in which to use different facilities (often far from their classrooms). Further, despite the fact that teaching is primarily female, schools continue to shame and/or disregard the needs of the menstruating body (Johnson, Waldman, & Crawford, 2020). In addition, the needs of the pregnant and post-pregnant body (that may, for example, need to breastfeed or pump) is institutionally silenced. Kimberly Wallace Sanders (2003) powerfully describes how classroom interactions about teacher pregnancy moves teaching away from the pure male space of intellect and makes the body visible. Because teachers are expected to be available to students throughout classes, before and after school, during class changes, and often during lunch, they are consistently forced to ignore their own basic physical needs.

Teachers' sacrificing of their physical needs extends into the physical spaces in which they spend the entirety of their professional lives. Discussions about the habitability of school buildings—most often focused on the insufficiency of those structures—are almost always focused on their suitability for students (Kozol, 2012). While these discussions are important, the stakeholders most affected by a crumbling infrastructure are seldom considered. It is teachers who spend decades in buildings that are often crumbling and unsafe. In our own K–12 experiences we have worked in buildings that have had problems with mold, rats, dust (which contributes to problems with asthma), windows that were either nonexistent or nailed shut (leading to searing hot or numbingly cold temperatures), broken walls, leaking pipes, and cramped conditions. Poor ventilation, long a problem in schools, is only now being seriously addressed due to the pandemic (Mooney, Stein, & Steckelberg, 2020). In short, due to the nature of their jobs, teachers are virtually locked into buildings that may be causing significant harm to their physical well-being.

Resistance

The kinds of hegemonic notions encapsulated by the mind–body divide are, by definition, kept below the surface, difficult to challenge and even more difficult to overcome. Generations of students, parents, educational policymakers, and teachers have been enculturated to focus on the body on the one hand (e.g., in popular culture) and to deny the body on the other (e.g., in schools). In the former, the body is sacred; in the latter it is profane. This divide is both harmful and hypocritical. We believe that it is up to critically minded educators to begin to break down this unhealthy dichotomy—to chip away at the foundations of an inequitable and untenable system.

While we do not expect any one teacher or group of teachers to tear down the deeply ethnocentric, androcentric, and logocentric practices of educating the mind while ignoring the body, there are myriad ways that teachers can enact change in their classrooms and schools. Teachers can, individually and collectively, engage in overt and tacit resistance—to be what we have called "guerrilla warriors" in a struggle for more socially just schools. In what follows, we provide a list of steps teachers might take to recognize and celebrate the importance of the body. (It is important to note here that we have not included body-based recommendations that only pertain to students, e.g., free lunches and school-based health care.) We do not aim here to be comprehensive but to spark further discussion:

- Advocate to school policymakers, administrators, teachers, and parents the need for research-based, holistic sexual education that comes not via a standalone course at the middle or high school level but that is integrated throughout K–12 curricula. Teachers can further advocate for a pleasure-based approach that acknowledges that human sexuality is intrinsic to wellness (rather than a risk to be mitigated through a framework of harm reduction).

- Critique, challenge, and circumvent school dress codes for both students and teachers. Highlight for school administrators, parents, and students the social and cultural norms—and the inherent biases—implicit in the ways that "appropriate" school dress is authorized (and by whom).
- Make our own teaching bodies visible through classroom discussions about the tacit and normalized erasure that comes deeming menstruation, pregnancy, pain, and other forms of embodiment as "inappropriate."
- Acknowledge the importance of the body across curricular/content areas and recognize that these issues are culturally relevant and culturally sustaining pedagogies that engage students in learning.
- Insist that the concept of "taboo" has no place in education; that classrooms should be places wherein we name and address difficult issues rather than silence them.
- Create a dialogue about school rules governing the use of bathrooms and challenge those rules via individual classroom-based policies. Respect that bodies have physical needs that do not vanish in institutional spaces.
- Integrate ethnic studies, anti-racist, feminist, LGBTQ+, and disability education into school curricula wherever possible and therein challenge both the Cartesian separation of body from mind and the meritocratic myth of a body-blind society.
- Support and add to the effort to keep guns—inarguably the most dire threat to students' and teachers' bodies—out of schools. Be informed about the issues and use social media and connections with parents to forge a stronger anti-gun voice.
- Publicly question the connections between militarism and military recruitment in schools and other forms of violence (thereby refusing ideologies that support violence when it is governmentally sanctioned). Make connections to militarism on a global scale and militarism on our streets—how the goal of both is to harm the body.
- Openly discuss the idea of physical pleasure (in any and every form) as *intrinsic* to the purpose of education. Recognize that aim for education must be for the greater good, and this has to include an understanding that the bodies we all live in are significant to our lives.

In trying to bridge the artificial body–mind divide, we remind teachers that though this endeavor is overtly political, there can in reality be no separation of education from the political. As Paulo Freire noted, teaching is an inherently political act (1970). While teaching in ways that respect the body may be controversial for some, it is no more political (yet far more harmful) than refusing to do so. Hope and healing are intrinsic to our bodies; it is through embracing this fact that we can begin to undo some of the pain that we are collectively and individually experiencing. We believe that teachers are uniquely positioned—individually and collectively—to throw a wrench into the machine, to pause or at least slow it long enough to allow for a return to the organic, the corporeal, and the sensual. We look forward to the moment when teachers and students can take pride in knowing and celebrating where their bodies are in classrooms.

Part III

Arts and Creativity

11

Songs in the Key of Healing Hope: Listening as Soul Care

Robert Lake

Dear Teachers,

I am writing to you as our entire planet is in throes of a second wave of one of the worst pandemics in recorded history. As of this writing there have been over two million deaths across the globe and four hundred thousand of those have been in the United States (CDC, 2021). There are approximately 37.5 deaths per minute worldwide and about two deaths every minute in the United States. Now with the availability of various and sundry vaccines for Covid-19, we are all still keenly conscious of the many battle fronts that challenge our minds and souls as well as our bodies. As teachers, we are more aware than ever that we are being called upon to *be* the embodiment and presence of hope in a period of history that minute by minute is filled with sounds of weariness, sickness, and confusion. By now, I think we have learned so much more about the vital importance of cultivating the healthy habits of wearing masks, frequent handwashing, social distancing, and physical exercise. Of equal or perhaps even greater importance is the need to cultivate daily habits of soul care that enable us to live above and beyond the fray of pettiness, hatred, and despair more than ever. I am reminded of a bumper sticker I saw once on the car of someone who works in a dentist's office. It read "Your teeth: Ignore them and they will go away." Pain exists to help us locate what needs our immediate attention. The same is the case where the health of our inner being is concerned. Ignore the pain of mistreatment or pain in any form and the toxicity of despair eats away at your inner life, which in turn has an effect on every other part of your life.

As these days, weeks, and months have passed I have thought many times about what medium would be best for what I want to say. I chose to write in the "epistolary genre" (Freire, 1996; Nieto, 2015; Kress & Lake, 2012) because for me it is less constrictive and more personal in expressing matters of the heart. Those of you who are familiar with my approach to teaching know that I have asked students and colleagues to write in this fashion in class assignments or in several books I have edited or coedited on crucially important issues such as critical pedagogies of care, hope, and imagination. In this letter, I want to share with you some of the healing sounds that have sustained hope through times such as the one we find ourselves in at this moment. These songs or sounds have become part of who I am as a person just as much as any physical part of me. So today please bear with me as I take you on a personal journey of sounds that in pondering the memory of them nourishes and invigorates my inner being.

I need to stress emphatically before I begin that this is not intended to be a technique or a prescribed method of "wellness." These songs and sounds are so much more than nostalgia. They are part of my being and sense of place. My hope is that in sharing my journey that you will be reminded of the ways you have found to renew yourself wherever you are at this moment. I am strongly curious to hear what soul care sounds and looks like to you. So, for now, please walk with me for a little while. I will start by remembering a time when the gift of music strengthened my hope for healing when I was literally fighting to stay alive. Then we will stop to hear an extraordinary poet /activist Wendell Berry as he transcends "despair for the world" (Berry, 1999) by listening to "the peace of wild things" (p. 30). Along the way, we will hear, learn, and reflect upon all these sounds while we stop to savor the rustling leaves in a forest of quaking aspen trees. Finally, I will take you to one of my first classrooms to discuss a pedagogy of gratitude through the praxis of appreciation.

Where Dreams Are Born

Over thirty years ago, I was extremely sick with a dangerous case of pneumonia. The doctor that was assigned to me suspected it was Legionnaires' disease, but conditions were too critical and time was too short to wait on the results of a test for this rare condition. He administered a regimen of antibiotics intravenously and put me on oxygen and a feeding tube. I was hospitalized for ten days and could barely speak or focus my thoughts. Family and friends would come in and help care for me. One friend who was also a nurse practitioner brought in a cassette player and a tape of instrumental acoustic piano music titled *Songs Unspoken* by Douglas Trowbridge (1985). The last track on the first side is titled "Where Dreams Are Born." This hauntingly beautiful melody still strongly resonates within me all these years later. During this past year of sheltering in place, I was thrilled to find the original studio recording of it available on streaming sources. The four words in the title literally describe the healing process that was going on inside me in and through my vivid dreams. Actually, I cannot remember if I was dreaming while awake or asleep. More than likely it was somewhere in between those two states. In these dreams, I was back home playing with my children around a set of swings in our backyard. A dramatic turn toward full recovery began as I was able to envision a future with my family. I am forever grateful for every act of care, every thought and prayer that brought me to conscious awareness of an urge to live and be with my family once more.

During these long and weary months of sheltering in place, I have thought much about why certain expressions of sound nourish our soul and create and sustain empathy. Why is it for example with certain songs that we can literally understand and feel every single note in multiple dimensions as if the person playing it knew what you were going through from the inside out? As I listened to *Where Dreams Are Born* recently, I was conscious of that deep resonance that was so much more than the actual melody and rhythm itself. I could hear oneness of spirit and soul, emotions and the touch of finesse of human hands on a piano that had to come out of the pianist's innermost being because it was bringing life to my own depths. I was curious to learn if there was a story behind the song itself and began an internet search to see if there was anything I could learn about the pianist and composer of this remarkable song as well as the *Songs Unspoken* album. I found a way to contact the artist on his website and was absolutely amazed to learn the story from the artist himself in reply to my question. By the way, his full name is Richard Douglas Trowbridge Souther. He used his two middle names when recording this album. I was thrilled that he responded to my email the same day. He stated that while he was working as a sound engineer in a recording studio, he contracted botulism from a tuna salad sandwich. This bacterial disease attacked his nervous system and he lost his short-term memory and motor skills, which made it impossible to play the piano. He even had to relearn how to tie his shoes and how to speak again. His doctors said it was miraculous that he survived. After a few years in recovery, he received a call from a friend asking if he would consider recording an album of mostly improvisational solo piano music. He describes the session:

> We had three days to complete it, almost no budget and the sessions would all be early morning. I had just broken a digit on my left-hand ring finger but felt it was a wonderful opportunity and said, "Yes, let's try and see what happens." I asked the producer and engineer to just record everything because I wouldn't remember what I did from one take to the next. I'd made myself a few chord charts but that was it. The Lord would have to make it happen if it was going to happen at all. My long term memory stayed intact and was where I'd go to draw on the feelings connected to each song on the album. Early on in the recording process "*Where Dreams Are Born*" happened.
>
> (Souther, June 9, 2020, personal communication)

There are many things that could be addressed at this point. But what Richard stated about drawing on the feelings connected to each song describes his *soul* in motion or action. You cannot give what you have not become yourself. His song had the power to touch my depths, because he was playing from his depths. I was particularly struck with the fact that Richard drew strength and inspiration from a place much deeper than the conscious level of notes, chords, and time signatures. As I searched for the song, I found a few cover versions and while the notes were beautiful, they could not convey the same message because the song Richard played was one he had become. He played from a place *Where dreams are born* and that is why and where his song was able reach me.

This in and of itself is certainly not a new phenomenon. Music as healing has been practiced by Indigenous tribes across the earth since the dawn of human communication. There are countless cases of the power of music in restoring and creating neural pathways that enable mind/body connections and coordination through the multidimensional dynamic of rhythm, language, and emotion. (For much more on this, see Mannes, 2013; Levitin; 2019, Sacks, 2008.)

Listening to Wild Things

When the pandemic first began to force school closings and my classes moved completely online, I posted a poem by Wendell Berry (1999) on the front page of our class website because of the sheer beauty of the language. The students loved it and several of them asked if they could use it in their assignments in one fashion or another. Here is the poem[1]:

> When despair for the world grows in me
> and I wake in the night at the least sound
> in fear of what my life and my children's lives may be,
> I go and lie down where the wood drake
> rests in his beauty on the water, and the great heron feeds.
> I come into the peace of wild things
> who do not tax their lives with forethought of grief.
> I come into the presence of still water.
> And I feel above me the day-blind stars waiting with their light.
> For a time I rest in the grace of the world and am free. (p. 30)

I have always found bird songs to be a source of great comfort. This is especially the case during this pandemic. The songs of birds have been a source of hope and great comfort to many during this pandemic. In fact, the National Audubon Society's bird identification site reports that it has "doubled over that period last year," and unique visits to its website are up by half a million. The prestigious Cornell Lab of Ornithology has seen downloads of its free bird identification app, Merlin ID, shoot up 102 percent over the same time last year, with 8,500 downloads on Easter weekend alone (Flaccus, 2020, n.p.). People across the globe are spending more time listening and drawing strength from these messengers "who do not tax their lives with the forethought of grief" and remind us with every call that there was life before and there is life beyond this nightmarish present moment.

I am reminded of an afternoon last winter, a few weeks before the pandemic forced the closure of our university. I was riding a bike on a nature trail near campus and I heard that song that took me right back to my days in the upper Midwest. It was the call of a red-winged blackbird. The sound drew me to stop; I looked around and there he was, perched on a cattail singing and chattering away. This bird shows up even before the robin in the spring with a message that signals that the end of winter is here, believe it or not. His song rings out clearly by announcing that as long as the earth revolves around the sun, there is life beyond now. That is what I heard in this soul nurturing song as it renewed my interior language that is our "house of being" (Heidegger, 1977, p. 213). I heard the singing of a red-winged blackbird with the inner ears of the soul and was revived.

Quaking Aspen's Song

The largest and one of the oldest living organisms on earth consists of a single organism forest of Quaking Aspens named the Pando forest in Utah. Pando is a Latin verb meaning

"I spread." Indigenous tribes used this tree for medicine. Here is a description from the United States Department of Agriculture (USDA) website for this National Park.

> Pando is an aspen clone that originated from *a single seed* and spreads by sending up new shoots from the expanding root system. Pando is believed to be the largest, most dense organism ever found at nearly 13 million pounds. The clone spreads over 106 acres, consisting of over 40,000 individual trees. The exact age of the clone and its root system is difficult to calculate, but it is estimated to have started at the end of the last ice age. Some of the trees are over 130 years old. It was first recognized by researchers in the 1970s and more recently proven by geneticists. Its massive size, weight, and prehistoric age have caused worldwide fame.

(USDA, 2020, n.p.)What fascinates me about this tree is the sound of the leaves as they tremble in the wind. Listen to the "song" of these leaves rustling for a minute or so on any streaming service of your choice. This sound is not one I can hear live and in person today, but it is still a part of who I am. When I was growing up, there was one of these trees in our next-door neighbor's yard. I could see it from my bedroom window on the side of the house right next door and probably no more than 150 feet away. The sound of the leaves trembling with the slightest breeze was a constant present experience until we moved to another house. I am now reminded that nature is always in motion, never static and yet this tree has so much more going on underground in the unpredictable spread of rhizomes.

Right now, the quaking aspen song is vitally important metaphoric reality in a world where Western dualism is so deeply entrenched in the "either/or" approach to everything. In their groundbreaking work on continental philosophy *A Thousand Plateaus: Capitalism and Schizophrenia*, Deleuze and Guattarri (1980/2017) discuss in depth (and I greatly paraphrase and summarize here) that rhizomatic growth is not hierarchical. You cannot predict or trace out its growth in a static pattern. There is not the typical thesis, antithesis and synthesis swinging of the pendulum level of logic or even a single "third space" approach to drawing rational conclusions. When I hear the sound of the quaking aspen leaves, I am reminded of the dynamic flourishing of rhizomatic growth as a metaphor of imagination that refuses the traps of word games and grows right under territorial walls and zero sum, politicized thinking as in "if you are not a ______ then you must be a ________ or else you are a _____" As teacher/researchers we can lead in thought and word as we listen and think rhizomatically, by refusing rootbound hierarchies of knowledge that often territorialize, essentialize, and standardize. The rhizome metaphor brings with it an understanding that is not stuck in the either/or of binary dualism or "moving up" the ladder of more power. "Do not try to fence me in," she sings. "I can grow under fences and make connections to any other part of the rhizome." Keep singing your song Quaking Aspen. In the sound of your leaves joining the sunlight and wind, we remember that breakthroughs in imagination and becoming take place in the unpredictable and wild ways that defy and transform the present deadly threat to life through what the natural philosopher/artist/scientist Bob Miller described as "hardening of the categories" (Miller in Cole, 2003, p. 180).

Praxis of Gratitude

Our last stop in this journey is a revisit to one of my first experiences of teaching a few years after my recovery and release from the hospital. My wife and her family had been involved with helping refugees from Southeast Asia learn English, find housing and employment after the end of the war in Southeast Asia and a wave of refugees arrived. I was inspired through their example to be volunteer teaching assistant. I was welcomed with open arms into a high school with my guitar to teach English through song. One of the first songs I used in my weekly visits to an ESL classroom was a children's song by Raffi (1980) titled "Thanks a Lot." It fit what I was doing perfectly as a beginning level low risk way of learning and practicing pronunciation because it is loaded with vocabulary such as "thanks for the sun in the sky, thanks for the clouds so high, thanks for the animals, thanks for the land, thanks for the people everywhere, thanks a lot, thanks for all I've got." At the end of the year, we had a recital and my students did a wonderful job of singing that song and several others so enthusiastically. At the end of the concert, I was presented with a t-shirt that said "Thanks a lot" on the front in big letters and all their names written with fabric paint covering the rest. The other teachers encouraged me to "get your Masters in teaching ESL and join us." It took a while, but I eventually did. This story provides the context for an ongoing application to all I have mentioned in this letter because it has helped keep my inner being in tune with songs and sounds in the key of healing hope. It is simply this: the more you express gratitude and appreciation for life, the more your capacity to experience and appreciate life increases too. It starts right where you are today. For example, on a particularly stressful day last week I expressed my appreciation and gratitude for our garbage service as I wheeled the garbage can out to the road. That led me think of so many other taken for granted things over the next week, including the new roof on our house, my new shoe strings and the ability to keep them tied tight. I am grateful that the act of thinking and writing this letter has in itself been a form of personal soul care. I am grateful that the words "thank" and "think" are from the same root words (Online Etymology Dictionary, 2020, n.p.). When I am appreciatively grateful, I am doing my clearest thinking too and vice versa.

Grateful to be here,
Dr. Robert Lake

12

Creating the Play Space: Human Encounters Explored through Theater Processes

Isabelle Gatt

Imagine entering a dark room dimly lit with candles set on the floor in a semicircle and, in the middle, a tall slender young man with slightly disheveled light brown hair, sitting on a stool playing the saddest of melodies on a vintage sunburst color acoustic guitar. The audience is silent and fully immersed in the atmosphere created by his music. He is looking at his fingers on the neck of the guitar as he makes it weep. The young man closes his eyes for a long moment as his fingers navigate through a complex improvisation, which brings the melody to an end. Silence. His eyes are still closed, and he suddenly looks up directly at the audience sitting on cushions on the floor close to him just beyond the semicircle of candles. It feels like he is looking directly at each and every one of us in the audience. Then in a deep, gentle voice, he takes his time to disclose his intimate story:

> *I have had three women in my life who have loved me and whom I have loved insanely. My mother, oh my dear mamma, she thought the world of me, she loved me from the second I was conceived and through my life till her end … an end I feel responsible for. She suffered so much as she watched me getting deeper and deeper in a spiral of addiction. She gave me everything and, in return, I gave her false hopes over and over again. I am so sorry and now I miss her so. You only have one mother, only one love as pure as that.*

Pause, eyes glistening as the young man still looks straight into the eyes of the audience. Deep breath.

> *And then Angela, my first love, we were only thirteen when we met. It was love at first sight. She was slim with long blond silky hair with a middle parting. Then she had the deepest blue for irises, oh yes how I would get lost in those eyes. We were so happy together, life was simple, and we felt so free. We grew up together so I could read her thoughts before she could speak, and she would look into my eyes and understand me without the need for words. It was all so pure and beautiful … sheer magic every time we met … until I got lost in the chaos of my habit. Then I would not look into*

> *her eyes for fear that she would know. She did get to know; once I looked into her eyes and I could see the pain she tried to hide. I made her suffer so, I made her cry, and you know what? I could not, would not, feel anything. She tried everything to make me stop, I was slowly destroying her, and then I pushed her away and she finally left.*

Pause.

> *My third woman*

Pause. His voice quivers with emotion.

> *Oh, she was so beautiful. I don't have the words to describe her. I fell under her spell. Every night she would hold my head on her lap and caress my hair as I looked into her unfathomable and wildly luminous black eyes until I would fall into the sweetest and most colorful of dreams. I do so long for her.*

Sad look on his face and he lowers his head to look at the neck of the guitar and make it weep again, softer and softer till he stops. All is still except for the flickering of candles.

For some time, there is absolute silence in the audience as what he was talking about sinks in. The disturbing realization that an intelligent man, let's call him Paolo, in the final months of his rehab, a man who had put in such hard work to get his addiction under control, still spoke with fascination about drugs, the fact that he still had a dangerous vulnerability at this point, sent shivers down my spine.

The memory of that evening in 1992 is still distinctly vivid in my mind. This was my first experience working with theater in a residential drug addiction treatment center. The experience opened up new understandings, fresh perspectives, and made me realize the potential of using theater and the arts as triggers and mediums for self-expression, discovery, and growth. I had been invited to participate in this seminar led by Giorgio Testa in this rehab center in Naples by Loredana Perissinotto. Giorgio, a practicing psychologist and theater practitioner was a collaborator of Loredana, a lecturer who had been one of my most insightful Theatre Studies lecturers at University. To this day, I consider her one of my gurus. She had extended the invitation to me and she was also at the seminar. The participants, thirteen in all, included two men in their final stage of rehab and various professional theater practitioners and drama educators.

For one whole week, we lived together and worked intensely on Sophocles' Philoctetes using a workbook designed by Giorgio. The workbook "activities" included coloring in pictures, reading excerpts of Philoctetes, and storytelling by Giorgio and participants that provided the links to the excerpts. The booklet included short writing tasks—answering questions in role, or a character's thoughts, stimuli for discussion, and creating our own individual presentations leading up to a collective creation based on triggers from the tragedy. The seminar used process drama techniques to help the participants inhabit the Greek tragedy; they were techniques familiar to me as I used them in schools during drama lessons, as a drama teacher at the time, and for theater in education (TIE). I was familiar with these strategies (hot seating, thought tracking, freeze frames, teaceher in role, etc.), and I knew how effective they were, but this text, the context, and the adult audience made this experience and the reflections different and all the more profound. For one thing, I had never really worked with anyone who had been substance dependent. I could, however, see how an experience such as this seminar was valid for the addict, but more so for the audience/other participants.

Paolo's autoethnographic performance humanized the drug addict, helping the audience understand the meaning, the pain, the confusion, and the struggles of his addiction, as well as his trajectory through his rehabilitation. Autoethnographic performance has a powerful effect, in that, the experiences shared are a method of inquiry into the perfomer's life, a space to engage with issues of reflexivity, identity, embodiment, transformation, and empowerment (Barbour, 2012). I distinctly recall the breathless silence at the end of the performance, as what Paolo had just shared sank in. My heart went out to Paolo who had the courage to tell his story so beautifully. Paolo liked to play music and write poetry, but he was not a trained actor. Yet, his performance was as good as that of a professional as he used vocal timbre, pauses, pacing, emotion, facial expression, eye contact, and silence to full effect. This was his own intimate story; it flowed aesthetically, physically, and verbally. This was more than the telling of his story but included critical self-reflexive discourse in performance. My reflections, as I processed what I had just witnessed that evening, were also about how the Greek tragedy and the process drama techniques had affected the group even by the third day and how fast the process managed to bond the group for such disclosure to take place.

When I had arrived, I was warmly welcomed in the group, the participants were all Italian, and save for Prof. Perissinotto, they were all strangers to me. Yet, I felt like I had known them for a long time by the end of that first day. Though our trajectories in life were different, I remember this strong feeling of bonding by the end of that day. In my notes for the first day, I had noted how Giorgio managed to create a safe, supportive atmosphere through the way the day had been structured, with the work done with sensitive pacing and guidance. Each one of us was given time to express and reveal ourselves and a chance to highlight our similarities and celebrate our differences. Through his manner, leadership skills, and careful planning, Giorgio had managed to create a play space, using theater and the arts as triggers and mediums for self-expression, discovery and growth. That space in the rehab center had been turned into a site of possibility for the seminar participants to make it what they wanted it to be; the participants felt safe to play, explore, and risk using Sophocles's Philoctetes as a pre-text and a pretext for rhizomatic exploration to help a group of individuals work out life's challenges. The process worked on physical, psychological, and emotional levels. Philoctetes acted as a point of access to exploring, discovering, and creating both on a personal level as well as that of the communal group.

The process encouraged individuals to be open to multiple ideas and opinions and to finding ways to communicate, collaborate, share, and cocreate communication performance praxis, which in turn was open to discussion, reflection, deconstruction, and reconstructions. By the third day, Paolo performed this autoethnographic performance, sharing with us his "social transgression." Linda Park-Fuller (2000, p. 26) argues that the very telling of one's story, the disclosure of what so far has been untold, kept secret, well hidden or silenced, mainly because such discourse struggles with societal preconceptions borne of the dominant politics, the very telling of it, becomes a transgressive act.

As a resident at the rehab, Paolo would have had group therapy sessions with the others at the residency where he would have shared his personal story. This was with others who had similarly struggled with addiction. Group therapy is a process that helps develop a sense of fellowship, sincere compassion, and ultimately makes for emotional healing. But, in this case, the dynamic was different; Paolo was opening up to a group of individuals who did not share his drug addiction experience, and therefore, even though the group had gone through various trust-building exercises and a comfortable play space had been established, the risk he was taking was even more daring when he shared his transgression. The fact that he explored his personal journey, his pain and struggle, first through the readings and discussions of Philoctetes and later narrated this through this solo performance, in which he acknowledged his remorse, took courage. It takes courage to recognize your errors, courage that is often unacknowledged in a world that is essentially content to persist in denial.

I remember talking to Paolo on the final day of the seminar week, and he expressed his happiness at a newfound self-confidence, a sense of self worth and that he had discovered, that besides his music and poetry, even theater helps him experience intense sensations besides a warm feeling of community. In my notes, I had noted down, in the final pow-wow he had said:

"*… nuova esperienza che mi ha dato sensazioni intensi… ho sentito che potevo rischiare perche mi sono sentito protetto da un senso di gruppo che me ha dato il tempo per scoprirmi…. facendo delle cose nuove…. … il lavoro mi ha dato una carica. Sembra che il tempo questa settimana si è dilatato e vi conosco tutti da una vita. Grazie*"

"*… a new experience that has given me intense sensations … I felt that it was safe to risk because I felt protected by a sense of group that gave me the time to discover myself … doing new things… the work has energized me. It seems like time was dilated this week and that I have known you all a lifetime. Thank you.*"

Exploring Greek Tragedy: A Play Space for Unspeakable Vulnerability

This was the first of two seminars using Greek tragedy which I had participated in with Giorgio. Since then, he has devised some ten different booklets and delivered thirty seminars. The workbook texts are for Greek tragedies mostly, though he has also used Shakespeare's tragedies and more modern works like Chekov and Pinter, for example. I discussed the process of planning the trajectory of such work with Giorgio asking him to explain his objectives for such work. Giorgio is a practicing psychologist, but he is also a theater practitioner, and he made it clear that these theater projects were separate from his work as a psychologist. He delivered these out of his love for theater and his belief that reading tragedies, beautiful works within a group, and delving deep through dramatic and other artistic strategies is good for adolescents' well-being with possibilities of moving beyond the personal aesthetic experience, expanding boundaries into the community.

His aim was to work with adoloescents and young people on such tragedies that focused on the figure of the adolescent. The methodology consisted of working on the text that was interspersed with different exercises using drama processes or other art strategies. He said that in hindsight there are three clear objectives. The first objective is for a group of people to experience Greek tragedy and to delve deep into it through the reading and exercises. So, the main objective was theater pedagogy, that is to understand the particular dramaturgy in Greek theater. Secondly, to sensitize the participants to the didactics of reading theater, what happens when we read, specifically when we read Greek tragedy aloud? So the objective there is of a didactic nature—interpreting a theatrical text, a Greek tragedy, exploring it collectively, and working together on the text, which can act as a catalyst expanding on each individual's boundaries. The third is to explore the character, discussing the tragic characters to understand them, possibly finding aspects that resonate with you.

A Collective Exploration of Greek Tragedy: The Risk of Growing

The aspect of collective reading, where all participants are on the same level, all making a contribution is, in itself, an educational experience. This is an intensive reading of a tragedy, made more meaningful through the workbook texts and the artistic activities done with a group of people, who come to live together for one whole week, sharing this experience. Giorgio says the therapeutic aspect comes about essentially because of the meeting of a group of people who experience the beauty and the artistic power of Greek tragedy when delving profoundly into it.

Giorgio speaks about the preparation stage for such a workbook, which he plans in detail with much thought and reflection. Each exercise is intended to help understand important aspects in the tragedy, for example the drawings, some individual and some collective, sometimes in silence and at times in discussion, helped understand certain aspects such as how an adolescent deals with pain, with risk-taking, which is what ultimately helps him/her grow.

The focus of the tragedy workbooks is always on the adolescent. In fact, for the title of each project, Giorgio never uses the actual title of the tragedy; the protagonist becomes the adolescent. So in tackling Sophocles's Philoctetes, the main focus is on Neoptolemus not Philoctetes. The seminar was titled "Neoptolemus—between Bow and Wound: The Risk of Growing, the Risk of Reading." This adoloescent, Neoptolemus, is caught between the pull of Odysseus and Philocteties as Odysseus tries to manipulate him into deceiving poor Philocteties. This is a serious moral dilemma he is faced with, having to choose whether to obey Odysseus and, in doing so, decieve Philoctetes by stealing the fabled bow and poison-tipped arrows given to him by Heracles, or to do what was right by the tormented Philoctetes, a soldier who had already been betrayed by his comrades and generals.

Philoctetes had been left to die on the deserted island of Lemnos while on their sea voyage to make war on Troy. Here was a vetaran who had been disabled while going to war when he was bitten by a snake. His comrades were repulsed by the stench of his infected snakebite wound and his continuous howls of agony. Consequently, he was left to fend for himself on a deserted island. At first, the young Neoptolemus goes along with Odysseus's orders and takes the weapons from the wounded veteran by tricking him into thinking he was on his side, but he struggles with his sense of honor and friendship with Philoctetes as he weighs the betrayal of a friend against the greater good of the country. He feels remorse at having "*used disgraceful lies and sly deceit to catch a man*" (Sophocles, ca. 409 B.C.E./2017, l. 1582–3) and would have much preferred "*to fail in something honorable, than to win out with treachery*" (ibid., l. 114). Neoptolemus reflects at length and argues with both Odysseus and with Philoctetes and finally takes the courageous decision to do what is morally right as opposed to acting in a politically ambitious way. He decides not to lie again to Philoctetes and to give him back the bow knowing full well the risks he was taking in doing so but believing this was the moral thing to do.

Another good reason for choosing this particular play for the seminar was the theme of suffering, the theme of illness and pain. Philoctetes, is after all, about a hero in pain and others' responses to it. Such a theme makes the audience/listeners aware of the vulnerability they share with Philoctetes. The Chorus's complex description of the sounds that Philoctetes makes in his suffering immediately immerses us into living a life with pain and in solitude (Allen-Hornblower, 2013). Philoctetes is about the protagonist's wounds, agonizing wounds, wounds to which witnesses respond differently, the wounds that isolate you. It is about the rancor that isolates you and entrenches you further in a fixed place. Philoctetes left alone with his pain, was stuck in a fixed place, anchored to his pain, his drama. One of the tasks, which Giorgio had set the group, was to physically express Philoctetes' pain as a group. This was a physical group exercise—no talking allowed, done in total silence, the pain expressed was individual but the collage of the collective had a profoundly powerful effect. I remember it to this very day, one could only hear each other's breath and feel the pain.

It was the following morning, during a discussion giving feedback as to how participants were feeling that Paolo expressed the desire to perform a solo that evening. By day three, Paolo felt welcome and safe enough in the group to express his pain. He felt that the group would receive his story just like we had received Philoctetes'. He offered to do this out of his own free will; he had a story he had to tell.

The power of reading tragedy collectively, with its raw and powerful emotions, has been explored by other theater practitioners working with diverse at-risk communities. There is a timelessness and depth in these ancient tragedies that touches people profoundly and my research has revealed various treatment programs that focus on classic to modern tragedies.

Theater-Based Healing Programs Using Tragedy to Explore Personal Trauma

Stephan Wolfert (Wiggins, 2019) developed a theater-based treatment program for military veterans he aptly named DE-CRUIT, as the veterans are recruited but never DE-cruited, as in, unwired from war and properly reintegrated in society. Wolfert was himself an army veteran who had left the army due to severe traumatic stress disorder and he came to theater when he came across a performance of Richard III and recognized the humanity and vulnerability that he shared with the protagonist, Richard III, who, like him, was a veteran having serious challenges adapting back to living in society (Pennacchia, 2019). Through this realization, he developed the DE-CRUIT program where veterans work with Shakespearean tragedies to construct their own personal trauma as a performance (Ali & Wolfert, 2016). When working with Shakespeare's verse, they can easily relate to what is said in the soliloquies, in some instances these describe their own trauma, their pain, their suicidal thoughts; the verse provides them with the aesthetic distance from their trauma to be able to express it to a room full of strangers, the audience who can relate and empathize with their vulnerability (Pennacchia, 2019).

What is particular about the DE-CRUIT outreach theater programs is that it is a veteran led model, with veterans supporting each other in healing and recovery from social, physical, and mental health problems. One way of doing this is by working on their self-confidence through theater. The training on breathing, voice, posture, embodiment, and rehearsing scripted verse and the routinized techniques of physical and mental grounding in preparing for recitation with DE-CRUIT has the added benefit of nurturing the self-assurance to look and speak confidently at a job interview (Ali et al., 2019). Considering veterans have serious challenges in job-seeking, this is of utmost importance.

A study of the DE-CRUIT program reveals how the imagination opens up emotional and psychological space for the exploration of trauma through the human capacity for storytelling and meaning-making, which promotes recovery (Ali, 2019). *Mimesis*, which Alisha Ali (2019) defines as a form of simulated story in theater in which we can imagine ourselves, activates our imagination when we witness theater in such a way that it allows us to imagine possibilities for our future selves thus rendering the experience therapeutic.

Bryan Doerries, a theater director, has been working on a public health project that involves the readings of Sophocles's war plays by professional actors, including Adam Driver, Frances McDormand, and David Strathairn, to soldiers, addicts, extreme storm survivors, and other vulnerable minorities in society. In his project called Theater of War, he presents readings of Greek tragedies, compelling stories of human suffering, such as Sophocles's Ajax and Philoctetes to military, prison, addiction, palliative care, and civilian communities across the United States and Europe. Most of the people who attend suffer from depression, posttraumatic stress disorder, and suicidal thoughts due to their war or other induced injuries. By bringing these timeless plays to military audiences and their families, Doerries attempts to create dialogue and community while destigmatizing the psychological injuries of war, of illness, of life. After the reading, the audience members disclose their trauma and their challenges in readjusting to civilian life away from war. I have watched some of the work online, and the stories people in the audience share after listening to the readings are indeed of mythical proportions. Doerries contends that

> tragedies are designed … to validate our moral distress at living in a universe in which many of our actions and choices are influenced by external powers far beyond our comprehension—such as luck, fate, chance, governments, families,

> politics, and genetics. In this universe, we are dimly aware, at best, of the sum total of our habits and mistakes, until we have unwittingly destroyed those we love or brought about our own destruction.
>
> (Doerries, 2016, p. 13)

This resonates perfectly with the content of Paolo's story, it is as if he felt that the tragedy we were exploring gave him the permission to take a risk and share his story of destruction. Brené Brown (2012) writes that vulnerability is both at the core of difficult emotions like fear, grief, and disillusionment, as well as the birthplace of love, joy, empathy, and creativity. In recognizing our vulnerability and daring to be vulnerable, we become open to experiences that bring purpose and meaning to our lives (ibid.).

A 2020 Interview with Giorgio Testa

I interviewed Giorgio Testa in February 2020 about his work on Greek tragedy, which he has been doing for the past thirty years, and he was adamant that his main objective was not to do therapy but to offer meaningful theatrical experiences. He goes on to say:

Credo che tutti hanno bisogno di essere curati ... per ogn'uno di noi, l'occazione di incontrare la tragedia è, comunque, un momento di crescita. Non era la psicologia che mi rivoltava a questo ma il mio amore per i greci. La mia pista era la pista antica, non era la pista moderna di terapia, ma terapeutica nel senso profondo, no? Aristotile diceva che la tragedia faceva bene per quelli che la fanno, quelli che la vedono, ... quando Aristotile diceva che la tragedia induceva la catarsi, lui usava un termine medico, quella parola si usava quando uno prendeva la porga, come quando una era disintossicato da tutte le tossine del anima. La catarsi induceva il terrore e la pieta, era un termine medico, una metafora molto forte.

I believe that everyone needs to be treated ... for each of us, the opportunity to meet tragedy is, in any case, a moment of growth. It was not Psychology that compelled me to do this but my love for the Greek classics. My track was the ancient track; it wasn't the modern therapy track but therapeutic in the deeper sense, you get what I mean? Aristotle said that Greek tragedy was good for those who do it, as well as, for those who see it. ... When Aristotle said that tragedy induced catharsis, he used a medical term, that word was used when one took a purge, as when one was detoxified from all the toxins of the soul. Catharsis was induced terror and pity, it was a medical term, a very strong metaphor.
G. Testa (February 2020)

Giorgio emphasizes the importance of experiencing tragedy collectively, coming into contact with important aspects of life, death, power, ambition, arrogance, injustice, war, and so forth, through tragedy, within a group and being able to express yourself, your opinions, your thoughts, disclosing your truth. That is what makes this process therapeutic; to be able to be yourself in the greatest freedom with others with no fear of judgment interpretation/ misinterpretation. In the work I did with Giorgio during seminars with various at-risk communities, the play space was always created using classic tragedies as a stimulus for potential moments of *affective experiences of aliveness* (Sloan, 2018), moments where we found the courage to dare to disclose our vulnerabilites, our pain, our fears, our hopes, our desires as well as our joys symbolically through theater.

13

"What Happens If I Open That Door?": Art, Truth-Telling, and Healing in a Poetry Course for Prospective Teachers

Laura Apol

I am a poet in a college of education. I read poetry, I write poetry, I teach poetry, and I teach a course called "Reading, Writing, and Teaching Poetry." My students are planning to be teachers, but most have had little poetry-related experience. Most often they are hesitant, if not terrified, about reading, writing, and teaching poems. My job, then, is to convince them—first and foremost—of the power of poetry, to help them discover and find a voice for what they have to say.

This is a course I helped create, and I have taught it at least once a year for about a dozen years. I know the trajectory—initially, students are resistant; they write their first poem and share it in the first class (that's the big hurdle). Some drop the course *right then*; others go on. Most move slowly, over weeks and months venturing further and further into the world of poetry, finding words—through and beyond assignments—for the things they care about (the school football team, a breakup, graduation, the death of a pet). They go to readings (sometimes mine); they read books of poetry (sometimes mine). The course concludes with an evening event titled "Trillium," where they bring guests and we light candles and they give public voice to their poems, proud and pleased.

But 2018 was different. I had been away from the University for a year—on leave following the sudden death of my twenty-six-year-old daughter, Hanna, to suicide. As a poet who has long believed in the healing power of poetry, I had spent much of the year writing about her death (*A Fine Yellow Dust*, 2021b). The process of creating the Hanna-poems was healing, but I was terrified of returning to teaching—particularly teaching young women (who make up most of my education classes); particularly teaching poetry.

In some ways, the semester unfolded as usual. I threw my energy into finding poems and crafting assignments that would help my students encounter and develop voices that were meaningful and powerful and transformative. Outside the classroom, my newest book, *Nothing but the Blood* (2018)—a book written before Hanna died, but containing several poems about her—came out. I did readings from the book; I gave talks about the healing power of poetry; and I ended the course a week early because I was attending a Critical Suicidology Conference at which I would present a paper about being a mother, a poet, and a scholar writing about my daughter's death.

As expected, my students began the semester in predictable ways. They read, they wrote, they shared—safe things, from a distance. They were "good students" who did what was required. In the course, they wrote weekly poems. They met in small feedback groups, responded to their group-mates' poems, and shared their writing in whole-class read-arounds. But when they came to my office for a mid-semester conference about their writing, student after student broke down and cried—not about the course or their poems but about other aspects of their lives. Many confessed to suffering from anxiety and/or depression; many talked about therapy and medication. They were struggling, many of them, and in my office, they were speaking about those struggles.

I thought of what was creating so much upheaval in their lives. There was global warming, with wildfires raging uncontrolled in the West; at the southern border, children were being separated from their parents and held in metal cages; despite allegations of sexual assault, Brett Kavanaugh was being confirmed as a Supreme Court Justice. At our own institution, a doctor accused of sexually abusing hundreds of young girls was sentenced to prison; a $500 million settlement was made with victims and the president of the university resigned. Even without knowing the particulars of my students' stories, there was much to bring them anxiety and depression.

But they were not writing about the troubled and troubling aspects of their lives. Instead, they were still writing "safe" poems about their pets, their roommates, a cabin up north, autumn leaves. "How can I write the poems I need to write?" one of them asked me through tears. "What happens if I open that door?" She was afraid of what would happen if the door opened, if painful truths were exposed and explored. We all were.

There is a long scholarly history of therapeutic writing and the healing potential writing contains (Fox, 1997; Pennebaker, 1997; DeSalvo, 1999; Anderson & MacCurdy, 2000; Orr, 2002). I was well-acquainted with that history as a practitioner and as a workshop facilitator, including a decade of work in Rwanda using writing to facilitate healing among survivors of the 1994 genocide against the Tutsi (Apol, 2015, 2017, 2019, 2021a). But the upheaval in this class was something new. Like my students, I, too, was avoiding opening doors. I didn't know how to hear their stories without hearing my own loss, and I wondered if they were more distressed than students in previous years or if I simply was more attuned.

Opening the Door: The Poems

In those mid-semester conferences, I encouraged students to use their writing as a place to explore complicated aspects of their lives. In the weeks that followed, a few began to take steps toward opening. They wrote tentatively, then more bravely, taking greater and greater risks with their words—first one, then another. Julia, a Latinx student, made the first breakthrough; soon after we met in my office, she brought to class a poem that upended some of the taboos of language and subject matter the students had imagined (were never told) a "class" would have in place. Her poem, "priceless," laid out in uncompromising detail the price on her body as a Latina, concluding that she would pay full price (plus tax) for herself because she was worth it.

Heather, who early on had written in indirect ways about the death of her mother when she was young, wrote more directly and poignantly about that loss in a poem in which she described visiting the funeral home when she was five. Marisa wrote about the murder of her boyfriend's father, and Lily came out as lesbian in a poem she titled "Pride." Lily also wrote about her frustrations visiting the campus health center for treatment for anxiety, and eventually wrote what to her was her most risky poem—a poem in which she talked about Black Lives Matter, gay rights, why Holocaust jokes aren't funny, and "family values" that include automatic weapons and holding children at the border. Courtney wrote a poem of address to the student with special needs in her teacher education placement classroom. Kailin wrote about her panic disorder; she also wrote about her grandfather in the hospital (he died during the semester). Caroline wrote—for herself, during class, on the back of a school flyer—a poem about disliking flowers because they reminded her of the years-earlier death of her five-year-old sister. Megan revealed that the love poem she had written near the start of the course was for a girlfriend, not a boyfriend. And Cyntara wrote a poem titled "9:10 a.m." about a class she was taking in which she as a Black woman had a significant problem with race-based insensitivity on the part of the instructor.

These were a few of the students who had asked what might happen if they "opened that door." These are the doors they eventually opened. They shared their poems, gave one another feedback, encouraged each other by example to write honestly about their own lives.

Although these poems—and others—were a response to it, the question "*What if I open that door*?" still hung over the class, right through to the end of the semester. The students were proud of the distance they had come, poetically, and the ways our class had been transformed from a class to a community. But they were unsure what the journey meant, beyond the poems they had written and shared. As well, I felt a little like a voyeur; I, too, had made a journey in our weeks together, but I had made the journey in silence and I felt the need to tell them what they had meant to me, what our time had meant, and to answer, from my own life, the question about doors and the writing of what was hard.

Finishing the Class: Poetry as a Healing Art

Near the conclusion of the semester, we held our "Trillium" reading—an event where many of them shared publicly the risky, heartful poems they had written during the semester. In the class that followed—the penultimate class of the term—we talked about our reading, our pride in each other, and our pride in what we had created, together and as selves. I saved the last fifteen minutes for something I had prepared in advance. We had only one class left before we parted, and I wanted to talk with them about my experience when it came to writing, healing, and opening doors.

"You know we're not meeting during exam week," I began. "I'll be giving a paper at a conference in Perth, Australia. It's a Critical Suicidology Conference." They were all listening now. "The title of my paper is, 'Writing for Healing after a Daughter's Death: A Researcher-Poet-Mother's Journey.' I'll be talking about the death of my daughter, Hanna." I went on, "I know this has been a difficult semester for many of you. And you have asked all semester about writing the hard things, about what happens when you open that door. Many of you wept in my office; if you think you were the only one, look around—many of your classmates wept, too." I paused. "It was a difficult semester for me, too. This is the first course I've taught since Hanna died. She was twenty-six, and her death broke my heart. Writing is what saved me. So I want to share with you something I read at the Unitarian Church earlier this semester. It's called 'Poetry as a Healing Art.'"

The piece was about eight minutes long, and it included four poems from four times in my life when poetry was healing for me: after the Oklahoma City bombing ("After the Bomb," Apol, 1998); during my work with survivors of the 1994 genocide against the Tutsi in Rwanda ("Eucharist," Apol, 2015); following the death of my mother ("The Gift of *Yes*," Apol, 2018); and, finally, after Hanna's suicide. Since I had told them in advance the title of the talk in Perth, they were not surprised when I got to the final poem. I read:

> In this last year, I have done the hardest writing, the hardest work in writing I could have imagined. In April 2017, Hanna, my adult daughter, died. For all her life, Hanna had been my muse—her brightness, her spiritedness, her provocations. I didn't know how I could bear her absence, but I also couldn't imagine that I could turn anywhere *but* to words to thrash around in these, my deepest questions and struggles, my excruciating sense of loss and pain. For a whole year I wrote … and as words formed on pages, as I went back and moved lines, deepened images, found structures that could hold my brokenness, I felt moments of peace. I found language for what was unspeakable.
>
> This poem was written on the nine-month anniversary of her death. Nine months is the duration of a pregnancy, and I was highly aware that I had carried her for nine months forward into her life, and now I had been carrying her for nine months after her death. The poem is called "Gestation."
>
> **GESTATION**
>
> The last time I counted months
I was waiting
                for her—she, the rhythm
beneath my stretched
skin. An elbow, a heel,
head up, head down—lotus, bridge,
crescent, mountain,
                        warrior.

The last time I counted months
she was moving
                toward me, my body
readying
to push her into the world.
Now I am counting months again.
Today marks as long
for her to pass
                        from sight
as it took her to arrive,
gestation reversed,
a telescope
            turned backward on time.
She has grown smaller,   smaller,
until only I know
                her turns, her slides,
                        her flips and kicks.
She is once more the secret
I keep
        at my center—the delicate curve
of spine, the translucent eyelids,
                        closed.

(Apol, 2021b, p. 52)

I concluded with a quote from poet, Jay Parini, about poetry being "a language adequate to our experience"—however incomprehensible, broken, or raw that experience might be. When I finished, they were silent, absolutely silent. Some wept. Then I said, "You have asked—yourselves and me—if you can write the poems you need to. But I'm telling you, *you must*. *You* need the writing of those poems. And others need those poems to be written, too."

Then I thanked them, wished them a good week, and we were done. The next week, our last week together, they brought in flowers; they had made a card, and they lingered to say goodbye. They wrote to me in the weeks that followed to tell me what the class had meant.

Revisiting Our Journey: From a Class to a Community

Months after the class concluded, I invited my students to think with me about what had happened in our time together. From a class of twenty-two women and one man, eleven women met to brainstorm together, ten wrote up their memories, and nine participated in individual interviews.

We talked about what had made the class memorable; many mentioned the sense of community that had evolved over the semester. According to these students, the course began as any course, but at some point, things changed. Courtney explained,

"Each week slowly transformed us more and more from a class to a community." Heather said, "At first I thought, 'oh, it's just a poetry class, I'll just write some poems and see if I can get a good grade,' but as it progressed I thought, 'I want to pour my heart into these poems, and I want my classmates to hear every single word I'm saying and hear the emotion that I put into it.'" Lily wrote, "[The class] became a space where each of us became genuinely interested in what others had to say. It was a community tied together by poetry."

As well, students spoke of a shift toward taking more risks, being more open and vulnerable in their poems. For Julia, the shift came when she finally fought back against the racism she was experiencing in her work life. She said, "Toward the end, [my poems] did get more aggressive. I had gone from super-emotional and upset to angry instead." Cyntara felt that her poetry got more real when she wrote with honesty about the class in which she experienced conflict with her instructor. She said, "That poem was my breaking point; it let me say what I wanted to say without saying it to that person. After I wrote that poem, it didn't get better but I accepted it for what it was. Definitely that poem was my shift into including more of *me* in my poetry."

Once a few members of the class began to write with more honesty, others in the class found themselves following. Heather said, "Seeing everyone in class open up more, that's what made me think, okay if they're willing to be vulnerable, I can too. That's the point where I started being more real in the class." Megan summed it up this way: "Without our realizing it, the poems were changing our class."

Writing poems that were more honest and took more risks led to greater feelings of connection and empowerment. The poets knew they were in the company of others who shared their experiences (either literally or as readers), and they were encouraged by the responses of those around them. Kailin saw this vulnerability as a source of strength; in reference to writing about and sharing a poem about her anxiety, she said, "This is something I'm standing for, standing against, standing up to—my anxiety—and feeling powerful in my own skin. I wrote a poem about something I don't usually talk about, so for me to do that was powerful to myself."

By the end of the course, the final Trillium reading became an "arrival" for the poets and their poems, and a high point for the group's sense of community. Megan wrote, "The event is hard to describe unless you were there, but there was an energy that had a combination of fear, excitement, anxiety, and love. We were all rooting for each other because we had put in our own thoughts to help make each other's poems and performances more powerful."

Writing and Healing in a University Course

From the vantage of months and years, I talked with participants about their experience of our time together. They talked about truth-telling, gaining clarity through writing, and viewing poetry as a source of healing. Megan explained, "By taking this class we were all pushed out of our comfort zones and asked to embrace just how meaningful and impactful poetry can be." She added, "Truth-telling is something that brought our class together because people were vulnerable enough to really say the things that were on their mind, not just have their guard up like every other person in every other class that we go to. Truth-telling is something that can make change." And Cyntara wrote, "My poems extended a hand from my heart that I was afraid, and will probably always be afraid, to share with others."

Writing often brought clarity to the writer; Caroline described it this way: "When I finished a poem, I knew how I felt, I was less confused. It made me feel like I was getting things out." And Courtney said, "Sometimes a line would come up and I would gain a deeper understanding of how I felt about a certain situation. It was always within myself. Almost like my body putting this line on a piece of paper and my head processing it and listening to it." As Heather noted, "Sometimes writing poetry brought out a much deeper truth inside of me that I didn't have a clue was there."

In many cases, writing was also a source of empowerment and healing. Marisa, in writing about the death of her then-boyfriend's father, explained, "it helped me come to terms with certain things and it allowed me to express myself emotionally in a way that I had not before." Cyntara said that after writing the poem about her experience as a Black woman in a course in which she felt marginalized, the class did not change, but the poem gave her an opportunity to shift how *she* felt about the class and "look [her] teacher in the face." As she put it, "Writing allows you to let go without the consequences of what letting go can do." Julia wrote at length about the ways writing had been important to her in navigating the difficulties of the semester:

> I never made the conscious decision to use my poetry in an attempt to heal myself from the trauma I was enduring, or bring light to the issues I wrote about. It just sort of happened naturally. Throughout the semester, as things in my life continued to snowball, I took comfort in the words and the lines I could produce … My writing during this time was just representative of me trying to work beyond my grief for my past self to a place where I could be okay, or maybe even strong.

And Lily summed it up like this: "Poetry comes from a place of heartbreak, of love, of pain, of awe, and most importantly, of what it means to be human. Poetry is healing, and in this class, we were able to find together what this meant to us, as a group and individually."

Letting Down Walls and Closing the Circle

The final part of my conversation with each participant was about the personal sharing I had done at the end of the course. I saved this topic for the end of the interviews to help give them a sense that I was looking for information rather than affirmation, and I framed the question as openly as I could. I reminded them of our second-to-last class, when I talked about writing and healing in my own life. *How had it felt? Was it an appropriate thing to do? What did they make of it, take from it?*

Nearly all of the participants viewed my reading as a fitting conclusion to the course and the themes of the course. Marisa said, "I feel like you waiting until the end of the class, at the end of the semester, let us know that the whole time we were doing this there was a purpose for it—how writing helped you and could help us," and Lily recalled, "It was surprising and people were shocked but not in a bad way. Throughout the semester, we knew that writing was a thing of healing, but it was never explicitly said. After that happened, it made it explicit. Writing is art, writing is activism, writing is healing in personal ways." Cyntara saw it as a testament to the power of writing; she said, "That moment made me realize that writing can be the best outlet when it comes to dealing with things that you have to deal with. It was mind-blowing to hear you carrying that experience and that weight with you and then to release it. It was like Wow."

Julia remembered experiencing the moment in a very personal way, given the difficulties of her semester. She said,

> It gave a different viewpoint to the things I was going through. My mom was always like "don't do anything. I love you;" just hearing how you were so affected by your daughter … I connected to it immediately. The poems you read were so—it really hit me … and I thought to myself, *this is your sign, get your life together*. It was really powerful.

Many of the participants saw the sharing as a way that I participated in the course as a colleague rather than a professor; in her course reflection, Megan wrote, "Our last class was when we really left it all on the table … as Laura shared a piece of herself with us. We saw our professor let her walls down and share her experiences, thoughts, and feelings with us … Personally, I had never seen a professor so willing to share the realities of life." Courtney said in the interview,

> After all that we'd shared in groups, and in the class, you were now giving it back to us and showing us how deep we can get, how many layers within ourselves we can tap into … it inspired me that you were now showing that you used poetry and you continue to use it as a way to heal. It closed that circle of it being a community, and I started writing about it when I got home.

Some of them saw possibilities for their own writing and their lives. Caroline said, "I remember thinking, Laura's being really vulnerable and sharing a huge moment with us, and that kind of opened me up to think okay I don't need to be as afraid; I can be vulnerable and I can write these hard moments." Heather, too, was encouraged in her own writing; she said, "For me it was like, all right I'm not the only one. If she can do something like that and write something like that, who's to say I can't." And Kailin said, "I think it touched all of our hearts because you were saying I'm with you, I stand with you, I'm also going through something, you're not alone … it really tied things up for our class. Yup, we've grown together, we're in this together, we've done this and poetry has made us stronger."

This Course Helped Heal Me

The students who thought with me about our journey together, the voices that are included in this chapter are, of course, self-selected. These are the students who *wanted* to keep thinking about writing and poetry. And it goes without saying that the journey we made together in that particular semester is not one that can be replicated; there is nothing that can be generalized or transferred across contexts. And yet, there are things we learned about writing, vulnerability, honesty, and healing that speak to heartfelt and soul-filled teaching and learning beyond the bounds of the course.

Listening to one another—deeply, without judgment—made space and created a sense of trust that allowed student writers to take risks. Over and over the participants talked about the ways this sense of community allowed them to feel heard, to feel understood, to feel less alone.

Through listening and sharing, students found they had much in common—not superficially, but in ways that allowed for deep connection. Long-lasting friendships formed in the class; the participants remembered, even months and more than a year later, poems that had been shared that stayed with them because of their vulnerability and power.

There was space in the class for honesty, even when that honesty was difficult or when the ideas in the poem might make others in the course uncomfortable. Julia aimed to be an "interrupter" with her poems; Cyntara spoke out as a Black woman in a predominantly white institution; Lily not only came out as a lesbian but argued against anyone who might view her sexuality as problematic.

The openness and risk-taking begun by just a few extended to others in the class. As individual students saw and heard their classmates giving voice to hard things, to things that mattered, many felt a pull to explore and contribute things that mattered to them as well. Playing it safe, treating assignments as if they were merely assignments became the exception rather than the rule.

Students were empowered through their own vulnerability and their willingness to grow a voice. They found that choosing to write their grief, anger, confusion, and pain led to healing and sometimes to change—even if the change was an internal shift or a feeling of being seen and known. Cyntara put it like this:

> This was the class that allowed me to express my feelings at the times I needed to the most. This was the class that I have probably been the most vulnerable in … I am not one to publicly share my feelings. I do not like to cry in front of others, I do not like to be vulnerable to others and I really do not like the spotlight. But this class made me do it all.

The confidence that was the result of truth-telling and community extended beyond the bounds of the class. The next semester, Lily delivered a speech on depression and anxiety at an event about mental health; "I would never otherwise have done that," she explained. "This class helped me find my voice." And from the vantage of eighteen months, Cyntara said,

> Writing and having the experience of my group helped me develop as a writer, and critiquing and praising helped me to develop a voice … Even this past year, I have seen myself speak up a little more because … it's important for me to use

my voice, especially in the spaces where no one looks like me and no one has my experiences.

It was Marisa who put it most succinctly: "This class helped heal me." I felt the same. In sharing part of my story as a way to demonstrate the ways writing can be healing, I knew I was taking a pedagogical risk. I also knew I was modeling for my students something that could reach beyond the boundaries of the classroom and the semester. Most importantly, I knew I was joining my students as together, story by story and poem by poem, we recognized and lived out the healing power of poetry, of community, of truth-telling, and, ultimately, of opening—and walking through—doors.[1]

14

The Distresses and Hopes of Beginning Teachers: Five Arts-Based Research Explorations

Gene Fellner

Destiny

Destiny O. teaches at an elementary charter school in Brooklyn. She carpools to and from work with four of her colleagues. For her master's research thesis, she recorded their daily conversations as they drove through the streets of New York City. She then selected the themes that, day after day, continually arose within their discussions. In her thesis, "Conversations of Distress, Narratives of Teacher Burnout," Destiny emphasized two of the main themes that emerged from her study—the unending accumulation of daily tasks expected of teachers but never officially acknowledged and the lack of support teachers get from administration. For each of theme, Destiny created what we might call collective verses composed from direct quotes of her colleagues (for an example, see Figure 14.1).

> [The verses] were meant to emphasize the distress teachers go through but non-teachers rarely hear about. ... Many people say teachers are "lucky" because we have the summers off, yet these are the same people who do not even know the half of what goes into teaching.

When one day in class Destiny projected her verses on the screen, the other master's students, also beginning teachers, spontaneously began to read them aloud, creating a chorus that joined the resonating text of distress to the relief of knowing that their individual experiences were not theirs alone. Though exuberant laughter accompanied the readings, it was a laughter of catharsis, an outpouring of self-recognition in a text that spoke with and for them. In this way, the reading of the verses facilitated a brief moment of community self-healing that a typical research paper would not likely do.

Destiny's research echoes many more traditional research studies about teacher burnout, but unlike those studies, her purpose was not to prove or establish statistical facts. Rather, she sought to *evoke* (not explain) the experience of teachers, inviting empathy through purposefully selected and artistically composed teacher statements that represented an authentic picture of their daily lives. She sought to "reconfigure"

From Destiny's findings on tasks expected of teachers

Wow. It's so unfair what they expect out of us.

From the second we come in we're doing something to the second we leave.

I don't even have time to pee.

Oh, God forbid I pee.

Or God forbid we have a lunch break.

We literally don't have a second to ourselves.

It's always a meeting or something that has to get done.

I couldn't even make my copies today.
Is anyone else going to do it for me? No!

Guys... What about that random fire drill in the middle of recess?

That was pretty chaotic.

Figure 14.1 Destiny's findings on tasks expected of teachers.

a common concept (what it means to be a teacher) so that it could be seen newly and "vicariously re-experienced" (Barone & Eisner, 2012, p. 20). Far from making any claims about objectivity, often thought of as a research requirement, Destiny's personal experiences and attitudes deeply guided her study. She felt a need to illuminate her own distress with teaching as an act of self-healing and of advocacy. Though Destiny had intended to address her work to non-teachers (something she may still do), she was surprised and gratified by her peers' reactions, "The teachers in the room vented, sharing out their [own] experiences of distress. I feel very fortunate to know my research was meaningful and served a purpose." Through her artistic representation of teachers' voices, Destiny's research served to heal and sustain.

Patricia Leavy (2009) writes about how the "therapeutic, restorative and empowering qualities" of art can serve to heal and affirm both its maker and its audience (p. 9). For many teachers in their first years of teaching (42 percent never make it past those years; see Ingersoll et al., 2014), research that employs art in all or some aspect of its process can likewise "heal" and "affirm." Arts-based research approaches can empower teachers (Schaefer & Clandinin, 2019) and help them focus on "who they are in relation to the larger narratives of which they are a part" (p. 64). Such research may be more important than the typical types of studies my students do in the two semesters devoted to writing a literature review and doing actual research. Teacher education rarely attends to the emotional cost that teaching can exact from a conscientious teacher, especially given the high ideals teacher education preaches and that many teachers embrace but find little evidence of in the schools that hire them. Indeed, the ideals many teachers bring into the profession with them often get lost in the struggle to simply survive. Arts-based research, through verse (as in Destiny's case) or through other artistic modes, seeks to evoke experience, generate empathy, give voice to the underrepresented, further understanding and reorient. It is well suited to address the lived experiences of beginning teachers, the emotional damage that often accompanies those experiences, and the need for recognition, catharsis, and advocacy.

Drawing on the Work of Victoria Restler

The students in my research class are all preservice special education teachers (PSTs) though most already teach with a general education license. They tend to investigate issues like differentiation, classroom management, and attitudes toward inclusion. Though many learn about research concepts and how to structure a thesis, relatively few believe their research helps them become better teachers or improve the profession. Meanwhile, the work entailed in producing the research paper often intensifies the stress they already feel as full-time teachers rather than helping them navigate their early teaching experience. But my research course took a revelatory turn when I introduced my students to the arts-based research of Victoria Restler (2017) that evoked—through videoed interviews, art, and performance—the invisible work that teachers do. On a Tumblr blog (http://thosewhocanproject blog.tumblr.com/), Restler asks teachers what they do in a day that can't be measured and we hear teachers discuss the countless unquantifiable things they do that aren't included in the official job description. Additionally, on a Vimeo site (https://vimeo.com/196373346), using a red magic marker, Restler writes the word "research" on a blank sheet of paper and then overwrites that word with what teachers have told her they are thinking and doing throughout a routine school day. When she's done, all you see is a worn, thick, red wound in the center of the paper. My PSTs were excited by Restler's work. They felt it spoke directly to their experiences as teachers in ways that scholarly articles rarely do. Restler's work affirmed that their own sense of being overwhelmed by the requirements of their job was not a reason to feel guilty or incompetent. Indeed, the echoing of their own despairs and hopes affirmed the worth of their daily work, made them proud of their accomplishments, and made them feel less alone. For many, this was the type of research they wanted to do though none of them considered themselves artists or were educated in art the way Restler was. It was the type of evocation research they needed to do to take care of their own spiritual health as they taught and to advocate for teachers everywhere who are denied the support and respect they deserve.

It was Restler's work that initially inspired Destiny O; it also inspired Sarah D'Abravia (pseudonym), Rachel Terrifia (pseudonym), Arlinda Lela and Samantha Corallo, who worked on a project they titled "Invisible Labors." Each approached the project differently but all with the intent of channeling the lived experience of a teacher. For each of them, the researcher was "viewed as a viable data source" (Leavy, 2009, p. 38) and in this way they challenged the traditional (unachievable) demand of research objectivity. Each did an auto-ethnography of sorts, presenting themselves within the context of their profession in a personal style that rejected academic jargon (Leavy, 2009), thus potentially appealing to a broader audience than does traditional research.

Sarah

Sarah, a first-year kindergarten teacher, became aware of the distresses that accompany teaching during her student-teaching days:

> Far too often, another teacher … would make negative comments to me like, "Are you sure you want to become a teacher?" or "Change your major now before it's too late," … or my personal favorite, "Those bright eyes and that big smile will fade before you know it, honey."

It was only after having her own class, however, that these comments resonated disconcertingly with her own experience. Her tendency toward anxiety began to be aggravated by the unexpected but "overwhelming amount of miniscule tasks and decisions that take place throughout a day in the life of a teacher." About her research, titled "A Day in the Life of a Teacher with Anxiety," Sarah wrote:

> [I] conducted a think aloud which I audio recorded and transcribed … over a five-day span. Each day I chose a different hour to ensure my research would cover different activities and settings. I then reviewed the transcript and selected pieces to highlight. Finally, I put together a video based on my findings in order to evoke feelings in the viewers.

That video (see four frames, Figure 14.2), echoing Restler's work, slowly overlays her hourly "tasks and decisions" on top of each other, creating a muck of darkness from which the possibilities of emergence seem remote. Sarah found her own research:

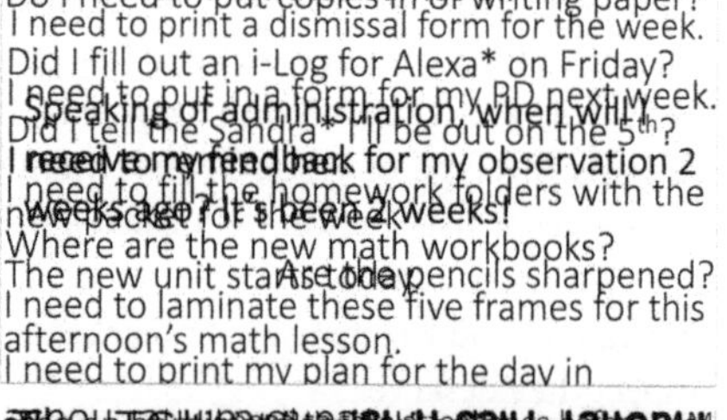

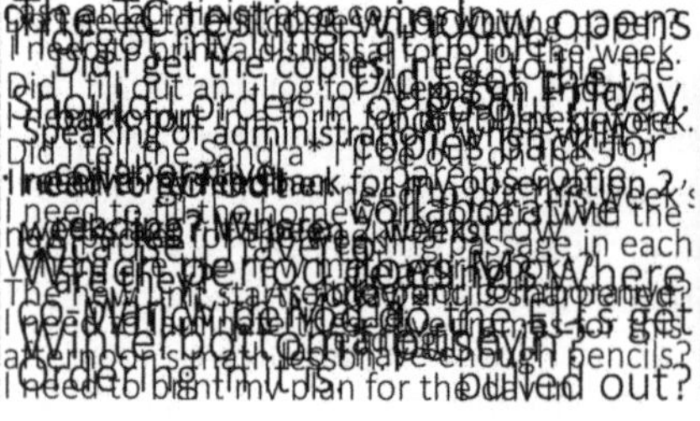

Figure 14.2 Sarah's video, four frames.

> Eye-opening. … It allowed me to view myself in a different light … to reflect on my thoughts, ideas and concerns … and to recognize things that are truly important. I strongly believe I would not be able to begin this process if it weren't for this autoethnography.

But her research had political as well as therapeutic goals. Her video sought to represent the discarded voices of teachers. To that end, she insists her research also advocates for the underrepresented, an objective often associated with arts-based methods (Barone & Eisner, 2012):

> While it is helping me to cope, it is equally important to find ways to eliminate these issues instead of just finding ways to deal with them. It is imperative to raise awareness on anxiety within teachers so we can demand a work environment that is conscious of the mental health of teachers. … Teachers cannot meet the needs of students if their own needs are not met. … Work should not be the root of anxiety.

Sarah's video is creative, self-reflective, emotionally rich, and politically powerful. Like much of arts-based research, it "leaves unresolved and unsettled the very problems it engages" (Fellner, 2019, p. 550), creating an opening through which the viewer can enter and participate.

Rachel

Rachel, who has dreamed about being a teacher since she was a child, created lists of the invisible labors she did in what was supposed to be her downtime including during lunchtime, evenings after school, and mornings before class. In this way, she attended to her own experience, an aspect of care and healing (Kwah & Fellner, 2020). Rachel wrote in her paper accompanying the lists:

> All my relatives and friends would reassure me with my intentions of becoming a teacher, "You have the whole summer off" or "A teacher is a great job for a woman. You get home early, can cook for your family, take care of your kids, and you're off holidays."

The reality was different, "Our day does not end when the last bell rings. In fact, for most of us, the next day has just begun." Her lists (e.g.,, see Figure 14.3) raised her self-awareness of how she spent her time and of all the things "a teacher may do in twenty-four hours that are not taken into consideration." Rachel recorded not only the activities themselves but took

> descriptive notes of my feelings, responsibilities and tasks that I do to fulfill my role as a teacher behind the scenes … This overwhelming list clarifies many of the things teachers do that are not in our contract or job description. … As a first-year teacher … I cannot imagine continuing in this profession for the next forty years.

THE NIGHT BEFORE

- **Preparing for Monday.**
- **Creating colorful anchor charts.**
- **Messed up, created new chart.**
- **Back hurts from being curled over on the floor.**
- **Using personal ink, paper, and materials (that I will never be reimbursed for) to print out guided reading booklets because the race to the copy machine the next morning isn't worth the hassle.**
- **Print 26 booklets, cut, put together in order, staple.**
- **Grade papers because the original ones that I graded last Sunday were lost within the building.**
- **Message parents back and forth.**
- **Vincent is out sick tomorrow. I wish I could call out.**
- **Where did this anticipated weekend go?**
- **Incoming call from co-teacher about plans for Monday. An hour and a half gone.**
- **Sunday dinner? I'll try to make it next week. So much that is not accounted for.**
- **Idea: Punch in time spent at home on online time clock.**
- **Watching videos of other teachers teaching lessons and writing notes because I'm expected to know the correct way to teach every topic and subject under the sun as if I were an encyclopedia.**
- **Finding pictures, printing more to somewhat fulfill my role as a "differentiator".**
- **Creating graphic organizers and powerpoints to help these lessons come alive!**
- **Oops, forgot to remind parents to send in their children with red shirts tomorrow! Here we go... "Good evening parents. Please remember to..."**
- **Boom. Goodie bags = 2 hours gone.**
- **Reorganizing reading and writing groups.**
- **E-maling technology teacher to see if our class may sign out ipads tomorrow.**
- **Figure out chaperones and which students still need to hand in permission slips.**
- **Time for family? Time for myself? Sanity?**
- **Limited.**

Figure 14.3 Rachel's list of activities.

Rachel's research contribution is a cry for attention and for a transformation in the teaching profession. Her lists reveal the toll that teaching takes on some of its practitioners. Joined with those of Samantha and the verses of Destiny, they also begin to build what Barone and Eisner (2012, p. 162) call a "preponderance of evidence" of teacher mistreatment and highlight "significant questions" about the systemic disregard for teachers that most people "might have overlooked otherwise" (p. 166). The lists of seemingly endless bullet-pointed activities and thoughts personalize the academic discussion of teacher-burnout and retention common to journal articles on the subject.

Arlinda

Arlinda and Samantha, in contrast to Destiny and Rachel, used arts-based methods not merely as a way of presenting evidence but as the medium of data collection. Through video, they brought the viewer as close as they could to the lived teaching experience, one that conveyed the frustrations of teaching as well as its sustaining joys. Their videos, which included the sounds and faces of children, classroom artifacts, and the movement through school spaces, joined "bodies, things, and time and space" in a continually changing scenario" (Pink, 2007, p. 244) that was authentic to the true life of a teacher.

Arlinda, her camera clipped to her shirt, video recorded six hours of her first-grade classroom and then edited it down to fourteen minutes, speeding up some sections "to show how fast our days go despite all that goes on," slowing down others "at the points that stuck with me at the end of the day … I wanted to show the audience that amidst the hectic day those moments are the ones that keep me going because they're so lovely or because they were the most challenging." The camera, jostled by her body as she engages with her students, "invites … empathetic engagements" (Pink, 2007, p. 250). The viewer's body moves with Arlinda's:

> My goals for this video were to show people what it is like being a teacher for a day. What it looks like, what it feels like and what it sounds like. … I think the video content was raw and authentic to what my day consists of. … I intend my audience to be anyone but specifically people who say things like "Teachers are just babysitters", "Teachers get paid enough", "Teachers have the easiest job ever." I think any teacher can relate to this video. … We all feel anxious, pressed for time, underappreciated."

Arlinda wanted the video to speak for itself, for the viewers to converse with the video just as they would with a work of art. She didn't want to present findings; she wanted viewers to come to their own findings after taking "another look" (Barone & Eisner, 2012, p. 145) from a new perspective. Sarah Pink writes that "walking with video provides ways of … sensing place" (2007, p. 243). Arlinda's video asks viewers to walk *with* her in her school, almost *through* her, so that they can sense her experience. Of course, they can never empathize fully. Still, artistic methods might be the best vehicle for helping the viewer feel as she feels in her teacher-body. The video images, filled with faces of children, cannot be included here for confidentiality reasons, and still images would not capture the often frenetic classroom activity conveyed through Arlinda's experiments with video speed. Instead, I have included one image of the classroom itself with its cacophony of student work and another of a happy but screaming child made unidentifiable through blurring of the image (see Figure 14.4). In a short text written after completing the video, Arlinda wrote:

> I think this video was powerful. It was different than I expected but I really loved and enjoyed making it. It was what I wanted to portray but I knew I couldn't put it

Figure 14.4 Two images from Arlinda's video.

into words. It was raw and real and gives a feeling that I don't think I could've given to the audience through writing.

Samantha

Samantha, like Arlinda, video recorded what she did in a day, but she juxtaposed her video with answers to a questionnaire that she distributed via social media. The questionnaire asked participants what they thought early-childhood teachers did in a day. In the video, in images I can't reproduce because of confidentiality concerns, Samantha comforts her pre-K students and engages in activities like playing ball and finger-painting. Justin Bieber's *Children* plays in the background, a marker of time, place and culture in a world that includes the school. Interspersed within the twelve-minute video are replies to her questionnaire (see Figure 14.5), mostly answered by teachers, affirming the important and unrecognized work teachers do. There are also some disdainful comments from non-teachers that are robustly challenged by the actual footage of Samantha in her classroom. The video and comments create a dialog between different attitudes toward teaching and different sensory mediums. As with Arlinda's research, Samantha uses image, movement, and sound (the children laugh, ask questions, scream) to present daily teacher responsibilities that find no mention in the official job description. Like Arlinda, Samantha invites us into her experience through empathic walking with her. Similar to the other PSTs highlighted in this chapter, though maybe more explicitly than some, Samantha also wanted her research to generate change in the teaching profession. In a short piece accompanying her video, she wrote:

What do teachers do all day?

Give students a sense of
;ecurity + a safe place to be

give huge hugs and wipe tears and boogies from little faces. They nurture, care, protect and provide help when needed which is 99% of the day. They laugh, play, sing and dance! They teach children to be creative and use their imagination. They read and they teach how to read. They potty train, they teach how to talk, they teach how to write their names. They teach how

They nurture minds and create safe spaces. They inspire creativity, answer endless questions, wipe runny noses, magically heal booboos, teach kids how to deal with their feelings, develop organizational and time management skills, turn lessons into play/fun activities, and ensure kids that it's ok to ask for help.

Early childhood/elementary school teachers are more than just teachers. They have all the responsibilities they are role models, care givers, friends, the enforcers ,solver of disputes, ect ect. Everything that A child would need

Figure 14.5 Replies to Samantha's questionnaire.

> Teaching goes deeper than what is presented at the surface. There are people who agree that we, teachers, lay the foundation for a lifetime of learning and there are those who believe we do the bare minimum and collect a paycheck. Here is what I have to say: Teaching is the most rewarding and joyous job I have ever had the pleasure of being a part of. It is arduous and strenuous … it can fill your heart while also having the ability to break it. …. We take on the responsibilities that include, but are not limited to, a caretaker, therapist, nurse, mentor, comedian, inventor, and actor. … Our days do not end when the last child waves goodbye. Our minds do not turn off when we turn the key to lock the door of our classroom. We are on a continuous loop of planning, assessing, modifying and creating for the next day, because we know that our children, ALL of them, deserve to be reached in any and all ways possible.

Her video ends with a statement of defiance:

> Teachers aren't given a budget big enough to supply kids with the tools they need to make each kid feel like they belong and will learn. Our educational system is a joke. Teachers aren't super-humans, but they try every day to be, to help change the lives of the kids they interact with. … Our love for teaching exceeds our distaste for a system that refuses to listen to the voices of those they are hurting. It is time for you to open your mind and see what our children need, what our teachers need—people who stand with them, not against them.

Concluding Thoughts

By the time my PSTs enter my research class, they have taken subject content, methods, and pedagogy courses, and most are in their first year or two of teaching. The goal of the research course, building on that knowledge, is to enable them to become teacher-researchers able to interrogate questions about education that confront them in the space of the classroom and also in the larger world, and to navigate those questions in ways that will benefit their students and themselves. Simultaneously, they seek to be a part of a school community that is welcoming, nurturing, and stimulating. Unfortunately, the schools our teachers enter at the beginning of their careers are often none of these things for teachers themselves. Our teachers often feel emotionally battered by their first years in the profession, which contributes to the high teacher attrition rates (Ingersoll et al., 2014), thus creating an unstable environment in which to teach and learn.

The five PSTs whose research I discussed in this chapter chose to address this battering because it was the immediate issue they needed to confront in order to survive as teachers. They didn't seek to prove anything about the stress that overwhelms so many of our teachers but to document that stress through multisensory texts that bring the reader/viewer along for the ride. Though none of them were artists, they chose arts-based methods because these methods are uniquely suited to (1) self-care through attending to and sharing personal teaching experiences; (2) healing through building collective self-recognition and teacher solidarity; (3) evocation of experience by making "vivid" what the reader/viewer might overlook (Barone & Eisner, 2012, p. 156); and (4) advocacy, by giving voice to those who have been ignored. Facilitating all these objectives, arts-based research helped sustain many of my PSTs as they faced systemic dysfunctions in the educational institutions in which they are primary laborers. Of course, arts-based research, like art itself, won't speak to every viewer/reader whose own embodied experiences of life will shape how they see, feel, and think. It does, however, offer a possibility of piercing set ways of viewing the teaching profession while providing much needed sustenance, care, and healing to teachers in the most vulnerable stage of their teaching career.[1]

15

Committing to Black Girl Joy in the Social Studies Classroom: A Hip-Hop Feminist Approach

Damaris C. Dunn

Blk Girl Soldier

Jamila Woods's (2016) song "Blk Girl Soldier" names freedom fighters Rosa Parks (sexual assault investigator), Ella Baker (mother of the civil rights movement), Audre Lorde (warrior poet), Angela Davis (prison abolitionist), Sojourner Truth (women's rights advocate), and Assata Shakur (revolutionary). She reminds listeners that these freedom fighters "taught us how to fight," while simultaneously fighting anti-Blackness and anti-womaness. Woods sings, "the cameras love us, Oscar's doesn't … aint nobody checkin for us," expressing society's love of Black culture but not Black women which makes Black women invisible. "Blk Girl Soldier" is a counter narrative that moves Black women freedom fighters and those who follow in their footsteps from margin to center. Their stories are battle paths and road maps for Black girls, but these women are often etched in history as passive interlocutors not agentive changemakers whose lives should be fully written and critically analyzed in social studies curriculum and standards (Gay, 2004; Aldridge, 2006; Woodson, 2015). Black girls in schools need access to historical Black women's power and accomplishments to reorient their understanding of the roles of Black women throughout history. They also need encouragement to see themselves beyond enslavement. Centering Black women and girls in the social studies classroom is not only equitable and just; it moves social studies toward a vision of social justice while fueling joy and healing for Black girls.

I conceptualize Black women's joy as a relentlessness to fight and liberate all people while simultaneously healing themselves and others on a path toward freedom. Woods's (2016) "Blk Girl Soldier" song underscores this conceptualization in the celebration of these Black women as freedom fighters who should be seen and heard. Thus, depicting their full stories as well as their joy and healing is crucial for Black girls in schools because much of the existing curriculum centers on their oppression. Dillard (2012) reminds us that (re)membering is a reclamation of one's identity and spirit, linking one's individual history to the collective "we." By (re) membering Black women's joy as expressed and shown throughout Woods's (2016) *HEAVN* album, we can begin to understand the manifold complex identities of Black women and girls. Social studies classrooms that recognize the multiplicity of Black women and girls' identities beyond oppression and erasure are critical to Black girls thriving.

As a Blk girl soldier and former New York City social studies educator, I am keenly aware of the ways in which schools suppress Black girl joy. For instance, in Massachusetts, an elementary school apologized for having a Black girl play the role of an enslaved person (Mikkelson, 2017). While classrooms should be sites for healing, they often reproduce racist and classist ideologies. Due to lack of cultural competency and anti-Blackness, Black girls are often seen as too loud (Evans-Winters & Esposito, 2010; Morris, 2016). Their joy is policed and surveilled so much so that they "scare the gov'ment," as Woods (2016) sings in "Blk Girl Soldier." The very spaces that should protect them reify their marginalization, shun their hair, perpetuate erasure, question their silence, and push them out at alarming rates (Morris, 2016). As an advocate for Black girls in and out of the classroom, I fight/write for their joy to wear their hair, to be, and to sing Black girl songs in spite of neoliberalism, racism, sexism, and poverty; joy for Black girls is healing and justice.

Activist, singer, poet, and editor, Jamila Woods's (2016) *HEAVN* album serves as a blueprint for how to successfully engage Black girls in order for them to thrive and heal in and out of schools. *HEAVN* centers Black women and girls, providing language for their intersectional identities while affirming their joy. *HEAVN* sits within hip-hop as a dialogical aesthetic that comes out of Woods's work and relationship to the Chicago community. Dialogical aesthetic breaks down the existing barriers between the artist and community; it is emancipatory in nature and opens up conversation around a particular idea or topic (Kester, 2004). This chapter will situate Woods (2016) within hip-hop feminism as an educational framework for Black girls to know joy in the social studies classroom. Each section is named after a lyric or song from Woods's (2016) album to highlight the importance of committing to Black girl histories, healthy relationships, and healing. The chapter will end with a call to action for creating *HEAVN* for Black girls in schools.

"You Go Ahead to Make a Place for Us"

Hip-hop has always been a place for Black American, Puerto Rican, and Afro-Caribbean peoples to creatively resist (Caponi-Tabery, 1999); therefore, the use of hip-hop as a tool to guide educators to embrace and engage Black girl histories, healthy relationships, and healing is worthwhile and in alignment with the goal of centering the most vulnerable. At its inception, hip-hop was a youth-sanctioned battle cry, a vehicle for truth-telling, and a joy-filled space in which youth used their voices to talk back to racism and classism. As the culture globalized, hip-hop's dialogical aesthetic morphed into a capitalist endeavor, commercializing the art form, making it male dominated and misogynistic. In 1999, journalist and award-winning author, Joan Morgan, coined the term "hip-hop feminist" to acknowledge the impact that misogyny had within the culture, while also recognizing that hip-hop was/is a space that empowered and served as an identity marker for women and girls. To be a hip-hop feminist was to "be brave enough to fuck with the grays" (Morgan, 2000, p. 59). Morgan ascribes the gray area as the liminal space of contradiction, the space that recognized that you could hold the art form close while critiquing it. Collins (1990) acknowledges that as a socially oppressed group, Black women's social thought is not only informed by academic theory, it also exists within art making, which makes our standpoint different from other groups. Music tells our stories. Woods's (2016) album exemplifies the Black feminist aesthetic within hip-hop that celebrates Black women's and girls' histories, healthy relationships, and healing as an integral part of her art.

Within a twenty-year span, the literature on Black girls and hip-hop feminism has grown (Durham, Cooper, & Morris, 2013; Lindsey, 2015; Sankofa Waters, Evans-Winters, & Love, 2018); yet, research on Black girl joy is limited. One space that centers Black girl joy is Saving Our Lives Hear Our Truths (SOLHOT) in Chicago. Ruth Nicole Brown (2013) developed SOLHOT as a multigenerational space for Black women and girls to express themselves through hip-hop (Durham et al., 2013 p. 727). At SOLHOT, Black girls interrupt, resist, and talk back to structures that seek to dehumanize them. SOLHOT allows me to see the social studies classroom as a potential fissure for Black girls to see themselves as worthy of joy.

To create such spaces, educators must first confront the ways anti-Blackness, hypervisibility, and invisibility are barriers to Black girl joy in and out of schools. Black girls' bodies are often hypersexualized and surveilled and controlled. While they make up 16 percent of the school population, they are the only group to undergo negative outcomes across the discipline continuum (Morris, 2019). As Ananama et al. (2016) assert, schools have become "sites of racialized and gendered terror for Black girls" (p. 2). Educators must commit to seeing Black girls as fully human, move away from working with them in a hierarchical manner that undermines their humanity and renders them invisible, and move toward partnership with Black girls to make their educational experiences more worthwhile. To make Black girl joy a reality in their classrooms, educators must problematize erasure and begin "accounting for the lived experiences of Black people across gender, age, sexuality, ability, ethnicity, citizenship status, and religion" (Lindsey, 2018, p. 166).

Joy is the pulse of hip-hop; it is also integral to social change (Love, 2019). Walker (1993) defines joy as resistance, while African American studies scholar, Imani Perry (2020) in conversation with writer Kiese Laymon, described it this way, "Joy is never the evasion of the depth of wounds. It's a sustaining life force." Joy is the enemy of injustice; it is steeped in an orientation of the spirit and continues to push Black people forward. Like Black girls in schools, "Blk girl soldiers" knew joy and pain. As such, the social studies classroom can be a site for social change and resistance, by which Black girls can tap into the sustaining life forces of Black women who came before them. By centering Black girl joy and giving Black girls the space to articulate themselves for themselves, schools can undo spirit murdering (Love, 2019) and policing of Black girls' bodies.

Cooper (2018) states, "Joy arises from an internal clarity about our purpose" (p. 274). What if schools committed to asking Black women and girls what brings them joy? How might school be a place for healing? Cooper (2018) asks that we consider joy as praxis. "When we lack joy, we have diminished capacity for self-love and self-valuing and for empathy. If political struggle is exercise for the soul, joy is the endorphin rush such struggles bring" (p. 275). Joy for Black girls is necessary, and when we commit to joy for them, we commit to joy for all. *HEAVN* emphasizes three themes that Black girls need to experience joy: knowing personal history and herstories pertaining to Black girls, developing healthy relationships, and healing.

VRY BLK (History)

In her song "VRY BLK," Woods (2016) belts, "Im very I'm very black, black, black, Can't send me back, back, back, You take my brother, brother, brother, I fight back, back, back, back." VRY BLK is a celebration, and its repetitive nature mimics a Black girl hand game. But under its playfulness is the story of erasure of Black women and girls. In her *New York Times* article, Kyra Gaunt (2020) says Black girl's play, "resists the dehumanizing dictates of a white, patriarchal culture ... Girls' musical play ignores the antipathy toward Black lives." Woods's articulation of "VRY BLK" is a joyful resistance of what it means to constantly save the entire Black race except Black women and girls. Woods's playfulness in "VRY BLK" necessitates a deeper look into how Black girls' ways of knowing and being are apparently one thing, but in actuality they mean something entirely different. (Re)membering the lived experiences of those women who "taught us how to fight," Kelley (2002) asserts,

> the crux of the problem: [is] the relative invisibility of black women ... The black community is too often conceived as an undifferentiated group with common interests. The men and many of the women who lead these movements see the yoke of the race and class oppression and accordingly create strategies to liberate the race. (pp. 137–8)

Even in the fight to negotiate freedom, Black women were grouped within the larger fight for all Black people, leaving them on the periphery of the conversation about their own liberation. Black women's subversiveness and tactful approaches to the struggle for liberation were not all struggles. Black women of the past had joy as do Black women and girls of the present. A perfect example of this is the recent presidential election. Black women organizers across the country band together to register voters and apprehend voter suppression. Hence, it is widely acknowledged the nomination of president-elect Joe Biden and the first Black vice president-elect Kamala Harris are result of Black women's commitment to envisioning the world anew. The social studies classroom can be a starting point for cultivating and nurturing Black girl joy, empowering Black girls to know present and current history.

By bringing Black women historical figures to center social studies, teachers and their students begin to recognize that Black women are more than their oppression. This reconciliation is the beginning of much needed healing between schools and Black girls. Imagine the Black girl joy that might emerge from a history lesson on why hair braiding was integral to freedom or on the importance of organizing and community work taught by Black women educators (Vickery, 2017). The social studies classroom that centers Black girls includes speeches from Ida B. Wells, first lady Michelle Obama, and vice president elect Kamala Harris. The social studies classroom is a homeplace where Black girls are seen and heard; this unearthing of herstories is joy embodied.

Popsicle, Assata's Daughters (Healthy Relationships)

Woods's (2016) "Popsicle" interlude shows the interconnectedness between Black girls across place and space. In the interlude, Woods (re)members an encounter with other Black women. She asserts:

> So, one day these random girls are at my office, and one girl's like, y'all remember how to play Rockin' Robin? And we all broke out into formation, and we were like … Popsicle, popsicle, a bang-bang we was rockin' in the treetop …and we like all knew how to play Popsicle together. And then like all of the people who weren't Black were just looking at us like … "Did y'all go to elementary school together?" It was literally like the best inside secret that I felt like I had ever had. That's one of my favorite things about blackness.

These Black girls, strangers to each other, but akin to Blackness, girlness, and Black girl games is joy. Gaunt asserts, "Black girls' musical games promote the skillful development of musical authority that reflects blackness, gender, individual expressive ability, and the very musical styles and approaches that later contribute to adult African American musical activities" (Forman & Neal, 2004, p. 251). These hand games take place in school yards and parks, making them nearly universal to Black girls and revealing their collectivity as a possible place to develop healthy relationships.

Safe spaces and places (Brown 2013) that mirror the Black girl experience are sites for joy. Affinity spaces like SOLHOT and Assata's Daughters in Chicago affirm and encourage Black girl joy. Historically, Black women's literacy societies were places of possibility and Black genius (Muhammad, 2020). Social studies educators can also look to the Black radical tradition to inform their understanding about creating classroom spaces for Black girls' thriving. In "Popsicle," we see how Black girlness might be exercised by some Black girls. To create such spaces, Black teachers should also be present. "As role models, parental figures, and advocates, they can build relationships with students of color that help those students feel connected to their schools" (Griffin & Tackie, 2016, p.1).

Healthy relationships sound like call and response, which invites participation from Black girls. Notice in Woods's "Assata's Daughter":

> It is our duty to fight for our freedom, (It is our duty to fight for our freedom), It is our duty to win (It is our duty to win), We must love each other and support each other, (We must love each other and support each other), We have nothing to lose but our chains, (We have nothing to lose but our chains).

Assata Shakur was a former member of the Black Liberation Army and a fierce revolutionary who fled to Cuba to seek asylum. Centering the history of Black women and highlighting their words as tools of liberation is empowering and can make social studies classrooms live up to ideals of social justice. In my own work, I used call-in response in an affinity space that my former Black women colleagues and I cocreated with Black middle schoolers in the Bronx. Every Monday, members of My Black Is Beautiful closed our meetups with this universal Black girl mantra. Both Black girl hand games and mantras that embody the Black radical tradition have been sites by which Black women and girls have been able to connect their life force, resistance, and joy. Additionally, Black girl–centered inquiry and focus groups can help social studies educators nurture Black girl joy. Finally, Black girls should have space to be alone, though not ignored, in schools should they need it. Black girls must be seen as worthy of space and place that mirrors their experiences and acknowledges their humanity.

Holy (Healing)

"Holy" is a step toward healing and a roadmap for social studies educators in moving toward Black girls joy in the classroom. Woods (2016) sings, "Though I walk through the darkest valley I will fear no love, Oh my smile my mind reassure me I don't need no one, Woke up this morning with my mind set on loving me." Walking through interlocking oppressions, Black women and girls experience pain; their holiness is a type of joy, the salve that allows them to move forward despite the pain. hooks (1994) sees education as a "practice of freedom" when healing and education are inextricably linked. As educators reorient their classrooms from anti-Black spaces to spaces that value and center Black joy, they enable Black girls to show up as their full selves, to know love and joy. What would it mean for Black girls to love themselves? What would it mean for Black girls to be whole? Classrooms and schools that commit to creating loving spaces where Black girls are whole commit to a path of healing.

Classrooms that render Black women's history and healthy relationships important promote healing through reconciliation. We acknowledge certain parts of ourselves, while recognizing the parts that are hurt no longer control us. Such internal clarity, which Cooper (2018) uses to define joy, is integral for Black girls' healing. Yet, healing is not the absence of pain; it can be difficult, making counselors and social emotional learning vital in schools. Histories that center Black women and girls' lived experiences can be painful, but if educators commit to developing space for Black girls, then we have already begun creating possibilities for healing. Hip-hop at its inception was youth sanctioned; it was a space where youth talked back to the institutions that undermined their very existence, a site where Black and Brown youth experienced joy, an embodied part of the healing process. Though hip-hop has drastically changed since its inception, it still remains a space by which to talk back. It was through rap, dancing, and storytelling that healing was ever present. Social studies classrooms can also be sites of healing where creativity and history can work in tandem to unearth and center the complex histories of Black women and girls.

HEAVN for Black Girls: Committing to Their Joy

Jamila Woods is just one artist; however, if we delved into the work of other Black women artists the possibilities for joy and healing centered frameworks for Black girls would be endless. Black women artists show the complexities of Black women and girls' stories and name their interlocking oppressions in ways that acknowledge pain but uplift joy. Freedom for Black women and girls has always begun in the mind. Walker (1983) insists that Black women "dreamed dreams that no one knew—not even themselves, in any coherent fashion—and saw visions no one could understand" (p. 402). Black women recognized interlocking oppressions and looked beyond existing spaces to cultivate grounds for liberation. We must say Black women's and girls' names—death by sleep (Breonna Taylor), noise complaint (Rekia Boyd), eviction (Elanor Bumpers), and wellness check (Atianna Jefferson)—are unacceptable ways to die. We should commit to Black women's and girls' joy in classrooms, instead of when they are hashtags on social media.

It is crucial to commit to history curricula that critically engages conversations and inquiry about race with Black women and girls at the center; reorient spaces for Black girls to develop affinity relationships; and recognize the folx who Black girls have relationships with outside of school. We must also acknowledge a commitment to healing. Healing does not mean damage never existed; it means damage no longer controls our lives. We commit to Black girls' healing by acknowledging their complex histories and developing spaces for them to process and grow. Hip-hop is a model for what youth-sanctioned joy looks and feels like. Woods's (2016) *HEAVN* is a framework for enacting joy for Black girls.

As a Blk girl soldier, I commit to the fight that looks beyond existing school classrooms and dreams up classrooms where Black girls know joy. When we (re)member Black women as cultural workers, learners, and healers we commit to a world that is equitable and just. Black joy is a "sustaining life force" (Perry, 2020) and resistance; it is not ephemeral, it is soul work. It is what pushed Rosa to investigate sexual assault against Black women, propelled Ella to spearhead the civil rights movement, encouraged Audre to pen prose of civil and social injustices, emboldens Angela to continue the abolition of prisons, compels Jamila to sing Black girl songs, and encourages me to imagine a Black girl joy beyond our wildest dreams.

Part IV

Community and Connection

16

Folding Cranes of Hope: Assembling Leadership through Critical Pedagogy

Robin Brandehoff

The school hallway was lined with plastic fold-up picnic tables, each adorned with a flimsy plastic sheet and beautifully wrapped gifts and baskets donated by teachers and staff. Gifts were visible or labeled and each had a decorated shoebox with a tiny slit for a raffle ticket. Our principal hoped to give our students a memorable Christmas and a shot to win themselves or a loved one a gift by earning raffle tickets during the last week of school before winter break. We knew this meant that not every student would walk away with a prize, but it was a way to break up the monotony and depression that often hangs like a heavy shroud around at-promise kids when the holidays approach—especially those who are food or housing insecure.

I worked with the principal to host this event. We had our office helpers—senior students who needed extra credits for an elective and something viable to put on their resume—to help us wrap gifts. It seemed like a simple and straightforward task, but it was an experience (of many) that taught me both humility and the importance of establishing relationships with youth using elements of critical pedagogy (Freire, 1972). One young female, around age twenty, was very excited to help. She told me, "I've never gotten a present before. How do you wrap it?" I had learned early in my career to not let my face betray what I was thinking, and in this moment, I was thinking, "Wait. You've *never* received a present? You don't know how to wrap one? How is that possible?" But I checked myself, smiled, and cued up my tagline of: "Lesson time!" She laughed and we sat in a corner on the cement floor of the office, allowing our conversation about home and growing up to fold its arms around us like origami poetry.

It was in these confined spaces of transcendent mentorship that I found myself appreciating my role and purpose as an educator most. During this conversation, she and I smoothed out our misunderstandings about each other to create crisp folds of new meaning. This lesson began as a technique of wrapping presents, but within those folds of paper, our conversation marked the stages of a mentoring relationship where we each learned a compelling fact about the other. Like gift wrap, we both shielded aspects of our life with a distracting façade. I talked about growing up in the projects and she shared with me that she did not live in a traditional house. She, her mom, and her siblings lived on the outskirts of an agricultural field saved for its farmworkers.

Their walls were cinder block and their roof was a wavy sheet of metal one might remove and salvage from the side of an old shed. They did not have running water or a toilet, so they would dig a hole on the side of their home to relieve themselves and showered at a friend or family member's house when they could. She told me she hated winter because the fields would flood and there was no way to keep her dirt floor clean, but that summer was worse because the heat brought out the smell of their surroundings.

I did not know any of this before we sat down to wrap presents, which began to feel like tangible pieces of privilege. Even the discount wrapping paper felt excessive in my hands as I sat there listening to this child open up about her life. I began to feel shame as images flashed in my mind: her brother would fall asleep in my class and how frustrated I was that this was a daily occurrence; I would try to exercise patience with him but often failed. Or, how this young girl's reputation among teachers and her propensity to fight marred my view of her before she entered my classroom. Through my shame, I wondered who here was teaching whom? My lessons on English grammar and writing expository essays were necessary to fill our school's data requirements. Her lessons of humanity, slipped beneath intricate folds of gift wrap and conversation, taught me more about the purpose and trajectory of my work than years of schooling and long days in professional development meetings. This was only one student, only one of many lessons folded delicately around honest conversations which could not be learned from a textbook or lecture, only one of many conversations wrapping around my heart over the years.

Measuring Folds and Limitations: School, Students, and Community

Much like many schools in rural and agricultural areas, our school lacked many basic resources, a stark reminder that our students lived on the margins of society. The school's focus was to use the flexibility of a charter program to provide a safe and educational space for at-promise students to finish out their remaining high school credits and potentially earn experience and a certificate in a trade such as construction, child development, or criminology. In fact, the school's first construction students were the labor force to transform the building from an old mechanic's shop into a functional school building with classrooms, walls, and a ceiling. The general student population was Latinx with a handful of Black and white students, many of whom would flow in and out of the school depending on their personal situations, work schedules, and family obligations. Some students would drift in and out of the juvenile justice system. Most of our students were removed from the traditional high school due to low grades, a result of having little English literacy support as multilingual learners. Many were removed for poor attendance and/or negative behaviors, gang affiliation, fighting at school, or having a criminal record.

Despite the students' negative reputations, shouldered from their years in the formal educational system, they gifted us with their wit, empathy, and a jarring perspective of the world which pointed out the sociopolitical and educational systems' inability to address the students' needs. They were unafraid to call out our shortcomings in the classroom, and their exceptional ability to balance multidimensional cultures and languages educated us (the teachers and administrators) on ways to recreate our curricula and assessments. Our students came to us with funds of knowledge (Moll et al., 1992) extending far beyond the scope and capital of mandated academic testing. They taught us that all they needed to excel was a positive and caring staff and the opportunity to prove themselves because they had a lot to share with the world.

Folding Foundations by Gifting Blankets

The winter celebration tables stretched along the walls of our main corridor, piled high with movie gift baskets, Nike sneakers, makeup bags, and even a coveted pair of wireless Beats headphones. As I chatted with students about their choices and strategies ("do I place *all* of my tickets in one gift box to strengthen my chances, or do I spread out of my options and maybe get more gifts?"), I noticed Chad standing in front of a cozy green-flannel blanket wrapped up in a big red bow with a pair of house slippers tucked into its ribbon. He stretched one hand out to touch the soft fabric and a smile crept across his face.

I asked him what was up. With his usual beaming Chad-smile, he talked about how soft the blanket was. "Yeah … I didn't see it until now, but I put my other tickets in them other boxes. Shit. Had I known about this, though? I woulda put ALL my tix in here!" He laughed and I laughed with him. He continued,

> See, I been living in the garage and like, it's aight in the summer when it's hot. It's too hot sometimes. But in the winter, like now, it's so cold. And sometimes the rain comes in under the door. I sleep on the floor. I got a mattress, but I don't have no blanket. Shit, ma'am. I wished I'da known about this blanket." He had one ticket left and at this point he held it close to his chest and paused as if in prayer. With a deep breath, he dropped it into the shoebox slit and smiled at me. "Well…who knows, right?

"Yeah, Chad. Who knows? I hope you get it, though."

"Yeah, ma'am, me too. Me too." He laughed again and walked away to join his friends.

I felt I only had one choice: I took the box behind a corner and crimped the edges of Chad's ticket, so it was clear which one was his. I told our principal about our exchange, and she just smiled and tilted her chin up, a silent recognition and green light blessing.

During the rally that morning, as we chose tickets at random and handed out prizes, it was easily the best day of the year. Every student was happy. Every teacher choked back tears. And I made a big show of digging around in the orange shoebox for a ticket to a green-flannel blanket. Chad was shocked that he won and chose to wear his house slippers all day—even while playing basketball at lunch.

Our students often enter our classrooms with beaming smiles and cheer, but many have giftwrapped themselves to cover parts of their lives from the world's gaze. It takes building a relationship and (sometimes) the right timing for us to unwrap those layers and learn deeper truths. Chad had been my English student for two years and was also in my Leadership Class. His uniform shirt was always fresh and pressed, his shoes were always spotless, though maybe a bit older. His hair was impeccable, and he worked hard every single day to get his work done, collaborate with others, and contribute to discussions. I never would have guessed Chad didn't have a blanket. Had I not wandered over to talk to him, I would not have known his story, and maybe luck would have been on his side as I drew out a ticket for the blanket, but his chances would have been slim.

Creasing Papers into Petals: Establishing a Leadership Class

In class, my students and I focused on short-term goals and aspirations for academic achievement and personal wellness. Instead, we completed assignments and tasks, but more importantly, we focused our energies on strengthening our collective collaboration, whether that was between partnered classmates, small groups, or individual students and myself. This was not always easy, especially since so many students represented opposing gangs. With a lot of patience and reflection, we learned that we were more similar than we anticipated, and together, we had more resources and knowledge to share than when we were at odds.

Our mentorship was developed and nourished outside of class: at lunchtime on the blacktop, I learned who was friends with whom and connected different students by engaging them in a larger conversation. There, I had more time for one-on-one conversations, and students could come and hang, even if they did not want to talk. The shared silences spoke volumes about what a student was going through and how much they needed the company of another person. In these moments, I learned that my students wanted an opportunity to give back to their school community and feel important, which inspired the birth of our Leadership Class.

The Leadership Class was an elective course and students were voted into the class by the faculty and staff. To be voted in, students needed to have two or more of the following qualifications:

1. Charisma and leadership among the student body
2. Passing grades
3. Good attendance
4. Desire to be in the class
5. Needed a space to belong

The final roster was an eclectic mix of students with a variety of talents and gifts who learned to converse and collaborate with each other to succeed.

In our first class together, we sat in a circle, which forced us to see each other and equalized the distribution of power. I was their co-conspirator (not their teacher) within this circle. We discussed what it meant to be a "leader" and what "leader" meant in relation to school. "Popular" students listed off what leadership meant: role model, set a good example, help classmates and teachers, not get in trouble, and share knowledge. As leaders, they wanted to make the school a "real" school with extracurricular activities, dances, and school assemblies.

The "loners" (a descriptor they used of themselves) remained quiet and would not interject or interrupt their louder classmates. One of the "popular" females noticed this and pointed to her quiet classmates, "You guys haven't said anything yet. What do *you* think?" That interjection bridged a sociocultural divide and sparked a series of changes in how students engaged with each other. The "loners" spoke up and suggested that dances and football games were out of reach, but school assemblies were possible. In a gratifying cacophony of "Ohhhh!" our Leadership Class took flight with ideas and possibilities—a thousand paper cranes with hope reflecting off their shiny wings. As a class of one, we began planning our very first of many school assemblies.

Folding Lessons into Assemblies

The Leadership Class began the fall semester by brainstorming our first school assembly. Students passionately examined and questioned the resources that their school and community lacked which I would softly challenge, folding in a critical perspective and prompting them to consider why our school was not afforded the resources, sports, and extracurricular activities as "traditional" schools. We examined resources in their neighborhoods and compared them to the resources in other areas of their town where middle- and upper-class families lived. We critiqued and questioned power structures, but we also focused on the immense community cultural wealth (Yosso, 2005) that their neighborhoods and families provided. As their teacher, I guided them to critically examine their oppressions as well as their gifts. As their co-conspirator, I helped them unearth a vocabulary to defend their perspectives and give them opportunities to exercise their own power, knowledge, and resourcefulness.

By creating space in our class to challenge oppressions and question the sociopolitical structures, students felt safe enough to open up about their experiences. They shared testimonies of trauma—poverty, violence, and loss—alongside aspirations for the future. Most wanted families and a house of their own. All wanted to travel or leave town altogether so their family could feel safe. They wanted peace, and to not be afraid of dying young or getting caught up in gang life. They wanted to stop losing people they loved.

One such conversation began over the loss of a classmate's brother who was caught up in the gang life but managed to graduate the year prior despite every barrier set in his path. He was popular in the neighborhood and with students because he was a hard worker but always down for a good laugh on the basketball court or in class. It is wrong to say that any youth in this town "chooses" the gang life given that poverty and fieldwork are common and opportunities few. Still, this young man entered a gang and paid with his life. In a close community such as ours, such sudden loss always hits hardest. My Leadership Class struggled to process his loss while balancing the need to support their friend. That day was stifling, as if our breath was pressed out of us beneath a heavy weight. The only word we could utter was, "Why?"

Together, we arranged our desks in a circle and sat in silence. Some kept their heads down on their desk. Others sat silently, tears running down their cheeks. Some scrolled on phones or popped an earbud in, angrily bobbing their heads to music. In moments like these, words are never enough. I patiently and silently waited with them and among them until someone, after twenty-five minutes, erupted with an outburst which pierced the air like a gunshot.

"It's just so fucked up, ma'am!" Paul, a close friend of the younger brother, with an earbud still in his ear, spoke but continued to stare down at his desk, his mouth pressed in a firm, head shaking in a soft "no" motion.

Students nodded in agreement. One looked at me and said, "Why is it so hard to just have a normal life?"

We talked well passed the final bell. Students held their classmates' hands or nodded to each other from across the circle as a silent recognition of shared pain. We discussed the limitations that existed for youth of color in this rural area where opportunities for steady work only existed in factories or fields. Two students had decided early that instead of folding into the fields like their parents, they would "get out" by going into the military. We discussed the depression and anxiety of living in places marred by violence, and we shared our aspirations for the future too. Students countered their self-proclaimed "fates" and rewrote their scripts with new chapters inspired by the experiences of those they lost. Together, restricted and overwhelmed by our grief, our stories of trauma became stories of remembrance of fallen victims.

These deeply honest conversations emerged through discussions in class but also through journaling and poetry writing. When planning for school events, students formed their own groups to work on the events' specifics and execution. In these collaborations, students shared personal experiences and recognized how much they had in common. Class projects and school service events were opportunities to share and heal while creating short- and long-term goals. This unique class allowed me to mentor students academically and professionally by mapping out their courses to graduation, building their resumes and cover letters, or filling out paperwork for social services. These short-term goals led to building long-term plans including pathways through college, trade school, or the military, and plans to save money to eventually move out on their own.

By the end of the fall semester, we realized our strengths were serving our school well. We put on several assemblies complete with silly games, prizes, and whole school announcements—but the class wanted to accomplish more. The district psychologist was impressed and suggested our class enter a state-wide competition on educating youth about mental health awareness. The regional portion of the competition took place in a neighboring city, and the project task was to create a public service announcement about mental health awareness and resources for teens. The students set themselves to work by establishing a research team, planning the public service announcement (PSA), and assembling an artistic team to direct, film, and edit the commercial. We used our shared experiences of sociopolitical, historical, and racial oppressions, and we discussed our journeys with and through mental health, including how we unwrapped ourselves from under the folds of anxiety. We realized for many students bullying preceded anxiety and depression, and the students determined that bullying would be our video's theme.

The students decided our video would have one main character, Juan, an overweight young man who walked the halls, getting shoved, yelled at, and laughed at as he tried to get to class. He wore balloons on his body with bold lettering spelling out words and racial slurs that people often called him. This portion of the video was shot in black and white, set to melancholy music. When Juan exited the main school building onto the blacktop, the camera angle changed to focus on a small group of students gesturing for Juan to join them at the benches. Chad played a character who did not want Juan to join them. He looked disgusted, and when the other group members invited Juan anyway, Chad stormed off camera. Juan's new friends stood around him and removed the balloons from his clothes, folding him into hugs and high fives. The music became uplifting, the film slowly switched from black and white to vivid color, as Juan and his new friends set the balloons on the ground and stomped them out of existence. Once they "Stomped Out the Hate," which was the title of our video, Chad came back to the group and apologized to Juan, who forgave him with a hug.

Reversing Folds and Taking Flight: From Teacher to Co-conspirator

We shot everything on our phones and one student conducted all of the video editing at home. We knew that this work was important and that the theme of mental health was not limited to bullying. By now, my role as their Leadership teacher had changed to the role of a mentor and *co-conspirator*. My students knew that I "had their back" and would support them in their endeavors, stepping in to guide them back on track as needed, but ultimately working with them to find a way to make their aspirations possible.

We held a brainstorming session to step up our work. The students decided they wanted to use their research and video to host an assembly centered around mental health, including its various definitions and forms, ways to recognize that someone may need help, resources that existed nationally and in the city nearby, and opportunities for students to share their own experiences and seek help. The students also collaborated with me and the school counselor to create proposals and guidelines for a peer counseling program where the Leadership students would be available to listen to their peers, hold "office hours," and recommend resources (which were provided to them through pamphlets and business cards by the school counselor). The students even created mini cards with important hotlines and information that they planned to pass out to the student body after the assembly. These cards had a tear-away piece that stated, "If I give you this card, it means that I need support." These Leadership students recognized the limitations of available resources in their community and chose to create resources of their own. After almost a year of collaboration and discussions around the social and political oppressions they faced on a regular basis, these students created alliances out of the pages of our self-written playbook of leadership and critical pedagogy.

The Finished Product

The assembly was nearly ninety minutes in length, by far our longest assembly ever hosted. The research on mental health and resources that our students presented was met with rapt attention and many questions. The video was applauded and comments of "that was dope!" rang through the air. Juan, the star of the video, received accolades for weeks, and our shy and quiet video editor became a mini celebrity on campus. Despite the concern of teachers that the informational cards would litter the campus like confetti, not one card was discarded. Instead, students slipped these leaves of hope between the folds of their wallets or into the empty space between their cell phone and its cover. Following the assembly, the students expressed that there was a chance they or someone they knew would need those cards in the future, and they did not want to lose them.

The students received honorable mention in the regional contest, and we dressed up to travel into the city to present our commercial and accept our award. In addition, many of the students chose to attend and walk a 5K for National Alliance on Mental Illness (NAMI) in the city early on a Saturday morning. These excursions, where students ventured outside of school were rare and unsupported by the district, meaning that the school was unable to provide transportation. Yet the students found a way to team up and attend anyway—another example of their passion, determination, and resourcefulness to achieve their goals, folding together into cranes of hope and healing.

17

The Elders' Pedagogy: Teaching as Survivance in the Academy

e alexander

Introduction: Setting the Stage

Like hooks, my upbringing led me to inherently understand Freire's work in ways that strengthened my professional praxis yet conflicted with the operative philosophy of colleagues.

Learning from My Elders

I am a country girl—raised by a mother from the Deep South, and a father from Coal Country. My parents taught me to take life slowly, cultivate authentic relationships, speak/act in earnest, and treat people with kindness. The values and modus operandi that I cultivated through my upbringing were reinforced in my early career: I received my master's degree in a therapeutic field, in a region away from Turtle Island, with Indigenous scholars and practitioners who wielded anti-colonialist frames that challenged presumed western norms of individualism, materialism, capitalism, and heteropatriarchy. My family and mentors instilled values in me that supported my successful pedagogical practice as a young educator:

1. *Humility*: No one, including leaders, is above scrutiny or making mistakes because we are all imperfect; we must make decisions in consultation with our communities.
2. *Community*: We should think and act with the needs and well-being of the collective in mind, because any one person's thoughts and actions will impact someone else.
3. *Organic intellectuals*: Knowledge, and the value and utility of it, can come from anyone—regardless of their social position and the origin of their learning.
4. *Ethics of care*: We should always act in ways that will support the well-being, safety, and happiness of everyone in our proximity whenever possible.

While these values underpinned my success with students, they also made me a target for misogynoir among coworkers. Misogynoir refers to specific ways that anti-Blackness and misogyny align to pathologize Black womxn (Bailey, 2014). To protect myself from this violence, I invoked an additional value from my Elders.

5. *Survivance*: Considering the subjugation that Black people continue to suffer in the west after half a millennium, we must continue to work toward living a fully actualized life of thriving. Doing so is resistance against western imaginations of our dehumanized purposes, conditions, and social positionings.

My Campus and Work Environment

I returned to Turtle Island after graduation and entered college administration at a tumultuous time in modern history. The region of the country to which I moved had long struggled with racial exclusion and settler violence, raced and classed segregation, a low-wage economy that progressively pushed people into poverty, and abuse of illicit substances. Amid these challenges came the rise of Black Lives Matter, and advocacy efforts to protect both lands from the North Dakota Pipeline and Dreamers from deportation. The region was in a crisis that I was completely unprepared to navigate: I had trained in a faraway place less touched by all of those issues, and was very unaware that the region was a quiet epicenter for them. Further, my university believed itself to be inclusive and progressive—despite being homogenous relative to its state population and unwilling to confront its history or culture of racism and classism. While it congratulated itself on facilitating advocacy efforts for sexual and gender diversity, it never initiated efforts toward intersectional justice in any form.

My position was in a very high-demand student affairs unit that supported approximately one-fifth of the institution's students. Such units at universities are known for being all-encompassing and requiring even entry-level professionals to quickly cultivate a wide repertoire of skills: budgeting, programming, training, et cetera. I had the task of administrating a cohort of first-year students that was even more affluent and less diverse than the overall campus population, and that was heavily involved in Greek Life. As a Black womxn, my position also included taken-for-granted invisible and emotional labor: mentoring and advising BIPOC students who were not under my purview; participating in initiatives beyond my portfolio because they were diversity-related; navigating misogynoir at the hands of anyone who was not a Black womxn as a part of workplace conditions, and so on. I was told that I was hired to enact social justice concepts through student-facing programs, training, and support. I later realized that I was a "diversity hire" because that campus unit previously had no Black womxn on its professional staff.

Practicing Liberation

My experiences with my students greatly contrasted those with my coworkers: despite being at the bottom of my unit's hierarchy for reasons that I explain later, I had complete agency with students as a supervisor—which provided me the opportunity to enact liberatory practices (hooks, 1994) in my work. Here, I detail my practices for dismantling power through four approaches that reflect lessons from my Elders: (1) being a student/teacher; (b) encouraging self-awareness; (c) centering care and authenticity; and (d) promoting community wellness.

Being a Student/Teacher

I came into my position with two understandings: (a) people should ever stop learning and (b) anyone has the potential to be a student/teacher of anyone else. Our academic years began with student staff training several weeks before all students arrived on campus. On day one with my team, I established our group dynamic as one of mutual teaching and learning—affirming that each member had years of experiential expertise, talents, interests, knowledge, and other assets to contribute to our collective strength. I also acknowledged that as their supervisor, I did not know everything, would make mistakes, and was doing my best in my role based on my knowledge and positioning in the world. I welcomed my teammates to advise me on how to do my job better, and to let me know if ever I was harmful. In alignment with being their student, I (a) progressively spoke less in group spaces to encourage communal sharing, (b) structured our training such that team members led different portions, and (c) primarily acted as facilitator and participant. In most cases, I only interjected to exercise authority in matters related to unit policy or procedures. However, even in such instances, I asked for assessment on whether policies and procedures were (a) effective in their purposes, (b) non-harmful to students, and (c) in support of our unit's proclaimed aims. I also welcomed feedback on my performance through anonymous surveys, comment boxes, white board polls, and the like.

These approaches in cultivating an environment wherein everyone was a student/teacher yielded a culture of trust within my team, and members carried this approach to sharing power into their relationships with our student cohort. Students felt as though they could come to my teammates and me in earnest with ideas, needs, and constructive feedback for collective growth. In concert with practicing self-awareness, I cultivated a close-knit community over time wherein students knew that as a positional authority in their on-campus lives, my intention was to lead them as informed by their input. Because I held students' voices in such high esteem, all of them became more confident in their own knowledge and abilities to contribute in our community as citizens of it. In short, my practice of being a student/teacher gave my students room to use their strengths in effecting changes that they wanted to see within our space.

Supporting Self-Awareness

While learning work duties and departmental protocols was essential for my teammates to be successful, I stressed to them that learning about ourselves was just as important if we were to collectively carry out duties in service to our community. I anchored developmental time in examining and sharing who we were with each other: motivations for working in our unit, family and community values and norms, personal (dis)likes, biases, and positionalities. Thus, we gave as much attention to self-exploration as we did to organizational knowledge. I emphasized the importance of us creating an ecosystem wherein we leveraged each other's strengths to resolve issues and reach goals. My aim was to support the team in understanding ourselves beyond performances of our positional power. As a result, we forged a bond of mutual care that resembled a familial unit before our students arrived on campus.

My team carried these practices and sentiments over into working with our cohort. We not only set expectations for keeping our community safe and respectful but provided students with opportunities to explore and utilize their strengths as assets in support of that goal. Many of my teammates repurposed our training activities for community-building, which encouraged students to explore who they were both in relation to their precollege environments and independent of them. By doing so, our students grew in several crucial ways. First, they realized that many of their behaviors and proclivities reflected their upbringing. Second, they realized that they did not have to remain the same people in college that they were prior to arriving and would also likely change throughout their careers. Third, they better understood how their social positionings informed their actions, and then consciously chose to act in support of their longer-term goals. For example, affluent students began interrogating the elitism that they learned in their families as they befriended lower-income peers, realizing that they were raised to demonize poverty and to not engage people with relatively less material wealth. The students in our cohort blossomed. They also shifted from seeing our program as an annoying college requirement to seeing it as a space wherein they could safely explore themselves and learn with others.

Centering Care and Authenticity

Care has always underpinned my promotion of self-awareness and authenticity in students/teachers. I wanted each of my students to live as healthy, happy, and full of a life as they desired, without impeding on others who were doing the same; encouraging them to do so was easiest for me through role modeling. From the beginning of my tenure, I shared about my motivations for working in our unit, goals for the cohort, values, norms, (dis)likes, biases, and positionalities—as a queer Black womxn, from a rural working-class background, and first-generation college attendee. Many aspects of who I am differed from those of my students: most of them were white legacy college attendees who were from the region in which we lived. Hence, I had to manage my authenticity against stereotypes that some students projected onto me. I was loud and assertive, and sometimes spoke with a Black Southern twang; I wore my hair in afro-natural styles; although I donned business attire as did my colleagues, I neither could help my body type nor felt compelled to apologize for it; and I engaged some aspects of Black culture that have been coded as negative throughout American history (e.g., listening to rap music) without shame. Yet I also embodied characteristics that challenged stereotypes of Blackness: I was a queer vegetarian whose hobbies included outdoor activities, wellness practices, arts and crafts, and board and video games.

I acknowledged all aspects of myself with my students, and sometimes made connections through them (e.g., debating with them whether Kendrick Lamar or

Tupac Shakur was the better rapper—and providing sociohistorical contexts to justify my points of argument). Doing so challenged my students to interrogate their implicit biases that coded certain aspects of my Blackness or Black womxnhood as negative and others as neutral or positive. I sometimes explained these social discourses to students if a developmental moment presented itself; other times, I simply lived my life. Regardless, students began to confront supremacist ideas with which they had been socialized throughout their lives to identify Black people, Black womxn, and performances of "the academic professional." These confrontations prompted their self-awareness and pursuit of more self-exploration.

While my team's work encouraged students to create environments of care and authenticity through pedagogical practices that I introduced in our trainings, my opportunities to enact both most often arose during conduct hearings after students had violated campus policies. Hearings allowed me to gain understanding of students' behaviors using a restorative care ethic. Alongside them, I explored harms that they contributed to in relation to policies; we did so with students' personhoods in mind to include their norms, social positions, personal needs, and relationships within the cohort. As often as possible, my sanctions included elements of self-exploration and community engagement as informed by students' strengths. Doing conduct in this manner demonstrated to them that I prioritized their authentic selves, self-awareness, awareness of their impacts on others, and community inclusion while holding them accountable for our collective wellness. I also used conduct to interrogate systemic oppression by examining how certain policies challenged or perpetuated disparities in criminalizing students by race, class, gender, and ability. Students came to understand that I cared about them as people within their subject contexts, even when they violated policies and caused harm.

I once had a hearing with a student whose behaviors had caused members of the cohort to feel unsafe. Upon meeting with them, I learned that they suffered addiction after learning to use drugs from their family to cope with anxiety and depression. We spoke openly about their dependency. To do so, I had to begin our conversation by letting them know: "If you're using, I'm not going to judge you … but your honesty will help me in best supporting you in whatever you need." Through their expressed desire to get sober and learn better coping skills, their sanction included participating in a recovery course and hosting a program of their choosing for our cohort. The student's program provided healthy coping skills for mental illness and was very useful for others later in the year who experienced anxiety or depression.

Promoting Communal Wellness

Collectively, my approaches to my work supported the wellness of the cohort: my teammates became invested in the health and safety of one another and our group because I prioritized doing so from the beginning of each academic year. Our students grew to enact lessons from my Elders—passed from me to my team, and from my team to the cohorts—to address community needs and concerns whenever they emerged. A shining example of this occurred after a pivotal political event. Its results caused a range of reactions throughout campus: a minority of students celebrated triumphantly while most experienced panic or shock. On their own, our students organized story circles wherein they sought to understand how each other's values and priorities informed their political choices and reactions to the event. Although hate crimes occurred off campus and tense discussions continued on campus through the week following the event, our cohort members who favored the result wanted to understand how they could support their peers who felt unsafe in light of it. I followed up with everyone throughout the week to offer support, while still managing my own emotions about the result. Our students never needed intervention from my team—but expressed concern for us and invited us to join their community dialogues.

Misogynoir and Survivance

My approaches allowed me to ascend over time into working more effectively than most of my colleagues with regards to cultivating students who coconstructed a learning community that valued mutual self-awareness, authenticity, care, and wellness. However, these approaches created tensions with my unit's professionals—namely its leadership—because they challenged the unit's corporate hierarchical culture. Moreover: while my approaches would have supported my coworkers in actualizing the values it espoused, they were taken as a threat specifically when they came from me and I was punished for enacting them in professional spaces. My differential treatment is misogynoir. Here, I brief how my practices created challenges with my colleagues.

Refusing to Be a Student/Teacher

During onboarding into my position, my supervisors were very welcoming and expressed that I should share ideas with them to support better unit outputs. I read this as their openness to being students as well as teachers in relation to supervisees. Believing their encouragements, I made suggestions for addressing structural oppressions in our protocols, policies, cultural norms, etc. that threatened our proclaimed ideals of social justice. I framed observations as concerns about community harm and suggestions as supporting community wellness.

My leadership's responses to my suggestions, and to those from other BIPOC colleagues of color, clarified that they did not view themselves as students but only as teachers. I was chastised about my tone and lack of collegiality and evaluated as subpar in professionalism—despite my success with students, invisible labor in supporting coworkers in their duties, and cultivation of campus networks beyond the requirements of my job. My senior leadership characterized me as "strong," "passionate," and "assertive." I never heard about their reactions to similarly constructive contributions from white colleagues at my level of our unit. However, I observed those colleagues holding temporary teacher roles while leadership held temporary roles as their students. Effectively, this created a dynamic wherein only white professionals could be teachers among professionals within our unit. My BIPOC coworkers suffered repercussions for offering constructive input, but repercussions seemed worse for BIPOC womxn than for BIPOC mxn. Supervisors sometimes extended invitations for advancement to these mxn; they punished BIPOC mxn by systematically excluding us from departmental processes—including those directly under our purviews—rapport-building office chats, mentorship, and networking.

Lacking Self-Awareness

In realizing that my supervisors did not want to cultivate an inclusive student/teacher environment among professionals, I also learned that they were not open to cultivating a deeper self-awareness in support of embodying their proclaimed values. Early in my tenure, I suggested that we engage in professional development to assess our biases, prejudices, and preferences—just as we required of our students through training, programs, and services. I posited that addressing structural oppressions in the unit required us to each understand our contributions to and disruptions of them, which in turn necessitated developmental self-work. Colleagues at my level of the unit agreed and welcomed this co-learning, but leadership argued it as "nonessential" because "there was not enough time" for it given "more pressing matters." Again, I was coded as "passionate" about social justice, "critical," and "an advocate." My "advocacy" came to a head several times when I took formal steps to address intersectional violence against me after my unit failed to do so. Because of my coexisting race, gender, class, regional origins, and body type, I was targeted multiple times by white colleagues about conditions wherein none of my coworkers was addressed. My aggressors should have taken my self-advocacy as a signal to learn about how they perpetuated oppression; instead, they reimagined my self-advocacy as offenses against them! During each ordeal, leadership supported them emotionally and professionally—treating them as victims and me as a disrupter, while neglecting my harm. Colleagues at my level of the unit confirmed their observation that our supervisors were discriminating against me. However, they were unwilling to openly act as allies for me lest they also became targets. Their silence, along with my aggressors' behaviors and leadership's alliance with them, pathologized me further as a Black womxn in my workplace.

Disregarding Communal Wellness, Care, and Authenticity

My leadership's refusal to be students/teachers or to develop self-awareness alongside their supervisees reflected their lack of care for our communal wellness, despite them having conditionally good relationships with select colleagues. I joined my unit in a junior position: reporting to a coworker than whom I had more years of professional experience, and than whom I earned less money, only because my master's degree was not in education. This positional and salary discrepancy persisted such that all but one of the BIPOC professionals were in junior positions, reporting to white-presenting coworkers than whom we had more diverse portfolios and practical knowledge because our credentials were less aligned with traditional pipelines into academic jobs. This raced and classed hierarchy led to the mistreatment of coworkers BIPOC professionals in our unit, and group distrust that eroded our sense of workplace community. Our leadership failed to address the structural violence and its impacts until white colleagues brought their attention to it; they never acknowledged that BIPOC colleagues had previously raised these concerns of disparity, and they never apologized for the harm that it caused us.

Additionally, their personal disregard of most non-white professionals signaled their lack of care for us as people such that authentic rapport was a nonstarter. My supervisors only ever engaged me at work about work: they never showed interest in my culture, hobbies, or lived experiences, as they did with white colleagues and masculine colleagues of Color. Other than following up about my ability to continue working after emotional or traumatic events, they also never inquired about my well-being or personal needs. Leadership's overall lack of interest in me led them to pathologize me such that they problematized almost all my actions—actions that reflected my authentic self as a person and a pedagogue. Because they minimized me in these ways, I had no cultural capital as a Black womxn and my coworkers never truly invested in me (e.g., their unwillingness to act as allies for me). At my departure from my role: I had received accolades and recognitions from the institution for my contributions, but almost no one took accountability for the harm they inflicted on me by way of misogynoir—and, no one ever really got to know me. The violence I suffered, all while practicing liberatory pedagogy with my students, was erased by hegemonic organizational practices that likely sustain the status quo of that unit: it continues to function, and I am still healing from my time there years later.

Reflecting: Survivance through Pedagogy

The harms that I suffered arose from tensions between my Elders' teachings manifested as pedagogical practices—teachings that align with those from hooks' childhood (1994)—and a white bourgeoisie culture in higher education administration that rejects those values. I led within my role through what Freire calls "authentic help" (as cited in hooks, 1994, p. 54) by uplifting my students as organic intellectuals, from whom I also learned, to understand and support the development of a healthy community. I also did my work with a lens of "mutual humanization" (Freire, 1999, p. 56) through two of hooks' (1994) pedagogical practices, and encouraged my colleagues to adopt them when working with each other:

1. *Engaged pedagogy*: commit[ting] to self-actualization that promotes the educator's own well-being, as requisite to empowering students, and
2. *Transformative pedagogy*: building community in learning spaces to both support openness and honor each learner's voice

Presuming that these practices were ubiquitous in academia, I did not anticipate that they would make me a target of misogynoir by educators! Nor did I anticipate that my Elders' teachings would conflict with my unit's culture such that my practices would become forms of survivance in that space. That I experienced violence for encouraging liberatory practices, while leadership preached those practices as integral in our work with students, suggests that my supervisors viewed our unit as a hierarchy wherein they were fully actualized experts whose roles were to deposit knowledge

(Freire, 1999) into everyone else as their less-actualized subordinates. Further, that they rewarded white colleagues and masculine colleagues of Color for contributing their voices to professional discourses, while punishing Womxn of Color for doing the same, suggests that they viewed us as their absolute inferiors. Nevertheless, I persisted in engaging pedagogy beyond their imaginations in ways that humanized everyone within my purview and promoted their collective wellness, while resisting my own dehumanization. That is survivance.

18

Between Wholeness and Restoration

dorothy vaandering

My biggest fear in life is to cause others harm. Yet, I know that in spite of this fear, without a doubt, I will do so. Along with everything beautiful that makes me human, this is a given. It comes from the opportunity I've been granted in my createdness to be free.

My next biggest fear in life is to be harmed. Yet, I know that in spite of this fear, without a doubt, I will be harmed. Along with everything beautiful that makes others human, this is a given. It comes from the opportunity we've been granted in our createdness to be free.

Many philosophers have written about this over time. Rabbi Sacks (Hynes, 2016) said in response to people's propensity to blame religion for violence that the cause of violence in the world is not the system, but the human heart. It is the human heart that creates systems and it is the human heart that can change those systems. Poignantly, Jean Vanier (2008), who posthumously was found to have caused great harm to those under his care, harm that he never acknowledged or addressed, perhaps was grappling with this dark side of humanity when he said, "I believe every act of violence is also a message that needs to be understood … We must ask: 'Where is the violence coming from? What is its meaning?' "

Out of my search to be less inclined to cause harm and to find healing, I have encountered and then embraced restorative justice as a "way of being" because at its core it seeks to address the impact of harm for all involved. From this experience, I have felt its mystery as my fear has been diminished and my curiosity piqued. What is it about restorative justice that makes this possible? What is it about its integration into education that is transformative? How can it be a critical pedagogy for healing?

Practice does not exist without theory or outside of one's worldview. However, for many, theory and worldview reside in our un/subconscious and we make assumptions about what draws us to certain practices. As an academic, I have a responsibility to ponder and grapple with this phenomenon and then make the insights practical. This act of praxis—"action *and* reflection *for* transformation" (Freire, 1970, 51, emphasis added)—guides my search for what lies at the root of restorative justice and describes my move to engage in critical pedagogies of healing that impact individuals and communities and revives our collective connections. In particular in this chapter,

I describe how restorative justice as healing praxis challenges me to confront the systemic injustice of colonization, my role in it, and responsibility for creating spaces/ communities that are free from harm.

What Is Restorative Justice?

There are many variations of restorative justice and restorative justice education. For greatest clarity and to recognize their similarities and differences, a comprehensive understanding of *justice* is required as a first step for ensuring it is not coopted to support agendas intrinsically designed to benefit some and burden others (Vaandering, 2011). In the *Little Book of Restorative Justice Education* (Evans and Vaandering, 2016), we write:

> *Justice* honors the inherent worth of all and is enacted through relationship. This is evident when it is used in the terms social justice or primary justice. [Justice] embraces respect, dignity, and the protection of rights and opportunities for all and exists in all relationships when no one is wronged. This is a foundational definition that supports a secondary or judicial definition where justice is understood mainly as a response to harm or crime.

Without explicitly identifying primary justice as the condition where the inherent dignity, worth, and interconnectedness of all human beings with each other and their environments is respected, secondary justice in its efforts to address harm or crime loses its reference point or purpose (Wolterstorff, 2006; Vaandering, 2011). Secondary justice then focuses on laws broken and punishment, where punishment never satisfies, and those harmed are left alone under the assumption that punishments are the required response. It promotes exclusion from community for those directly impacted.

In defining *restorative*, we go on to say:

> *Restorative*, as an adjective for both primary and secondary justice, describes how an individual's or group's dignity, worth, and interconnectedness will be nurtured, protected, or reestablished in ways that will allow people to be fully contributing members of their communities. (p. 7)

When using *restorative*, as an adjective for both primary and secondary justice, we accept that justice is a state of wholeness where people's dignity, worth, and interconnectedness are nurtured; it is "present in social relationships when people are enjoying what they have a right to … present in social relationships when no one is wronged" (Wolterstorff, 2006). *Restorative* also acknowledges that between wholeness and restoration there is breakdown, people and their environments are wronged and harmed.

In restorative justice, I found solace for my deep desire to not cause harm for I recognized that when I did, I was upset because at my core I knew I was diminishing another human being in a way I didn't want to be diminished. Yet in causing harm or being harmed, restorative justice was telling me I did not have to fear being excluded, but rather could look forward to belonging.

Pulling back the curtain on what lies between wholeness and restoration in what follows, I describe the invitation restorative justice extends to move toward discomfort and away from fear allowing healing to become reality.

Brokenness?

Like bell hooks (1994),

> I came to theory young, when I was still a child … I came to theory because I was hurting … I came to theory desperate, wanting to comprehend—to grasp what was happening around and within me. Most importantly, I wanted to make the hurt go away. I saw in theory then a location for healing. (p. 59)

Tragedy and trauma have not been a part of my life, and as such I have and continue to live a very privileged life. As a child raised by immigrant parents struggling to eke out a living as dairy farmers in southwestern Ontario in the 1950s and 1960s, I knew that my six siblings and I were loved and that my parents had devoted all their efforts to being sure our needs were met. I also knew this was a faith response for them, an expression of thanks to God who created this world and was taking care of them. So then, where was my hurt that drove me to theory young?

Included in their gratitude and commitment, my parents lived in fear that they were disappointing God, that their children would reject God, and that heaven would be denied them. This resulted in adamant commitment to their perceptions of "right and wrong" and their constant struggle within their church community. As a child, I watched intently as my parents fought, grieved, and joined groups that found solutions in splitting the community and rejecting/banning members that did not comply. As my siblings and I grew, that struggle became part of our family structure, and when we did not comply, the solution was threat of banishment, of not being welcome at home. Though I knew my parents meant well, this created pain and alienation. As an adolescent, I was desperate to comprehend the grown-up conflict surrounding me and to find a better way. As an adult, restorative justice has brought understanding and is now deepened as I realize the significance of identifying what is being restored when I engage with its practices.

Freire's (1970) concept of humanization made sense to me: humanity's ontological vocation to become more "fully human" implied that our current state is limited. I interpreted this as "brokenness" with a need to return to our potential—people with dignity, worth, and interconnectedness. Recently, however, I have come to see my assumption of "brokenness" as perpetuating an understanding that human beings are objects in need of fixing. Freire's intention was to move people from being objectified and manipulated by oppressive power, to being subjects who are capable of making choices to be more fully human. In the context of pandemic and a renewed civil rights movement, wholeness has taken on new meaning for me. Bigelow (2020) in an article aptly titled "The Freedom *to Harm vs. the* Freedom *from Harm*" along with Sacks

(Hynes, 2016) who identified the human heart as the source of violence, remind me that in addition to human beings having dignity, worth, and interconnectedness, they also have the capacity to choose selfishly or what they do not intend. This critical element describes Freire's call to each of us to take up our vocation of becoming more fully human. It also is at the core of what Paul (57 CE), Hebrew theologian and academic, exclaims when he says, "I have the desire to do what is good, but I cannot carry it out. For I do not do the good I want to do, but the evil I do not want to do" (Rom. 7:18–20).

When I am whole, I stand at the precipice of being able to choose either to work for myself and others to be free *to* cause harm, or for myself and others to be free *from* being harmed or harming others. I become more fully human when I choose to nurture environments free *from* harm because I am engaging with my interconnected nature, to *nurture* dignity and worth for others; I am choosing humanization. When I choose personal gain, I am choosing to be free *to* harm, engaging with my interconnected nature to undermine the dignity, worth, and connectedness of others; I am choosing dehumanization. Simply wanting to make the choice to live for the freedom from harm, however, doesn't ensure that I will do it perfectly. In fact, another characteristic of being human is our inability to choose consistently. But *knowing* that I can be intentional about this allows me to work for healing and restoration when I slip into causing harm or have been harmed.

Between wholeness and restoration is *the choice to cause harm and the capacity to be harmed.* Restorative justice is a way of being that recognizes these characteristics of humanity so that when we cause harm, or when we have been harmed, *it is also human to need the opportunity to rectify the impact of that harm.*

Fixing or Healing?

Though it is easy to dismiss one's intent as *semantics* when using different terminology, the words I use reveal much about my frame of reference. By latching onto *brokenness* as a condition of humanity, I was inadvertently reinforcing the perspective that humans are objects. If I am broken, then I need to be *fixed.* When I explored other contexts in which I might use the term, I realized most related to objects—my car is broken, the glass broke, my cellphone is broken; I rarely use it to describe living things—I say the hydrangea bush is wilting, my dog is sick, Joe has cancer.

What encouraged me to use the term *broken* to describe people? I am coming to realize this has come from living a privileged life in a Western world grounded in empirical evidence as the primary way of understanding life. It comes from a culture that elevates a healthy (!) economy (note the organic nature of this phrase) as our common goal, where people are valued primarily as commodities along with natural resources that can contribute to an accumulation of wealth, where *growth* is about quantity, not quality (Yunkaporta, 2019). It is also a term that feeds a deficit mindset where we are encouraged to think we can "fix" ourselves or more significantly, others. I was brought up short on this when reading Adair and Howell's (2007) list of characteristics of dominant and oppressed groups. Each characteristic of the dominant group exuded confidence in feeling they could *fix* others, while those in minoritized groups had absorbed that they were lacking or broken, unable to contribute to dominant society. As a member of this dominant group, I now see that my Westernized teacher preparation included encouragement to consider what I could do *for* students and others in my community. Schooling endorsed the dominant agenda to elevate Western thought and ways of being by seeing some as broken and needing to be fixed—by me.

Inherent in the term *fixing* is complete dependence on external sources, experts who provide repair, either sought out by myself for my own repair or imposed by others who notice my deficiencies. Interconnectedness is ignored and my capacity to know myself is diminished, robbing me of my inherent dignity and worth. My organic humanity with its capacity to *heal* is diminished. *Healing and woundedness* are terms that recognize life as being multifaceted and interconnected, terms that know that both our external and internal environments are critical to our health. At one point, I called my adherence to the term *broken* in the context of restorative justice a "theory of brokenness" (Vaandering, 2006). In this chapter, I consider how this perspective comes from that place of privilege that defaults to objectifying life looking for quick fixes. I move to wondering if "a theory of woundedness and healing" is more apt. Or could it be that "a theory of harm" better acknowledges that it is our capacity to choose to cause harm and our capacity to be harmed that lies between wholeness and restoration and is the reason restorative justice is found to be effective?

So What? A Critical Pedagogy for Healing

I am a white, privileged educator of European descent who benefits from past and present-day colonialism. I have felt it, I feel it; I have seen it, I see it; I have done it, I do it—and it is because of restorative justice that I have become viscerally aware of what a colonized education is and how I have both experienced and contribute to it. In Canada, colonialism, a system where outsiders decide to settle among and take control of the original peoples and lands for their own benefit, has earned the official descriptor of "genocide." It has been proven that the federal, provincial, and territorial governments explicitly intended, pre and post Confederation, to wipe out Indigenous peoples and their cultures through death or assimilation (Sinclair, 2011). Education was one of the key vehicles through which colonialism was carried out. Residential schools (1831–1996) tore Indigenous children away from their families and communities as a result of laws decreeing mandatory attendance (Woolford & Benvenuto, 2015). Mainstream public schools for non-Indigenous children remaining with family and community, were given curriculum explicitly designed to leave out any reference to First Peoples other than stereotypical details characterizing them as uncivilized, unsophisticated, and/or savage. Conveniently ignored was any reference to treaty agreements and the Canadian governments' and citizens' (ir)responsibility in carrying these out. Combined, both types of schooling resulted in education as a colonizing tool employed to dehumanize people for the purpose of benefiting a few (Sinclair, 2011).

I am a product of an incomplete and biased curriculum that left me with a perspective that Canada was a land of hope and opportunity for people like my parents, and that Indigenous peoples were ungrateful for all the gifts bestowed on them by a peace-loving country and its citizens. My very DNA, which can be traced for generations to Dutch ancestry, leans toward being comfortable as a dominator. For years, I was oblivious to this, not needing to wake up each day conscious of my skin color or heritage, always looking over my shoulder to be sure I was safe, and never feeling out of place in a classroom as a student or teacher because my story wasn't told. As a result, I perpetuated this thinking and way of being, *simply by being me.*

And then graciously, while learning with my students one day, I heard this quote from an Inuit guest in our class:

> I am not saying that any of this is your fault or even that your grandparents did any of it. I'm saying that it happened, and it happened on your people's watch. You're the one who benefited from it. It doesn't matter that you're way downstream from the actual events. You're still drinking the water.
>
> (Lakota Elder Dan in Nerburn, 2009, p. 148)

How do I stop drinking the water?

Ironically, though I came to restorative justice through Western faith-based initiatives, its humanizing principles have brought me to the humble, persistent, resilient modeling of the First Peoples of this land, who I now know deserve the credit for keeping restorative justice alive through horrific circumstances. From them, I see a commitment to living free *from* harm, which contrasts starkly with prominent oppressive pedagogies that are committed to living free *to* harm.

So then, how is restorative justice, grounded in a theory of harm, a critical pedagogy for healing? Kincheloe (2004) defines critical pedagogy as "*the concern with transforming oppressive relations of power in a variety of domains that lead to human oppression*" (p. 45). Restorative justice leads me to turning toward myself and the institutions I am comfortable in and seeing how my/our choices, past and present, continue to benefit a few and burden many (Vaandering, 2010). Restorative justice education can best be characterized as (1) creating just and equitable learning environments, (2) nurturing healthy relationships, and (3) addressing harm and transforming conflict (Evans & Vaandering, 2016, p. 5). It does this first of all by explicitly acknowledging that all human beings and their environments are worthy and interconnected, deserving of dignity regardless of who they are or what they have done and then, allowing this to inform all interactions within the educational experience—curriculum, pedagogy, school policy, the physical layout of the school, caregiver–school relationships, relationships with colleagues, students, et cetera. This occurs primarily through a pedagogy where all involved in the school can share, be heard, and explicitly respond. At present, circle dialogue and open-ended question frameworks best characterize restorative justice pedagogy.[1] Pranis (2017) likens these as opportunities for honing our skills for deep listening[2] (Dobson, 2014) that will nurture communities and cultures characterized as "free *from* harm."

This becomes our way of being and will be seen in every action and word, the small things as well as the more complex concerns that arise. The following are examples:

- Students learning addition, invited to share what is happening in terms of their understanding, never made to feel inadequate or superior, simply part of a group that is learning.
- Educators seek support from colleagues describing what is happening, what impact it is having and their needs for moving on. They are heard, not responded to with microaggressions that dismiss them as being inadequate.
- Parents at odds with each other when they pick up their children after school invited by the administrator to a facilitated dialogue.
- The student loudly mocking peers they perceive to be "gay" is not sent home for three days because policy indicates that that is the required response. Rather the class is invited to have a series of circle dialogues on what allows them to work at their best in the class, what happens to undermine cohesiveness,.
- Educators who recognize their potential for implicit bias use circles to get to know the needs and strengths of all students regardless of race, gender, religion, and class.
- Educators encourage youth and community leadership, stepping aside and authentically allowing others to design activities that would meet their needs.[3]

As I began to consciously engage this critical pedagogy for healing in daily experiences of being an educator, the opportunities for turning toward the reality of colonization began to present themselves. I was practicing making choices in small decisions so that as my colleagues, students, caregivers, and neighbors continue expressing their experiences of systemic injustices, I am better able to listen deeply, accepting, not fearing, the discomfort of knowing I am part of the problem. Through the guidance of restorative justice principles and practices, I move toward holding myself accountable and taking responsibility for repairing harm I cause and confronting harm I see others experience. We cannot change what we do not know. Restorative justice education quite literally creates spaces for authentic communal knowing and being where sharing and listening to stories will reveal what we do not know. At this nexus point, we engage in becoming more fully human, as we are invited to choose to be free *from* harm and causing harm, where we honor each individual's capacity to express their needs in a communal context, and where community listens and responds with support that will nurture healing rather than hinder it.

As the words of Lakota Elder Dan (Nerburn, 2009) woke me up to the reality that I am drinking the water downstream of colonization, the insights of an Elder in northern Ontario provide support for how I can respond. "You don't measure progress in inches and feet, exclusively … but in degrees … the first thing that you need to do, when you change, is you need to point your head in a different direction, before you've taken a single step" (Kirlew in Rigden & Ballantyne, 2018). Engaging in restorative justice education as a critical pedagogy for healing, and identifying what lies between wholeness and restoration, takes away debilitating fear and replaces it with anticipation—because my head is pointed in a different direction.

19

Fraying Lives: Toward a Pedagogy of Healing

Gregory Tewksbury

The pandemics of coronavirus, systemic racism, wealth inequality, and the climate crisis are evocatively described by Arundhati Roy as a "portal" (April 3, 2020). The "portal" she contends can be a "gateway between one world and the next." We are positioned at this juncture, a transition between an insidious market rationale striving to dominate more and more aspects of life—what Paulo Freire (1998) calls the "scourge of neoliberalism, with its inflexible negation of the right to dream differently" (p. 23)—and the need to "reimagine everything" as Grace Lee Boggs (2012) calls us to do. This is our task, to create new narratives of healing. Freire elaborates,

> Narratives of liberation are always tied to the people's stories, and what stories we choose to tell, and the way in which we decide to tell them, form the provisional basis of what a critical pedagogy of the future might mean.
>
> (Freire 1993, p. xii)

A critical pedagogy of healing is situated here to create and embody processes of inquiry, communities of support and solidarity that will allow us to tell the truth about what this society has done to its people and communities, so that we can imagine ourselves and communities differently. "The time has come for a new dream. That's what being a revolutionary is" (Boggs, 2012).

The theme of healing affords us an entry point to understanding and coming to grips with a wide array of deep-seated social, cultural, and psychological needs long ignored, erased, and marginalized in the current era of violence, othering, and uncertainly. Further, a pedagogy of healing provides a window, when understood critically, that enables us to envision broader and more humane social and historical relationships: how we have been injured and what cultural actions and contexts are needed to address the complexity of these wounds.

In this essay, I argue that the elements of a critical pedagogy of healing are already implicit in Freire's writing and practice. The forms of knowledge and "cultural actions" that engage with issues of social and economic inequality, racism, and marginalization vital to the formation of a pedagogy of healing were already present in Freire's literacy work as seen in the "cultural circles." In his literacy work, organizing land reform, and voter mobilizations, cultural circles were spaces for community affirmation as well as learning to analyze common problems and craft collective solutions (Freire, 1974, p. 81). Ginwright (2010) captures a vital aspect of this pedagogical approach: "Healing is like a dance between the individual and the community … In black culture, community is about fostering hope and justice. Community can be an important buffer against trauma and can promote the healing necessary for activism" (p. 77).

This chapter illuminates a new rendering of Freire's insights, one that pays careful attention to and critiques popularized notions of individualized self-care with the urgency and necessity of developing a social analysis. Freire calls to us to "re-invent" his pedagogy and project. This challenge is as relevant as it is urgent today. The path and challenge that Freire, and Antonia Darder among others, set out is to see a critical pedagogy of healing "as a road yet to be made, which because it is unknown, must be traced out step by step in our organic relationship with the world" (Darder, 2020, p. 45).

This chapter develops the four tenets of a critical pedagogy of healing—reflection as enabling entry into understanding; analysis of social relations with sustaining curiosity; creative agency, to transform oppressive relations; and the construction of a "relational home." We can create a "relational home" where our injuries don't have to be hidden, and they can be worked through and transformed together. Injury, analysis, healing, and action are nurtured in the organic way Darder notes through a pedagogy of healing.

Building on Patel (2016), I liken critical pedagogy to her view of research where "core to this framing is learning as a constant becoming and unbecoming, a constant inquiry and coordinate taking" (p. 77). Ai-Jen Poo, Director of the National Domestic Workers Alliance, describes this creative tension and importance of keeping this formative tension in view and in our practice:

> We have tools to heal from trauma as individuals. And we have some tools to change policy, systems, and culture. But rarely do the two meet; … And when we're trying to heal as individuals we often attempt to do so in a vacuum, as if the therapist's office or the meditation cushion were islands in a sea devoid of systems of power and privilege.
>
> (in Haines, 2019, p. x)

This awareness of and commitment to "inquiry and coordinate taking" offers a path to critical pedagogy that can shift the narrative of fraying lives by recognizing the connections between individual problems and experiences and the social context in which they are embedded.

With the collective trauma that the nation is facing, "we must ask how do we make sense of pain, wounds and injuries felt by so many but impact[ing] communities of color disproportionally … We must acknowledge our pain and embrace hope at the same time" (powell, June 2, 2020). This tension centers my analysis of and reflections on how to best understand what a critical pedagogy of healing can mean and how to see it as an "educative practice" (Freire, 1998, p. 21).

A Pedagogy of Healing as Educative Practice

Freire refuses to see people's stories as static and history as closed to possibility. He offers guideposts to "call us out beyond ourselves … of our being as something constructed socially and historically" (Freire, 1998, p. 25). When involved in the complex process of naming and working through the trauma, hurts, and wounds inflicted by oppressive relations, "presence," a concept central to his later work, provides a bridge between individual experience and the ways we locate it in the social contexts of our lives. Rather than seeing these domains as separate, Freire calls to us to create expressions, narratives, and creative acts that will enable a " 'presence' that can reflect upon itself, that knows itself as a *presence*, that can intervene, transform, can speak of what it does, but that can also take stock of, compare, evaluate, give value to, decide to break with and dream" (Freire 1998, p. 26). Angela Davis (2019) offers a powerful historical insight complementing Freire:

> It is dangerous not to recognize that as we struggle we presage the world to come, and the world to come should be one where we acknowledge the collectivity, connections and relations and joy … If we don't start practicing collective self-care now, there is no way to imagine much less reach a time of freedom.

Naming the places of creative ferment where a "presence" of healing can emerge offers an outline of pedagogy that enables a new narrative of self and social transformation—the core "educative practices" of a pedagogy of healing. These creative locations are grounded through dialogue and problematizing everyday experiences, where people make sense, heal, and act on the underlying conditions that led to the wounds. As Haines (2019) argues in her insightful work, *The Politics of Trauma*, "If we do not understand and integrate the shaping power of institutions, social norms, economic systems, oppression and privilege alongside the profound influences of family and community, we will not fully understand trauma or how to heal from it. We will not understand how to prevent it" (p.11).

Educative practice, then, is a primary occupation in the *Pedagogy of Freedom*. This "educative practice" has core elements of an emerging pedagogy of healing: critical sensibilities, or the shaping of curiosity that problematizes the everyday text of one's experience. Further, how a critical pedagogy of healing embraces and is dialectically transformed by the needs and rigor of healing.

Critical Dispositions and Core Sensibilities of a Pedagogy of Healing

Curiosity and problematization are critical dispositions and core sensibilities of consciousness vital to a pedagogy of healing. First, is the centrality of curiosity—what Freire (1998) calls the "flame of resistance … that sharpens their capacity to risk, for adventure, so as to immunize themselves against the banking system" (p. 32). This constitutes the heart of practices animating the pedagogy of healing, and it applies to more than just the school or classroom setting. As we struggle to think and reflect on the texture of our lives and the ways we can be trapped by the forces of silencing and oppressive relations, curiosity as a "flame" can enable us to insert ourselves into a permanent process of searching and healing.

Curiosity, then, must reach beyond the latest new thing or trend. It requires a different disposition, a critical sensibility. "Curiosity as a restless questioning, as movement toward the revelation of something hidden, as a question verbalized or not, as search for clarity, as a moment of attention, suggestion and vigilance, constitute an integral part of the phenomenon of being alive" (Freire, 1998, pp. 37–8). Curiosity as a knowing practice of aliveness embodies a disposition toward personal life that enables a criticality toward social and historical experience. Criticality activates a stance "to ask questions, and to call into question." But it is also the curiosity embedded in our unfolding and unfinished subjectivity—the knowledge we have of ourselves as persons who can be more than we are at this moment. "For we have built into all of us," Audre Lorde writes (1988 p. 54), "old blueprints of expectations and responses, old structures of oppression, and these must be altered at the same time as we alter the living conditions which are the result of those structures."

Problematization is a key way that people's curiosity enables their freedom and provides the opportunity to engage their own history and the social world in which they find themselves and in which they struggle to transform. "Problematization is so much a dialectic process that it would be impossible for anyone to begin it without becoming involved in it" (Freire, 1974, p. 153). Problematizing dialogue breaks the crust of being a spectator in one's own life. "In entering into their own world, people become aware of their manner of acquiring knowledge and realize the need to know even more" (Freire, 1974, p. 155). The critical self-consciousness emerging out of this process of reflection is a powerful and necessary grounding for constructing the threads of a storyline for a pedagogy of healing. Problem-posing around the potent narrative threads or generative themes "inaugurates" the dialogue vital to the formation of a sustaining educative practice—enabling a confidence and faith that things can be different and we can make them so. In this way, problematization underscores the restorative project driving a pedagogy of healing for self and social determination: A pedagogy of healing, then, enables us to figure out collectively how to think, imagine, analyze, and transform in the face of the uncertainty, hurt, injuries and precarious relation of domination we face as individuals, in our communities, and society.

Freire as an Intersectional Theorist

A central pillar of Freire's pedagogy offers a path and a practice to visualizing and locating the "sites of these shaping institutions." Freire (1970) explains, "The investigation of what I have termed the people's 'thematic universe'—the complex of their 'generative themes'—inaugurates the dialogue of education as the practice of freedom" (p. 86). A generative theme captures a central dynamic of an issue or period and affords the opportunity to see interconnections among aspects of social reality often hidden or seen as distinct. In this way, the generative work of critical pedagogy is to be the connective tissue of the lived experience of oppression. In this light, Patricia Hill Collins observes, "While not typically categorized this way, the *Pedagogy of the Oppressed* can be read as a core text for intersectionality … Freire rejects a class-only analysis of power relations in favor of the more robust power-laden language of the 'oppressed' … invoking 'intersecting inequities' of class, race, ethnicity, age, religion and citizenship" (Collins & Bilge, 2016, pp. 160–1). Some of the main themes of our era that are fulminating injury are outlined below.

This reading of Freire as an intersectional theorist provides a way to conceptualize the forces of injury that shape sites of harm and proliferate social relations of fraying deepening both our grasp of the wounds and enriching our ability to identify core social relations. These are the "dynamic and interconnected relations of power" (Tewksbury, 2016).An important and often forgotten corrective to critical analysis, one that Freire strove to always keep in sight, is a focus on theory and practice of change. Awareness of the split between individual isolated suffering—with its attendant trauma—and the need for "collective self-care" that Angela Davis emphasizes is an important step in "unseating" systemic forms of oppression.

There are many examples of the dynamics that lead to fraying lives or what Glaude (2020) calls the layering of catastrophe. The Poor People's Campaign (poorpeoplescampaign.org) report, *The Souls of Poor Folk* (April 2018), coauthored with the Institute for Policy Studies, analyzes four key areas of "dynamic and interconnected relations of power": Poverty and Inequality; the War Economy and Militarism; Ecological Devastation and the Denial of Health Care; and Systemic Racism. Here I will address two of them, though, of course, they are all interconnected.

Suffice to say that inequality in wealth and income has dramatically increased in the last decade. In New York State, from 1979 to 2012, income for the top 1 percent grew by 307 percent while the income for the bottom 99 percent grew by only 8 percent. On the national level, three men, Bezos, Gates, and Buffett own as much wealth as the bottom half of all Americans. During the pandemic, Bezos from Amazon took in $13 billion in one day! Stiglitz remarks, "What happens when a society's wealth distribution becomes lopsided? … Growing inequality is the flip side of something else: shrinking opportunity" (May, 2011). The power messages of neoliberal psychology seek to blame and individualize "failures." A critical politics of care evokes a necessary corrective, what "Young (2006) calls the "social connection model" of responsibility that focuses on eliminating the background conditions of structural injustice" (Ghazavi, 2020, 49).

In this moment of systemic racism nationwide, uprisings have been sparked by the continuous murders of Black, Indigenous, and People of Color (BIPOC). Yet, with the entire country seeing the knee on the neck of George Floyd for eight minutes and forty-six seconds and the cry again of "I Can't Breath!" something happened—wounds were opened anew and the crust of white supremacy and indifference was shattered in an unexpected way across the country and around the world.

Breonna Taylor (say her name), a young emergency medical technician (EMT) risking her life in the midst of the pandemic is shot dead in her own home, by police with "no-knock." We suffer with her partner unable to save her. The wound is opened deeper and we relive and comprehend how deep infectious and systemic racism goes. Many days passed and the police officers were not held to account for her murder.

Then around the same time Ahmaud Arbery, a known jogger who is Black was hunted and shot in the back. The killers went home and the police in Georgia did nothing until a video emerged. Protests erupted; scrutiny brought action. It was later revealed in the transcript the killer said, "Yea, we got that f——ing N——." While this is horrifying in 2020, it is not surprising and perhaps too easy to denounce the bold old-time racism by saying, "I am not like that." The deeper work resides for whites in the America around what Wendell Berry calls *The Hidden Wound*, "I have been unwilling until now to open in myself what I have known all along to be a wound—a historical wound, prepared centuries ago to come alive in me at my birth like a hereditary disease and to be augmented and deepened by my life" (Berry, 2010, p. 3). How do we as individuals and communities heal? In the aftermath of the murder of George Floyd, William Barber, cochair of the Poor People's Campaign, wrote, "If we take time to listen to this nation's wounds, they tell us where to look for hope. The hope is in the mourning and the screams, which make us want to rush from this place. There is a sense in which right now we must refuse to be comforted too quickly" (May 30, 2020). The impulse "to be comforted and move quickly" is the default reaction to an extended consideration of the uncomfortable historical truths of systemic racism, settler colonialism, wealth inequality, and climate change.

Images for a Critical Pedagogy of Healing

The conceptual and practical work that constitutes a pedagogy of healing has many different influences and tributaries of knowledge and wisdom. Freire's praxis is rooted in adult literacy and cultural circles that facilitate what Maxine Greene (2009) calls "contextualized storytelling by which … the influences of social life on their becoming, of race and gender, of traditions of the stories told to them" (p. 143). Included in these stories are the ones of family strength and resilience, joy and suffering as well as the dominant narratives teaching people their place and aspirations. Darder (1996) offers a vantage point to apprehend the complexity of a language of healing originating from culture. We must "hold a concept of culture as an enacted phenomenon. It is dynamic and occurs only with the process of human interaction, within the context of community and relationships … we must recognize how the link between culture and power is at work in the production and legitimation of knowledge (p. 15). To trace the emerging shape of a critical pedagogy of healing, we need to attend to the creative expressions and formative acts of knowing that signal the way the dominant narratives—the stories—are told to us about who we are, our place in the world and what we are capable of.

Certainly for me as a white man of working-class background, this has been a struggle sometimes rich and powerful and often times invoking troubling threads in my life's journey. As Darder writes, "[our] own personal struggles—particularly for those of us from working-class and racialized populations—are as demanding as the larger societal struggles we wage" (Darder, 2020, p. 65).

A critical pedagogy of healing deepens a person's capacity for self-reflection, to analyze and sustain curiosity of the social forces shaping their world. This capacity building—the radical notion of collective self-care—is vital to knowing oneself and one's struggles and being able to act to both change the world, know oneself more deeply and to change oneself. This knowledge born in struggle against oppression offers vital insights and avenues for the restoration of our humanity and relations with nature, while we struggle together with the shards of oppression planted inside us. The living practice of a pedagogy of healing has taken place around specific injuries that need to be seen as an intersectional whole and worked with as such. In her work with many women-led people of color organizations, Haines has utilized many of the approaches offered in this essay. Ai-Jen Poo remarks on the need for "unprecedented cultural conversation and truth-telling about the reality of sexual violence (police brutality) [that can] move us towards healing and long-overdue solutions" (p. xi).

This process is what Margaret Walker (2000) calls "healing and annealing," where annealing is a process where a substance—metal or glass—is heated and allowed to cool slowly in order to remove its internal stresses and to toughen it. At its core, this is what a pedagogy of healing strives for in forging new knowledges and practices, and a new self and society.

A recent article in the *New York Times* (Whitfield, 2020, p. D3) titled "Black Yoga Collective Makes Space for Healing" offers insight about what it means to practice curiosity, problematization, and generative themes. Before the collective, an African American woman reports going into yoga classes that were white spaces where she received an icy reception. "The spiritual component was totally missing. It wasn't about healing. It felt like everyone was there just to show off how much more stretchier they were than another person." Collective healing is alienated in this white space, as it enacts its unquestioned and assumed superiority. Opening up space to dialogue led to the formation of a Black collective where after yoga sessions people broke bread and talked about issues like police brutality and racism. Haines states that after doing such work for more than two decades, "I believe we cannot heal, or help others to heal deeply, unless we integrate into this work an analysis of social conditions and how they shape us" (p. 59). This yoga collective is an example of what she calls "sites of change"—moving from a framework of power-over to a power-with orientation.

This development in critical pedagogy is captured beautifully by Cities of Peace cofounder Aurora Levins Morales (2016) in her statement on Towards Reflection, Transformation and Healing:

> It is part of our task as revolutionary people, people who want deep-rooted, radical change, to be as whole as it is possible for us to be. This can only be done if we face the reality of what oppression really means in our lives, not as abstract systems subject to analysis, but as an avalanche of traumas which leave a wake of devastation in the lives of real people who nevertheless remain human, complex, and full of possibility.

This sentiment and its evolving practices capture the imagery of activism, healing, and pedagogy articulated by Grace Lee Boggs (2012):

> We have to do what I call visionary organizing. We have to see every crisis as both a danger and an opportunity. It's danger because it does so much damage to our

> lives, to our institutions, to all that we have expected. But it is also an opportunity for us to become creative; to become the new kind of people that are needed at such a huge period of transition (p. 44).

As we continue to create a critical pedagogy of healing, we need to find ways to keep the initiation to visionary organizing open. We want this to be as alive for others as it is for us. This bridging work across differences must become "a fund of necessary polarities between which our creativity can spark like a dialectic" (Lorde, 1984, p. 111). This is the ethical imperative to liberate us from the particular shackles of our histories and to offer a protocol, a pedagogy of love, that guides our work. To help us get centered and find the collective strength we need to do our work. To embrace our frayed lives and find our "relational homes" in communities of mutual respect, affiliation and caring. "And each one of us, somewhere in our lives, must clear a space within that blessing where she can call upon whatever resources are available to her in the name of something that must be done" (Lorde, 1988, p. 129). Clearing this space, to imagine and address our injuries and create collective acts of healing and transformation is the power a critical pedagogy of healing can offer in these difficult times, full of despair and yet hopeful for opportunities to draw a new map with a more fully human future for us all and the earth.

20

An Autoethnographic Account: How Black Teacher-Coaches Counter-Narrate New Social Constructs to Inform Pedagogy for Healing

Alex Chisholm

If reflection can be used as a method for rewriting the stereotypical narrative of Black teacher-coaches being limited to sports or physical education positions, then my personal accounts reveal the possibilities of how athletic experiences can be employed to inform pedagogical practices for Black and Brown students. Accordingly, this autoethnographic account was inspired by Goings's (2015) *The Lion Tells His Side of the (Counter)Story*, which demonstrated the power and validity of personal reflection in scholarly writing. Consequently, I write this to revisit my own journey and also to trouble the misconceptions about Black educators who serve dual roles as teachers and athletic coaches in K–12 education.

While playing youth sports in my adolescence, I came to notice that my athletic coaches were Black community members (fathers, mother, aunts, uncles, brothers, sisters), while my classroom teachers were white men and women who pushed academics during the week, and occasionally supported my athletic interests as spectators on the weekends. Although I understood that my small city upbringing warranted a close-knit community where most people contributed to the whole child, I began to internalize the social construct that educational spaces were inherently white and athletic spaces were naturally Black. For example, my first football experience as a six-year-old was with a set of three Black coaches; meanwhile, I did not have a Black classroom teacher until I was a sixteen-year-old sophomore in high school.

While my hometown boasts 52 percent Black or African American population, I always wondered why Black coaches rarely entered our classrooms as teachers for academic instruction. After all, these were the people who were offering life lessons—teaching me how to conduct myself when confronted by police, offering words of wisdom on how to navigate school curriculums that failed to include the heroes and heroines who looked like me, and who knew how to break any situation down in a way that made me more knowledgeable. Moreover, it was their communal bonds and willingness to share their athletic and life experiences that made learning restorative, which often alleviated the disconnect I felt in school. Since this absence of a merger between athletics and academics appeared to be racial in nature, I began paying attention to the narratives offered through film and media in my teens hoping that my assumptions would not be reverberated.

Over the past twenty years, films depicting educational and athletic progress for students of color have been dominated by what novelist Teju Cole termed the white savior industrial complex. Anderson (2013) asserts that this savior mentality produces a "confluence of practices, processes, and institutions that reify historical biases to ultimately endorse white privilege" (p. 39). If we leave it to Hollywood and media interpretations of effective teaching of Black and Brown youth where educational and athletic spaces merge, we are complicit in the distortion of a powerful narrative that already exists. This narrative not only illuminates a truth, but it is also grounded in the socialization of a marginalized group who navigates complex barriers within an educational system that prioritizes Eurocentric values. This set of beliefs is often disseminated through the commercialization of popular culture through film. As a result, Black and Brown educators, coaches, and youth are inaccurately depicted.

The 1996 film *Sunset Park* portrays a talented yet dysfunctional urban, African American high school basketball team that needed to be "polished and saved" by their white nonathletic coach (Rhea Perlman) who took the position for a stipend. The motion picture *Finding Forrester* combined academics and athletics as a talented, Black inner-city basketball player developed a passion for literature from a socially isolated novelist (Sean Connery). In these narratives, Black and Brown youth are often the subjects of a story that says being "saved" by their white teachers through sport is rewarding. It further permeates a deficit frame of thinking that all Black students in urban spaces are less fortunate and will benefit from being "fixed" by someone of another hue.

Other films such as *Coach Carter* and *Remember the Titans* have centered Black coaches and students as their focus. Coach Carter (Samuel L. Jackson) and Coach Boone (Denzel Washington) show determination in bringing out the best in their athletes off the playing field. Coach Carter's approach is centered in teaching life lessons about right versus wrong and self-respect through discipline. Nevertheless, in this Hollywood narrative, the real-life story of Herman Boone was abbreviated, and his roles as a teacher and Black Student Union adviser were excluded. It makes one think about how he may have employed his athletic experiences to inform classroom teaching. It brings the imagination to wonder, in what ways could he have enhanced the critical consciousness of Black and Brown youth, especially at the pivotal moments of integrating schools or navigating the most impoverished neighborhoods? While these narratives reveal the ability to overcome adversity, harmful omission of bringing Black and Brown students' critical consciousness to the light in conjunction with their athletic prowess reproduces stereotypes that justify white supremacy. Furthermore, it prevents a more accurate understanding of Black students and teacher-coaches and how their pedagogies may be useful for healing.

In the sections that follow, I promote a discussion_about critical pedagogies for healing by Black educators who serve in dual roles as classroom teachers and athletic coaches within secondary education. The aforementioned examples in film show how the narratives of teacher-coaches are portrayed to perpetuate deficit perceptions of

Black teacher-coaches and athletes. Throughout this chapter, I reference counter-narratives as a conceptual tool to provide a lens for contextualizing and supporting the assertion that, "Counternarratives speak to the realities of marginalized groups, allowing us to name our own realities, as opposed to having reality defined for us by their grand narrative" (Duncan, 2016, p. 53). The grand narrative of Black male educators in particular as the commodified physical education teacher intersects with the stereotypical football and/or basketball coaching role. Therefore, youth who absorb such narratives unconsciously internalize the notion that Black teacher-coaches lack the skill to teach academic subjects. For this reason, I contend that in order eliminate such microaggressions against Black and Brown teacher-coaches and youth, self-empowerment, racial healing, and critical consciousness in our classrooms is a necessity.

Thus, the purpose of this chapter is to highlight the potential for Black teachers who occupy dual roles as coaches to leverage such roles and experiences in utilizing sport and athletics as a gateway to increasing the critical consciousness, self-empowerment and racial healing potential for Black and Brown youth (Duncan-Andrade & Morrell, 2008). To accomplish this, I would like to (a) offer a short autoethnographic account about how Black teacher-coaches act as healers through the application of critical pedagogy, (b) speak to the challenges that Black teacher-coaches face and the importance for answering the call to consciousness as educators, and (c) share the what it means to rewrite the narrative of the Black teacher-coach. My hope is that this chapter will initiate further discussion and exploration of this concept in the world of education and sport.

Critical Pedagogy for Healing

Socialization theory and narrative storytelling provide a base for understanding how Black teacher-coaches come to recognize their positions and counter racial constructs. According to Freire (1972), critical pedagogy, which is meant to challenge students to analyze power structures and inequality, is another theoretical approach that can be applied to how Black teacher-coaches can inform teachers on praxis for developing powerful counter-narratives about urban school failure. Jeffrey Duncan-Andrade and Earnest Morrell (2008) outline a study about what coaches can teach teachers through the lens of critical pedagogy. The authors asked the following research questions pertaining to the positionality of coaches and their use of sports to impact change in and outside of the classroom: (1) Could sports be used to develop a collective culture that aims to transform oppressive social norms? and (2) Can critical pedagogy help coaches to foster such a critical collective consciousness and agency with their teams? The findings of this study not only suggest that Black educator-coaches can impact student achievement for this particular group of learners, but also serve as implications for how schools can learn to value the benefits of having them as liberated instructional leaders.

In his book *Black Youth Rising: Activism and Radical Healing in Urban America*, scholar Shawn Ginwright (2010) speaks to healing as a way to cultivate critical consciousness of marginalized groups who are subject to racism and oppression. Ultimately, the goal is to raise consciousness to the point of action. This process of healing is one that Black teacher-coaches have the potential to implement through teaching in order to empower Black and Brown youth. In one of their many roles as doers, teacher-coaches have the ability to align themselves with community members to promote hope. When combined, Ginwright (2010) and Duncan-Andrade and Morrell's (2008) works suggest that the education profession could largely benefit from examining and changing the way that the coaching profession uses praxis to improve instruction for maximum effort and performance of students. In fact, it has the potential to promote healing and action. As stated in the study, teacher-coaches should continue to focus on:

1. putting the needs, goals, concerns, and interests of students first;
2. providing consistent social, emotional, and academic support that values each individual student's identity yet sets goals differently under the same set of principles;
3. providing instruction both on the court and in the classroom that calls for students to challenge dominant structures and narratives;
4. developing the same sense of community and collective achievement (teamwork) with your students and community that you build with your athletes;
5. developing learning and relationship cultures that are counter hegemonic in their outcomes and processes; and
6. creating time and space for self-reflection by students and teachers. (Duncan-Andrade and Morrell, 2008)

In the tradition of ethnographic research, I kept records of text messages and audio recordings of conversations with fellow teacher-coaches that I worked alongside during my tenure as a high school history teacher and assistant varsity boys' basketball coach. While maintaining records of myself as the subject of study, I also constantly referred back to the film depictions of Black teacher-coaches and scholarly literature that emphasized critical pedagogies in Duncan and Morell's study, and the writing of Ginwright. Through my storytelling and conversations with peers, I realized that I cannot, nor will I, try to speak for every Black teacher who coaches. To do so would be to generalize and assume that all Black teacher-coaches share the same sentiments, feelings, and approaches to sport and academic teaching. However, my personal stories align with the very concepts found in the research.

In an informal interview, one theme that often came up was the unspoken expectation of Black teacher-coaches. A colleague (Coach Gregory) and I had extensive dialogue on understanding the purpose of this role. I stated that,

> understanding your position is first and foremost, whereas Black teacher-coaches are often hired by school systems to both encourage and discourage Black and Brown youth. For example, coaching requires role modeling, mentoring, and motivating, while we're also being asked to discipline or punish students' sport participation when they fail to meet academic requirements.

In other words, teacher-coaches are asked to celebrate and capitalize Black and Brown youth's athletic success yet hold it against them when Eurocentric knowledge is not retained, regurgitated, and reproduced according to state standards. Here, the first step to healing is to abolish playing the contradictory roles of being the promoter of athletic success, and the inhibitor of emotional and academic support. Dismantling this role for healing entails emphasizing students' well-being and raising their critical consciousness to question why such opposing roles exist from a historical standpoint. Therefore, as Duncan-Andrade and Morrell (2008) asserted, youth can develop learning and relationship cultures that are counterhegemonic.

In a separate, and more formal interview, another colleague (Coach Raymond) asked, "Why is critical pedagogy needed? What concepts are behind breaking content down for students, and how it becomes relevant through sport?" Somewhat overwhelmed by the layers within these questions, I stopped and thought before speaking. I eventually replied,

> Critical pedagogy is necessary because Black and Brown students will benefit when they learn through a lens that helps them navigate any system that has been built to condition a negative self-efficacy within themselves. Coupled with culturally relevant teaching, which empowers students' ability to think critically on political and emotional issues with reference to who they are and what they know, they are more likely to accurately analyze and assess social constructs.

(Ladson-Billings, 1994)In an English classroom, the incorporation of athletics could be implemented by having students trace historical Black athletic protest ranging from Tommie Smith and John Carlos's 1968 Mexico City Black power fist gesture to Colin Kaepernick's 2016 kneeling during the national anthem objection and make a list of demands on the injustices they face within their schools.

Ultimately, Black teacher-coaches have the potential to center instruction around the core values of Black and Brown students in a way that enhances their critical consciousness. A good and successful start not only begins with teacher-coaches who resemble them in skin color, but also in community and cultural similarities. Allowing Black and Brown students to see themselves within the literature and having that extra commonality of sports and athletics demonstrates a willingness to target their interests, concerns, and needs in an educational space. It further establishes stronger community ties and teacher-coaches implement learning goals with ingenuity and creativity.

Facing the Challenge: Role Conflict and Answering the Call to Consciousness

Duncan-Andrade and Morrell's action steps listed prior, along with my counter stereotypical narratives that communicate the importance of Black teacher-coaches are not foreign. They actually combine the work that other scholars know to be effective in educating Black and Brown youth. These steps stand in solidarity with Dr. Love's

(2015) writing of communities of practice, Dr. Ed Brockenbrough's (2015) standing in the gap of fatherhood, and the need for care and concern to be role models of positive behavior. However, this requires a skill set and presents a set of challenges, as teaching and learning typically does.

In my fourteen years of teaching and coaching, I've learned that athletics and academics are two arenas in which Black educators find themselves balancing the roles of both teacher and coach. There is potential for Black teachers in dual roles as coaches to foster the utilization of sport as a gateway for increasing consciousness and healing, however it comes with no guidebook and little recognition for long hour days of dedication and frequent planning. Gena Dagle Caponi (1999) writes:

> Perhaps in no arena of present-day cultural life in this country is the African American aesthetic so visibly on display as in sports. Yet, Scholars have rarely considered the hardwood court, gridiron, or baseball diamond within the expressive domain in which literature, music, dance, and speech exist.

Despite having irrepressible qualities and working without widespread acknowledgment in academic literature, Black teacher-coaches also face challenges such as role conflict and role overload with the stress of balancing two distinct roles (Connor & Bohan, 2018). Lock and Massengale's (1978) contribution on interrole conflict highlights the demands of when two or more roles compete with one another. Evidently, all teacher-coaches experience conflicting demands, and role overload occurs as a result as those demands increase.

In addition to navigating the demands of coaching and teaching that lead to role conflict and overload, Black teacher-coaches stand in as role models, parental figures, and advocates. Dr. Ed Brockenbrough (2015) specifically speaks on Black males in education by stating as follows:

> The valorization of the authoritative Black male patriarch in American society at large provides an important backdrop for understanding the experiences of Black male teachers … Black male teachers have been cast as ideal role models and surrogate father figures for Black youth, especially Black boys, who may lack adult male figures in their homes and neighborhoods. (p. 500)

In *Here's Why Black Teachers Are So Important to Education and to Our Children*, author Kelley D. Evans argues that Black teachers are more likely to serve in schools full of Black students to help those students feel a sense of connection to their school and communities. While it can be perceived as an added pressure or challenge, it also serves as a call to consciousness, or understanding that there is an unspoken duty to give back in a way that it was not available in your own youthhood. This self-prescribed responsibility lends itself to a cultural connection that exists in representing Black and Brown youth in sport and in education. Dr. Bettina Love (2015) reiterated Wenger, McDermott, and Snyder's (2002) point in stating that "individuals sharing knowledge through situated learning activities—such as apprenticeship, coaching, and storytelling—foster ongoing participation, which moves members into the role of doers, and 'doing' is an essential component of communities of practice" (p.111). Simply, Black teacher-coaches have the ability to serve as action-oriented educators; however, navigating such complex responsibilities presents the potential for stress, and difficult time management.

Rewriting Our Own (Counter) Narratives

In this chapter the use of the counter-narrative, specifically through autoethnography allowed me the opportunity to communicate the importance of Black teacher-coaches and the possible positive effects that Black and Brown youth stand to gain. This includes but is not limited to learning about their history through sport, while understanding how to counter white society's notion of Black intellectual inferiority (Duncan, 2016). The application of critical pedagogy and the creation of culturally relevant classrooms breaks down those constructs and allows dreams to build. Those dreams are further solidified when coming from a shared social and cultural affinity for dismantling stereotypes that hinder scholar athletic learning.

The Black teacher-coaches' significance lies in their ability to move in and out of academic and athletic spaces, further emphasizing that education exists wherever there are lessons to be learned. Therefore, Black teacher-coaches are capable of encouraging Black and Brown students to believe in their own abilities and thus imagine and create new realities in a manner that disrupts the implicit messaging that academia in an inherently white space while athleticism is a separate Black space. In essence, healing for Black and Brown students in education stems from critical teaching to awaken consciousness, as well as the counter-narratives that provide self and cultural preservation.

Part V

Space, Place, and Land

21

The Politics of a Revolutionary and Humanizing Praxis: The Story of Liberation, Victory, and Regression in Tucson

Curtis Acosta

In a speech to the Claremont Graduate School in 1989, Paulo Freire articulated the beauty and promise of what can be produced in a classroom by living and learning in community. It is also antithetical to the experiences of many students in the United States who have survived the hostility, drudgery, and pain in our education system for generations. Yet, Freire's words still resonate with me because he does capture the ethos for what we created in partnership with the youth of Tucson in our now defunct MARS classes, and what can happen when a community of learners is liberated from cultural deficit stereotypes and threats to their bodies and souls. Freire promises an education experience filled with the desire to learn more once students feel safe and free.

> When I speak of serious education I am also speaking about happiness. I cannot understand how it is possible to have an education through which we believe that studying is something difficult, impossible to be done, and exclusively painful … But we need education that does not make students afraid of studying, but curious, full of desire to study; because every time we begin to study, we must have in ourselves the certainty that at some moment we will become full with pleasure. And this is the moment in which we arrive to knowledge.
>
> (Freire in Darder, 2002)

It was revolutionary to witness the extreme pleasure that learning brought us during the years that the MARS program thrived in Tucson, before it was destroyed by the state of Arizona in 2012. I reflect about the laughter and joy. I relive the healing and humanity of our students who were seeing themselves in the stories and curriculum of our classes and feeling relief—they were not insane, broken, or deficient as the institutions of our country purported them to be. They engaged in a process of conscientização, or critical consciousness, to heal deficit notions of their intelligence, creativity, and humanity. Many students entered our classrooms believing the stock narratives of who they were as Chicanx or disenfranchised youth. They had not found a decolonial education space where they could interrogate and analyze their homes, barrios, and lives. Once they did, our classrooms ceased to be sterile rooms of disconnection—they became community and familia.

During those amazing years, the most impactful moment of our theoretical and pedagogical work as a collective was when we began to embrace our own cultural funds of knowledge, namely, the MesoAmerican Indigenous epistemologies that elders shared with us from their knowledge and understanding of the *tonalmachiotl* (Aztec sunstone). Although we had embraced the pursuit of critical consciousness, the magic that would eventually be our source of strength through the years of racist legislative attacks had not been fully realized. It was the Nahui Ollin, or "Four Movements" in Nahuatl, that provided the framework to fully apply the lessons of *Pedagogy of the Oppressed,* critical race theory, and cultural asset-based pedagogies like *Funds of Knowledge.*

Indigenous Epistemologies and the Smoking Mirror

When I first learned about the Nahui Ollin, I knew I fell short of creating a fully humanizing classroom. No matter how I tried to cultivate conscientization, it was the balance of the four elements Tezcatlipoca, Quetzalcoatl, Huitzilopochtli, and Xipe Totec that was key to unlearning colonized education and charting a new path. I had always asked my students to reflect on their learning and connect literature to their lives, but the concept of Tezcatlipoca inspired me to be more intentional about critical "self-reflection." In English, Tezcatlipoca means "smoking mirror." The ancestors understood that self-reflection was difficult but also active. One needed to seek their image through the smoke in order to truly find oneself. Thus, I built critical self-reflection into every curriculum unit and as daily practice in our writing time. I felt the more practice we had looking within and sharing what we discovered with one another, the easier it would be to critically self-reflect in our lives outside of the classroom.

Having self-reflection as a foundation made learning our precious and beautiful knowledge, our Quetzalcoatl, more impactful. Whether it was new knowledge from authors like Luís Alberto Urrea or Ana Castillo, or ancient knowledge from our ancestors, learning became sacred because we connected it to our lives through critical reflection. School is filled with knowledge; yet, we often struggle to make content accessible and impactful for youth because we eliminate the cultural component of why the information is so important. The Indigenous principles of the Nahui Ollin highlighted the absurdity of decontextualizing our learning from our humanity.

This was emphasized further with the principles of Huitzilopochtli and Xipe Totec. Huitzilopochtli translates to "hummingbird on the left"; it was meant to symbolize the "will to act." The Mexica viewing the hummingbird as the avatar for action made perfect sense to me. There are not many animals that work has hard as the huitzilin. However, I was confused about what it meant to be on the left until an elder asked me what organ was on the left side of our bodies. Our hearts. The will to act with a heart like a hummingbird. Indefatigable. The final concept of the Nahui Ollin was Xipe Totec, which symbolized the shedding of skin or transformation. As human beings, we need to be mindful of our own growth and changes, which is why the practice of self-reflection is so critical. Otherwise, we can never learn from the knowledge that has been gained from our personal and collective actions. Our ancestors' conceptualizations of qualities of being human provided a framework to reflect upon the gaps in the educational experience I was attempting to construct as a teacher. The elements spoke to me intimately; they were connected to thousands of years of Mexica wisdom on how to be a better human being. Huitzilopochtli seemed to come to life and glare at me, and I could not hide. How were the youth in my classes living and acting their learning beyond an essay or classroom presentation?

The humanity and brilliance of maestro Paulo became clear when I stared at the images of the Nahui Ollin and reflected on the wisdom of the ancestors. The Nahui Ollin unlocked what Freire expected of us all along—to put our precious and beautiful knowledge toward the work of emancipation. The Nahui Ollin became the framework for pedagogical and methodological changes that led to the most significant gains my MARS colleagues and I had seen in regard to the activism and liberation of our youth. Students' academic gains exploded since they were having a fully human educational experience that did not stop at the classroom door. The sound of the bell was just a suggestion of ending, not the release of torture and pain that youth often exhibit when a period ends. Instead, class blended into class, which led to community organizing, community education, civic engagement, and activism. It did not matter that we did not have MARS Science or Math classes, the students were bringing their consciousness and "will to act" with them and they excelled. The walls and gates of the school could not confine their passion to change the world.

Our students began to live the Freirean concept of tri-dimensionalization. "People can tri-dimensionalize time into the past, present, and future; their history, in function of their own creations, develops as a constant process of transformation within which epochal units materialize. These epochal units are not closed periods of time, static compartments within which people are confined" (Freire, 1993, p. 101). Our students were looking into the smoking mirror of Tezcatlipoca, in order to commune with the generations that came before them through studying the art, stories, and history of the Chicanx movimiento in our classes. They applied their new knowledge toward revolutionizing their barrios through art, protest, organizing, and activism in an attempt to transform Tucson for future generations. Tri-dimensionalization was echoed in MesoAmerican Indigenous funds of knowledge since it was so closely aligned to the idea of the seven generations. According to our Mexica elders, we must live each day in honor of the seven generations that came before us and for the seven generations to follow. This Indigenous knowledge is also shared with other Native cultures on Turtle Island and serves as a connection to the original stewards of this continent. Having a generational understanding of our place in the world also created a more salient bond to our raices (roots) for both youth and teachers alike. Our path toward liberation through education was much larger than ourselves and the contemporary moment.

Historicizing our experiences provided a potent lens to access our humanity in the midst of some of the most dehumanizing experiences in the modern history of Arizona. As the vile anti-Mexican, anti-Immigrant rhetoric of Tea Party Republicans increased, our youth were fully grounded in the knowledge of this tierra—how stolen land, broken treaties, and slave labor became the engine for Empire. Our classrooms were the spaces to resuscitate hope for our students, for them to breathe liberation, even as the attacks of Arizona state officials became intensely personal to all of us. Indigenous epistemologies such as the Mayan concept of In Lak Ech, or "you are my other me," and the Nahui Ollin provided a foundation and process of humanization, empathy, and love for all in the classroom regardless of the political vitriol. Maestro Paulo spoke about a similar process in his letters to Guinea-Bissau.

> Authentic help means that all who are involved help each other mutually, growing together in the common effort to understand the reality which they seek to transform. Only through such praxis—in which those who help and those who are being helped help each other simultaneously—can the act of helping become free from the distortion in which the helper dominates the helped.
>
> (Freire, 2016, p. 3)

Without question, the youth in my classes were the most significant voices in establishing my identity as Xicano. As a biracial person, who had grown up in a world before that word became popular, I was lost before I became a teacher. It was through our process of humanizing the academic space where I could reflect with my students about who I was, and who I was becoming, while they were doing the same. The strong voices of speeches and art that comprised the academic content of our courses were intimately connected to our lived experiences. Humility was embedded in the fact that we were all in the process of our own journey of Xipe Totec and our collective journey together. There was no hubris, or false teacher–student hierarchies established from institutional power and privilege. We were all learning and growing, flaws and all.

Split and Sacrifice

Largely because of the transformative power of our classes, MARS came to an unnatural end due to the intervention of the state of Arizona. Our students and teachers were vilified by powerful officials as anti-American. Arizona legislation banned our literature, art, and history. Our intellectual and cultural heritage, and all the contributions our ancestors and elders made to the greater American and global story, had been made illegal to teach to our own children. Our classes were ethnically cleansed; the violence of that act still resonates in Tucson today.

Our teacher collective of nearly fifteen years fractured. Only a few of us continued the path of resistance, refusing to comply with racist demands of the state, continuing the struggle for justice through the courts. My good friends Sean Arce, the former MARS Director, and fellow teacher Rene Martínez were fired. I severed ties to the school district in solidarity with my colegas. A few colleagues felt trapped and paralyzed, while others chose a different path, submitting to anti-Chicanx normalcy to further their careers.

Lifelong relationships were lost. Marriages were tested and some lost. Families were torn apart. Health has suffered. Days after I was deposed for six hours by the state of Arizona in our lawsuit against the state, I suddenly lost the ability to hear in my left ear. Doctors believe it was a virus, but I cannot help to think it was the stress of the struggle. I share these wounds with you to illustrate how white supremacy and Empire wreaked havoc upon something beautiful. Yet, we still had the will and strength to keep fighting.

Pain and heartbreak were an indelible part of the sacrifices made in the pursuit of justice. It was our responsibility and honor to resist through action and embody the love we had for our antepasados who suffered so much more. Through these sacrifices, we gained a historic legal victory for Mexican American youth and Ethnic Studies programs throughout the nation. I am forever indebted to the sacrifice of Maya and Sean Arce, an amazingly powerful daughter–father combination, who were key leaders in our continued struggle. Maya Arce was the longest serving student-plaintiff in our lawsuit against the state of Arizona. She was also a witness on the stand, like her father, Sean, and me. Her courage still inspires me and fuels my work. Maya was plaintiff for our victory at the Ninth Circuit Court of Appeals in 2015, paving the way for triumph two years later. The history of our case has also served as legal precedent by the solicitor general of Washington state in their challenge of the Muslim ban, as well as precedent to protect Deferred Action for Childhood Arrivals (DACA) from the inhumane policies of Trump's administration. In Lak Ech in action.

> Love is at the same time the foundation of dialogue and dialogue itself. It is thus necessarily the task of responsible Subjects and cannot exist in a relation of domination … Because love is an act of courage, not of fear, love is commitment to others. No matter where the oppressed are found, the act of love is commitment to their cause—the cause of liberation.

(Freire, 1993, p. 89)It is important that their sacrifices and story of the Arces are not forgotten, since many times the story of women of color and youth are erased from history. Thus, we honor the Arces for the sheroes and heroes that they are. They endured personal and familial sacrifices, surviving the racist attacks of Arizona state officials, as well as the Tucson community that blacklisted Sean, forcing him to leave Tucson to restart his life and career in California.

Victory, Yet Regression

With the backdrop of a divided community, our small collective continued to pursue justice, to hold the destroyers of MARS accountable in federal court. As the trial opened, I took the witness stand to enlighten the court of the beauty and power of MARS, as well as the Draconian actions of the state of Arizona dismantling our classes and banning books like *Pedagogy of the Oppressed.* It was not long into my cross-examination before the Arizona attorneys attempted to smear my use of a speech by Ernesto "Che" Guevara. In the following exchange the state revealed its racist view of our ability to teach material that some may see as controversial.

Ellman: One of the materials identified there is entitled "At the Afro-Asian Conference in Algeria," by Ernest Guevara, better known as "Che Guevara." Do you agree that was one of the materials used in the Latin literature class?
Acosta: Yes. I taught that once.
Ellman: That's not a novel or a play or a poem, is it?
Acosta: No, it's a speech.
Ellman: It's a speech he gave in 1965, is that right?
Acosta: That's correct.
Ellman: And in this speech it says: It is imperative to take political power and get rid of the oppressor classes. Do you remember that from the speech?
Acosta: I don't.
Ellman: Do you have any reason to believe that that's not in the speech?
Acosta: [No].
Ellman: And the speech text also states …: If the imperialist enemy, the United States, or any other, carries out its attack against the underdeveloped peoples and the socialist countries, elementary logic determines the need for an alliance between the underdeveloped peoples and the socialist countries. Do you remember language to that effect in the Guevara speech?
Acosta: Without the speech in front of me, sir, no, I don't. …
Ellman: So can we assume for our purposes here that it is?
Acosta: Sure.
Ellman: Don't you agree that that teaches your students class-based resentment and ideology?
Acosta: No.
Ellman: No. And why is that?
Acosta: Well, I had a pretty solid liberal arts background, and we learned many different philosophies from many different points of view. And so, to me, because we're reading something doesn't put it in the proper context of how we were analyzing it or how the students were asked to analyze it for my classroom.
Ellman: This is an English language course offered for core credit, correct?
Acosta: Sure.
Ellman: And you believe there's independent literary value in Che Guevara's speech in 1965?
Acosta: It wasn't a staple of my curriculum, but I don't—yes, there is value in that, of course.

(*González et al. v. Douglas et al.*, 2017, June 26, pp. 114–16)

Even though I lived this exchange just a few years ago, it still does not seem real. However, it has left me with numerous questions regarding how the state of Arizona perceived our classes:

- What criminalized this speech?
- Was it the ideology?
- Was it the fact that I was Xicano?
- Was it the activism of the youth of color in our classes?

Regardless of the answers, the evidence remains clear: some youth can peacefully protest without being harmed or seen as foreign criminals, others cannot. Some teachers are free to use this content without it being characterized as indoctrination or criminal behavior, others are not. Nearly every day on mainstream and social media, folks of color and other historically oppressed people are told these facts and lived experiences are fiction. Of course, I was elated that the federal courts found the opposite to be true.

In August 2017, Judge A. Wallace Tashima was clear that there were racist and careerist motivations behind the attacks on our program by the former attorney general and state superintendent of Arizona. The law that banned MARS was found to be unconstitutional; it violated the First and Fourteenth Amendment rights of Mexican American students in both enactment and enforcement.

> Considering the evidence, the Court is convinced that A.R.S. § 15–112 was enacted and enforced with a discriminatory purpose. Huppenthal's anonymous blog comments are the most important evidence, as they plainly show that he harbored animus. The circumstantial evidence corroborates that direct evidence, and confirms that other actors held the same views. Given this wealth of evidence, the Court finds Horne and Huppenthal did not testify credibly regarding their own motivations. The passage and enforcement of the law against the MARS program were motivated by anti-Mexican-American attitudes.
>
> (*González et al. v. Douglas et al.*, 2017, pp. 38–9)

The story of MARS proves the importance of critical pedagogy and the journey toward conscientization for all of us. Without political clarity, we would have succumbed to the racist law and harmed the Ethnic Studies movement by bending our knee to a dangerous law and precedent. As Angela Valenzuela wrote in *Subtractive Schooling*, "authentic caring must be imbued with such political clarity" (Valenzuela, 1999, p. 110). As educators, youth, parents, and community members, we possess more power than we are told. We must resist the narratives meant to keep us from our collective strength to change our neighborhoods, cities, and world. Regardless of the lack of political will from Chicanx politicians and fake progressives in Tucson, we were able to hold the bigots in our state government accountable, while the courts affirmed the transformative impact of MARS.

Unfortunately, the Tucson unified school district (TUSD) school board and many different constituencies in Tucson continue to demonize and resist MARS. Although the school board is made up of individuals across the political spectrum, they have in common a vehement opposition to bringing MARS back in the way that it was proven to be a success. Years after our court victory, we still have no Mexican American/ Raza Studies in Tucson regardless of the historic win for Ethnic Studies, and there is a strong possibility that MARS will not return for a generation or more. Yet, there is always hope, and this story itself offers proof that staying faithful and committed to the beautiful struggle will produce liberation that can restore our humanity. Thousands of our former students still speak about our classrooms as being a home. That home is gone now, and to borrow from one of my literary heroes Langston Hughes, MARS in Tucson remains a dream deferred.

Yet, the legacy of our classrooms and the academic success of our students lives on through Xipe Totec (transformation). Although we lost our sacred classroom spaces, new collectives of teacher-activists were born. My comrades on the Education for Liberation Network advisory board were the first to help me heal. Through our organizing for Ethnic Studies, both regionally and nationally, we created a national Ethnic Studies Assembly at our biannual conference, Free Minds, Free People. I have been blessed to assemble a brilliant team of educators at the Acosta Educational Partnership, where we engage in critical and humanizing education and Ethnic Studies collaborations with communities and school districts throughout the country. I am also honored to still be connected to former MARS colleagues through the Xicanx Institute for Teaching and Organizing where we continue to share the revolutionary work of MARS. Even before our legal victory, I felt that it was critical for MARS to live on by sharing the lessons that we learned from surviving this struggle, so that such regressive actions do not destroy the brightest lights of youth liberation again. These radical collectives were a lifeline to doing just that.

Xipe Totec resides in the inspiration of struggle during a dark and anxious time in our nation and the world. It is proof that diverse groups of people can work, sacrifice, and seek justice together. And, that the people will prevail. In the wake of the elimination of Mexican American/Raza Studies in Tucson, Ethnic Studies programs have surged across the United States. This victory provided the legal precedent—a shield—for new programs to grow and mature so that racist and discriminatory attacks will not crush them in their nascent state. The dream is alive, no longer deferred, and we will realize it one day soon together.

Let us all look into the smoking mirror and reflect upon our individual and collective roles at our universities, school districts, schools, and in our communities in pursuit of the radical dreams of Paulo Freire and our own ancestors.

- How do we cultivate our radical dreams?
- How do we nurture and care for each other while we are in crisis, as we struggle against the inhumane policies and practices of white supremacy that threaten the lives of our youth, families, and communities?
- How do we heal from the volatility of the attacks and mend ourselves so that we can continue to live lives of joy?
- How do we breathe in the power of those that came before us and live lives of hope in an increasingly cynical and inhumane time?

I share our MARS story, as one who is not broken for what was lost. I am proud of the scars we obtained from essential sacrifices for the people. The wounds from our struggle and the aftermath in Tucson have not wounded my heart. I am invigorated by those sacrifices and filled with hope in the generation that now takes to the streets demanding justice, liberation, and humanity—all the young people who remind me of the powerful MARS youth that came before them and our once united Chicanx community in Tucson over a decade ago. My heart explodes in joy for the days of struggle ahead.

22

Schools for Liberation: Creating Leadership for a New World

David S. Greene and Janet Wells Greene

Learning to Read a Changing World

As we write this in the summer of 2020, a rebellion is underway on the streets of the United States and across the world. It has been energized by a reaction against recent police murders of Black men, women, and other members of marginalized groups. In addition, the coronavirus pandemic, poverty, lack of adequate health care, and systemic racism have exposed the profound failures of our capitalist economic system in every area of society. More and more of the population is hungry, impoverished, out of work, disabled and marginalized while the wealth of the world flows into the pockets of the few. Eight billionaires in the United States have more wealth than half the population of the whole country. In 2019, more than seven hundred people in the United States died from poverty every day—even before the pandemic began. Underlying the oppression and intensified exploitation of a multinational working class are the contradictions of a system that is failing to meet the basic needs of the majority of the population (Galea et al., 2011: 1456–65; Bezruchka, 2014: 190–9; Barnes, 2020).

Out of these conditions, a spontaneous movement is developing that is largely unaware of its history, its position, or its potential. People are coming forward with questions and dreams of a better future (Buchanan et al., 2020). In these times, education for liberation has an important role to play: it can help build communities that are empowered by a knowledge of history, shared experiences, and a vision of justice for all. This kind of education is needed to develop conscious leadership and organization to fight against encroaching fascism and repression.

How will this education take place? As Paulo Freire (1985: 102) has said, "It would be extremely naïve to expect the dominant classes to develop a type of education that would enable subordinate classes to perceive social injustices critically." In other words, mainstream institutions rarely support emancipatory education. But we can carve out space both inside and outside mainstream institutions to create an independent mission in order to educate both our communities and their emerging leaders (Horton and Freire, 1990: 199–226). Critical pedagogy and popular political education need the freedom to allow people to name, understand, and thereby heal the divisions within our society by joining together to overcome injustice and oppression. As educators begin to lead the fight for education for liberation, they will transform learning from a tool for elitism to a tool for democracy. It is out of such a collective fight that new leaders will come forward and a new society can be born. The Reverend William Barber, a leader of the Poor People's Campaign, has a name for these new leaders. He calls them "Repairers of the Breach"—people whose deeper understanding and love for humanity lead them to work together against the injustices in society (https://www.breachrepairers.org/mission). Central to this new version of community empowerment and leadership development is a respect for the lived experience of poor and working people (Hunt and Pieper, 2016: 440).

Educators and leaders must learn to listen well and earn the trust of the communities in which they live and work through a process of dialogue, shared experience, and collective action.

Can you start a school or space for this kind of learning in the community where you live? We think the answer is "Yes!" This chapter is a serious reflection on our work with others to create a space for education for liberation in rural central Ohio. The examples we will share are specific to our situation in a small, conservative rust belt town, where after several years of work, we invited others to join us in creating the Freedom School in Licking County. We hope our experience will inspire others to do the same.

We see ourselves as educators in the tradition of resistance. We are both working class people who feel that education should do more than merely give people credentials. We met when we helped establish the Southern Appalachian Labor School at the West Virginia Institute of Technology in 1979. We were inspired by Myles Horton and Paulo Freire to help people understand the power relationships and the world in which they live. We worked as educators in alternative and mainstream institutions for over forty years, pushing for education that would allow people to see their lives in a larger context.

The following discussion is designed to help others think about how to engage a community and begin to understand relationships between people and identify leaders. We will draw on our experiences over the years which taught us, through trial and error, that to understand the world you must first listen and learn—from leaders of existing institutions, from people directly affected by unequal power relationships, and from those who are actively engaged in resistance.

Listening in the Community

Our experience of building a school for liberation began in 2008. The housing crisis which rocked America impacted us as well. We had to leave Brooklyn, New York, after twenty-three years and return to live near Janet's family in Newark, Ohio. There, we found a community in foreclosure. Following nearly twenty years of layoffs and plant closings, factory workers and white-collar workers were now losing their homes in the mortgage crisis. Slum landlords and house flippers were increasing in number, and within a few years, nearly half of formerly owner-occupied dwellings in this town of fifty thousand people had become rental property. Good union jobs were in short supply. Instead, people were funneled into non-union low-wage jobs through more than sixteen temporary employment agencies. The jobs were not nearby, and there was no public transportation.

The first step was to learn about the impact of these changes. We studied the local media. We talked to friends—old and new. We accepted invitations to do volunteer work at a food pantry, attended church, book discussions, weekly city council meetings, local history programs, and public talks at local colleges. We read local history.

We knew something about the city from our work in Newark in the 1980s, when Janet was a reporter on the local newspaper, and David was a counselor and factory worker. Charity organizations had multiplied in two decades into what amounted to a nonprofit volunteer industry, including more than thirty-two food pantries in the county network. While there were countless other opportunities to volunteer to help the poor, and much discussion about what to do for the poor, there was little or no public conversation about the causes of poverty.

Listening to the People Directly Affected

A major part of the critical education process for empowerment is talking with and listening to marginalized people. What working people and the poor themselves say about their needs and the solutions to their problems is often quite different from the perceptions and solutions put forward by well-intentioned reformers and educators. Myles Horton (1990: 20), in his early days as an educator, described how he learned "to talk to others and [get] help from them. I learned to listen .... They were the experts on their own lives and their own experiences. And those experiences could have something to teach me even if I didn't see it at the moment." There are many places to have these conversations.

In 2010, we decided we wanted to grow some vegetables, so we got involved with two fledgling community gardens. One garden was the project of a woman who lived in an affluent community outside Newark. She owned land in a low-income, multiracial neighborhood near the railroad yards on the East Side of town, known for its mix of rental property, Habitat for Humanity houses, and rent-to-own housing. This well-intentioned woman tried to start a community garden without consulting anyone in the community, a strategy that directly contradicts Paulo Freire's teaching that we must begin with the problem a community identifies for itself. The neighbors started a petition to stop the garden, but we were unaware of the opposition when we agreed to help her with planting. On our first venture into the neighborhood, residents came out of their houses and confronted us, saying, "Ain't gonna be no garden here!" "We don't want rats in our grass!"

We were taken aback, but at once asked, "What do you want?"

"We need sidewalks," they said. "There are old people in wheelchairs who get stuck in the mud and little kids have to play in the street." People were very clear about their needs.

This neighborhood became one of the first sites for the kind of education that would lead us to the formation of the Freedom School. It is also an example of how education for liberation means choosing sides. We told the landowner that we wouldn't be gardening with her after all. David met with the neighbors to strategize about the best way to get sidewalks. They decided to contact a progressive city council woman to meet with them and listen to their needs. They wrote and circulated a new petition for sidewalks which they presented at City Council and spoke eloquently about the needs in their community. They won partial victories. We all learned much about the role of some of the power brokers in the city. Best of all, we connected with people who eventually became involved with the Freedom School.

The second community garden, where we actually did plant some vegetables that summer, was on the south side of town, near a factory in a neighborhood with many Section 8 rental houses (federally subsidized homes for the poor owned by private landlords). This neighborhood had few resident homeowners. Its garden became another space where we learned more about what the Freedom School needed to be.

This garden was also a work in progress. It had a board made up of representatives from churches, city government, garden clubs, a nearby college, and the county extension office. Its mission was to beautify the neighborhood and to address the problem of food for the poor in a neighborhood that had no grocery store. The board agreed to let us have a plot but warned us that it was a dangerous neighborhood and that "There were 'murderers' down there." We were not deterred.

We learned many things from the gardeners during the six years we were able to be active. David, who loved to work in his plot, was at the garden for hours each day. He volunteered to be a "garden coordinator" to assign plots, hold weekly meetings of gardeners, and help people learn from each other. It was a diverse group. Some gardeners were unemployed or on welfare because of plant closings, or disabilities from heart attacks, cancer, or workplace injuries. Others were widows or displaced homemakers whose spouses had abandoned them. One woman had been a commercial driver of big rigs—the eighteen-wheel trucks—before she became too ill to work anymore. A young man had lost his house after his wife died, but he was still working while living, as he put it, "out of my car." Some people were experienced gardeners, others were beginners. David encouraged people to share gardening techniques with each other. We had monthly potluck picnics and people enjoyed getting to know each other. Janet learned that several gardeners had been professional cooks and bakers earlier in their lives. She organized a committee to share their knowledge and healthy recipes. Together they wrote a cookbook, gathering recipes from other gardeners and information about planting and harvesting vegetables. We also got to know other people who lived near the garden.

We saw the impact of slum landlords on the neighborhood during that first summer. One man, whose rented house was poorly maintained, said, "The real issue here is housing." He gestured at his house, with its peeling paint and broken stairs, and added, "If you think this is bad, you should see my sister's rental. Maybe you could help her out."

Uncovering Power Relationships and Structures

David went to visit the sister. Her house had no hot water, backed-up plumbing, thin walls with little protection from the cold, vermin, and other health and safety issues. She pressed the landlord to improve the property, but he retaliated by giving her an eviction notice. David accompanied the woman to her hearing at Eviction Court; they saw her landlord talking and laughing with the magistrate outside the packed courtroom. Her Legal Services lawyer presented the case against the landlord; David also testified as to the condition of her house. She was evicted anyway, but the magistrate ruled that she could have an extra three days before the bailiff would come to put her out in the street. With an eviction on her record, she would find it difficult to rent a decent place.

As popular educators, we have often used public hearings to illustrate how power works in a community. It is important to observe the workings of public bodies over a period of time. We observed that even though few tenants had lawyers, most landlords had legal representation. The tenants, hoping for justice, explained the reasons why they were behind on the rent. The litany of problems revealed the precarious financial state of many households, the absence of public transportation, and the presence of many chronic and serious health problems in the community. In addition to these financial reasons, some tenants had tried to withhold rent to force the landlord to fix the property or to defend themselves against physical or sexual abuse from the landlord.

Even though advocates try to help people at the point of their eviction, by the time someone gets to court, it is usually too late to stop the process. Between sixty and eighty families were evicted from rental housing *every two weeks*, and we saw the numbers rise. Eviction Court became one of the many sites we used for education over the next few years.

The housing and financial crisis had also reached into the offices of the lawyers who worked for Legal Services. Cutbacks in state funding meant that only three lawyers remained to serve people in four counties. Most tenants were unaware of their rights or the law. The local head of Legal Services had written a booklet called *Landlord Tenant Rights and Responsibilities*, but very few people had seen it. We soon made it a tool for education and organizing.

Empowering the Community

As we learned more about the many issues that surfaced in Eviction Court, we met some amazing people who had been working on these issues in relative isolation. Some people were focused on trying to improve public transportation, find housing for the poor, feed the homeless, stop the attack on unions, improve race relations, uncover the high rates of cancer in the community, as well as trying to get the city to inspect rental property and regulate landlords. We shared what we had seen and began to talk about getting together to do education that empowers people.

People struggled to understand what exactly we meant by education for liberation. It was not the traditional model of a school. We invited them to meet in churches, bars, living rooms, union halls, parks, libraries, school rooms, fast food restaurants, and community centers. They in turn invited others to join our conversations. When they asked, "Where is this school?" we answered, "You are in it right now."

We also read books. One of the first books we studied together was Myles Horton's *The Long Haul*, about the beginnings and history of the Highlander Folk School, founded in 1931 to support labor organizing and later the Southern movement against segregation. There was an enthusiastic response. So many people wanted to read and talk about this new kind of education that we had to set up eight or nine book groups over the course of several months. People joined in to work on committees for a film series and a newsletter. In early 2011, we showed the first film in our series at the public library. The newsletter attracted even more attention. We were surprised by how much interest and activity arose from this small beginning.

We encouraged people to write for the newsletter, and they did. Soon the Freedom School helped form autonomous community groups to work on a number of issues: transportation, housing, unemployment, labor, health and the environment, and civil rights. The Freedom School worked with these committees to organize education and reflection that would help their work.

Reading the World: Power

We made the city part of our curriculum. We took groups to public meetings to observe how policy is shaped. With guidance from those who had been working on these issues for years, we took people to City Council, Eviction Court, County Commission meetings, and meetings of the county Transit Board, at first to listen and later to speak about the needs of the community. Some people were surprised to see how little regard local government had for the needs of people for housing and transportation; others already knew it from firsthand experience.

Many in the community remembered better days when neighborhoods were filled with people who walked to work at nearby factories. The abandoned industrial landscape inspired Janet to read and talk with people about the town's industrial history. With the help of faculty at local colleges and local historians, she developed industrial history tours of Newark. These tours became another way for people to learn from each other about their common history as well as understand the process of deindustrialization that resulted in so much poverty.

We called ourselves the Newark Freedom School after the schools of the Civil Rights Movement. It was a loosely organized, unincorporated group of volunteers with boundless enthusiasm because these were the issues affecting their lives. People offered their skills in support of activities. Some people contributed money to reprint the *Landlord/Tenants Rights* handbook for housing workshops; others always brought cookies to meetings. People designed T-shirts, business cards, and buttons. These were important steps because they signaled that a real organization was forming for education, even though it was small. When we did incorporate as a nonprofit organization in 2012, we had a diverse and experienced pool of people who agreed to serve on the board (https://www.thefreedomschoolinlickingcounty.org).

Our efforts were dwarfed in the spring of 2011, when there was an explosion of activity across the state of Ohio in response to proposed legislation to do away with collective bargaining for public employees. We were surprised by the huge numbers of people who mobilized in opposition to this anti-union legislation. We joined with hundreds of others to be trained to collect signatures on petitions opposing the legislation. The goal of this massive ninety-day campaign was to stop Senate Bill 5, which the Teamsters Union called a "War on Workers." In June, the state American Federation of Labor and Congress of Industrial Organizations (AFL-CIO) submitted more than 1.3 million signatures and stopped the bill. People saw clearly that there is strength in numbers.

Shortly after the petition victory over anti-union legislation, the local labor council bought forty-eight copies of *Labor's Untold Story* (Boyer & Morais, 1979) for community discussion groups led by the Freedom School. The book, a popular retelling of labor history, is a classic in the field of worker education. Our experiences reinforced our belief that even though established institutions rarely support emancipatory education, it is possible to carve out space both inside and outside of them for independent education in our communities and for their emerging leaders (Horton & Freire, 1990). Our educational activities, including book groups, community forums, films, and labor history tours, benefited from the advice, support, and participations of progressive people working in local institutions, including unions, colleges, and churches, who helped build the process of emancipatory education by providing support, meeting spaces, student workers, and inviting us to do programs.

If you intend to try to do this kind of education, you need to understand that you need to be tough, that you need to stand your ground, and that it will sometimes be a fight. Because education to develop leadership and promote organizing for social change is rarely in line with the goals of other organizations, there will be conflict. For example, some people thought our model should resemble the League of Women Voters—neutral research to inform the public. Yes, we said, but people need to take sides on issues. Some wanted us to be a place where college students could get experience in service learning. Yes, we said, but the priority of this work is building organization and leadership in the community. Others expected that the school would be an arm of the Democratic Party. We staunchly insisted that our mission would be education on issues, not partisan politics, and we would work with everyone who wanted to uncover the ways in which people are deprived of power and dignity. Some people encouraged us to deliver charity or uplift the poor by teaching job skills, General Educational Development (G.E.D.) classes, or better behavior through programs like Bridges Out of Poverty. We did not see that as our mission. As Martin Luther King said, "True compassion is more than flinging a coin to a beggar; it comes to see that an edifice which produces beggars needs restructuring" (King, 2015: 214). We want to provide opportunities for education to expose and eliminate the conditions that caused people to be unemployed, poor, and uneducated. Most importantly, when some educators insisted that people who cannot read cannot learn, we disagreed. People can learn from their own lived experiences and the experiences of others and become teachers for liberation. Our educational programming clearly demonstrated this principle. For example, the Freedom School sponsored a nonpartisan forum for candidates for city council at the public library, with questions submitted in advance to the candidates from community groups formed by the Freedom School. The community groups were made up of people of different races, political parties, religions, income groups, educational levels, and neighborhoods. They had joined together to learn more about the issues directly affecting their lives.

There is no question that building the school has been hard and challenging and that our labor to create dialogue, action, and reflection within oppressed communities has been successful but has also been perceived as a threat to the existing power structures in the county. We have, consequently, often been denied access to meeting spaces, information, resources, and support, because education for liberation endangers the maintenance of social control. Despite these challenges, the Freedom School's labor persists. We retired from the board in 2019, after ten years of leadership, but the Freedom School in Licking County continues to evolve. Our goal now is to encourage others to develop schools and political organizations necessary to change the world. Let us know if we can help or talk with you about ways to create a Freedom School in your community.

23

"The Gift of Setting Alight the Sparks of Hope in the Past": Ancestry and History in Pedagogical Praxis in the Brazilian Amazon

Inny Accioly, Benedito Alcântara, Aldineia Fernandes Monteiro, and Aldenice Monteiro

This text was written in July 2020, during the coronavirus pandemic, when Brazil reached the mark of 94,000 deaths and 2.7 million confirmed cases (Brazil, 2020). So far there have been reported nine thousand deaths and two hundred and forty-five thousand cases of coronavirus in the Brazilian states of Pará and Amapá, the Amazonian macro-region where the project "Young Environmental Guardians from Riverside Communities" takes place. The project is developed by the Pan-Amazonian Ecclesial Network (REPAM), the Amapá-Pará Educational Institute (IEAP), and the OLMA Observatory with the support of the Macapá Diocese, the Federal University of Amapá, and the Fluminense Federal University.[1] In a small school in the Marajó Archipelago, young people from riverside communities meet once a month with educators from different regions. Because of the pandemic, activities were suspended in March 2020.

By using the lens of history and ancestry, this chapter analyzed the project's pedagogical praxis, interrogating the present of the Amazon, which is threatened by corporations and stained by the blood of the murdered generations of peoples who fought against colonization, slavery, and expropriation (Benjamin, 1940; Bâ & Cardaire, 1957). Here, history and ancestry are folded into an act of negating what is, in anticipation of what could be. The praxis is guided by the intersubjective, community, and intergenerational dialogue, on the dialectics of denunciation and announcement (Freire, 1994). History is reconstructed from the perspective of the colonial and capitalist systems' victims, aiming at restoring the "Deep Amazon" and constructing another future.[2] The historical-critical materialism contradicts the idea that considers history as a heap of facts and actions that are overlapped in a chaotic and disconnected way. "Where we see the appearance of a chain of events, he [the Angel of History or the historical-critical materialist] sees one single catastrophe, which unceasingly piles rubble on top of rubble and hurls it before his feet" (Benjamin, 1940, p.6). As a result, analyzing the Afro-Amerindian History means looking at the catastrophe of colonization and slavery, which are the roots of the current time. The rubble, hurled before our feet, are the annihilated peoples who fought for freedom, land, and the right to exist.

In the Latin American grassroots movements' praxis, there is a tradition of calling the murdered brother's or sister's names and answering "present." In remembering the dead, it is affirmed that they live in every person who engages in their struggle.

> Are we not touched by the same breath of air which was among that which came before? Is there not an echo of those who have been silenced in the voices to which we lend our ears today? … If so, then there is a secret appointment between the generations of the past and that of our own. For we have been expected upon this earth. For it has been given us to know, just like every generation before us, a weak messianic power, on which the past has a claim.
>
> (Benjamin, 1940, p. 2)

Against the linear and quantitative view of history, in the quote above Benjamin presented a qualitative perception of temporality, rooted in remembrance and in the messianic/revolutionary rupture of continuity (Löwy, 2002).

Ancestry brings to light the dimension of a past that is present and that points to a future of liberation, which needs to be constructed. It is opposed to the Cartesian mentality that dissociates the material and the spiritual dimensions and, therefore, conceives the human being in its entirety. Furthermore, it reveals knowledge from times before colonization, which resisted through oral tradition (Bâ, 2010). This is knowledge about nature and human organization, which are intertwined with stories of resistance to colonial control, enslavement, and expropriation. This way, ancestry refers to the roots that connect each human being with his/her past, with previous generations, and with their ways of life.

Both historical and ancestral past lay claim to the lives of the oppressed and inform the present about their confidence, courage, humor, cunning, and steadfastness in their struggle. Critical educators cannot reject this claim with impunity. They have the ethical duty to fight for all lives that have been denied throughout history and for those that will still be, especially in the current socio-environmental and economic catastrophe (Dussel, 2012). The critique is the starting point of the struggle for life. However, it is not possible to criticize the current system without the recognition of the "other" (whose life is denied to the limit) as an autonomous subject, free and equal in his/her humanity. In this chapter, it is argued that the recognition of ancestry is an important step toward the reconstruction of collective ties. Linking education and ancestry, therefore, would redirect the teaching-learning process to its collective and historically situated character.

Lenses of History and Ancestry on the Current Amazon

> On Saturday, before the sunrise, I took the road to go to *Ariri* to reconnect with Mother Earth Pachamama. Diving into the water, listening to the rain from the bottom of the river, embracing the trees and plants, and being silent inside and

> out. At night, passing *andiroba* and *pracaxi* oils on my body, massaging each bone joint, relaxing the muscles, crying and crying, contemplating the creation and the human saga in pandemic times. After 4 months, I've cut my hair kneeling on the *trapiche*, immersed in the river waters. I spent hours in the hammock, sleeping, and dreaming. I heard the forest's sounds and moans. May the tears fertilize the gardens that I cultivate. May the bleeding wounds recover the vital link in our existence. We are in the middle of 2020. We are in the middle of the world, on the Equator. We have come this far. We will keep moving on![3]

That night, the full moon emerged on the Amazon River, from the direction of the São José de Macapá Bay. It was 2019. Nobody wanted to miss the moon show and that is why some people took photographs using cell phone cameras. The Saturday night's dialogue meeting of the project "Young Environmental Guardians from Riverside Communities" was scheduled for after dinner. At the expected moment, the *trapiche* was crowded with students, educators, and some children running around. The geography teacher started the dialogue: "Let's take an imaginary tour in the Amazon, to understand its different realities, which have crossed centuries and which are still involved in so many mysteries and challenges." In the Brazilian Amazon, the lens of history points to the "single catastrophe," which "unceasingly piles rubbles" (Benjamin, 1940, p. 6) of genocide since the Portuguese colonization in 1500, and which nowadays hurls before our feet the multiple tensions between the ancestral peoples' culture and knowledge, the Portuguese colonizer's culture and the capitalist ideology of progress that claims for the economic exploitation of the forest.

The ancestral native peoples have developed a real cartography of the Amazon region by mapping the rivers' path and living in coexistence with the forest. They have developed knowledge about curing and preventing illnesses using herbs, fruits, and seeds. This knowledge is orally transmitted over several generations. This way, they consolidated wisdom about the tides, the climate, fishing, and river navigation. The rhythm of the rains and the rivers' waters marks the local culture creating a peculiar relationship with time. For example, the 2,500 islands of the archipelago where the project takes place are flooded twice a day. Thus, the waters' time gains more importance than the chronological time since the waters impose strict limits on navigation. Over the centuries, rivers were the "roads" and boats and canoes were the means of transportation. Likewise, the river is the backyard, the space for leisure, and socializing and it also plays an important role in providing part of communities' daily food that comes from fishing.

> The river and the riversides' communities are part of one whole. While the river provides food and fertilizes the banks when waters go up and down, the riversides' communities historically protect the river. This can be noticed in the legends from the Amazon, like the *Iara* legend (Mother of the Waters), the big snake legend— that eats the ones who do not respect nature – and many others. These legends express the 'humanization' of nature and the 'naturalization' of humans.
>
> (Cruz, 1999, p. 105, our translation)

Since 2007, the riverside communities have been recognized as traditional communities by the Federal Decree that instituted the "National Policy for the Sustainable Development of Traditional Peoples and Communities" due to their social organization, their practices, and knowledge. The ways they relate to the river and the forest are connected to times before European colonization: "knowledge is a light that exists in man. It is the inheritance of everything that our ancestors came to know and that is latent in everything they transmitted to us, just as the baobab tree already exists in its seed potential" (Tierno Bokar apud Bâ & Cardaire, 1957). Most of this knowledge came from Indigenous heritage which conceives human beings as a material and spiritual totality connected to forests, rivers, and all beings.

According to Marx, nature is the inorganic body of the human being and, therefore, his physical and spiritual life is linked to it:

> Nature is man's inorganic body – nature, that is, insofar as it is not itself a human body. Man lives on nature – means that nature is his body, with which he must remain in continuous interchange if he is not to die. That man's physical and spiritual life is linked to nature means simply that nature is linked to itself, for man is a part of nature.
>
> (Marx, 1959, p. 31)

However, colonization established the mode of production based on the exploitation of nature and slave labor, which drastically affected native peoples' and African peoples' ways of relating to nature. Both the descendants of Africans who escaped from slave labor in plantations and took shelter in resistance territories (*quilombos*), and the surviving Indigenous peoples are now recognized for their importance for environmental protection.

The 1988 Brazilian Constitution guarantees the rights of Indigenous peoples and the peoples from *quilombos* to land and the preservation of their culture. However, the intensive and predatory mining and agribusiness threaten their rights and transform the rural zones into areas of permanent conflict. The Indigenous and African peoples' historical resistance has strongly marked Amazonian cultures. In the early nineteenth century, the Indigenous, Black and mestizo people played an important role in one of the biggest popular revolts in Brazilian history (the Cabanagem revolt). The rebels removed the representatives of colonial power in the Amazon (Pinheiro, 1999). During the war that lasted around six years, 40 percent of the local population died (Chiavenato, 2007). Although the rebels did not achieve their goals of autonomy and slavery abolition, the spilled blood fertilized the Amazon and the Brazilian territory with strength and inspiration for fighting for justice.

In 1822, Brazil declared independence from the Portuguese Metropolis and in 1889 the republican regime was established. Since that time, the rubber boom has promoted waves of migrant workers from Northeast Brazil to the Amazon. This also resulted in a large expansion of European presence, provoking great cultural transformation. In the twentieth century, governmental projects that have encouraged migration to the Amazon in order to stimulate large-scale agriculture and commercial exploitation of the forest, as well as the construction of highways and hydroelectric power plants, have intensified conflicts over land ownership, which increased cases of assassination of community leaders (REPAM, 2020).

The conflicts led the peasants, the Indigenous peoples, and the traditional communities to organize themselves into unions and grassroots movements for struggling for rights and the preservation of the Amazon Rainforest since this is a condition for maintaining their ways of life. Chico Mendes, a rubber tapper, a trade union leader in a small town called Xapuri, in Acre State (North Brazil), became world-famous and inspired environmentalist movements worldwide due to his activism for preserving the forest and advocating for the rights of peasants and Indigenous peoples. In 1987, he was awarded the United Nations Environmental Program Global 500 Roll of Honor. The following year, he was assassinated. Mendes was the ninetieth rural activist murdered that year in Brazil (Hall, 1997). More than thirty years after his death, Chico Mendes is still a reference, for example, in the curriculum of the Department of Environmental Education at Korea National University of Education (South Korea). As Mendes stated, "At first, I thought I was fighting to save rubber trees, then I thought I was fighting to save the Amazon rainforest. Now I realize I am fighting for humanity" (Da Rocha & Possamai, 2015).

The strength of Brazilians' ancestry proves that "the dead do not die, on the contrary, they feed the struggle for land and remain present in the journey" (Souza, 2016, p. 360). Thus, history and ancestry are intertwined to found a concept of time created on the act of "brushing History against the grain." According to Benjamin, "the only writer of History with the gift of setting alight the sparks of hope in the past, is the one who is convinced of this: that not even the dead will be safe from the enemy, if he is victorious. And this enemy has not ceased to be victorious" (Benjamin, 1940, p. 4). The enemy's victory is perpetuated by a "banking education system" that serves oppression and control and, therefore, cannot hide its necrophilic imprint (Freire, 1994). This system's primary task was to annihilate traditional knowledge and destroy ancestral awareness. This resulted in mentalities that were educated to deny the past, despise the elders, and the knowledge that came from oral traditions (Barros et al., 2018).

Education, Ancestry and the Project "Young Environmental Guardians from Riverside Communities"

As mentioned before, linking education and ancestry is a possibility for redirecting the teaching-learning process to its collective and historically situated character.

> In the act of knowledge, it is not possible to deny the individual dimension of the subject. But I think that this dimension is not enough to explain the act of knowing. The act of knowledge is social. ... My individual practice of knowing a certain object occurs in a social practice that determines my individual approach to a certain object. It is necessary that the student ... recognizes the social dimension of his individual act of knowing.
>
> (Freire & Guimarães, 2014, p. 185)

The act of knowing is social, in the sense that "it is not the consciousness of men that determines their existence, but their social existence that determines their consciousness" (Marx, 2008, p. 47). Thus, the conscience of the individual is constituted in society, in the material and inter-psychic relations in a given historical time (Vygotsky, 1997).

The ancestry's approach makes it possible to broaden the historical analysis and reconstruct it from the remembrance, the liberating anamnesis, the affirmation of life in face of its permanent negation. However, pedagogical practices should be rooted in the victims' perspective (the oppressed) and the community's intersubjective dialogue (Dussel, 2012). The liberating anamnesis, the rescue of the ancestral learning, takes place when individuals come together motivated by a common interest of transforming their quality of life. In a second moment, the individuals find themselves connected in a vital link for the maintenance of their own lives, which extends to the maintenance of all lives on earth. Then, from the common concerns, there is an understanding of the interdependence that connects them to the previous generations. The knowledge transmitted by the elders gains centrality as it allows children and youth to access memories of a past that they did not live but that was fundamental for their current presence in society as historical subjects capable of promoting social transformation and breaking the linearity of history.

In the project, the ancestral learning is constructed through the dialogues between the youths, the elders, and the children. The main goal is to reinforce the youths' commitment to the Amazon and the riverside territories, reaffirming the principles of the defense of life, *buen vivir* (good living), and socio-environmental justice.[4] The pedagogical praxis of rescuing the ancestral spirituality is guided by the popular critical education theoretical-practical framework. The purpose is not to go back to the past—besides being impossible, it is not desirable—but to construct common ancestral futures that oppose the commodification of forests, waters, land, and the whole of life.

The project is hosted by a school built of wood, without doors or windows, integrated with the forest and the Amazon River. It was conceived by two strong women (Aldineia and Aldenice, who are local residents) and plays an important role in providing access to high school education. Often, the lack of public services leads youth to leave the community. One weekend a month, students travel in small boats to the project meetings. Some spend two hours sailing on the river. Teachers from different states and countries conduct the collective teaching-learning rituals, which start when they arrive at school, with the welcoming hugs, and continue during the group activities and talks, the meals—that are special moments for sharing local foods (açaí, fish, shrimp)—and in the evening relaxing time with regional music and dances. The teaching-learning rituals only end when everyone finds a place to hang the hammock to sleep and rest. Sleeping in hammocks is an Indigenous' habit that is part of the Amazonian culture. The term teaching-learning ritual expresses that both are not separate and that they reach a ritualistic dimension with the *mística*, which is rooted in the liberation theology inspired by Freire's concept of *conscientização* (Freire, 1994). It's an important part of some grassroots movements' political mobilization for inspiring and conveying knowledge about collective memory (Issa, 2007). Despite being a Catholic legacy, the *mística* in the project takes contributions from Indigenous, and African religiosity.

The following narrative is an example of how it is established:

> We are in the first activity of the first day of classes in 2020. In the center of the hall is the "mandala of life" (made of local trees' leaves, seeds, fruits, oils, herbs, and symbols of the Amazonian culture), whose aromas and colors create the atmosphere for the pedagogical praxis. It is a solemn moment. Children, youth, and elders are standing in a great circle. Two babies are on their mothers' lap. They represent the future that we want to construct in the present. The mothers guide their babies so that each person can be blessed by them. These new lives are celebrated as a way of celebrating life on earth. Life is also represented in the elements of water, earth, and fire, which pass from hand to hand so that each person can look, smell, and be connected with them. The invited educators who came from far do not know the elements that are in the mandala. So, the youth enthusiastically teach them about their culture and traditional medicine.

The dialectical analysis from local to global is constructed as the invited educators share their life stories and their worldviews. This leads to a more critical perspective that raises new questions: Why are there so many people going hungry in a place so rich in biodiversity? From this question, one comes to local problems such as the conflicts over land ownership and the injustices around the commercial chain of *açaí* – the Amazonian fruit extracted by communities for feeding their families and for exporting.

The methodology of the Theater of the Oppressed made it possible to perform a scene about a fictional public hearing at the city hall for addressing conflicts over land tenure and child labor. This enabled the recognition of the oppressive local reality. This way, the teaching-learning rituals recall stories of murdered activists (such as Chico Mendes) for taking the strength, wisdom, and inspiration from them. The acts of remembering and dreaming, therefore, are connected with the purpose of breaking the linearity of history for building a new future.

Conclusions

The ability to intertwine the historical-critical perspective of time with ancestry in a transformative praxis aiming at transforming society characterizes leaders such as Chico Mendes and Paulo Freire. For this reason, their legacies remain alive. The connection with ancestry can pedagogically contribute to reestablishing the links of collectivity broken by colonialism and shattered by the neoliberal school, which is rooted in individualism and competition. Therefore, the critical educator has great importance in the current socio-environmental catastrophe that is killing Indigenous peoples and traditional communities. In the Amazon, it is said that when elders die, it is as if several libraries are set on fire. Thus, it is up to the present generation to keep the flame of traditional knowledge alive, which can nourish pedagogical praxis in struggles for justice and liberation.

24

Thy Will Be Done: Radical Love as Self-Other Healing Praxis

Patricia Krueger-Henney and Perpetual Anastasia Hayfron

This chapter is a dialogic, intergenerational, and cross-racial space unfolding between us. We follow a question-and-answer-approach, creating a written conversation between two womynx born during different generations and raised and schooled in different parts of the world. We were brought together in a doctoral program at a public university and are deeply cognizant of the ways that academia's traditions position us on opposing ends along hierarchized power dynamics: student–teacher, advisee–advisor, mentee–mentor, younger–older, pre- and post-dissertation. From day one of having met in the academic classroom, we practiced and modeled a radical love and respect for each other that intentionally abandons, if not betrays, knowledge traditions that promote and protect racialized meritocracy and the status quo. We spilled our excitement for and about each other's nonnegotiable articulations of our daily refusals into late night messaging. Even amidst the Covid-19 pandemic raging on top of previous and unresolved pandemics (i.e., growing Black maternity death rates, food insecurity among trans lives), our linking to each other via phone conversations and text messaging "has not missed a beat" (Perpetual, personal communication). Instead, we have remained deeply invested in each other's pursuit of finding health amidst rampant white supremacy, anti-Black racism, ableism, misogyny, and hetero-patriarchy in and outside of academia.

We turn to Black feminist writer Toni Cade Bambara who opens her novel *The Salt Eaters* (1992) with candid insight to restoring our (Black, Brown, Queer, working class, immigrant womyxn's) health: "Just so's you're sure, sweetheart, and ready to be healed, cause wholeness is no trifling matter. A lot of weight when you're well" (p. 10). We, too, deliberately choose "healing" over our "wellness." The concretized, racist, and Westernized definitions of what it takes and means to be or get "well" are not meant for us. Institutionalized and state-sanctioned forms of wellness surveille and control our bodies and lifeworlds. We were not born "well," and the current industry of corporatized "wellness" ensures that we will never be "well" to thrive. We don't want to be "well." Instead, we seek our healing as a set of ongoing practices that we define among and for ourselves. "Healing" in this sense is our collective fugitive declarations of our humanities and futures.

The systematic subordination of people is fundamental to understanding the intimate interconnections between global settler colonialism and postcolonialities that are driven by land theft and appropriation, racialized capitalist economies that chase after the commodification of land and life, and the devastations these maintain particularly in economically under-resourced lives. However, these systemic forces of violence transcend time-spaces and blast right through our raced, classed, and gendered lifeworlds. Having access to more remote spaces in academia during the past few years did not protect us from physical and mental injuries that ongoing horrors, terrors, and traumas have etched into our bodies. Both of us have been diagnosed with medical conditions that make the functioning of our bodies regularly painful, sometimes impossible. We ask, how do we restore, recover, and protect ourselves, our bodies, as we walk through deadly minefields? What are some immediate as well as more sustainable remedies that do not pave healing into dependence on profit-driven and privatized cures (i.e., Big Pharma)? Can we demand liberation with the same terminology of "healing" that also declares our death sentences?

Here, we speak openly about our beliefs and practices of healing as simultaneously accomplices to maintaining our collective fight against the systemic erasure of our lives. We posit healing is a praxis, fueled by radical love for self and others, built by individual commitments to and hinged on collectivized desires toward enacting liberation from economic exploitation and social oppression. To know about and do the work of healing with this purpose means protesting, resisting, and refusing to participate in the re|production of the injustices and inequalities current globally hegemonized economic and social relations spew into every realm of our lives. As individual-collective labor, we contest healing births individual visions to be linked with collective enactments of freedom. Moreover, healing work is political, a "Source of Self-Regard" (Morrison, 2019) and others concurrently. Healing is protesting, and as Audre Lorde wrote, "I see protest as a genuine means of encouraging someone to feel the inconsistencies, the horror, of the lives we are living. Social protest is to say that we do not have to live this way" (2008, p. 163). We seek our healing with and through each other's courage.

While healing fueled by love cannot cure or dismantle actual structures of capitalist, white supremacist hetero-patriarchy, healing practices sustained by "a hermeneutics of love" (Sandoval, 2000, p. 136) embrace risk taking to find multiple pathways leading to healing. And healing grounded in radical love can be a powerful antidote to defragment our socially constructed differences. As Toni Cade Bambara accentuates, we offer hope for the living, thank those who came before us (but are not afraid to disagree), and refuse to participate in state-sanctioned traditions and rituals that destroy and kill us. Healing as radical knowledge of self and others in action can move us to do this freedom-seeking work.

In the section that follows, we braid together themes from a conversation we recorded in which we each answered six key questions about healing in our lives. We do not offer analysis and categorization of our own words. We will not allow the radical love-abiding healing we frame here to be shoved under the rug of academic conventions. Radical healing is dangerous, and it cannot be tamed and contained. It will move freely into the lives of those who have wanted and needed it for what seems forever. We conclude by recasting healing as a praxis of radical self-other love for freedom.

We Done Resurrecting Ourselves: Declarations of Loving Our Lives

What is my origin story with regards to healing?

PAH: My story of healing began when I was conceived. This is not something I have been consistently and consciously aware of throughout my life. My mother, my muse, the source of my foundation, prayed to Our Lady of Perpetual Help for a girl when she found out she was pregnant at forty-six. She named me, a Ghanaian-Liberian girl born Monday, a Virgo, after the Virgin Mary herself: Perpetual Anastasia Adjwoa Baiswa Hayfron.

From a young age, I was conditioned to be silent to survive. I was teased and bullied from kindergarten until high school for various things including how I was dressed. When I told my mother, she told me to "ignore it" and do my schoolwork. Since birth my mother dressed me up, my love of accessories and shoes is birthed from her. She always made sure her children were "presentable" leaving the house. By the time I entered high school I learned to suffer in silence *and* look damn good doing it. The nonnegotiable standard my mother had set for herself in regard to dressing her children is something I adopted for myself and cultivated into a survival mechanism for twenty-seven years.

My muse is a devout catholic; I was born into colonization and generational self-hate. My fate premeditated and involuntarily sealed when I was baptized as an infant in my father's Methodist church. My muse's self-betrayal became my biggest conquest, and that has led me to the divinity I was stripped off as an infant. Healing is something I will do for the rest of my life as radical self-love is my birthright.

PKH: I may not have called my curiosities about the always-present urgencies for social change "healing." Neither would I have linked my commitment to teaching and learning to "healing work," at least not in the ways I speak of these terms now as an adult. "Healing" echoes throughout most social media platforms these days, especially since Covid-19. This global pandemic has laid bare structures and mechanisms of globalized capitalist nastiness. But we have always been in trouble. The lives of BIPOC[1] peoples were never guaranteed in time-spaces where settler colonialities reigned. I spent my adolescence and early adulthood feeling tormented while entering conversations about social change and racial justice with the same terminologies that also uphold white supremacy and thus our subordinations. "Healing" is one of those terms; it tends to privilege individual needs over communal approaches to maintaining health that will benefit all.

Growing up on both sides of the Atlantic, I experienced first-hand the contradiction between healing self and collective healing. After a ten-hour flight, I would leave behind or arrive to spaces of economically saturated European nation-states, or systemically underdeveloped sovereign nations in the Caribbean. The socialized health-care system of one settler nation-state was directly enmeshed with the plundering of resources of the territories it had colonized centuries before. I knew then I would refuse to look at peoples' lives through the cataracted gaze of white settler coloniality. This meant being consistent about making my teaching and researching pedagogies answerable to people's lives. Just as I demand from myself, I invite students to think of their future teaching and researching purposes. This self-reflexive dialogue is guided by questions like, Whose side is my research on? Who gets hurt? Who benefits? What is my endgame with this research?

Where have I run myself into the ground?

PAH: I've run myself into the ground when choosing the comfort of others over my own to feel/be loved, while never believing those who showed they loved me because it wasn't coming from the people I thought I wanted it from the most. Aunty Nikki Giovanni said on the "Daughters of Series" by Girl Trek (2020), "why are you looking for approval from people who don't look like you!?" This is another area I've been raggedy with myself: devouring perfectionism and washing it down with institutional bleach (Guishard, 2009), creating a false sense of external stability while ignoring my internal mutilation, my silence overall as it pertains to various aspects of myself and my life. My absorption of parenthood at six eliminated my childhood innocence. I've had to break my silence for my parentified, inner child to heal. Rationalizing pain so I don't have to feel it has been my ultimate self-betrayal.

PKH: I live for the beehives among us; I understand my individual being and living in this world as intimately connected to my families and communities I do not restrict to shared biology. So, I run myself into the ground when I give into forces that exploit the ways I am generous with my labor, energy, and creativity; I run out of steam when I am isolated from my collective being. Racialized capitalism commodifies and exploits laboring bodies without taking into account the mental and physical toll this takes on us and our communities. I have grown "sick and tired of being sick and tired" (words of Fannie Lou Hamer) when I have allowed academia to take over time-spaces we need for ourselves. As a student and faculty, I have repeatedly told myself, "I will not let [name of university] kill me."

Where and how has the world run me into the ground?

PAH: My muse was my first bully, then from primary school to high school I was bullied. For any of my experiences as a Black human to be relevant in academia I must cite my primary sources. It is ridiculous yet clear that we, Black womxn, are mandated to constantly re-traumatize ourselves in order to prove to the white mind an abuse that is historical and ongoing (Evans-Winters, 2009). The Black body and mind battle lifelong assaults of micro and macro aggressions from the time Black people are born, as a result of reigning social structures that legitimize white supremacy. My chances of dying in childbirth as a result of my identity are quadruple in comparison to white womxn as a consequence of this. The children that I may or may not have the opportunity to raise in the future are more likely to die while driving, walking, simply existing … because of the color of my skin. They will be born with the epigenetics associated with my survival tactics. This grave world has taught me to neglect my multiplicity and compartmentalize it in order to survive. School systems were not created for Black students like me in mind. What it takes to be considered a scholar in the eyes of the institution, I see as a death sentence for my spirit. However, I am anxious about whether my lived experiences are worthy for my academic pursuits because they are not in accordance with "institutional standards." Instead, institutions have run me into the ground by neglecting my multiplicity, leaving me anxiously second-guessing myself at every turn, which is a struggle every day. Hence, by acknowledging my rage while pursuing my doctorate, I have encountered deep love and honor. In the words of Robin G. Kelly (2018), "Black study and resistance must begin with love. … To love this way requires relentless struggle, deep study, and critique" (p. 164).

PKH: None of our social institutions were originally purposed to hold our collective thinking, strategizing, or guard our practices of care for each other. I do not trust and neither do I rely on academic spaces to do this for us. We cannot seek love and acceptance from places that built their futures by banking on our destruction. Hence my social relations are deeply political, particularly with BIPOC, immigrant, gender-fluid persons, and non-white womxn. As much as we relax in the company of each other to speak truths to our daily struggles, us coming together is always guided by the intensity of "when's their next strike against us coming? Because it is coming!" Having to be on guard 24/7 will never allow us to breathe deeply, think openly, and love freely. The nonstop murdering of Black and trans lives, whether in public or within the privacy of home life, speak to how this country is free to kill Black and trans bodies. In academia, I have experienced this erasure of the space between life and death through "spirit murdering" (Love, 2019) that reduces our existence to "a life of exhaustions, a life of doubt, a life of state-sanctioned violence, and a life consumed with the objective of surviving" (p. 39). It is an ontologically tight space that defaults us to being breakable, exploitable and always replaceable. We are drained of our creative sparks that can set free our love and joy for each other.

How do I heal myself?

PAH: I pay attention to what I deserve, being hypervigilant about unconsciously lying to myself and others because "I don't want anyone to think." After twenty-seven years of not being my fully expressed self in all areas of my life, I am committed to deconditioning from self-betrayal and the suppression of my multiplicity to survive a world that hates me (Cooper, 2018). My destiny doesn't require anyone's approval. I show gratitude to the highest by *choosing* to show up as the best version of myself, unapologetic in my truth. I have healed by choosing my own comforts over others' in order to give love. Once I unlearned the things I thought I loved, I began to receive the love I deserved, and I realized, radical love is my birthright. I used to fear how others perceived me when I was surviving. In the midst of this pandemic, we have been forced to be still and see we aren't small in comparison to system and structures, as white supremacy has brainwashed us to believe. In releasing my own shackles of survival and engaging in the process of creating, I have been able to return to my roots and acknowledge the divinity of my ancestors, igniting my own flame of divinity.

PKH: The words of Fred Moten and Stefano Harney have tossed me many lifelines. They explain, our work toward mobilizing each other within the confines of academia toward forms of freedom is to be "in but not of the modern university" (2013, p. 26). For these spaces of "the undercommons," the authors question, "What is that work and what is its social capacity for both reproducing the university and producing fugitivity?" Doing subversive academic work through teaching, service and research has meant positioning my teaching practices and the learning I facilitate against the currents of conventions. I take great care of my teaching. I am a knowledge mobilizer who intentionally teaches and learns *against* Eurocentric, settler colonial, heteronormative, and ableist traditions of my discipline (education). Teaching and learning against mainstreamed, whitewashed knowledge can create a strengthened collective critical consciousness among us. Unlearning what we have internalized to know about ourselves and each other has healing powers because it steers us through questioning master narratives that perpetuate and protect one-sided stories (and lies!) about us and our communities. Knowledge mobilization is utterly relational and willfully heals injuries committed against us by curricular violence (Patel, 2019). Moreover, healing through knowledge mobilization is guided by a fearless, radical love for naming all that is not yet; it fosters our fugitivity that "is (in) the invention of escape, stealing away in the confines, in the form, of a break" (Harney & Moten, 2013, p. 51). Knowledge mobilization as a healing practice also contributes to the protection of well-being of others, and I teach future accomplices to declare, "this is how I want to be loved, seen, heard. This is what I want you to know about me, and us. And if you don't stop hurting me, I will know what actions I need to take to make sure I am going to be okay."

Who else participates in my healing work?

PAH: *Me*! My mother. My friends. My Virgos PKH and JME. My ancestors. My babies. Mother Mercy. God. My Grandmothers. Black Womxn! Cannabis.

PKH: My students, my elders, partner, my children (also beyond blood-relations), my ancestors, chosen families, and me. Everything I do, whether for myself or for others, is a collective undertaking. In fact, my co-conspirators remind me constantly of the importance of resting, reflecting, pausing, and eating healthy while doing movement-nourishing work. I tend to overlook these self-healing practices.

How are others benefiting from your healing work?

PAH: On September 6, 2018, at 4:39 p.m., the world began to unravel for me. I was in your (PKH's) TLC class and you stated, "Unlearning what we know is hard and unsettling … it's often painful to be groundbreaking. Many people get depressed and cynical." This is exactly what has taken place for me in the pursuit of unlearning in order to survive and embrace my rage. If it wasn't for your radical love and presence, I would not have had the insight to recognize my pain was worthy of acknowledgment. At a time when I was filled with despair, you said, "I know you are in pain, write about it!" Your radical love unapologetically honors my rage; your encouragement of my healing made me incapable of suffering in silence. The institution isn't worthy of you and they can never kill you because unconditional love never dies. Your love is uncomfortable, because there is no growth in comfort, but it's invigorating at the same time. Your presence and spirit transform the classroom to a sanctuary.

PKH: One of the first things you (PAH) said to me for this project was: "we die every day, and we resurrect ourselves every day." This past year you showed me your courage to surmount an internalized expectation to reinvent ourselves after each racist and misogynist blow we receive. You taught me that there is a limit to how much pain and self-degradation we can endure. In your rage I see you claw after the love and strength you have for yourself. It runs deeply and next to other people's fed-upness with the nastiness in our world. The joy and range of your rage is infectious and intimidating. Just gorgeous! It is magnificent that you have chosen the infinities of you over the deadly predetermined destinations of you! Your strategic refusals to secure your self-growth ignites our collective getting-out and getting-free.

Conclusion

The labor of healing through and with radical love for each other, whether through teaching and learning, birth assistance, mentoring, or community organizing, does not rest on the assumption that BIPOC, immigrant, gender-fluid, poor, and working class people are broken. The healing we speak to disagrees with current trends in healing that focus on personal self-care and benefiting, if not protecting, individual wellness (Delaney, 2020). This dominant narrative about healing is not grounded in collective practices of healing as both starting point and final destination. We emphasize that our practices of healing are not grounded in the brokenness of our bodies and lives.

The healing we speak to does not necessitate causality between injury and healing. We do not enact healing practices *because* we wait for events to strike and injure us, discriminate against us, marginalize us, and attempt to destroy us. Our radically loving healing does not wait; we engage in healing work *despite the* struggles and the injuries. We choose healing as a way of knowing and moving through life while seeking the company and wisdom of each other. We seek our futurities *despite ongoing* supremacy, oppression, and dispossessions committed against us. While our healing work is surely responsive to daily racist and transphobic assaults on ourselves and communities, our healing labor is not vindictive of ongoing systemic violence. We participate in our radical healing practices and pedagogies because *through and with* them we seek and demand better living conditions for all. Radically loving healing positions us at a threshold between what has not worked for us, has perpetually endangered us, that we no longer want, and creates social systems, resources, and shifts us toward collective responsibility for nourishing "care webs" (Piepzna-Samarasinha, 2018, p. 33) that are more equally accessible to us. Healing that positions us at this threshold is freeing, liberating, but moreover, fugitive from oppressive and subordinating forces in our lifeworlds. This healing is mobilizing. It moves us collectively.

25

Deflecting the Echoes of Settler-Colonialism: Resilience and Healing While Working with Maya Youth

Donna DeGennaro

In November 2019, I received shocking news. The office of a nonprofit I started was found disheveled and nearly empty. What once was the "home" of Unlocking Silent Histories (USH), a program designed to equip Indigenous youth with the tools to capture their heritages through their perspectives, was vacated. Local leaders who the community and I entrusted to oversee the program pawned an accumulation of computers, cameras, and other documentary equipment gathered over seven years.

The once vibrant energy that inspired the creation of USH quickly dissipated. The exhausting and exhilarating ride, destroyed in a heartbeat. When I mustered the courage to tell my critical education community, nonprofit colleagues, and Maya partners, I received immediate support. Each revered USH and recommended that I rest. Heeding their advice, I paused the organization after working with the remaining program leaders to salvage what we could of the year.

The distance from both the incident and the project resulted in much needed healing. Ceasing the program allowed me to engage in important reflection regarding the complexities, pervasiveness, and inner workings of a settler-colonial past and present. Moreover, time away made visible the powers of community connections to transcend it. To be clear, settler-colonialism is a form of colonization where settlers make their "new" land a permanent home by taking resources and obtaining indentured servants, explicitly for their benefit (Veracini, 2010). Settler-colonialism is a pervasive system that engraves oppressive power systems; it is not a singular event. In European settler-colonial nations, its values are Eurocentric, claiming ethnic and moral superiority over those colonized, and coalescing around dispossession and dehumanization of Indigenous peoples' lands, resources, and cultures (Wolfe, 1999, 2006).

Critical educators confront settler-colonialism in ourselves, our institutions, and our work. Consequently, we experience "unsettled times" in perpetuity. The echoes reveal the unyielding grips of settler-colonialism to outline the birth and "death" of USH. Each story awakens consciousness and evokes new strategies of action (Swidler,

1986). Writing this is part of healing for both myself and the communities from which I learn.

Echo 1: Occupancy and Escape

There is an irony that lies between becoming a critical educator and working as a professor. Ultimately, we live in a third space existing neither in our training or our employment.

As doctoral students, we utilize critical theory to confront institutions, structures, and power, pushing back on oppressive and marginalizing acts. Personally, I focused on the interrelationships among media, culture, and society, which revealed the dark history of using media to shape the image of historically disenfranchised peoples. Specifically, films like *Reel Injun* and *I am not Your Negro* highlights how media stereotypes and racializes Indigenous Peoples and Black Americans. The images burn into the social imagination, creating a collective memory and sealing the dominant narrative into the fabric of society (Delgado, 1991). These movies also show how social, cultural, and political establishments work together to maintain social control and create a master narrative where minorities are "muted and erased when they challenge dominant culture authority and power" (Ladson-Billings, 1998, 18).

As professors, we work in colonized and colonizing institutions while at the same time struggle each day to resist the vices of settler-colonialism, and struggling. Foremost, universities sit on dispossessed Indigenous land. To be sure, the Morrill Act of 1862 allowed states to take land from Indigenous Peoples and establish land-grant colleges (Lee & Ahtone, 2020). This act enabled the westward expanding empire of the United States, converting land into capital that profited from Native American soil (la paperson, 2017). In addition to dominating lands with physical structures, academies are steeped in settler-colonial values, replicating indistinguishable policies, practices, and curriculum (Masta, 2019; Patel, 2019). As massive colonizing machines, universities are complicit in the ongoing enactment of settler-colonialism by perpetuating other colonizing acts such as knowledge production, wars, media production, and government and educational policies (la paperson, 2017). Professors and employee's unwillingness to oppose or acknowledge the university's role in colonialism makes us participants in cultural, social, and educational reproduction (Bourdieu & Passeron, 1990). Folding "helplessly" into the system all members of the institutions succumb to colonizing systems that oppress us, our students, and our societies.

Critical educators rest in either reality. Instead, we hold steadfastly to the principles of emancipation, conscientization, critical conversation, and the quest for humanization (Freire, 1970, 1973). Champions of a liberatory pedagogy, we engage as a critical reflexivity, learning from and with the community. Because "attempting to liberate the oppressed without their reflective participation in the act of liberation is to treat them as objects that must be saved from a burning building" (Friere, 1970, p. 52).

Subscribing to the above, my research trajectory began to take shape. I established partnerships in urban and rural contexts to work through what it means to *live* critical pedagogy. From youth-direct web design workshops (DeGennaro & Brown,

2009), to digital story projects (DeGennaro, 2008), to video artifact critiquing media representations, and youth written and produced documentary shorts (DeGennaro, 2016), I, along with my young research partners, were exploring lived critical pedagogy. Listening to and learning from youth and their communities, we cocreated three foundational principles for counternarratives and liberatory pedagogy:

1. Local knowledge and voice are the foundations of authentic learning.
2. Community connected themes encourage critical and creative expression.
3. Youth have the capacity to direct their own learning and author their own stories.

These foundations guided the work that would later become the substructure of USH, which was founded on possibility and promise stemming from youth visions for using media to shift cultural narratives. While media is undeniably used by those in power to shape narratives, it also holds possibilities to (re)image and (re)present them (Solorzano & Yosso 2002). Counterstories have implications for voice, positionality, and authority. This is particularly salient for oppressed communities as many disenfranchised peoples know that their stories are a means of survival and liberation (Delgado, 1989). Similarly, while education functions as a conditioning instrument to assimilate children into the current settler-colonial system, it can become a practice of freedom and transformation.

Working outside settler-colonial values that assist in maintaining power, comes with risk. My colleagues made it clear that this work did not belong in their teaching institutions. Reviews of my tenure portfolio resulted in painting me as a "rebel" by dismantling my research, tainting my character, and attacking the legitimacy of my work. The devaluation of the transdisciplinary approaches I took to link theory with practice, scholarship with teaching, and service with the community (Solórzano & Yosso, 2001) became an unsettling time.

Not falling in line with the norm, however, also motivates. Were it not for this unsettled time, I would not have been compelled to take flight. This echo planted the seeds for USH's possibility to embed practices departing from and informed by my experience working in the margins.

Echo 2: Dispossession and Reclamation

Without hesitation, I took a leave from the university. I moved to Guatemala—the K'iche' Mayan word for "place of many trees." Home to twenty-one Maya nations, this country is deeply embedded in historical events that perpetually impact the approximately 75 percent of Indigenous people who live in poverty. The impoverished conditions are a direct consequence of Spanish settler-colonialism and the more recent armed conflict. The ghosts of settler-colonial Guatemala would be where USH was born and "died."

To begin, I traveled along steep winding roads and across the tree-lined sweeping mountains from Panajachel to Chirijox. Here, I met four Maya K'iche youth (ages ten to seventeen) who would be my partners in shaping USH. We worked free from traditional school structures, state and federal standards, and assimilating school practices. Celebrating community wealth held within familial, aspirational, social, navigational, resistant, and linguistic capital (Yosso, 2005), these burgeoning filmmakers drew upon and embraced their languages, practices, and experiences. The youth took ownership, choosing their own topics, moving forward in their visions, and speaking their mother tongue. There were no limits to content and no rigid timelines. At their pace, youth produced their films, while seeking guidance and support from one another. Their adobe homes provided a "non-school" feeling, where together we sat on floors, beds, or around tables to co-create goals, deconstruct video, and eat (always food!).

Physical spaces and freedom of content, however, does not immediately break us of our internalized conventions. Our disenfranchising histories and enculturated expectations that rise out of settler-colonialism clench our unconscious. I faltered into stereotypical assumptions, forcefully reminding myself to release them. Listening to and learning about the youth's everyday lives reformed my constantly challenged habits. The young hesitated, drawing on their conditioned routines of waiting for direction, asking permission, and outsiders shaping the end goal. Altering both of our patterned responses to imposing stratifying structures, we openly embraced that our roles would look different in this space.

Working toward liberation involves critical reflexivity, breaking oppressive habits, and building and rebuilding trust. A flourishing program evidenced our successful struggle toward liberatory learning spaces. "We explore the possibility that Indigenous Knowledge Systems might offer distinct spaces in which educators and their students might be exposed to broader notions of what teaching and learning are and can be" (Brayboy & Maughan, 2009, p. 3). By the end of two years, fourteen youth from two different locations completed thirteen films. This is impressive given the perpetual obstacles. Maya youth have endless family responsibilities and community obligations. Other impediments that interrupt their progress included power outages, weather events, and transportation issues. What was more, we completed these films with just three legacy Mac computers and a handful of basic GE HD1080p cameras.

Once completed, we organized film screenings. Local screenings were opportunities to discuss the issues facing their Indigenous cultures and to celebrate their rich traditions. It was also a chance to solicit feedback in order to polish their final cut. We presented these final cuts to larger expat audiences. Here young producers fielded questions as they provided a window into insider representations of Maya culture.

By the third year, three program participants moved into leadership positions. These leaders taught new groups of youth in K'iche, Kaqchikel, and Tz'utujil communities. As planned, I incrementally retreated from the project, allowing local talent to take ownership of the project. I moved back to the United States while the leaders continued their work. While in the States, I attended a Native American and Indigenous Studies Association (NAISA) conference. It was there that the project captured the attention of the Smithsonian National Museum of the American Indian (NMAI). After the NMAI film team vetted the films, the youth leaders were invited to present their films, and the films of their students in both New York and Washington D.C. locations. The exhibition entitled "Maya Creativity and Cultural Milieu" would position these young Maya Guatemala leaders center stage to explain and present their stories.

Positioning Maya Voices front and center, directly counters the history that "Indigenous identity as culture is frequently presented through the anonymous voice of museum authority, which is usually not Indigenous" (Trofanenko, 2006, p. 311). Three Maya youth claimed their rightful place of representing their stories.

Echo 3: Persistent Setter-Colonial Characteristics

Sitting on one of the world's major stages would not be the end to settler-colonial rumblings. As part of its persistence, settler-colonial bubbles to the surface along with the normalization of territory claims, impositions of values, and appropriations of resources. USH encountered each of these, eventually leaving it vulnerable to the deterrent of Indigenous sovereignty that settler-colonialism fuels.

Historically, Maya lives are set in and reflective of intense historical violence. Colonial settlers and missionaries alike expelled the Maya to the highlands regions of the country and worked to strip them of their languages, religions, and cultures. Today, many nonprofits arrive asserting that they want to "help" and "lift" the people out of poverty. Working to counter this narrative is an ongoing challenge within unyielding settler-colonial characteristics. At USH, youth sign documents declaring that their productions belong to them. We also persistently remind them that the organization is for and by its participants. As anyone doing community work knows, trust and relationships are critical. Both take decades, sometimes lifetimes, to build. Thus, our partner organization was seminal to USH's rapid expansion from one to nine communities in three years. Equally important is the Maya youth counter-storytellers willingness to share their wisdom. Yet, foreigners running nonprofits want to claim territory and people as "property," taking credit for any success. USH experienced this attempt to claim property when NMAI invited the youth to present their films. As Sleeter (1994) reminds us, in the wake of systemic racism, white people attempt to shift the spotlight to themselves, deflecting the attention from Indigenous People's major concerns. Organizations that claim ownership of the children and of their work, denies the legitimacy of local knowledge, agency, and capacity. Instead of celebrating the seismic shift in racial positioning, the settler ego emerged. Reestablishing their lives in this territory (Guatemala), the indentured servants (Maya youth) produced currency (global visibility) to claim their new home (leading in the nonprofit world).

In the ongoing colonial settler model, Western value systems persist. The omnipresence of ethnic and moral superiority surfaced during the struggle to shift the ownership of USH to the local community. Though many nonprofit organizations in Guatemala employ Maya women and men, the direct leadership positions are held by foreigners. This work structure illuminates the ever-present persistence to maintain the settler-colonial caste system. Reflecting again on the NMAI invitation as an example, our partner organization insisted that a long-standing employee of their organization could not "properly" represent it. This woman was instrumental in USH from the start, and she spoke four languages. The "Maya Creativity and Cultural Milieu" was intended to be about Maya knowledge, told by and represented by Maya, not to be about our nonprofits. Yet, "so strong is this expectation of holding center stage that even when a time and place are specifically designated for members of a non-privileged group to be central, members of the dominant group will often attempt to take back the pivotal focus" (Grillo & Wildman, 1997, p. 621).

Those of us working directly with USH crafted statements to counter this pattern. We wrote:

> *USH seeks to break boundaries and lead nonprofits into a model that lessens foreign influence and increases Indigenous leadership. Our model moves away from traditional operational roles where foreigners maintain decision-making power, so that youth quickly and seamlessly become leaders of the program. At USH, we have drawn on the understanding that we cannot "liberate" and uplift these communities, only they can do this as we take on a supportive and listening role.*

USH, which valued experiential knowledge, multiple perspectives of history, and racialized hierarchical phenomena as sources of fulfillment and communal empowerment (Valdes, Culp & Harris, 2002) needed to move away from foreigners speaking for Indigenous experiences or imposing Western values on their vision (Grillo & Wildman, 1997). Maya epistemologies of community, family, and collectivity, exist "in dramatic opposition to the dominant epistemology" (Pizarro, 1998, p. 65) into which foreign expats are enculturated. As a result, I detached USH from partner organizations to more quickly transition to local ownership, which unfortunately still relied on foreign assistance. My colleague, a critical filmmaker, organized interviews for a program coordinator and three mentors. She cast our net widely, drawing applicants from across the country, and we first hired the program coordinator. Juana was carefully vetted through a hiring committee composed of a Maya Guatemala with extensive nonprofit and community development experience, a board member—also Maya Guatemala—and our team. We unanimously agreed that a Maya Mam woman from Huehuetenango was our leader.

We realized that this shift would be difficult. Afterall, settler-colonialism paints Indigenous Peoples through a deficit lens. Settler-colonial look at their Indigenous counterparts as lesser, justifying settler's appropriation of human and material resources to conquer Maya territories. Conquistadors saw the nations densely populated and economically advantageous lands as an opportunity for labor and land exploitation. Similarly, a handful of USH foreign volunteers and philanthropists asserted their superiority, and when challenged entitlement emerged. An example of such an event centered on a hired US filmmaker. Over time, it became apparent that his actions were steeped in white supremacy. He used his role to place the spotlight on himself as someone with more and better experience than his colleagues. He increasingly asserted his white male privilege subordinating the USH leadership team, co-opting youth workshops, and commanding attention to himself during film presentations. In other words, he had "retained characteristics of the dominator" to manipulate for the situation to his benefit (Friere, 1970, p. 5). Juanna and I realized that he was not a fit. We thanked him for his services and told him that it wasn't working. In response, he confiscated the production equipment and held it hostage. Attempting to assert white privilege, he went to the courts and filed a complaint against Juana, assuming that the courts would be responsive to the narrative that Indigenous people denied him of his rightful claim to imparting his knowledge on the program.

Juana handled the situation professionally and with poise. She eventually repossessed the equipment and quickly returned her focus on the program, showing promise of local autonomy. She raised $1,000 at her first fundraiser. She led USH youth to be spotlighted on a local media program. She worked day and night providing positive experiences for the leaders and the participating youth. By the early part of 2018, we were on the brink of changing our organizational structure. We seem to be deflecting the immense weight of settler-colonialism's ugly characteristics; that was until they resurfaced.

It was then that Juana's husband Josué, who had also been working for the organization, was in a car accident. Josué was driving a car that he did not own. Uninsured, he quickly found himself in profound debt. To pay off that debt, he was slowly pawning the documentary equipment. Aware that something was not right, I made arrangements to transition the organizational oversight to a trusted Indigenous Guatemala "family" member. We set a meeting, but then I received a suspicious message from Josué. He staged a "terrible accident that rendered Juana unconscious." I sent my family member to the office and he found it deserted. The "accident" was a distraction to enable their escape. Josué contacted me a few times after the incident. He confessed to a lawyer, expressed remorse, and promised to return everything once his finances were restored. Not long after, the communications went silent. Josué, Juana, and their daughter vanished from the face of the earth.

Resting Inside of Healing

Healing from while within settler-colonialism is interminable. With every step, its reverberations show themselves. Our work requires ongoing attention to the social, cultural, and political undercurrents that surround and exist in all of us. As USH we believe(d) that "institutions must challenge themselves to move away from encouraging acts that are performative, into commitments for transformative change" (Red Shirt-Shaw, 2020, p. 2). Yet, the ever-present invisible hold that of settler-colonialism can quickly destroy what we attempt to transform. A colleague of my once said to me, you can try to work in the margins, but you are still under the auspices of looming superstructures. Once an idealist, I assumed we could supersede that reality. I was regretfully wrong.

A simple path would be to walk away entirely. Yet, healing requires pushing through the wounds. So many of us get tired, and we eventually retreat to a place that saves our sanity. Yet, if we retreat, oppression and systemic racism go unchallenged and unchanged. If we turn away from injustices, we are complicit. As critical educators we must and will continue to exercise resilience. My Indigenous Guatemalan partners inspire me. Each young filmmaker, each family, teaches me—resilience underlies survival. They remind us, as do the words of the late John Lewis, to "answer the highest calling of your heart and stand up for what you truly believe" and to "walk with the wind, brothers and sisters, and let the spirit of peace and the power of everlasting love be your guide" (Engle & Schulten, 2020). When I return to the communities with whom I've worked, we will continue healing while living critical pedagogy in action.

26

Healing in Urban Nature: On Place, Identity, and Land Relationships

Jennifer D. Adams

Barefoot on Concrete

In warm weather, I like to walk barefoot, feeling the textures of irregular stones embedded in sun-warmed concrete under my feet. My feet vacillate between hot/dry and moist/cool, passing over grass and moss growing between the cracks of pavement. The concrete earth is healing for me; I feel grounded and relational, as if roots are growing from my feet, reaching to the core of the earth, and energy emanating from my fingers and head-crown connecting me to all relations—animate and inanimate. Accessing this healing connection does not require me to venture further than what is around me.

I have always lived in urban spaces that defy romantic visions of verdant landscapes untouched by humans; yet, I have never felt deprived of nature. My mother, who is Jamaican, made these connections for me early in life. She filled our apartment with plants. She caught June bugs, dug up earthworms, and placed them in the middle of my hand where I felt them tickle and watched them wiggle. We lived twelve stories above the ground in public housing; I watched the sunrise out my east-facing bedroom window and noticed the oak trees as they went from bare to green to colorful to bare with the passing seasons. I collected acorns and made necklaces, as I did with soda-can tabs tossed in the gutter. Caterpillars wove cocoons on wrought iron fences surrounding Shady Rest Park and pigeons nested under the Brooklyn-Queens Expressway overpass. Nature was all around me, and I was part of nature even amidst the bricks, asphalt, and concrete.

This chapter reflects the complexity of how urban nature, experience, and identity are entwined within (1) layers of reality that move across time-space and (2) the epistemological and material engagements with lived and ethereal experiences that are internally constituted and embodied. I begin with a vignette that intersects my embodiment of urban nature with my Caribbean identity. I then question land relationships for Indigenous and African diasporic peoples and the conceptualization of the urban within a dualistic framework. This yields a re-envisioning of urban nature by disrupting dominant notions of what is nature and to whom it belongs and presenting a mindful practice of *being* in urban nature. These themes emerge as discrete but are interconnected through the rise and fall with my ontological experiences with urban nature, which is partly about geography but also about history, migration, land, place, home, and experience with my ongoing identity emergences.

Land Acknowledgment

I am a daughter of the Caribbean, born and raised in Lenapehoking, the Lenape homeland. I honor Indigenous nations and their land with gratitude and acknowledge the genocide and continuous theft of land and displacement of Indigenous in North America. I also recognize the stolen labor of enslaved Africans who resided in Manhattan during and beyond colonialism. I acknowledge the harm inflicted upon the Indigenous communities and people of color in the settler-colonial nations of the United States and Canada.[1] When I emigrated to Canada to take my job at the university, I first became aware of land acknowledgments as a formal statement. Each meeting opened with a land acknowledgment, stating that we, our university is situated on the traditional territories of the Blackfoot Confederacy, the Tsuut'ina First Nation, and the Stoney Nakoda as well as the Métis Nation of Alberta. While this recognizes the original stewards of the land, I have encountered numerous Indigenous peoples as homeless in these traditional territories, a visceral example of genocide and theft of land and culture Indigenous peoples have experienced in North American for centuries. It also made me think of the irreparable generational harm of the theft of Indigenous Africans from their lands, which led me to question the purpose of land acknowledgments. Aside from recognizing the intimate connections of Indigenous people to the land, what do acknowledgments do to promote sovereignty and dignity of Indigenous peoples?

I have asked Indigenous people about their feelings on land acknowledgments. I asked African-descended people, like myself, because we are not settler-colonizers but subjects of theft and genocide that shaped coloniality, and we continue to suffer related oppressions today. Although the histories of our land relationships are different, the contemporary context of Black and Indigenous suffering on Indigenous lands is very present and relevant. People's opinions ranged from not having the land acknowledgments without reparations to land acknowledgments being a critical step toward reparations. The binding threads were reparations and authentic reconnections to the land, ownership of land and sacred sites, and ownership of sacred objects. As a descendant of enslaved Africans, I have thought about what authentic reparations would look like without direct connections to land, which becomes more complex when one considers the Caribbean—the silencing of indigeneity, the continued presence of coloniality and issues of land ownership in relation to place, family, and plantation history. People of the Caribbean diaspora have carried these land connections with them as "immigrants" to colonizing nations and settler-colonial outposts of the United States and Canada. Just as family history—stories and genetics—shape individual identities, stories around land relationships shape collective histories and identities and bind people to various notions of home, place, and land. On Turtle Island, land acknowledgments are an important step toward historical justice; it is important to understand our own histories and relationships to land and place, especially the land on which we work and live and the land(s) that have shaped us as individuals, cultural communities, and a societal collective.

In some urban landscapes, like Calgary, Alberta, it is easier to visualize Indigenous connections to land through geology—two rivers meeting, cliffs that were buffalo jumps and the living landscape that features prominently in Indigenous stories. In landscapes like Brooklyn, New York, it is not as obvious. However, I can see the Lenape trail in the meander of Flatbush Avenue. Noticing endemic flora and fauna, I visualize how even designed and curated areas, such as Prospect Park, provided food and shelter in their pre-urban state. The waters that surround the city are rich with marine life that provide seafood for people who occupy Lenape land. Along the shorelines lay evidence of oysters, clams, and fish that live in the waters. My friend fishes these waters as a practice of healing. I collect quahog shells that Lenape people used for jewelry and currency because I am attracted to their rich purple hues.

I taught biology in a high school in Canarsie, one of the very few places in Brooklyn to retain the original name of the Canarsee tribe of the Lenape people. Flatbush Avenue, a main trail for the Canarsees, became the street that helped shape my identity as a Caribbean-American. It transverses the borough, connecting the formerly rich oyster beds of the New York harbor, forests, and savannah of Brooklyn to what is now Jamaica Bay. Similar to Flatbush Avenue, I imagine the trail was an important source of trading, hunting and social gathering for Canarsees. Today, a large stretch of Flatbush is considered "Caribbean Brooklyn," an important place of commerce and identity for Caribbean people who emigrated there starting in the 1960s.

In school we learned about Dutch and other European connections to New York City, all very reflected in place names we grew up experiencing. I don't recall hearing about Lenape people until I was an adult volunteering at the Smithsonian National Museum of the American Indian at the southern tip of Manhattan. Like many people of my generation, we learned about Indigenous peoples as "Eastern Woodlands Tribes" on visits to the dusty halls of the American Museum of Natural History. Today, those halls are still dusty and reinforce the false notion that Native peoples are nonexistent in New York City. Indigenous peoples exist in New York City and elsewhere and have been responsible for shaping the geography of the city through well-worn trails, sites of commerce, and building the iconic skyline. Similarly, we learned about the institution of slavery as a "Southern" issue. However, not only was there a slave market on what is now Wall Street, but enslaved people were forced to clear land, widen Lenape trails, and build the port—all critical in building generational wealth for European settlers and shaping the city to what it is today.

My research and writing about sense of place began with autoethnographic reflections of my place relationships. As science educator who is concerned with planetary well-being, I needed to understand how I related to places of importance to me. This was in response to place-based education literature at the time that aimed at connecting school subjects with students' lived places and experiences. I quickly realized, although I was born and raised in Brooklyn, I connected to this place in Caribbean ways. I identify as Jamaican or Caribbean-American. I developed a strong sense of Caribbean identity both because of my parents, mainly my mother's influence, and because of my interactions within the Caribbean diaspora in Brooklyn. This identity and connection to Caribbeanness did not come from being situated on land in the Caribbean, but through my interactions with family and community in Brooklyn, which like other Caribbean enclaves in colonial and settler-colonial contexts became an extension of the Caribbean. Identity is not only connected to interactions with physical places but also through conceptual spaces defined by notions of home and belonging, sense of self vis-à-vis community (Adams, 2014; 2013). Cultivating healthy relationships with place, land, and identity is critical in individual and community well-being. In settler-colonial contexts, this means (1) recognizing the fraught history over land, (2) understanding the relational ontologies that Indigenous and other people have with land; meanings about attachments to land that are deeper and meaningful than neoliberal ideologies of land ownership, and (3) being deliberate in learning about our own land and place relationships in relation to the first two. It is important to recognize the original caretakers of the lands that we currently occupy, the ones who were forcefully brought to these lands for free labor, and the role of those who have benefited from the theft of land and labor, and, in many cases, still retain power over land and labor in disruption of the latter.

Relative to geological time, land is enduring. Place is ephemeral. Sense of place is a function of the interaction between the two.

Detoxifying the Urban

Historically, urban spaces have been described in terms that imply scourge—both for the place and the people who occupy it. John Osborne, one of the early leaders of the American Museum of Natural History, was a eugenicist and unabashed racist. He wrote the forward to *The Passing of the Great Race*, where New York City is described as "*cloaca gentium* which will produce many amazing racial hybrids and some ethnic horrors that will be beyond the powers of future anthropologists to unravel." Dating back to the Roman Empire, Cloaca Maxima is the world's oldest sewer. In Latin *cloaca* refers to the anus, the orifice where waste is expelled from the body, usually solid and foul-smelling. The cloaca gentium is akin to the forty-fifth president of the United States referring to certain Black and Brown nations as "shithole countries." There is persistent language that positions urban places as terra sacer, "[a] wasteland whose inhabitants lack the liberal capitalist insights and technological know-how to properly occupy a city" (la paperson, 2014). The urban is unused because it is occupied by bodies that are inhuman/dysgenic and therefore justifiably gentrifiable, appropriatable, thiefable.

Ansfield (2015) extends Wynter's work to urbanization, describing the conceptualization of cities within the Enlightenment-era ideology that situated white European man, *homo economicus*, at the apex:

> The city often haunted Enlightenment thinkers, symbolizing an anarchic, indefinable, and uncontrollable mesh of bodies and structures. … [T]he city

> was seen as all that nature was not: toxic, human, degraded, fallen. Yet even in its hazardous fluidity and unruly rapidity, the city represented a fundamental achievement of Man: domination over an equally treacherous nature and implementation of human knowledge models onto a physical landscape. The city typified the promise and perils of the Enlightenment episteme. To subdue and organize the city and its constituents was to translate Enlightenment modes of rationality over a social and physical landscape. (p. 132)

However, this subduction and organization created substandard spaces that led to behavioral "deviances," which were reinscribed back on individuals, namely, Black and Brown bodies in urban spaces. Ansfield (2015) described this as "a geo-racial poetics of filth, … [an] enduring cartographic exercise … that ensures that black pathology remains fixed and immutable within the dominant mode of subjective understanding" (p. 132). Urban residents, especially those of us who are Black, Brown, immigrant, and/or poor are often positioned as removed from nature or unnatural. Disconnected, nature-deficient, entombed in concrete—urbanity is the antithesis of romantic green landscapes untouched by humans. Similarly, urban nature is positioned as unnatural; in order for one to get out into nature, one has to leave the city. This narrative fails to recognize the richness of urban nature, the interrelationships between land, people, nonhuman beings, and built structures that form the urban landscape. Just as humans have made their homes within built structures, peregrine falcons and redtail hawks nest on bridge stanchions and building ornaments. Opossums find their ways onto subways and racoons find food in what we discard. Just as humans have immigrated to new lands, portmanteau biota[2] have made their way to the city in the waters of ships' ballasts and through deliberate introductions for food, entertainment, or design.

People who grow up in urban environments become attuned to urban nature, the interrelationships of the adaptations of humans, animals, plants to concrete and asphalt structures. We notice seagulls flying in a particular way when snow is coming. In abandoned lots we grow community gardens that attract butterflies, bees, and migrating birds. We manage feral cat colonies and liberate racoons caught in dumpsters. We notice when endemic animals, like coyotes, return to the city and respond when domesticated ones, like cows, escape slaughterhouses. These connections comprise a nature that is both chaotic and congruence. To realize a sustainable future amid globally growing urbanity, people must connect with nature in ways that are resonant with cities and value the diverse human-nature interrelationships therein.

Black in Urban/Nature

In the spring of 2020, Christian Cooper was verbally assaulted by a white woman while he was birdwatching in Central Park, a large urban park, centrally located in Manhattan. It also an important stopover for birds during the seasonal migrations. Year-round Central Park and other parks in New York City are popular with birders and bird aficionados, but the migrations are more special. To preserve and recognize the importance of urban natural habitats, Central Park includes protected areas for birds, and dogs are not allowed off-leash. Cooper, a birder, asked a white woman to leash her dog which precipitated her calling the police on an "African American" man, thereby weaponizing his race because of her own indignation and fear. While the media has pegged this as a racial incident, and undoubtably it was, it was deeper than this. Cooper, a birder, had a special connection to this place and understood the significance of preserving it and taking care of nonhuman relations. This place is important to birds and people who appreciate birds for the diversity they bring to the urban environment. Yet, the police-calling woman exuded a sense of entitlement, ownership of the space, without having the same connection: it was affront that a Black man was requesting she follow the law. Although urban Black people are connected to the nature that is around us, we are often made to feel we are unwelcome, anomalies because "how do you know so much," or novices in our pursuits. I recall numerous incidents where I was addressed like this but one in particular comes to the forefront:

> "Mom, look at that pretty red bird!" I exclaimed, as we were walking to Prospect Park in Brooklyn, NY. I know my mother loves birds and loves red. "That is a very pretty bird," she responded, admiring the bird. As we chatted, an older white man overheard and patronizingly chimed in, "that is a cardinal!" His proud, smug expression read as if he had just enlightened our ignorant minds to the nature around us. But, I knew it was a cardinal. My mother who fed birds in our backyard knew it was a cardinal. I turned to the man and frigidly said, "We. Know." He hurried off; we continued our walk, noting the birds along the way.

While this tale may seem benign, to me it conveys how this man thought that I, a young Black woman, and my mother, a Black woman with an accent and therefore foreign, could not possibly have knowledge about a common urban bird. Perhaps the man had good intentions, but his comment came with false assumptions about being Black in nature. Such assumptions put us at extra risk when we try to enjoy the outdoors and require us to form support groups in order to feel safe in nature.

I worked for an outdoors education nonprofit while also teaching high school. I enjoyed the job as we did many outdoors activities with mostly middle and high school students, both within the city and in the state parks a few hours north. Local activities included canoeing, alpine tower climbing, overnight camping in Jamaica Bay, and "urbans" (backpacking trips through the city). Through my years with the organization, I encountered white counterparts who treated the job like an "urban peace corps," as if they were white saviors exposing inner-city youth to nature. They neither took the time to get to know the young people, nor gain an understanding of urban nature, engaging the young people in exploring their lived nature. It was their mission to get kids out of the city into "natural" spaces, leaving the city and all its filth in a distant glow.

Urban Forest Bathing

For the health and well-being of cities we cannot think of nature as something absent from, outside of, or in opposition to cities. We need to think of cities-as-nature and recognize how they afford health and well-being to its residents. By developing a relational stance toward urban nature, we can view cities as complex, interdependent organisms comprised of living and built. We would empathize with other humans and nonhuman organisms and care for each other like our lives depended on it, because they do. The recent pandemic has demonstrated we are connected and dependent on one another to keep whole. We have found ways to cope with mass uncertainty. Not being able to travel or even leave our communities or homes, we could forge connections that sustain mental and physical well-being through a mindful practice of connecting with urban nature through urban *shinrin-yoku* or "connecting with trees." Anecdotally, a high school class I worked with in Brooklyn, New York, did a study on students walking to school along different paths—tree-lined streets versus busier commercial veins and found less stressed with the former. These students found ways to make unconscious and conscious connections with urban trees, allowing them to experience and document reduced stress. This leads me to ask, how can we engage in *shinrin-yoku* in urban nature?

Forest bathing or *shinrin-yoku* originated in Japan in 1982 as a public health initiative that encouraged people make contact with forests to improve health and well-being. People take meditative walks through spaces with trees, without particular direction, paying attention to smells, sights, sounds, feels. According to Park et al. (2010), forest environments promote physiological responses that indicate lower stress than do city environments. While scientific research supports the benefits of soil, plants, and oceans to human well-being (e.g., Craig, Logan, & Prescott, 2016), the Western European discourse about *shinrin-yoku* runs the risk of defaulting to romantic visions of pristine forest, perpetuating the urban=bad/nature=good dichotomy, with the latter extending to describe people who occupy or live closer to those respective places. Wandering, being among the trees without a path or agenda, is central to *shinrin-yoku*. Cities offer opportunities to wander and be immersed in the beautiful chaos of urban nature. Many times, I have wandered Flatbush Avenue or other streets lined with flowerbeds, homes, and sidewalks. I meander through shops, enjoying the carefully curated displays of small businesses, while English sparrows search for bagel crumbs in tree pits and curbs. Sparrows, starlings, and pigeons follow main streets built by humans in preference over the small stand forest deep within Prospect Park. Amidst prewar buildings, I think about how these streets differed when my mother emigrated to Brooklyn in the 1960s. There are remnants of old shops, their faded signs painted directly on the bricks. Ivy creeps alongside the signs and across the top of the building along with other plants living on the bricks, drawing nutrients from the crumbling mortar and decaying moss between the cracks. On the sidewalk, ants carry crumbs to their dens. As a child, I squatted down and carefully watched them enter and leave a hole in the sandy soil. I crumbled Ritz crackers and watched tiny black bodies carry white crumbs to their lands below. I meander home from my dance class, down 6th Avenue, through Madison Square Park where squirrels manipulate humans for food with their cuteness while well-kept dogs play nearby. Evening walks bring the sweet scent of transpiration as trees and grass exhale water they produced all day.

During difficult times, these walks are comforting. The lighted pathways emanating through the trees of the Poets Grove in Prospect Park give me space to speak out loud and process my thoughts. I take the train to Coney Island, breathe in the ocean air, and bury my toes in the sand with the Cyclone, Wonder Wheel, and Parachute Jump illuminated and animated against the dark sky. The moonlight makes the sea foam glow while the salt sprays on my face. Rat prints remain in the sand as seagulls sit toward the wind, waiting for the sunrise, searching the sand and boardwalk for food that humans have left behind. *Shinrin-yoku* in urban nature requires patience in being able to navigate city streets and allow the experiences of connection with urban nature to emerge; curiosity to notice a sparrow, smell the trees within the urban air, and appreciate the hard work of a bee in search of flowers in potted gardens, and gratitude because urban nature sustains us, even in times of turmoil.

Medicinal Waters

There are spaces in the city where people seek out healing, practicing *shinrin-yoku* in urban ways. One such place where the city touches the ocean has been dubbed the Medicinal Waters of Off the Coast of South Brooklyn. People bathe here year-round to heal mentally, physically, and emotionally. We notice what lives below and above the waters—rock crabs scurrying along the sand in the shallows, recently rebuilt sand dunes of planted beachgrass, and individual seagulls that leave and return at different times of the year. Migrating birds, butterflies, and several species of cetaceans rely on these waters for sustenance and survival. People rely on these waters for the same; we are all urban denizens, whether permanent residents or just passing through for a season. The red-orange-pink sunset illuminates the sand and reflects off glassy buildings in the distant Manhattan skyline.

Urban landscapes are complex, as is the nature intertwined therein. The diverse relationships between people and urban nature do not ascribe to the unified romantic visions of nature. In contrast to the pristine, "man-versus-nature" of Western European episteme, urban nature is beautifully multifaceted and urban residents are attuned to this multiplicity. Urban nature defies control-seeking logic of Enlightenment thought and is the underlying reason why control-seeking people deem diverse urban places "anarchist" and filthy. Those of us who are urban-embodied are well aware of the beauty of urban nature. We rely on the energy of the urban collective for healing as we gaze beyond the skyscrapers to the birds soaring above the city's lights.

Afterword: Healing the Soft Tissue of Critical Pedagogues with a Radical Love

Shirley R. Steinberg

Paulo Freire introduced us to radical love over five decades ago; my critical pedagogical self cannot begin to have this discussion without acknowledging Paulo's embodiment and enactment of the notion of radicalizing love:

> The more radical the person is, the more fully he or she enters into reality so that, knowing it better, he or she can transform it. This individual is not afraid to confront, to listen, to see the world unveiled. This person is not afraid to meet the people or to enter into a dialogue with them. This person does not consider himself or herself the proprietor of history or of all people, or the liberator of the oppressed; but he or she does commit himself or herself, within history, to fight at their side.
>
> (Freire, 1972)

After spending a fortnight exploring and investigating *Critical Pedagogy for Healing*, I moved away from my laptop to a spiral notebook. This habit had been engrained over thirty years ago by Joe Kincheloe, who wrote on his belly on a red futon with our dachshund sleeping on him, just above his knees. Word processing was new in those days, and I pushed Joe to learn to apply words to keyboard instead of buying scores of notebooks. However, Joe continued to write by hand and actually reintroduced me to his notion of organic writing. I began to use colored Uniball pens, the ones with caps, noting what I researched in blue, drawing stars on specific items in red then connecting themes in green to join the ideas; I culminated in purple, noting what I found, learned, and where I would go. I use black to take out what I didn't like. None of this could be done on a keyboard, it had to be lined spiral paper and colored pens. I use hot pink in large sweeping circles to identify what I favor and to prioritize the writing. I would never call myself physically organic as I am pleased to find assistance for manual work, but when it comes to writing, I have to *be there with the stuff*. It is the stuff that keeps me honest, grounded, and physically connected to my writing. This short *Afterword*, then, is a retrospect of the *stuff* I am taking away from this book and blending with what I know and, more importantly, what I don't know.

I begin this piece with what I don't know, but what I want to know. In my trite 1960s style of reading the world, the notion of peace and the emotion of love wove through the book; I determined to begin with those words. The first site that I found was titled: Peace and Love Principle. I hadn't heard of this construct, but I was drawn to the purple tones on the website and it was clear to me I found the hook for my *Afterword*. Well, PEACE and LOVE turned out to be acronyms for the "common and well-known principles of soft tissue injury management" (*Physiopedia*, 2021). Laughing and starting to search again, I rolled with the idea of soft tissue injury, thinking that our lives, indeed were soft tissue, that the healing we seek is for the consistent injuries we incur in our private and public lives. Isn't that the point of our critical pedagogy for healing? We attempt to detect ways in which to be well, to teach well, to advocate well, to get our *stuff* together, to mend our soft tissue before it tears again. As beings who espouse criticality, a philosophical way in which to identify how power works, how disenfranchisement occurs, how oppression exists, we frequently plunge head on into a tunnel which re-shreds our fragile soft tissue. As pedagogues, we attempt to meld our vocation into our lives hoping to enact all the insights we garner on our journeys.

It's somewhat Sisyphean, this task of critical pedagogy. A set up, continually rolling our stone uphill, we stop to refresh ourselves with one another, slip backward a bit, then trod ahead. Our *stuff* is fragile, but we are able to mend it and push on, ever secure in knowing that we are doing the right thing. We attempt to heal and mend the world, and then we return home in need of healing and mending ourselves—the next day we go back to rolling the stone. Why do we try to heal what continually tears?

Fearless, optimistic, hopeful—we're still here. It can only be love. Writing in circles, I return to love to understand how we keep putting our *stuff* out there. That's what this book is, an homage to love, radical love, love of our homes, our families, students, colleagues, and how to stretch that love to include ourselves. It was in the fall of 1990 when Kincheloe and I were invited to fly to Boston to meet Paulo Freire. Newly married and beyond broke, we scraped money together to buy tickets and met Paulo in a tiny local Portuguese restaurant. We were there for hours, as he unveiled his thoughts about radical love (Freire, 1990). Paulo saw love as an artery to our hearts—our pedagogy. He named what we knew we felt, but hadn't put to words—the passion, commitment, and exhaustion of our work, certainly radical and most assuredly, love. Joe and I had that connected artery; Paulo's introduction to radical love spoke to us and allowed us to comprehend more completely the nature of our relationship (Steinberg, 2008). We saw ourselves as meshed not only with one another, but with our students and the community we served (Steinberg, 2017). Paulo's explanation of the radicality of critical pedagogical love emphasized how passion was necessary certainly for romantic love but equally as essential for pedagogical love. Reminding us of Whitehead's insistence that the act of teaching must, indeed include passion, my ultimate critical pedagogy goal is to never lose my passion, never to lose my *stuff*.

One could not claim critical pedagogy without emulating radical love (Flecha & Gomez, 2016; Gomez, 2004, 2014; Steinberg, 2010). As we embody the themes in this book, we are surrounded by our connections to radical love, through ourselves: healing, mindfulness, care, resilience—through our pedagogies: listening, inclusion, leadership, collaboration, the arts—through our communities: vulnerability, humanization, justice, reconciliation—through nature—we are in touch with the joy and wholeness, we embrace wellness, and we give gratitude. We seek to reside in the normal, hoping that our critically pedagogical normal is engaged in our need to heal, ever mindful that the soft tissue of life tears—and can be repaired.

There isn't a time in the history of earth's human beings that some sort of spirituality hasn't existed. Earthlings recall, recant, repel, or reclaim the spiritual in life, and certainly many enhance it in an afterlife. Healing is connected through constructs of love dwelling in different spiritual beliefs. The prophetic traditions of Judaism note duty, responsibility, and obligation as appendages to love (Weinberg, 2017). Theravada Buddhism sees love in different incarnations as romantic, familial, erotic, compassionate, all fitting into different levels of more or less elevated categories. All this, but with the stumbling block of impermanence—it's there, then it isn't, often a difficult axiom to internalize. Islamic mysticism sees a radical love as a spiritual humility, which includes a bountiful sensuality and intellectual depth (Sofi, 2019). Nouveau Christianity sees that we are "made from the same star matter [which is] connected from the same source worthy of the same unconditional worthiness" (Reints, 2014).

While working on this writing, my heart was most taken by the traditional radicality of Indigenous ways of love. I was recently introduced to Richard Wagamese, an Ojibwe from the Wabaseemoong Independent Nations in what is now called Canada, and found that he wrote of healing, authenticity, and love. In *One Drum,* he gives us the fourth Grandfather who "offered Love. The energy that heals all things is Love. To know Love is to know Peace. To extend Love is to create Peace" (Wagamese, 2019, p. 41). Going back to my association that peace and love are intertwined, Wagamese braids the understanding that the notions are ever connected. He goes onto muse of the Creator:

> The elders say that Creator is perfect loving energy. Within the realm of perfect love there is no judgment. If there is no judgment, then there can be no failure. In turn, if failure does not exist, there is no unworthiness. We are all one energy. We are worthy and we always were. We never have to qualify. And ceremony was born to allow us to remember that.
>
> (Wagamese, 2019, p. 72)

My mind soars with questions: Could critical pedagogy be our ceremony? Can we allow ourselves to open to peace and love, inviting them to enter our lives, our classrooms, our ideologies; releasing the fights we seem to feel pledged to provoke; revolting arrogance and leftist self-confidence and embracing gratitude? Can we find the perfect loving energy, renouncing fears of failure? Could we begin to heal by releasing anger? Can we stay critical, naming power without feeling the exhausting enmity our politics invite? How can we lovingly and peacefully manage and bind the soft tissue injuries we know we will continue to have?

This book, this union of critical friends seeking healing, has evoked our hearts and senses, allowed us to muse upon what is good, positive, and necessary for critical pedagogical healing. I have gratitude for those who shared wisdom, stories, and friendship in this volume and join hands to participate in the ceremony hoping for peace and love to walk beside us. I end with the wisdom of Marie Battiste (2013), who wrote:

> To understand education, one must love it or care deeply about learning, and accept it as a legitimate process for growth and change. To accept education as it is, however, is to betray it. To accept education without betraying it, you must love it for those values that show what it might become. (p. 37)

Notes

3 A Spirituality of Inclusion and Six Dispositions of Significance: Bringing Eternal Meanings to Our Pedagogical Practice

1. This chapter is adapted from my book, *The Thoughtful Teacher: Making Connections with a Diverse Student Population* (Rowman & Littlefield, 2021).
2. In brief, personalism is a philosophy that emphasizes the exceptionality of the human person from all other life form. This exceptionality suggests that not only are human beings more than matter but also that each and every human being is unique onto herself/himself (Kirylo & Boyd, 2017; Williams & Bengtsson, 2016). And while personalism is linked to the metaphysical, and possesses an integral link to the spiritual and belief in God, this does not suggest that all personalists are theists or believers in a god(s) (Williams & Bengtsson, 2016).
3. To further expound, for Mounier, while the starting point of ontological and epistemological reflection begins with the person, critically examining the dignity, status, and experience of what it means to be human, this starting point is also informed by a strand of humanism that is linked to the spiritual (as opposed to secular humanism). In other words, while all humanist thought is fundamentally grounded in a love for life, is socially conscious, takes responsibility, seeks to explore and discover new knowledge, new adventures, and works to ascertain solutions to human problems and challenges, the strand of humanism that is linked to the spiritual also sees that link as integral as to what it means to be human and to be a whole person (Kirylo, 2011; Cunningham, 1987; Edwords, n.d.).
4. For example, the way teachers think, prepare, and act regarding their pedagogical approach on a Cheyenne River Indian Reservation in the western part of the United States will differ from that of Tonawanda Indian Reservation in the northeast part of the country; will differ from working in the city of Chicago, Illinois, from that in Fort Hays, Kansas; will differ from working in Los Angeles, California, from that in El Paso, Texas, and so on.
5. Dorothy Day, who along with Peter Maurin, started the Catholic Worker Movement in 1933, which works to setting up houses of hospitality for the poor. As her fundamental driving motive, intent, and action for all that she did, Day adopted the phrase "love is the measure" from which she quotes St. John of the Cross (1542–1591) when he stated that "Love is the measure by which we shall be judged" (Forest, 1994, p. 81).
6. While there is a certain synergy between humility and belief in God, a higher power, or a transcendent entity, the notion of humility is obviously not solely confined with its link to otherworldliness. It is indeed a prolific human virtue that greatly works to illuminate the goodness, kindness, and "humanness" of what it means to be human.

8 In the “Being” and the “Doing”: Teachers’ Critical Embodied Pedagogies of Care

1. In order to protect participants’ confidentiality, all names of schools and teachers are pseudonyms.
2. Significantly, neither Sarah nor Amir racialize her queerness. I wonder how Sarah’s comfort with being queer in school spaces may also be tied to a greater likelihood of cultural acceptance as white woman.

11 Songs in the Key of Healing Hope: Listening as Soul Care

1. Copyright ©1998 by Wendell Berry, from the *Selected Poems of Wendell Berry*. Reprinted by permission of Counterpoint Press.

13 “What Happens If I Open That Door?”: Art, Truth-Telling and Healing in a Poetry Course for Prospective Teachers

1. I wish to thank the following students for their honesty, courage, vulnerability, and assistance in thinking back over our time together: Julia Alvarez, Lily Blake, Caroline Dimas, Courtney Fox, Kailin Greenhoe, Cyntara Herndon, Megan Isherwood, Heather McArdle, and Marisa Tringali.

14 The Distresses and Hopes of Beginning Teachers: Five Arts-Based Research Explorations

1. I am grateful to Samantha Corallo, Sarah D’Abravia (pseudonym), Arlinda Lela, Destiny O, and Rachel Terrifia (pseudonym) who generously gave me permission to cite their research for this chapter.

18 Between Wholeness and Restoration

1. See Boyes-Watson and Pranis (2014) and DeWolfe and Geddes (2019) for in-depth descriptions of circle dialogue approaches and open-ended question frameworks.
2. Dobson explains deep listening requires listeners remain curious and open, putting aside judgment and assumptions, working to truly hear what is being said. It expects that listeners may need to change.
3. See extensive list of examples in Evans, Morrison, and Vaandering (2019).

23 "The Gift of Setting Alight the Sparks of Hope in the Past": Ancestry and History in Pedagogical Praxis in the Brazilian Amazon

1. The REPAM Network develops important work supporting traditional communities to fight for rights and denounce violence against community leaders.
2. "Deep Amazon" is a concept under construction by native peoples and scholars of Amazonian epistemologies that attempts to break Cartesian and colonial logic, in an effort to recover an understanding of the world in which everything is interconnected and that goes beyond the usual exotic interpretations of the Amazon. For preliminary studies, see Kopenawa, Albert, and Dundy (2013).
3. This text written by Benedito Alcântara on June 29, 2020, in his online diary, narrates how nature is an intrinsic part of the local culture. Ariri is a small rural district surrounded by the Amazon Forest, 20.5 miles distant from the capital of the State of Amapá (North Brazil), close to the mouth of the Amazon River, where most residences are accessed only by boat. *Trapiche* is a raised, level small structure made of wood built beside the edge of the river for accessing riverside houses.
4. Here, *buen vivir* is understood as the political and ethical act of claiming the historical reparation of traditional knowledge and annihilated lives. This means repairing the past of traditional peoples' genocide that remains present.

24 Thy Will Be Done: Radical Love as Self-Other Healing Praxis

1. Black, Indigenous, and People of Color.

26 Healing in Urban Nature: On Place, Identity, and Land Relationships

1. This is paraphrased from the Living Land Acknowledgement Project: https://www.prosecution.org/living-land-acknowledgement.
2. Coined by Historian Alfred Crosby in *Ecological Imperialism: The Biological Expansion of Europe, 900–1900,* portmanteau biota refers to biological colonization/invasion of Europeans; the domestic animals, plants, pathogens, and vermin that were spread around the globe, often upsetting the balance of endemic ecosystems.

References

Introduction: Pathways toward a Soul Revival

Adjapong, E., & Emdin, C. (2015). Rethinking pedagogy in urban spaces: Implementing hip-hop pedagogy in the urban science classroom. *Journal of Urban Learning, Teaching, and Research, 11*: 66–77.

Braidotti, R. (2019). *The posthuman*. Polity.

Darder, A. (2014). A pedagogy of love: Embodying our humanity. in A. Darder (Ed.), *Freire and education*. Routledge.

Emdin, C. (2016). *For White folks who teach in the hood ... and the rest of y'all too: Reality pedagogy and urban education*. Beacon Press.

Freire, P. (1978). *Pedagogy in process: The letters to Guinea-Bissau*. Seabury.

Freire, P. (1987). *Literacy: Reading the word & the world*. Bergin & Garvey.

Fromm, E. (1955). *The sane society*. Henry Holt.

Gruenewald, D. A. (2003). The best of both worlds: A critical pedagogy of place. *Educational Researcher, 32* (4): 3–12. doi:10.3102/0013189X032004003. ISSN 0013-189X. S2CID 42948512.

Hope, D., & Limberg, J. (2020). Footing the COVID-19 bill: Economic case for tax hike on wealthy. *The Conversation*. Retrieved from: https://theconversation.com/footing-the-covid-19-bill-economic-case-for-tax-hike-on-wealthy-151945.

Kress, T. M., & Lake, R. (2019). Dreaming of "nowhere": A co-autoethnographic exploration of utopia-dystopia in the academy. *Educational Philosophy and Theory*. doi: 10.108000131857.2019.1665024.

Kress, T. M., & Lake, R. (2018). Walking with Freire: Exploring the onto-epistemological dimensions of critical pedagogy. *Interfaces Scientificas: Educacao*, 7(1). doi: http://dx.doi.org/10.17564/2316-3828.2018v7n1p47–60.

Kress, T. M., & Lake, R. (2017). The strong poetry of place: A co/auto/ethnographic journey of connoisseurship and learning. *Cultural Studies of Science Education*. doi: 10.1007/s11422-016-9804-y

Miller, J. (2000). *Education and the soul: Toward a spiritual curriculum*. SUNY Press.

Pinar, W. F., & Grumet, M. R. (2014). *Toward a poor curriculum*. Educators International.

The Children's Defense Fund (2020). The State of America's Children 2020: An urgent and preventable crisis. Retrieved from: https://www.childrensdefense.org/policy/resources/soac-2020-child-poverty/#:~:text=Children%20remain%20the%20poorest%20age,and%20older%20(10%20percent).

Thomas, P. L., & Kincheloe, J. (2006). *Reading, writing & thinking: The postformal basics*. Sense.

van Manen, M. (1991/2016). *The tact of teaching: The meaning of pedagogicathoughtfulness*. Taylor & Francis.

Chapter 1: And Let the Church Say "Amen": Racio-Spiritual Re-membering as a Pedagogy of Healing

Bell-Scott, P. (1994). *Life notes: Personal writings by contemporary Black women.* New York: W.W. Norton

Cone, J. H. (2011). *The cross and the lynching tree.* Orbis Books.

Dillard, C., Abdur-Rashid, D., & Tyson, C. (2000). My soul is a witness: Affirming pedagogies of the spirit. *International Journal of Qualitative Studies in Education, 13*(5): 447–62. https://doi.org/10.1080/09518390050156404.

Du Bois, W. E. B. (1903). *The souls of black folk.* Dover Publications.

Du Bois, W. E. B. (1968). *The autobiography of W. E. B. DuBois: A soliloquy on viewing my life from the last decade of its first century.* International Publishers.

Johnson, L. (2017). The racial hauntings of one Black male professor and the disturbance of the self(ves): Self-actualization and racial storytelling as pedagogical practices. *Journal of Literacy Research, 49*(4): 476–502. https://doi.org/10.1177/1086296X17733779.

Love, B. J. (2019, May 23). How schools are 'spirit murdering' black and brown students. *Education Week.* https://www.edweek.org/ew/articles/2019/05/24/how-teachers-are-spirit-murdering-black-and.html.

Love, B. J. (2010). Developing a liberatory consciousness. In M. Adams, W. J. Blumenfeld, R. Castañeda, H. W. Hackman, M. L. Peters, & X. Zúñiga, (Eds.), *Readings for diversity and social justice* (2nd ed., pp. 599–603). Routledge.

Morrison, T. (2004). *Beloved: A novel.* Vintage.

National Public Radio. (2008, March 31). Black liberation theology, in its founder's words. *NPR.* https://www.npr.org/templates/story/story.php?storyId=89236116.

Sharpe, C. E. (2016). *In the wake: On Blackness and being.* Duke University Press.

Williams, P. (1987). Spirit-murdering the messenger: The discourse of fingerpointing as the law's response to racism. *University of Miami Law Review, 42*(1): 127–55. https://repository.law.miami.edu/umlr/vol42/iss1/8.

Chapter 2: Toward a Critical Pedagogy of Spirituality and Healing

Dallaire, M. (2001). *Contemplation in liberation: A method for spiritual education in the schools.* E. Mellen Press.

Freire, P. (1972). Conscientizing as a way of liberating. In US Catholic Conference (Ed.), *Paulo Freire: The LADOC "Keyhole" series* (pp. 3–10). USCC.

Freire, P. (1997). *Pedagogy of the heart* (D. Macedo & A. Oliveira, Trans.). Continuum.

Freire, P. (1998a). *Pedagogy of freedom: Ethics, democracy, and civic courage* (P. Clarke, Trans.). Rowman & Littlefield.

Freire, P. (1998b). Cultural action and conscientization. *Harvard Educational Review, 68*(4): 499–521.

Freire, P. (1998c). *Teachers as cultural workers: Letters to those who dare to teach.* Westview Press.

Freire, P. (2000). *Pedagogy of the oppressed* (M. B. Ramos, Trans.). Continuum.

Freire, P. (2004). *Pedagogy of indignation.* Paradigm.

Freire, P. (2005). *Education for critical consciousness*. Continuum.
Kirylo, J. D. (2016). *Teaching with purpose: An inquiry into the who, why, and how we teach*. Rowman & Littlefield.
Kirylo, J. D., & Nauman, A. (2006). The depersonalization of education and the language of accountability: A view from a local newspaper. *Journal of Curriculum and Pedagogy*, *3*(1): 187–206.
Leopando, I. (2017). *A pedagogy of faith: The theological vision of Paulo Freire*. Bloomsbury Academic.
Mayes, C. (2003). Teaching mysteries. *ENCOUNTER: Education for Meaning and Social Justice*, *16*(3): 43–51.
Monbiot, G. (2016, April 15). Neoliberalism: The ideology at the root of all our problems. *Guardian*. https://www.theguardian.com.
Perkins, P. (2001). "A radical conversion of the mind": Fundamentalism, hermeneutics, and the metanoic classroom. *College English*, *63*(5): 585–611.
Purpel, D. E. (2010). Education in a prophetic voice. *ENCOUNTER: Education for Meaning and Social Justice*, *23*(3): 2–14.
Roberts, P. (1999). Freire, neoliberalism and the university. In P. Roberts (Ed.), *Paulo Freire, politics and pedagogy: Reflections from Aotearoa—New Zealand* (pp. 97–111). Dunmore Press.
Roberts, P. (1996). Rethinking conscientization. *Journal of Philosophy of Education*, *30*(2): 179–96.
Tillich, P. (2001). *Dynamics of faith*. Perennial Classics.
Weiler, K. (1996). The myths of Paulo Freire. *Educational Theory*, *46*(3): 353–71.

Chapter 3: A Spirituality of Inclusion and Six Dispositions of Significance: Bringing Eternal Meanings to Our Pedagogical Practice

Ayers, W. (2005). Education for a changing world. In D. A. Breault & R. Breault (Eds.), *Experiencing Dewey: Insights for today's classroom* (2nd ed., pp. 119–24). Kappa Delta Pi International Honor Society in Education.
Buber, M. (1958). *I and thou* (2nd ed.). Scribner.
Costa, A. L., & Kallick, B. (2000). Preface to the series. In A. L. Costa & B. Kallick (Eds.), *Discovering & exploring habits of mind*. (pp. xii–xvi). Association for Supervision and Curriculum Development.
Cunningham, L. S. (1987). Humanism. In J. A. Komonchak, M. Collins, & D. A. Lane (Eds.), *The new dictionary of theology* (pp. 498–500). Liturgical Press.
Dewey, J. (1933). *How we think: A restatement of the relation of reflective thinking to the educative process* (2nd ed.). Houghton-Mifflin.
Dewey, J. (1983). In J. A. Boydston (Ed.), *The middle works of John Dewey, Volume 14, 1899–1924*. Southern Illinois University Press.
Edwords, F. (n.d.). What is humanism. *American Humanist Association*. https://americanhumanist.org/Humanism/What_is_Humanism.
Eisner, E. (2006). The satisfaction of teaching. *Educational Leadership*, *63*(6): 44–5.
Forest, J. (1994). *Love is the measure: A biography of Dorothy Day*. Orbis Books.
Freire, P. (1994). *Education for critical consciousness*. Continuum.

Freire, P. (1998). *Pedagogy of freedom: Ethics, democracy, and civic courage*. Rowman & Littlefield.

Freire, P. (2005). *Teachers as cultural workers: Letters to those who dare teach* (expanded ed.). Westview Press.

Fromm, E. (2006). *The art of loving* (50th anniversary ed.). Harper Perennial Modern Classics.

Helminiak, D. (1987). *Spiritual development*. Loyola University Press.

Huebner, D. (1995). Education and spirituality. *Journal of Curriculum Theorizing: An Interdisciplinary Journal of Curriculum Studies*, *11*(2): 13–33.

Inglis, W. B. (1959). Personalism, analysis, and education. *International Review of Education*, *5*(4): 383–99.

Kirylo, J. D. (2011). *Paulo Freire: The man from Recife*. Peter Lang.

Kirylo, J. D., & Boyd, D. (2017). *Paulo Freire: His faith, spirituality, and theology*. Sense.

Kolander, C. A., & Chandler, C. K. (1990, March). *Spiritual health: A balance of all dimensions*. Paper presented at the annual meeting of the AAHPERD National Convention, New Orleans, LA.

Komonchak, J. A., Collins, M., & Lane, D. A. (Eds.) (1987). *The new dictionary of theology*. A Michael Glazier Book. Liturgical Press.

LaCaze, D., & Kirylo, J. (2012). A practical guide to a principled classroom. *Focus on Teacher Education: A Quarterly ACEI Publication for the Education Community*, *11*(3): 8–9.

Leean, C. (1988). Spiritual and psychosocial life cycle tapestry. *Religious Education*, *83*(1): 45–51.

Lovewell, K. (2012). *Every teacher matters*. Ecademy Press.

Mayeroff, M. (1971). *On caring*. Harper & Row.

Mother Teresa. (1983). *Words to love by ….* Ave Maria Press.

Mother Teresa (1996). *Mother Teresa: In my own words*. Compiled by Jose-Luis Gonzalez Baldo. Gramercy Books.

Mounier, E. (1952). *Le personnalisme* (P. Mairet, Trans.). Routledge & Kegan Paul (Original work published 1950).

Niebuhr, R. (1927). *Does civilization need religion?* Macmillan.

Noddings, N. (1992). *The challenge to care in schools: An alternative approach to education*. Teachers College Press.

Noddings, N. (2013). *Caring: A relational approach to ethics and moral education*. (2nd ed.). University of California Press.

Nouwen, H. J. M. (1983). *Gracias: A Latin American journal*. Orbis Books.

Nouwen, H. J. M. (2016). *The spiritual life: Eight essential titles*. HarperOne.

Palmer, P. (1993). *To know as we are known: Education as a spiritual journey*. Harper San Francisco (a division of HarperCollins).

Pugach, M. C. (2006). *Because teaching matters*. Wiley.

Purpel, D. (1989). *The moral and spiritual crisis in education: A curriculum for justice and compassion in education*. Bergin & Garvey.

Ritchhart, R., & Perkins, D. N. (2000). Life in the mindful classroom: Nurturing the disposition of mindfulness. *Journal of Social Issues*, *56*(1): 27–47.

Sawchenko, L. D. (2013). *The concept of person: The contribution of Gabriel Marcel and Emmanuel Mounier to the philosophy of Paul Ricoeur* (unpublished master's thesis). University of Calgary.

Warren, M. (1988). Catechesis and spirituality. *Religious Education*, *83*(1): 116–32.

Williams, T. D., & Bengtsson, J. O. (2016, Summer ed.). Personalism. In E. N. Zalta (Ed.), *The Stanford encyclopedia of philosophy*, https://plato.stanford.edu/archives/sum2016/entries/personalism.

Chapter 4: Pentecostal Pedagogy and the Rights of the Body as Restoration in Education

Bales, K., & Soodalter, R. (2010). *The slave next door: Human trafficking and slavery in America today*. University of California Press.
Cornelius, J. (1983). "We slipped and learned to read:" Slave accounts of the literacy process, 1830–1865. *Phylon (1960–)*, *44*(3): 171–86.
Emdin, C. (2020). A ratchetdemic reality pedagogy and/as cultural freedom in urban education. *Educational Philosophy and Theory*, *52*(9): 947–60.
Hinson, G. (2010). *Fire in my bones: Transcendence and the Holy Spirit in African American gospel*. University of Pennsylvania Press.
Jacobsen, D. (2003). *Thinking in the spirit: Theologies of the early Pentecostal movement*. Indiana University Press.
Judith, A., & Anodea, J. (2004). *Eastern body, Western mind: Psychology and the chakra system as a path to the self*. Random House Digital.
Livers, A., & Caver, K. (2003). *Leading in black and white: Working across the racial divide in corporate America* (Vol. 26). Wiley.
Rhoden, W. C. (2010). *Forty million dollar slaves: The rise, fall, and redemption of the Black athlete*. Broadway Books.
Thomas, T. (1992) *Tennessee* (song recorded by Arrested Development). *On 3 years 5 months and 2 days in the life of…* Chrysalis Records.
Turner, J. H. (2012). *Face to face: Toward a sociological theory of interpersonal behavior*. Stanford University Press.
Webber, T. L. (1978). *Deep like the rivers: Education in the slave quarter community, 1831–1865*. Norton.

Chapter 5: Embodiment and Buddhist Practices for Racial Healing and Social Justice

Bourdieu, P. (2000). *Pascalian meditations*. Stanford University Press.
DiAngelo, R. J. (2018). *White fragility: Why it's so hard for white people to talk about racism*. Beacon Press.
Garfield, L. Jay, 1995, *The Fundamental Wisdom of the Middle Way*, New York, Oxford: Oxford University Press.
Ginwright, S. A. (2016). *Hope and healing in urban education: How urban activists and teachers are reclaiming matters of the heart*. Routledge.
Hall, W. J., et al. (2015). Implicit racial/ethnic bias among health care professionals. *American Journal of Public Health*, *105*(12): e60–e76. https://doi.org/10.2105/AJPH.2015.302903.
King, R. (2018). *Mindful of race: Transforming racism from the inside out*. Sounds True.

Kwah, H. (2019). Bringing a dialogue between Buddhist multilogicality and evolutionary science into the science classroom. *Cultural Studies of Science Education*. https://doi.org/10.1007/s11422-019-09930-1.

Salzberg, S. (2011). Mindfulness and loving-kindness. *Contemporary Buddhism*, *12*(1): 177–82. https://doi.org/10.1080/14639947.2011.564837.

Selassie, S. (2020). *You belong: A call for connection*. HarperOne.

Sherrell, C., & Simmer-Brown, J. (2017). Spiritual bypassing in the contemporary mindfulness movement. *The Initiative for Contemplation, Equity & Action Journal*, *1*(1): 75–94.

williams, R. a. k. (2020a). https://angelkyodowilliams.com. Retrieved August 31, 2020.

williams, R. a. k. (2020b). *Zenchangeangel Livestream*. Retrieved August 21, 2020, from https://youtu.be/OhJ7AXJmLrA

williams, R. a. k., Owens, R., & Syedullah, J. (2016). *Radical dharma: Talking race, love, and liberation*. North Atlantic Books.

Chapter 6: Mindfully Running the Course(s): Self-Care as Critical Praxis

Darder, A. (2016). Freire and the body. *Encyclopedia of Educational Philosophy and Theory*. Springer. doi:10.1007/978-981-287-532-7_529-1.

Davidson, R. J., with Begley, S. (2012). *The emotional life of your brain: How its unique patterns affect the way you think, feel, and live—and how you can change them*. Hudson Street Press.

Freire, P. (1970). *Pedagogy of the oppressed*. Continuum.

Freire, P. (1998). *Pedagogy of freedom: Ethics, democracy, and civic courage*. Rowman & Littlefield.

Freire, P. (2007). *Daring to dream: Toward a pedagogy of the unfinished*. Paradigm.

Giroux, H. (1988). *Teachers as intellectuals: Toward a critical pedagogy of learning*. Bergan & Garvey.

Kabat-Zinn, J. (2015). Mindfulness. *Mindfulness*, *6*(6): 1481–3. doi:10.1007/s12671-015-0456-x.

Kincheloe, J. L. (1999). Trouble ahead, trouble behind: Grounding the postformal critique of educational psychology. In J. L. Kincheloe & S. R. Steinberg (Eds.), *The postformal reader* (pp. 4–54). Falmer Press.

Purser, R. (2019). *McMindfulness: How mindfulness became the new capitalist spirituality*. Watkins Media.

Tairako, T. (2018). Reification-thingification and alienation—Basic concepts of Marx's critique of political economy and practical materialism. *Hitotsubashi Journal of Social Studies*, *49*(1): 1–28.

Tobin, K., Powietrzynska, M., & Alexakos, K. (2015). Mindfulness and wellness: Central components of a science of learning. *Journal Educational Innovation / Revista Innovación Educativa*, *15*(67): 61–87.

Chapter 7: Immanence and a Pedagogy of Vulnerability: Teaching with Anxiety and Panic Disorder

Barad, K. (2007). *Meeting the universe halfway: Quantum physics and the entanglement of matter and meaning*. Duke University Press.

Braidotti, R. (2013). *The posthuman*. Polity Press.

Brunila, K., & Valero, P. (2018). Anxiety and the making of research(ing) subjects in neoliberal academia. *Subjectivity*, *11*(1): 74–89.

hooks, b. (1994). *Teaching to transgress*. Routledge.

Deleuze, G., & Guattari, F. (1987). *Capitalism and schizophrenia: A thousand plateaus*. University of Minnesota Press.

Mountz, A., Bonds, A., Mansfield, B., Loyd, J., Hyndman, J., Walton-Roberts, M., … & Curran, W. (2015). For slow scholarship: A feminist politics of resistance through collective action in the neoliberal university. *ACME: An International Journal for Critical Geographies*, *14*(4): 1235–59.

Price, M. (2011). *Mad at school: Rhetorics of mental disability and academic life*. University of Michigan Press.

St. Pierre, E. (2000). Poststructural feminism in education: An overview. *International Journal of Qualitative Studies in Education*, 13(5): 477–515.

Chapter 8: In the "Being" and the "Doing": Teachers' Critical Embodied Pedagogies of Care

Aaron, K., Ye, Y., & The WNYC Data Team (2015, September 15). More than 90,000 New York City students are searched before school. *WNYC*. Retrieved from: http://www.wnyc.org/story/school-metal-detectors/.

Bakare-Yusuf, B. (1999). *The economy of violence: Black bodies and the unspeakable terror*. London: Routledge.

Cariaga, S. M. (2018). *Pedagogies of wholeness: Cultivating critical healing literacies with students of color in an embodied English classroom* (doctoral dissertation), University of California at Los Angeles.

Collins, P. H. (1986). Learning from the outsider within: The sociological significance of Black feminist thought. *Social Problems*, *33*(6): s14–s32.

Ginwright, S. A. (2010). Peace out to revolution! Activism among African American youth: An argument for radical healing. *Young*, 18(1): 77–96.

Ginwright, S. (2015). *Hope and healing in urban education: How urban activists and teachers are reclaiming matters of the heart*. Routledge.

Haraway, D. (1988). Situated knowledges: The science question in feminism and the privilege of partial perspective. *Feminist Studies*, *14*(3): 575–99.

Kupchik, A., & Ward, G. K. (2011). Reproducing social inequality through school security: Effects of race and class on school security measures. In American Sociological Association's 106th Annual Meeting.

La Jevic, L., & Springgay, S. (2008). A/r/tography as an ethics of embodiment: Visual journals in preservice education. *Qualitative Inquiry*, *14*(1): 67–89.

Nieto, S. (2008). Nice is not enough: Defining caring for students of color. In M. Pollock (Ed.), *Everyday antiracism: Getting real about race in school* (pp. 28–31). New Press.

O'Brien, M. (2009). The impact of economic, social, cultural and emotional capital on mothers' love and care work in education. In K. Lynch, J. Baker, & M. Lyons (Eds.), *Affective equality: Love, care, and injustice* (pp. 158–79). Palgrave Macmillan.
Ohito, E. O. (2019). Thinking through the flesh: A critical autoethnography of racial body politics in urban teacher education. *Race Ethnicity and Education*, *22*(2): 250–68.
Orner, M., Miller, J. L., & Ellsworth, E. (1996). Excessive moments and educational discourses that try to contain them. *Educational Theory*, *46*(1): 71–91.
Pindyck, M. (2018). Frottage as inquiry. *International Journal of Education through Art*, *14*(1): 13–25.
Reimers, E. (2020). Disruptions of desexualized heteronormativity–queer identification (s) as pedagogical resources. *Teaching Education*, 31(1): 112–25.
Restler, V. (2017). *Re-visualizing care: Teachers' invisible labor in neoliberal times* (unpublished doctoral dissertation). City University of New York.
Restler, V. (2019). Countervisualities of care: Re-visualizing teacher labor. *Gender and Education*, *31*(5): 643–54.
Rolón-Dow, R. (2005). Critical care: A color (full) analysis of care narratives in the schooling experiences of Puerto Rican girls. *American Educational Research Journal*, *42*(1): 77–111.
Smith, D. E. (2005). *Institutional ethnography: A sociology for people*. Rowman Altamira.

Chapter 9: Healing in Collaboration with School Counselors: Hip-Hop and Spoken Word Therapy

Adjapong, E. S. (2017). Bridging theory and practice in the urban science classroom: A framework for hip-hop pedagogy in STEM. *Critical Education*, *8*(15), 5–23.
American School Counselor Association. (2019). *The ASCA national model: A framework for school counseling programs* (4th ed.).
Bacher-Hicks, A., Billings, S. B., & Deming, D. J. (2019). *The school to prison pipeline: Long-run impacts of school suspensions on adult crime* (No. w26257). National Bureau of Economic Research.
Ball, J. A. (2011). *I mix what I like! A mixtape manifesto*. AK Press.
Beck, A. T. (1963). Thinking and depression: Idiosyncratic content and cognitive distortions. *Archives of General Psychiatry*, *9*(4): 324–33.
Benton, J. M., & Overtree, C. E. (2012). Multicultural office design: A case example. *Professional Psychology: Research and Practice*, *43*(3): 265–69. https://doi.org/10.1037/a0027443.
Bowers, H., Lemberger-Truelove, M. E., & Brigman, G. (2018). A social-emotional leadership framework for school counselors. *Professional School Counseling*, *21*(1b), 1–9.
CASEL. (2016). SEL Research. Retrieved from http://www.casel.org/research/.
Chang, J. (2005). *Can't stop, won't stop: A history of the hip-hop generation*. St. Martin's Press.
Cholewa, B., Goodman-Scott, E., & Thomas, A. (2016). Teachers' perceptions and experiences consulting with school counsellors: A qualitative study. *Professional School Counseling, 20*(1). https://doi.org/10.5330/1096-2409-20.1.77
Cook, K., & Malloy, L. (2014). School counseling office design: Creating safe space. *Journal of Creativity in Mental Health*, *9*(3): 436–43.

Cook, A. L., & Krueger-Henney, P. (2017). Group work that examines systems of power with young people: Youth participatory action research. *Journal for Specialists in Group Work, 2*: 1–18. https://doi.org/10.1080/01933922.2017.1282570.

Cook, A. L., Levy, I., & Whitehouse, A. (2020) Exploring youth participatory action research in urban schools: advancing social justice and equity-based counseling practices. *Journal for Social Action in Counseling and Psychology.*

Creedon, T. B., & Cook, B. L. (2016). Access to mental health care increased but not for substance use, while disparities remain. *Health Affairs, 35*(6), 1017–21. doi:10.1377/hlthaff.2016.0098

East, D. (2019). *On my way 2 school. On the survival* [CD]. Def Jam Recordings.

Emdin, C. (2016). *For white folks who teach in the hood … and the rest of y'all too: Reality pedagogy and urban education*. Beacon Press.

Emdin, C., Adjapong, E., & Levy, I. (2016). Hip-hop based interventions as pedagogy/therapy in STEM. *Journal for Multicultural Education, 10*(3): 307–21.

Gallagher, M., Burnstein, E. T., & Oliver, W. (2018). *How affordable housing providers can boost residents' economic mobility*. Urban Institute.

Golberstein, E., Wen, H., & Miller, B. F. (2020). Coronavirus disease 2019 (COVID-19) and mental health for children and adolescents. *JAMA Pediatrics, 174*(9): 819–20.

Gopalan, M., & Nelson, A. A. (2019). Understanding the racial discipline gap in schools. *Aera Open, 5*(2): 2332858419844613.

Gelso, C. J. (2018). *The therapeutic relationship in psychotherapy practice: An integrative perspective*. Routledge.

Gershenson, S., & Papageorge, N. (2018). The power of teacher expectations: How racial bias hinders student attainment. *Education Next, 18*(1): 64–71.

Gershenson, S., Holt, S. B., & Papageorge, N. W. (2016). Who believes in me? The effect of student–teacher demographic match on teacher expectations. *Economics of Education Review, 52*: 209–24.

Gonzalez, T., & Hayes, B. G. (2009). Rap music in school counseling based on Don Elligan's rap therapy. *Journal of Creativity in Mental Health, 4*(2): 161–72.

Hannon, M. D., & Vereen, L. G. (2016). Irreducibility of Black male clients: Considerations for culturally competent counseling. *Journal of Humanistic Counseling, 55*(3): 234–45.

Hansen, J. T., Speciale, M., & Lemberger, M. E. (2014). Humanism: The foundation and future of professional counseling. *Journal of Humanistic Counseling, 53*(3): 170–90.

Hook, J. N., Farrell, J. E., Davis, D. E., DeBlaere, C., Van Tongeren, D. R., & Utsey, S. O. (2016). Cultural humility and racial microaggressions in counseling. *Journal of Counseling Psychology, 63*(3): 269.

Kelly, L. L. (2013). Hip-hop literature: The politics, poetics, and power of hip-hop in the English classroom. *English Journal*, 51–6.

Knopp, S. (2012). Schools, Marxism, and liberation. In S. Knopp & J. Bale (Eds.), *Education and capitalism: Struggles for learning and liberation* (pp. 9–40). Haymarket Books.

Levy, I. (2019). Hip-hop and spoken word therapy in urban school counseling. *Professional School Counseling, 22*(1b), 1–11.

Levy, I. P., & Adjapong, E. S. (2020). Toward culturally competent school counseling environments: hip-hop studio construction. *Professional Counselor, 10*(2): 266–84.

Levy, I., Cook, A. L., & Emdin, C. (2018). Remixing the school counselor's tool kit: hip-hop spoken word therapy and YPAR. *Professional School Counseling, 22*(1), 1–11. https://doi.org/10.1177/2156759X18800285.

Levy, I., & Travis, R. (2020). The critical cycle of mixtape creation: Reducing stress via three different group counseling styles. *Journal for Specialists in Group Work, 45*(4): 307–330, doi: 10.1080/01933922.2020.1826614

Lindsey, M. A., Chambers, K., Pohle, C., Beall, P., & Lucksted, A. (2013). Understanding the behavioral determinants of mental health service use by urban, under-resourced Black youth: Adolescent and caregiver perspectives. *Journal of Child and Family Studies, 22*(1): 107–21.

Lindsay, C. A., & Hart, C. M. (2017). Exposure to same-race teachers and student disciplinary outcomes for Black students in North Carolina. *Educational Evaluation and Policy Analysis, 39*(3): 485–510.

Patel, M. R., Israel, B. A., Song, P. X., Hao, W., TerHaar, L., Tariq, M., & Lichtenstein, R. (2019). Insuring good health: outcomes and acceptability of a participatory health insurance literacy intervention in diverse urban communities. *Health Education & Behavior, 46*(3), 494–505. doi:10.1177/1090198119831060

Parks, C., Wallace, B. C., Emdin, C., & Levy, I. P. (2016). An examination of gendered violence and school push-out directed against urban black girls/ adolescents: Illustrative data, cases and a call to action. *Journal of Infant, Child, and Adolescent Psychotherapy, 15*(3): 210–19.

Perreira, K. M., & Pedroza, J. M. (2019). Policies of exclusion: implications for the health of immigrants and their children. *Annual Review of Public Health, 40*: 147–66.

Prez, D. (2000). *They school. On let's get free* [CD]. Loud Records.

Rogers, C. R. (1957). The necessary and sufficient conditions of therapeutic personality change. *Journal of consulting psychology, 21*(2): 95.

Rose, T. (1994). A style nobody can deal with: Politics, style and the postindustrial city in hip hop. *Microphone Fiends: Youth Music and Youth Culture*, 71–88.

Sanchez, Y. M., Lambert, S. F., & Cooley-Strickland, M. (2013). Adverse life events, coping and internalizing and externalizing behaviors in urban African American youth. *Journal of Child and Family Studies, 22*(1): 38–47. doi: 10.1007/ s10826-012-9590-4

Schonert-Reichl, K. A., Kitil, M. J., & Hanson-Peterson, J. (2017). *To reach the students, teach the teachers: A national scan of teacher preparation and social & emotional learning*. Report. CASEL.

Smith Lee, J. R., & Robinson, M. A. (2019). "That's my number one fear in life. It's the police": Examining young Black men's exposures to trauma and loss resulting from police violence and police killings. *Journal of Black Psychology, 45*(3): 143–84.

Villodas, M. T., Pfiffner, L. J., Moses, J. O., Hartung, C., & McBurnett, K. (2019). The roles of student gender, race, and psychopathology in teachers' identification of students for services. *Children and Youth Services Review*, 104468.

Washington, A. R. (2018). Integrating hip-hop culture and rap music into social justice counseling with black males. *Journal of Counseling & Development, 96*(1): 97–105.

Weger Jr, H., Castle, G. R., & Emmett, M. C. (2010). Active listening in peer interviews: The influence of message paraphrasing on perceptions of listening skill. *International Journal of Listening, 24*(1): 34–49. https://doi.org/10.1080/10904010903466311.

Chapter 10: Sexual Healing: Confronting Disembodiment in Public Schooling

Ali-Khan, C. (forthcoming). Reflections from an in(descrete) body: Corporeality, capital and connection in the age of Covid. In K. Tobin & K. Alexakos (Eds.), *Wellness and well being: Educating the citizenry from pre-birth through death*. Brill | Sense.

Apple, M., & Christian-Smith, L. (1991). The politics of the textbook. In M. Apple & L. Christian-Smith (Eds.), *The politics of the textbook* (pp. 1–21). Routledge.

Bowles, S., & Gintis, H. (1977). *Schooling in capitalist America: Educational reform and the contradictions of economic life*. Basic Books.

Darder, A. (2010). Schooling bodies: Critical pedagogy and urban youth. In S. Steinberg & J. L. Kincheloe (Eds.), *19 urban questions: Teaching in the city* (pp. xiii–xxiii). Peter Lang.

Delpit, L. (1995). *Other people's children: Cultural conflict in the classroom*. New Press.

Freeburg, B., Workman, J., & Arnett, S. (2011). Rationales and norms for teacher dress codes: A review of employee handbooks. *NASSP Bulletin*, *95*(1): 31–45.

Freire, P. (1970). *Pedagogy of the oppressed*. Continuum.

Freire, P. (1997). *Pedagogy of the heart*. Continuum.

Foucault, M. (2010). *The Foucault reader*. Pantheon.

hooks, b. (1994). *Teaching to transgress: Education as the practice of freedom*. Routledge.

Johnson, T. (2004). "It's pointless to deny that that dynamic is there": Sexual tensions in secondary classrooms. *English Education*, *37*(1): 5–29.

Johnson, M. E., Waldman, E. G., & Crawford, B. J. (2020). Title IX and menstruation. *Harvard Journal of Law and Gender*, *43*: 225.

Kipnis, L. (2015). My Title IX inquisition. *Chronicle of Higher Education*, *61*(38): B6.

Kozol, J. (2012). *Savage inequalities: Children in America's schools*. Broadway Books.

Liston, D. (1990). *Capitalist schools: Explanations and ethics in radical studies of schooling*. Routledge.

Mooney, C., Stein, P., & Steckelberg, A. (2020, June 26). As America struggles to reopen schools and offices, how to clean coronavirus from the air. *Washington Post*. Retrieved from https://www.washingtonpost.com/climate-environment/2020/06/26/coronavirus-indoor-air-schools-offices/?arc404=true.

Owen, P., & Gillentine, J. (2011). Please touch the children: Appropriate touch in the primary classroom. *Early Child Development and Care*, *181*(6): 857–68.

Paris, D. (2012). Culturally sustaining pedagogy: A needed change in stance, terminology, and practice. *Educational Researcher*, *41*(3): 93–7.

Sin, M., & Koole, S. (2013). That human touch that means so much: exploring the tactile dimension of social life. *Mind Magazine*, *2*: 17.

Wallace-Sanders, K. (2003). A vessel of possibilities: Teaching through the expectant body. In D. P. Freeman & M. S. Holmes (Eds.), *The teacher's body: Embodiment, authority, and identity in the academy* (pp. 187–98). SUNY Press.

White, J., & Ali-Khan, C. (2020). Sex and sexuality in the Language Arts classroom. *English Education*, *52*(4): 383–309.

White, J. (2012). From textbooks to "managed instructional systems": Corporate control of the English Language Arts. In H. Hickman & B. Porfilio (Eds.), *The new politics of the textbook: A project of critical examination and resistance* (pp. 193–212). Sense.

Chapter 11: Songs in the Key of Healing Hope: Listening as Soul Care

Berry, W. (1999). The peace of wild things. In *The selected poems of Wendell Berry*: Counterpoint Press

CDC (2021). Data & statistics for Covid 19: Covid data tracker, Retrieved January 18, 2021 from: https://covid.cdc.gov/covid-data-tracker/#demographicsovertime

Cole, K. C. (2003). *Mind over matter: Conversations with the cosmos*. Harcourt.

Deleuze, G., & Guattari, F. (1980/2017). *A thousand plateaus: Capitalism and schizophrenia*. University of Minnesota Press.

Freire, P. (1996). *Letters to Cristina: Reflections on my life and work*. Routledge.

Flaccus, G. (2020, May 2). *Bird-watching soars amid Covid-19 as Americans head outdoors*. Associated Press. Retrieved from: https://apnews.com/article/94a1ea5938943d8a70fe794e9f629b13.

Heidegger, M. (1977). *Basic writings: From being and time 1927 to the task of thinking 1964.*: Routledge & Kegan Paul.

Kress, T. M., & Lake, R. L. (2012). *We saved the best for you: Letters of hope, imagination, and wisdom for 21st century educators*. Brill/Sense.

Levitin, D. J. (2019). *This is your brain on music: Understanding a human obsession*. Penguin.

Mannes, E. (2013). *The power of music: Pioneering discoveries in the new science of song*. Walker.

Nieto, S. (2015). *Dear Paulo: Letters from those who dare teach*. Routledge.

Raffi (1980). Thanks a lot. On *Baby Beluga* [cassette recording]. Troubadour.

Sacks, O. (2008). *Musicophilia: Tales of music and the brain*. Vintage Books.

Thank (2020). *Online Etymology Dictionary*. Retrieved December 15, 2020, from https://www.etymonline.com/word/thank.

Trowbridge, D. (1985). Where dreams are born [cassette recording]. On D. Trowbridge. *Songs unspoken*. Sparrow Records.

USDA (2020). *Pando: I spread*. In Fishlake National Forest. Retrieved from https://www.fs.usda.gov/detail/fishlake/home/?cid=STELPRDB5393641.

Chapter 12: Creating the Play Space: Human Encounters Explored through Theater Processes

Ali, A., & Wolfert, S. (2016). Theatre as a treatment for posttraumatic stress in military veterans: Exploring the psychotherapeutic potential of mimetic induction. *Arts in Psychotherapy*, *50*: 58–65. https://doi.org/10.1016/j.aip.2016.06.004

Ali, A., Wolfert, S., Fahmy, P., Nayyar, M., & Chaudhry, A. (2019). The therapeutic effects of imagination: Investigating mimetic induction and dramatic simulation in a trauma treatment for military veterans. *Arts in Psychotherapy*, *62*: 7–11.

Ali, A., Wolfert, S., & Homer, B. D. (2019). In the service of science: Veteran-led research in the investigation of a theatre-based posttraumatic stress disorder treatment, *Journal of Humanistic Psychology*. https://doi.org/10.1177/0022167819839907.

Allen-Hornblower, E. (2013). Sounds and suffering in Sophocles' Philoctetes and Gide's Philoctète. *Studi Italiani di Filologia Classica*, *11*(1): 5–41.

Barbour, K. N. (2012). Standing centre: Autoethnographic writing and solo dance performance. *Cultural Studies—Critical Methodologies*, 12(1): 67–71. doi:10.1177/1532708611430491.
Brown, C. B. (2012). *Daring greatly: How the courage to be vulnerable transforms the way we live, love, parent, and lead* (1st ed.). Gotham Books.
Doerries, B. (2016). *The theater of war: What ancient tragedies can teach us today*. Knopf Doubleday. Google Scholar.
Park-Fuller, L. M. (2000). Performing absence: The staged personal narrative as testimony, *Text and Performance Quarterly*, *20*(1): 20–42, https://doi.org/10.1080/10462930009366281.
Pennacchia, M. (2019). Theatre strikes back in the digital era: An interview with Stephan Wolfert, *Multicultural Shakespeare*, *20*(1): 37–49. https://doi.org/10.18778/2083-8530.20.04 20:1,3.
Sloan, C. (2018). Understanding spaces of potentiality in applied theatre, *Research in Drama Education: Journal of Applied Theatre and Performance*, 23(4): 582–97. https://doi.org/10.1080/13569783.2018.1508991
Sophocles (2017). *Philoctetes* (I. Johnson, Trans.). 409 BC Vancouver Island University Nanaimo. 2008. Revised 2012. Reformatted 2017.
Wiggins, D. (2019). Veterans find a path to healing through Shakespeare. *Mad in America*. https://www.madinamerica.com/2019/10/veterans-find-path-to-healing-through-shakespeare/.

Chapter 13: "What Happens If I Open That Door?": Art, Truth-Telling, and Healing in a Poetry Course for Prospective Teachers

Anderson, C. M., & M. M. MacCurdy (2000). *Writing and healing: Toward an informed practice*. National Council of Teachers of English.
Apol, L. (1998). *Falling into grace*. Dordt College Press.
Apol, L. (2015). *Requiem, Rwanda*. Michigan State University Press.
Apol, L. (2017). Writing poetry in Rwanda: A means for better listening, understanding, processing, and responding. *Journal of Poetry Therapy: Interdisciplinary Journal of Practice, Theory, Research and Education, 30* (2): 71–83.
Apol, L. (2018). *Nothing but the blood*. Michigan State University Press.
Apol, L. (2019). "Stories *as* change: Using writing to facilitate healing among genocide survivors in Rwanda." In H. Grayson & N. Hitchcott (Eds.), *Rwanda after 1994: Stories of change* (pp. 232–51). Liverpool University Press.
Apol, L. (2021a). *Poetry, poetic inquiry and Rwanda: Engaging with the lives of others*. Springer Nature.
Apol, L. (2021b). *A fine yellow dust*. Michigan State University Press.
DeSalvo, L. (1999). *Writing as a way of healing: How telling our stories transforms our lives*. Beacon Press.
Fox, J. (1997). *Poetic medicine: The healing art of poem-making*. Tarcher/Penguin Group.
Orr, G. (2002). *Poetry as survival*. University of Georgia Press.
Pennebaker, J. W. (1997). *Opening up: The healing power of expressing emotions*. Guilford Press.

Chapter 14: The Distresses and Hopes of Beginning Teachers: Five Arts-based Research Explorations

Barone, T., & Eisner, E. W. (2012). *Arts based research*. SAGE.
Fellner, G. (2019). The demon of hope: An arts-based infused meditation on race, disability, and the researcher's complicity with injustice. *Art|Reseearch International, 4*(2): 545–67.
Ingersoll, R., Merrill, L., & May, H. (2014). *What are the effects of teacher education and preparation on beginning teacher attrition? Research Report (#RR-82)*. Consortium for Policy Research in Education, University of Pennsylvania. Retrieved on June 31, 2020 from https://www.cpre.org/sites/default/files/researchreport/2018_prepeffects2014.pdf.
Kwah, H., & Fellner, G. (2020). Contemplative, visual arts-based research methods for self-care and transformation. In K. Alexakos & K. Tobin (Eds.), *Methodologies for multilevel research in teacher education*. Brill/Sense.
Leavy, P. (2009). *Method meets art: Arts-based research practice*. Guilford Press.
Pink, S. (2007). Walking with video. *Visual Studies, 22*(3): 240–52.
Restler, V. (2017). *Re-visualizing care: Teachers' invisible labor in neoliberal times* (doctoral dissertation). City University of New York.
Schaefer, L., & Clandinin, D. J. (2019). Sustaining teachers' stories to live by: Implications for teacher education. *Teachers and Teaching, 25*(1): 54–68. https://doi.org/10.1080/13540602.2018.1532407.

Chapter 15: Committing to Black Girl Joy in the Social Studies Classroom: A Hip-Hop Feminist Approach

Alridge, D. P. (2006). The limits of master narratives in history textbooks: An analysis of representations of Martin Luther King, Jr. *Teachers College Record, 108*(4): 662.
Annamma, S. A., Anyon, Y., Joseph, N. M., Farrar, J., Greer, E., Downing, B., & Simmons, J. (2016). Black girls and school discipline: The complexities of being overrepresented and understudied. *Urban Education, 54*(2): 211–42.
Brown, R. N. (2013). *Hear our truths: The creative potential of Black girlhood*. University of Illinois Press.
Caponi-Tabery, G. (1999). *Signifyin(g), sanctifyin' & slam dunking: A reader in African American expressive culture*. University of Massachusetts Press.
Collins, P. H. (1990). *Black feminist thought: Knowledge, consciousness and the politics of empowerment*. New York: Routledge.
Cooper, B. (2018). *Eloquent rage: A Black feminist discovers her superpower*. St. Martin's Press.
Dillard, C. (2012). *Learning to (re)member the things we've learned to forget: Endarkened feminisms, spirituality, and the sacred nature of research and teaching*. Peter Lang.
Durham, A., Cooper, B. C., & Morris, S. M. (2013). The stage hip-hop feminism built: A new directions essay. *Signs: Journal of Women in Culture and Society, 38*(3): 721–37.
Evans-Winters, V. E., & Esposito, J. (2010). Other people's daughters: Critical race feminism and Black girls' education. *Educational Foundations, 24*: 11–24.
Gay, G. (2004). Social studies teacher education for urban classrooms. *Critical Issues in Social Studies Teacher Education*, 75–95.

Forman, M., & Neal, M. A. (Eds.). (2004). *That's the joint!: The hip-hop studies reader*. Routledge.
Gaunt, K. (2020, July 21). The magic of black girls' play. *New York Times*. https://www.nytimes.com/2020/07/21/parenting/black-girls-play.html.
Griffin, A., & Tackie, H. (2016). *Through our eyes: Perspectives and reflections from Black teachers* (p. 3). Education Trust. https://edtrust.org/resource/through-our-eyes/
hooks, b. (1994) *Teaching to transgress*. Routledge.
Kelley, R. D. (2002). *Freedom dreams: The black radical imagination*. Beacon Press.
Kester, G. (2004). Dialogical aesthetics. *Conversation Pieces Community+ Communication in Modern Art*, 82–123.
Lindsey, T. B. (2015). Let me blow your mind: Hip hop feminist futures in theory and praxis. *Urban Education*, *50*(1): 52–77.
Lindsey, T. B. (2018). Ain't nobody got time for that: Anti-Black girl violence in the era of SayHerName. *Urban Education*, *53*(2): 162–75.
Love, B. L. (2019). *We want to do more than survive: Abolitionist teaching and the pursuit of educational freedom*. Beacon Press.
Mikkelson, D. (2017, October 19). *School apologizes for photograph appearing to show black slave girl on leashes*. Snopes. https://www.snopes.com/news/2017/10/19/school-apologizes-for-photograph/.
Morgan, J. (2000). *When chickenheads come to roost: A hip-hop feminist breaks it down*. Simon & Schuster.
Morris, M. W. (2016). *Pushout: The criminalization of Black girls in schools*. New Press.
Morris, M. W. (2019). *Sing a rhythm, dance a blues: Education for liberation of black girls*. New Press.
Muhammad, G. (2020). *Cultivating genius: An equity framework for culturally and historically responsive literacy*. Scholastic.
Perry, I. (2020, June 10). Imani Perry (@imaniperry) in conversation with Kiese Laymon: On the uprising since George Floyd's murder [tweet; thumbnail]. Twitter.
Sankofa Waters, M., Evans-Winters, V. E., & Love, B. L. (Eds.) (2018). *Celebrating twenty years of black girlhood*. Peter Lang US.
Vickery, A. E. (2017). "You excluded us for so long and now you want us to be patriotic?": African American women teachers navigating the quandary of citizenship. *Theory & Research in Social Education*, *45*(3): 318–48.
Walker, A. (1993). *Possessing the secret of joy*. Open Road Media.
Walker, A. (1983). *In search of our mothers' gardens*. Harcourt.
Woods, J. (2016). *HEAVN*. Jagjaguwar.
Woodson, A. N. (2015). "What you supposed to know": Urban Black students' perspectives on history textbooks. *Journal of Urban Learning, Teaching, and Research*, *11*: 57–65.

Chapter 16: Folding Cranes of Hope: Assembling Leadership through Critical Pedagogy

Freire, P. (1972). *Pedagogy of the oppressed*. Penguin Education.
Moll, L. C., Amanti, C., Neff, D., & Gonzalez, N. (1992). Funds of knowledge for teaching: Using a qualitative approach to connect homes and classrooms. *Theory into Practice*, *31*(2): 132–41. doi:10.1080/00405849209543534.

Yosso, T. J. (2005). Whose culture has capital? A critical race theory discussion of community cultural wealth. *Race Ethnicity and Education*, *8*(1): 69–91. doi.org/10.1080/1361332052000341006

Chapter 17: The Elders' pedagogy: Teaching as survivance in the academy

Bailey, M. (2014, April 27). More on the origin of misogynoir. *Tumblr*. http://moyazb.tumblr.com/post/84048113369/more-on-the-origin-of-misogynoir.
Freire, P. (1999). *Pedagogy of the oppressed* (new revised 20th anniversary ed.) (M. Ramos, Trans.). Continuum.
hooks, b. (1994). *Teaching to transgress: Education as the practice of freedom*. Routledge.

Chapter 18: Between Wholeness and Restoration

Adair, M. & Howell, S. (2007). Common behavioral patterns that perpetuate power relations of domination. *Tools for change*. file:///Users/user/Downloads/Common_Behavioral_Patterns_that_Perpetuate_Power_Relations.pdf
Bigelow, B. (2020). The freedom to harm vs. the freedom from harm. *Rethinking Schools*. *34*(4). https://rethinkingschools.org/articles/the-freedom-to-harm-vs-the-freedom-from-harm.
Boyes-Watson, C., & Pranis, K. (2014). *Circle forward: Building a restorative school community*. Living Justice Press.
DeWolfe, J., & Geddes, T. (2019). *The little book of racial healing*. Skyhorse Publishing.
Dobson, A. (2014). *Listening for democracy: recognition, representation, reconciliation*. Oxford University Press.
Evans, K. Morrison, B., & Vaandering, D. (2019). Critical race theory and restorative justice education. In T. Lewis & C. Stauffer (Eds.), *Listening to the movement: Essays on new growth and new challenges in restorative justice*, Wipf & Stock. https://zehr-institute.org/publications/listening-to-the-movement/.
Evans, K., & Vaandering, D. (2016). *The little book of restorative justice in education*. Skyhorse.
Freire, P. (1970). *Pedagogy of the oppressed* (2005 ed.). Continuum.
Hynes, M. (2016). Religion doesn't cause religious violence—A conversation with Rabbi Sacks. [Radio Broadcast]. CBC Radio. https://www.cbc.ca/radio/tapestry/religion-doesn-t-cause-religious-violence-a-conversation-with-rabbi-sacks-1.3511152/rabbi-jonathan-sacks-dies-at-72-1.3511173
hooks, bell. (1994). Theory as liberatory practice. In *Teaching to transgress: Education as the practice of freedom* (pp. 59–75). Routledge.
Hynes, M. (Host) (2016, April 1). Religion doesn't cause religious violence [Audio podcast episode]. In *Tapestry*. CBC Radio. https://www.cbc.ca/radio/tapestry/religion-doesn-t-cause-religious-violence-a-conversation-with-rabbi-sacks-1.3511152/tapestry-25-rabbi-lord-jonathan-sacks-1.3511173.
Kincheloe, J. L. (2004). *Critical pedagogy primer*. Peter Lang.
Nerburn, K. (2009). *Wolf at twilight: An Indian elder's journey through a land of ghosts and shadows*. New World Library.

Paul (57 CE). Letter to the Romans. In *Holy Bible: New international version*, 2011. www.BibleGateway.com.
Pranis, K. (2017, June 5–6) (workshop). *Advanced peacemaking circles training*. University of Waterloo.
Rigden, M. (Writer) & Barnsley, P. (Director). (2018, October 12). Colonial tea [television series episode]. In Barnsley, P. (Producer), *APTN Investigates*. APTN.
Sinclair, M. (2011). *What is reconciliation?* Truth and Reconciliation Commission, Ottawa. Video: https://vimeo.com/25389165.
Vaandering, D. (2006). Between wholeness and restoration: Theorizing restorative justice and restorative practice (unpublished). https://research.library.mun.ca/13611/1/beth06_vaandering.pdf.
Vaandering, D. (2010). The significance of critical theory for restorative justice in education. *Review of Education, Pedagogy, and Cultural Studies*, *32*(2): 145–76.
Vaandering, D. (2011). A faithful compass: rethinking the term restorative justice to find clarity, *Contemporary Justice Review*, *14*(3): 307–28.
Vanier, J. (2008). *Becoming human*. House of Anansi Press.
Woolford, A., & Benvenuto, J. (2015). Canada and colonial genocide, *Journal of Genocide Research*, *17*(4): 373–90. doi: 10.1080/14623528.2015.1096580.
Wolterstorff, N. (2006). Teaching justly for justice. *Journal of Education & Christian Belief*, *10*(2): 23–37.
Yunkaporta, T. (2019). *Sand talk: How Indigenous thinking can save the world*. World Text Publishing.

Chapter 19: Fraying Lives: Toward a Pedagogy of Healing

Barber, W. (2020). America must listen to its wounds. They will tell us where to look for hope. *Guardian*. May 30.
Boggs, G. L. (2012). Reimagine Everything. *Race, Poverty & the Environment*, *19*(3): 44–5.
Berry, W. (2010). *The Hidden Wound*. Counterpoint Press.
Cities of Peace. (2016). Teach-in Series. www.citiesofpeaceyouth.org/curriculum.
Collins, P. H., & Bilge, S. (2016). *Intersectionality*. Polity Press.
Darder, A. (1996). First person: Antonia Darder, interview by Cristina Valdez. *Race, Poverty & the Environment*, *6*(2/3): 14–16.
Darder, A. (2020). Conscientizaco. in S. L. Macrine (Ed.), *Critical pedagogy in uncertain times*. Palgrave.
Davis, A. (2019). Radical self-care. YouTube. https://www.youtube.com/results?search_query=angela+davis+radical+sel-care.
Freire, P. (1970). *Pedagogy of the oppressed*. Seabury Press.
Freire, P. (1974). *Education for critical consciousness*. Seabury Press.
Freire, P. (1993). Foreword. In P. McLaren & P. Leonard (Eds.), *Paulo Freire: A critical encounter*. Routledge.
Freire, P. (1998). *Pedagogy of freedom: Ethics, democracy and civic courage*. Roman & Littlefield.
Gayler, S. (2020). SAPPHIRE NOW unplugged: Racial Justice is a Movement, not a moment. SAP. https://news.sap.com/2020/07/eddie-glaude-at-sapphire-now-unplugged-racial-justice-is-a-movement-not-a-moment/
Ginwright, S. (2010). *Black youth rising: Activism, radical healing in urban America*. Teachers College Press.

Gharavi, V. (2020). Ethics at a distance. The politics of care. *Boston Review*. April 21.
Greene, M. (2009). Teaching as possibility: A light in dark times. In S. L. Macrine (Ed.), *Critical pedagogy in uncertain times*. Palgrave.
Haines, S. K. (2019). *The politics of trauma*. North Atlantic Books.
Lorde, A. (1984). *Sister outsider*. Crossing Press.
Lorde, A. (1988). *A burst of light*. IXIA Press.
Patel, L. (2016). *Decolonizing educational research: From ownership to answerability*. Routledge.
Roy, A. (2020). Pandemic is a portal. *Financial Times*. April 3.
Stiglitz, J. (2011). Of the 1%, by the 1%, for the 1%. *Vanity Fair*. March 31.
Tewksbury, G. (2016). *Schooling the market: Venture philanthropy, field building and the New Schools Venture Fund* (unpublished dissertation). CUNY Graduate Center.
Walker, M. (2000). On being female, black, and free. in J. Sternburg (Ed.), *The writer on her work*. W. W. Norton.
Whitfield, C. T. (2020). Black yoga collectives make space for healing. *New York Times*. July 27.
Young, I. M. (2006). Responsibility and global justice: A responsibility model. *Social Philosophy & Policy*, 23(1): 102–30.

Chapter 20: An Autoethnographic Account: How Black Teacher-Coaches Counter-Narrate New Social Constructs to Inform Pedagogy for Healing

Anderson, A. (2013). Teach for America and the dangers of deficit thinking. *Critical Education*, *4*(11): 28–47. https://doi.org/10.14288/ce.v4i11.183936.
Brockenbrough, E. (2015). "The discipline stop" black male teachers and the politics of urban school discipline. *Education and Urban Society*, *47*(5): 499–522. https://doi.org/10.1177/0013124514530154.
Caponi, G. D. (1999). Introduction: The case for an African American aesthetic. *Signifyin (g), sanctifyin', and slam dunking: A Reader in African American Expressive Culture*, 1–41.
Conner, C., & Bohan, C. H. (2018). Social studies teacher–athletic coaches' experiences coping with role conflict. *Journal of Educational Research and Practice* *8*(1): 54–71. https://doi.org/10.5590/JERAP.2018.08.1.05.
Duncan, K. E. (2016). *Teachers as resisters: black teachers using emancipatory pedagogies with black students* (doctoral dissertation). University of Georgia. https://getd.libs.uga.edu/pdfs/duncan_kristen_e_201605_phd.pdf.
Duncan-Andrade, J. M. R., & Morrell, E. (2008). *The art of critical pedagogy: Possibilities for moving from theory to practice in urban schools* (Vol. 285). Peter Lang.
Freire, P. (1972). *Pedagogy of the oppressed.*. (Myra Bergman Ramos, Trans.). Herder (original in Portuguese, 1968).
Ginwright, S. A. (2010). *Black youth rising: Activism and radical healing in urban America*. Teachers College Press.
Goings, R. B. (2015). The lion tells his side of the (counter) story: A black male educator's autoethnographic account. *Journal of African American Males in Education*, *6*(1): 91–105.

Ladson-Billings, G. (1994). *The dreamkeepers: Successful teachers of African American children* (1st ed., The Jossey-Bass Education Series). Jossey-Bass.
Locke, L. F., & Massengale, J. D. (1978). Role conflict in teacher/coaches. *Research Quarterly, 49*: 162–74.
Love, B. L. (2015). What is hip-hop-based education doing in nice fields such as early childhood and elementary education? *Urban Education, 50*(1): 106–31. https://doi.org/10.1177/0042085914563182.
Wenger, E., McDermott, R. A., & Snyder, W. M. (2002). *Cultivating communities of practice: A guide to managing knowledge.* Harvard Business Press.

Chapter 21: The Politics of a Revolutionary and Humanizing Praxis: The Story of Liberation, Victory, and Regression in Tucson

Darder, A. (2002). *Reinventing Paulo Freire: A pedagogy of love.* Westview Press.
Freire, P. (2016). *Pedagogy in process: The letters to Guinea-Bissau.* Bloomsbury.
Freire, P. (1993). *Pedagogy of the oppressed.* Continuum.
González et al. v. Douglas et al. Day 1 of Transcripts of Proceedings of Bench. Trial in CV-10-623-TUC-AWT (US Fed Ct. Arizona 2017).
González et al. v. Douglas et al. CV-10-623-TUC-AWT 468 (US Fed Ct. Arizona 2017).
Valenzuela, A. (1999). *Subtractive Schooling: U.S.-Mexican youth and the politics of caring.* SUNY Press.

Chapter 22: Schools for Liberation: Creating Leadership for a New World

Barnes, S. G. (2020). Predictable and possible. Kairos Center Policy Briefing. Retrieved from https://kairoscenter.org/policy-briefing-1-predictable-and-possible/.
Bezruchka, S. (2014). Inequality kills. In D. C. Johnston (Ed.), *Divided: The peril of our growing inequality* (pp. 190–9). New Press.
Boyer, R., & Morais, H. (1979). *Labor's untold story: The adventure story of the battles, betrayals and victories of American working men and women* (3rd ed.). United Electrical, Radio & Machine Workers of America.
Buchanan, L., Bui, Q., & Patel, J. K. (2020, July 8). Black Lives Matter puts another stamp on history. *New York Times*: A15.
Freire, P. (1985). *The politics of education: culture, power, and liberation.* Bergin & Garvey.
Galea, S., Tracy M., Hoggitt, K. G., DiMaggio, C., & Karpati, A. (2011). Estimated deaths attributable to social factors in the United States. *American Journal of Public Health 101*(August): 1456–65.
Horton, M. (1990). *The long haul: An autobiography with Judith Kohl and Herbert Kohl.* Doubleday.
Horton, M., & Freire, P. (1990). You have to bootleg education. In B. Bell, J. Gaventa, & J. Peters (Eds.), *We make the road by walking: Conversations on education and social change* (pp. 199–226). Temple University Press.

Hunt, E., & Pieper, C. M. (2016). *The third reconstruction: Moral Mondays, fusion politics, and the rise of a new justice movement*, by Dr. William J. Barber, II & Jonathan Wilson-Hartgrove. *Sociology of Religion*, *77*(December): 440–1.

King, M. (2015). Beyond Vietnam. In C. West (Ed.), *The radical king* (pp. 201–17). Beacon Press.

Chapter 23: "The Gift of Setting Alight the Sparks of Hope in the Past": Ancestry and History in Pedagogical Praxis in the Brazilian Amazon

Bâ, H. (2010). A Tradição Viva. In J. Ki-Zerbo (Ed.), *História Geral da África I: Metodologia e Pré-História da África* (pp. 167–212). UNESCO.

Bâ, H., & Cardaire, M. (1957). Tierno Bokar, le sage de Bandiagara. *Présence Africaine*,.

Barros, D., Pequeno, S., & Pederiva, P. (2018). Educação pela tradição oral de matriz Africana no Brasil: Ancestralidade, resistência e constituição humana. *Arquivos Analíticos de Políticas Educativas*, *26*(91): 1–31.

Benjamin, W. (1940). *On the concept of history*. http://www.efn.org/~dredmond/Theses_on_History.html. (also *Theses on the philosophy of history*. https://www.sfu.ca/~andrewf/CONCEPT2.html)

Brazil. Ministry of Health (2020, July 26). Data SUS. https://covid.saude.gov.br/.

Chiavenato, J. J. (2007). A hora da desforra. *Revista História Viva*, *45*: 84–91.

Cruz, M. M. (1999). Sítios agroflorestais na várzea do Careiro. *Revista de Geografia da Universidade do Amazonas*, *1*(1): 105–22.

Da Rocha, F., & Possamai, F. V. (2015). Chico Mendes and José Lutzenberger: Ecosystem management at multiple scales of government. In R. Rozzi et al. (Eds.), *Earth stewardship: Ecology and ethics* (Vol. 2). Springer.

Dussel, E. (2012). *Ética da Libertação na idade da Globalização e da exclusão*. Vozes.

Freire, P. (1994). *Pedagogia do Oprimido*. Paz e Terra.

Freire, P., & Guimaraes, S. (2014). *Partir da infância: diálogos sobre educação*. Paz e Terra.

Hall, A. L. (1997). *Sustaining Amazonia: grassroots action for productive conservation*. Manchester University Press.

Issa, D. (2007). Praxis of empowerment: Mística and mobilization in Brazil's landless rural workers' movement. *Latin American Perspectives*, *34*(153): 124–38.

Kopenawa, D., Albert, B., & Dundy, A. (2013). *The falling sky: words of a Yanomami shaman*. Belknap Press of Harvard University Press.

Löwy, M. (2002). A filosofia da história de Walter Benjamin. *Estudos Avançados*, *16*(45): 199–201.

Marx, K. (1959). *Economic and philosophic manuscripts of 1844*. Progress Publishers.

Marx, K. (2008). *Contribuição à crítica da Economia Política*. Expressão Popular.

Pinheiro, L. (1999, November). A revolta popular revisitada: apontamentos para uma história e historiografia da cabanagem. *Projeto História*, *19*: 227–41.

REPAM. (2020, June 16). *REPAM*. http://repam.org.br/?p=4815.

Souza, E. (2016). Crônicas da morte revivida na luta: uma etnografia da Romaria dos Mártires da Caminhada em Ribeirão Cascalheira (MT), Brasil. *Etnográfica*, *20*(2): 340–62.

Vygotsky, L. (1997). *Obras Escogidas Tomo I—Problemas Teóricos y Metodológicos de la Psicologia*. Visor.

Chapter 24: Thy Will Be Done: Radical Love as Self-Other Healing Praxis

Bambara, T. C. (1992). *The salt eaters*. Random House.
Byrd, R. P., Cole, J. B., & Guy-Sheftall, B. (Eds.) (2008). *I am your sister: Collected and unpublished writings of Audre Lorde*. Oxford University Press.
Cooper, B. C. (2018). *Eloquent rage: A black feminist discovers her superpower*. St. Martin's Press.
Delaney, B. (2020, January 30). We need to move on from self-care to something that cannot be captured by capitalism. *Guardian*. https://www.theguardian.com/commentisfree/2020/jan/31/we-need-to-move-on-from-self-care-to-something-that-cannot-be-captured-by-capitalism?CMP=share_btn_fb&fbclid=IwAR1j0ibSX2XZdUGkXMSUNbqDvFJvRQ5TjUcwOk7daxEh1oNVYo9iFiZ8vgg.
Evans-Winters, V. E. (2009). *Black feminism in qualitative inquiry: Writing our daughters' bodies*. New York: Routledge.
Guishard, M. (2009). The false paths, the endless labors, the turns now this way and now that: Participatory action research, mutual vulnerability, and the politics of inquiry. *Urban Review*, *41*(1): 85–105.
Harney, S. M., & Moten, F. (2013). *The undercommons: Fugitive planning and black study*. Minor Compositions.
Kelley, R. D. G. (2018). "Black study, black struggle." *Ufahamu: A Journal of African Studies*, *40*(2): 153–68.
Love, B. (2019). *We want to do more than survive: Abolitionist teaching and the pursuit of educational freedom*. Beacon Press.
Morrison, T. (2019). *The source of self-regard: Selected essays, speeches, and meditations*. Random House.
Patel, L. (2019). "Fugitive practices: Learning in a settler colony." *Educational Studies*, *55*(3): 253–61.
Piepzna-Samarasinha, L. L. (2018). *Care work: Dreaming disability justice*. Arsenal Pulp Press.
Sandoval, C. (2000). *Methodology of the oppressed*. University of Minnesota Press.

Chapter 25: Deflecting Echoes of Settler-Colonialism: Resilience and Healing While Working with Maya Youth

Bourdieu, P., & Passeron, J. C. (1990). *Theory, culture & society. Reproduction in education, society and culture* (2nd ed.). (R. Nice, Trans.). Sage.
Brayboy, B., & Maughan, E. (2009). Indigenous knowledges and the story of the bean. *Harvard Educational Review*, *79*(1): 1–21.
DeGennaro, D. (2016). *Designing critical and creative learning with Indigenous youth: A personal journey*. Sense.
DeGennaro, D. (2008). The dialectics informing identity in an urban youth digital storytelling workshop. *E-Learning and Digital Media*, *5*(4): 429–44.
DeGennaro, D., & Brown, T. (2009). Youth voices: Exploring connections between history agency and identity in a digital divide initiative. *Cultural Studies of Science Education*, *4*(1): 13–39.

DeGennaro, D., & Duque, R. (2013). Video of the oppressed: Insights into local knowledge, perspectives, and interests with youth. In T. Kress, C. Malott, & B. Porfilio (Eds.), *Challenging status quo retrenchment: New directions in critical qualitative research* (pp. 193–208). Information Age.

Delgado, R. (1991). Affirmative action as a majoritarian device: Or, do you really want to be a role model? *Michigan Law Review, 89*(5): 1222–31.

Delgado, R. (1989). Storytelling for oppositionists and others: A plea for narrative. *Michigan Law Review, 87*(8): 2411–41.

Engle, J., & Schulten, K. (2020). Is your generation doing its part to strengthen our democracy? *The New York Times*. https://www.nytimes.com/2020/09/15/learning/is-your-generation-doing-its-part-to-strengthen-our-democracy.html

Freire, P. (1973). *Education for critical consciousness*. Continuum.

Freire, P (1970). *Pedagogy of the oppressed*. Penguin Books.

Grillo, T., & Wildman, S. M. (1997). Obscuring the importance of race: The implications of making comparisons between racism and sexism (or other Isms). In R. Delgado & J. Stefancic (Eds.), *Critical white studies: Looking behind the mirror* (pp. 619–26). Temple University Press.

la paperson (2017). *A third university is possible*. University of Minnesota Press.

Ladson-Billings, G. (1998). Just what is critical race theory and what's it doing in a nice field like education? *International Journal of Qualitative Studies in Education, 11*(1): 7–24.

Lee, R., & Ahtone, T. (2020, March 30). Land-grab universities: Expropriated Indigenous land is the foundation of the land-grant university system. *High Country News, 52*(4): 32–45.

Masta, S. (2019). Challenging the relationship between settler colonial ideology and higher education spaces. *Berkeley Review of Education, 8*(2): 179–94.

Patel, L. (2019). Fugitive practices: Learning in a settler colony. *Educational Studies, 55*(3): 253–61.

Pizarro, M. (1998). "Chicana/o Power!" Epistemology and methodology for social justice and empowerment in Chicana/o communities. *Qualitative Studies in Education, 11*(1): 57–80.

Red Shirt-Shaw, M. (2020). *Beyond the land acknowledgement: College "LAND BACK" or free tuition for native students* [Policy brief]. Hack the Gates. https://hackthegates.org/wp-content/uploads/2020/08/Redshirt-Shaw_Landback_HTGreport.pdf.

Sleeter, C. (1994). White racism. *Multicultural Education, 1*(4): 5–8, 39.

Solorzano, D. G., & Yosso, T. J. (2001). Critical race and LatCrit theory and method: Counter-storytelling. *International Journal of Qualitative Studies in Education*. 14(4): 471–95.

Solorzano, D. G., & Yosso, T. J. (2002). Critical race methodology: Counter-story telling as an analytical framework for education, *Qualitative Inquiry, 8*(1): 23–44.

Swidler. A. (1986). Culture in action: Symbols and strategies. *American Sociological Review, 51*(2): 273–86.

Trofanenko, B. (2006). Displayed objects, indigenous identities, and public pedagogy. *Anthropology & Education Quarterly, 37*(4): 309–27. https://www.jstor.org/stable/4126368.

Valdes, F., Culp, J. M., & Harris, A. P. (Eds.) (2002). *Crossroads, directions, and a new critical race theory*. Temple University Press.

Veracini, L. (2010). *Settler colonialism: A theoretical overview*. Palgrave Macmillan.
Wolfe, P. (2006). Settler colonialism and the elimination of the native. *Journal of Genocide Research*, *8*(4): 387–409. https://doi.org/10.1080/14623520601056240.
Wolfe, P. (1999). *Settler colonialism and the transformation of anthropology*. Cassell.
Yosso, T. J. (2005). Whose culture has capital? A critical race theory discussion of community cultural wealth. *Race Ethnicity and Education*, *8*(1): 69–91.

Chapter 26: Healing in Urban Nature: On Place, Identity, and Land Relationships

Adams, J. (2014). Place and identity. In *Transforming Urban Education* (pp. 341–54). Sense.
Adams, J. D. (2013). Theorizing a sense of place in a transnational community. *Children Youth and Environments*, *23*(3): 43–65.
Ansfield, B. (2015). Still submerged: The uninhabitability of urban redevelopment. In *Sylvia Wynter: On being human as praxis* (pp. 124–41). Duke University Press.
Craig, J. M., Logan, A. C., & Prescott, S. L. (2016). Natural environments, nature relatedness and the ecological theater: connecting satellites and sequencing to shinrin-yoku. *Journal of Physiological Anthropology*, *35*(1): 1–10.
Paperson, L. (2014). A ghetto land pedagogy: An antidote for settler environmentalism. *Environmental Education Research*, *20*(1): 115–30.
Park, B. J., Tsunetsugu, Y., Kasetani, T., Kagawa, T., & Miyazaki, Y. (2010). The physiological effects of Shinrin-yoku (taking in the forest atmosphere or forest bathing): evidence from field experiments in 24 forests across Japan. *Environmental Health and Preventive Medicine*, *15*(1): 18.

Afterword: Healing the Soft Tissue of Critical Pedagogues with a Radical Love

Battiste, M. (2013). *Decolonizing education: Nourishing the learning spirit*. Purich.
Flecha, R., & Gómez, A. (2016). Joe L. Kincheloe: How love could change the world. In M. F. Agnello & W. M. Reynolds (Eds.), *Practicing critical pedagogy: The influences of Joe L. Kincheloe*. Springer.
Freire, P. (1990). Personal communication. Boston, MA.
Freire, P. (1972). *The pedagogy of the oppressed*. Continuum.
Gómez, J. (2014). *Radical love: A revolution for the 21st century*. Peter Lang.
Gómez, J. (2004). *El Amor en la Sociedad del Riesgo*. El Roure.
Peace and Love Principle. *Physiopedia News*, Charity Organization. (2021). https://www.physio-pedia.com/Peace_and_Love_Principle, last retrieved January 17, 2021.
Reints, B. (2014). *An author's guide to the pursuit of happiness*. Derbyshire.
Sofi, O. (2019). *Teachings from the Islamic mystical tradition*. Yale University Press.
Steinberg, S. R. (2017). Radical love. In H. Jansen & H. Letiche (Eds.), *Post-formalism, pedagogy lives*. Peter Lang.

Steinberg, S. R. (2010). "The anti-preacher: Radical love in a post-post world." *Cultural Studies <> Critical Methodologies, 10*(5): 364–5.

Steinberg, S. R. (Director, Producer) (2008). *Why critical pedagogy?* The Paulo and Nita Freire International Project for Critical Pedagogy. Montreal, Quebec.

Wagamese, R. (2019). *One drum: Stories and ceremonies for a planet.* Douglas & McIntyre.

Weinberg, N. (2017). *4 ways to wisdom.* ArtScroll Shaar Press.

Index

www.ingramcontent.com/pod-product-compliance
Ingram Content Group UK Ltd.
Pitfield, Milton Keynes, MK11 3LW, UK
UKHW020641100726
473098UK00008B/184

9 781350 192683